D0128403

CREATIVE STRATEGY IN ADVERTISING

CREATIVE STRATEGY IN ADVERTISING
TENTH EDITION

BONNIE L. DREWNIANY
School of Journalism and Mass Communications
University of South Carolina, Columbia

A. JEROME JEWLER
Professor Emeritus
School of Journalism and Mass Communications
University of South Carolina, Columbia

WADSWORTH
CENGAGE Learning™

Australia • Brazil • Japan • Korea • Mexico • Singapore • Spain • United Kingdom • United States

**Creative Strategy in Advertising,
Tenth Edition**
Bonnie L. Drewniany, A. Jerome Jewler

Senior Publisher: Lyn Uhl

Publisher: Michael Rosenberg

Associate Development Editor:
Megan Garvey

Assistant Editor: Jillian D'Urso

Editorial Assistant: Erin Pass

Production Manager: Samantha Ross Miller

Marketing Manager: Bryant Chrzan

Marketing Communications Manager:
Christine Dobberpuhl

Print Buyer: Justin Palmeiro

Art Director: Linda Helcher

Text Permissions Account Manager:
Margaret Chamberlain-Gaston

Senior Permissions Account Manager-
Image: Deanna Ettinger

Content Project Management:
Pre-PressPMG

Production Service: Pre-PressPMG

Cover Image: istockphoto.com © DSGpro

Compositor: Pre-PressPMG

© 2011, 2008, 2005 Wadsworth, Cengage Learning

ALL RIGHTS RESERVED. No part of this work covered by the copyright herein may be reproduced, transmitted, stored, or used in any form or by any means graphic, electronic, or mechanical, including but not limited to photocopying, recording, scanning, digitizing, taping, Web distribution, information networks, or information storage and retrieval systems, except as permitted under Section 107 or 108 of the 1976 United States Copyright Act, without the prior written permission of the publisher.

For product information and technology assistance, contact us at
Cengage Learning Customer & Sales Support, 1-800-354-9706

For permission to use material from this text or product,
submit all requests online at **www.cengage.com/permissions**
Further permissions questions can be emailed to
permissionrequest@cengage.com

Library of Congress Control Number: 2009943636

ISBN 13: 978-1-4240-6907-1

ISBN 10: 1-4240-6907-6

Wadsworth
20 Channel Center Street
Boston, MA 02210
USA

Cengage Learning is a leading provider of customized learning solutions with office locations around the globe, including Singapore, the United Kingdom, Australia, Mexico, Brazil, and Japan. Locate your local office at **international.cengage.com/region**

Cengage Learning products are represented in Canada by Nelson Education, Ltd.

For your course and learning solutions, visit **www.cengage.com**

Purchase any of our products at your local college store or at our preferred online store **www.CengageBrain.com**

Printed in the United States of America
1 2 3 4 5 6 7 14 13 12 11 10

{This book is dedicated to the memory of my brother, Michael Drewniany}

Contents

Preface   xiii

About the Authors   xv

1 **CREATIVITY:** UNEXPECTED BUT RELEVANT SELLING MESSAGES   1

Creativity Defined   2

Media: The New Creative Inspiration   3

Inspiration from Consumers   5

That's Entertainment, but Is It Advertising?   10

Ethical Issues   17

The Creative Challenge   18

Suggested Activities   18

>> BRIEFCASE: IKEA Thinks Outside (and Inside) the Box   21

2 **BRANDING:** IDENTITY AND IMAGE STRATEGY   26

Branding Defined   27

Brand Identity Elements   28

Projecting a Unified Message   33

Protecting Brand Identity   34

The Identity Strategy   35

Suggested Activities   35

>> BRIEFCASE: Now That's a Large Pizza!   36

3 **DIVERSITY:** TARGETING AN EVER-CHANGING MARKETPLACE   38

African Americans   40

Hispanic Americans   43

Asian Americans   45

Native Americans   46

Arab Americans   47

How to Reach Ethnic Minorities   48

The 50-Plus Market   50

People with Disabilities   53

Gays and Lesbians   54

Lessons That Apply to All Segments   55

Suggested Activities   57

>> BRIEFCASE: How Sweet the Sound   58

4 UNCOVERING INSIGHTS: THE BASIS FOR EFFECTIVE CREATIVE WORK   68

Step 1: State Your Questions   69
Step 2: Dig Through Secondary Sources   70
Step 3: Conduct Primary Research   75
Step 4: Interpret the Data   84
Future Steps in the Process   84
Common Mistakes in Research   85
Suggested Activities   86
>> BRIEFCASE: Icelandair and Baltimore Washington International Airport Take the Travail Out of Travel   88

5 STRATEGY: A ROAD MAP FOR THE CREATIVE TEAM   91

The Creative Brief   92
Writing the Creative Brief   92
Linking Strategy with the Thinking/Feeling and High-/Low-Importance Scales   102
Checklist for Creative Briefs   104
Suggested Activities   104
>> BRIEFCASE: Eat Mor Chikin or These Cows Are Goners!   105

6 IDEAS: THE CURRENCY OF THE 21ST CENTURY   111

How Do You Come Up with the Big Idea?   111
There's a Big Idea in the Creative Brief   113
Turn an Idea into a Campaign Theme   113
From One Big Idea to Hundreds of Ideas   114
Guidelines for Brainstorming   122
Using Criticism to Improve Your Ideas   125
Suggested Activities   126
>> BRIEFCASE: The Cows Are Singing, "California Here I Come!"   132

7 WORDS ON PAPER: CONNECTING TO CONSUMERS' HEARTS AND MINDS   138

Headlines Help Form Good First Impressions   140
Body Copy Tells the Rest of the Story   147
Mandatories: Writing the Small Print   149
Answers to Common Questions about Writing Copy   150
Guidelines for Writing Effective Copy   154
Checklist for Writing Copy   161
Suggested Activities   161
>> BRIEFCASE: North Carolina Plays a Starring Role   163

8 LAYOUTS: DESIGNING TO COMMUNICATE   166

Functions of Design   166

Design Principles   168

Gestalt Theory   171

Negative, or "White," Space   171

The Five Rs of Design   173

Selecting Type   175

Basic Ad Layouts   178

Inviting Readership   179

Creating the Finished Ad: Computers and Design   182

Designing Outdoor and Transit Ads   183

Answers to Common Questions about Design   183

Suggested Activities   185

>> B R I E F C A S E : Why Weight?   186

9 RADIO: CAN YOU SEE WHAT I'M SAYING?   191

Why Advertise on Radio?   191

The Theater of the Mind   192

Guidelines for Writing Effective Radio Spots   192

Approaches to Radio Commercials   197

Live versus Produced   200

Radio Script Format   201

Checklist for Radio Copy   203

Suggested Activities   203

>> B R I E F C A S E : Tom Bodett Sells Affordability and Comfort
for Motel 6   205

10 TELEVISION: THE POWER OF SIGHT, SOUND, AND MOTION   208

Combining Sight, Sound, and Motion   209

Preparing to Write Ads for Television   210

Formats for TV Commercials   213

Camera Shots, Camera Moves, and Transitions   216

Editing for Continuity   218

Music and Sound Effects   219

Getting It on Paper: The TV Script   221

Making It Clear: The TV Storyboard   221

TV Production   222

Checklist for Television   223
Suggested Activities   223
>> BRIEFCASE: Hoping to Connect with Someone a Bit on the Wild Side?   224

11 DIRECT MARKETING: THE CONVENIENCE OF SHOPPING AT HOME   229

Direct Marketing: An Old Idea Improved Through Technology   229
Advantages of Direct Marketing over Other Forms of Advertising   230
Direct Mail: The Next Best Thing to a Door-to-Door Salesperson   231
Catalogs: Bringing the Retail Store into the Home and Office   234
You've Got E-mail   235
The Internet: The Ultimate Direct Marketing Experience   235
The Interactive Team   237
Designing for the Internet: A Four-Stage Process   237
Banner Ads   244
Ethical Aspects of Direct Marketing   245
Suggested Activities   246
>> BRIEFCASE: A Big Idea for a Small Space   248

12 INTEGRATED MARKETING COMMUNICATIONS: BUILDING STRONG RELATIONSHIPS BETWEEN THE BRAND AND THE CONSUMER   253

Integrated Marketing Communications   254
Sales Promotion   254
Public Relations   260
Promotional Products   264
Special Packaging   265
Sponsorships   266
Cause-Related Marketing   267
Guerilla Marketing   268
Product Placement and Branded Content   268
Suggested Activities   269
>> BRIEFCASE: IKEA Embraces Change   270

13 THE LAW AND CREATIVITY: MAKING SURE YOUR GREAT IDEA IS A GOOD IDEA   274

Who Worries About Advertising?   275
Government Regulation of Advertising   276
Advertising Regulations: Time, Place, and Manner   277
Avoiding Individual Disputes   278
Invasion of Privacy and Right of Publicity   279
About Photographs   280

Copyrights 281

Ad Copy 284

Trademarks 284

Libel and Product Disparagement 287

A Final Word: Keep Creativity Out of the Courtroom 287

Suggested Activities 288

(>>) B R I E F C A S E : ITT Industries' Corporate Advertising Campaign:
Putting a Face on a Large Corporation 289

14 CLIENT PITCHES: HOW TO SELL YOUR IDEAS 293

The Presentation Is Half of the Battle 294

Pitching with Pizzazz 296

Guidelines for Making Presentations 298

Perils and Pitfalls of Presenting 299

How to Correct the Problems 300

Using PowerPoint Effectively 301

Suggested Activities 302

(>>) B R I E F C A S E : What Does "Urgent" Mean to You? 303

Appendix 1: How to Land a Job in the Creative Department 309

Appendix 2: Assignments 313

Index 321

Preface

There's a creative revolution going on in advertising today. In the midst of a struggling economy, advertising agencies are being challenged to find innovate ways to reach—and engage—consumers. Media outlets continue to evolve in directions that many of us find mind-boggling. From innovations in electronic media to guerilla efforts, there's almost no way to escape promotional pitches 24/7.

This creative revolution is featured throughout the book, including in several new briefcases. And while much has changed, much has remained the same. The three basic tenants of creativity—that advertising must be unexpected, relevant, and persuasive—continue to be true. So is the importance of basing your work on research and sound strategy.

As you read this book, you will be taken step-by-step through the process of creating messages that engage consumers. Woven within chapters are legal and ethical considerations. Since these issues are of such great importance, I invited Carmen Maye, a legal scholar, to devote an entire chapter to law and ethics. To my delight, she was able to translate legal jargon into "human speak."

I hope you'll enjoy reading this book as much as I've enjoyed writing it. I hope it inspires you to do great creative work. Perhaps you'll share examples of your work in future editions of this book.

I owe a debt of gratitude to my students, who are a source of inspiration. A tremendous debt of gratitude goes to A. Jerome Jewler, who developed the idea for this book and who was kind enough to include me as a contributor, starting with the fourth edition.

I would like to thank the following people who made this edition possible: my Development Editor Megan Garvey; Michael Rosenberg, Publisher; Jillian D'Urso, Assistant Editor; Erin Pass, Editorial Assistant; Bryant Chrzan, Marketing Manager; Margaret Chamberlain-Gaston, Text Permissions Account Manager; Deanna Ettinger, Senior Permissions Account Manager; and Pradhiba Kannaiyan, Production Manager. I would also like to thank the following reviewers whose insights helped greatly improve this tenth edition: William Florence, Chemeketa Community College; Dr. Michelle Seelig, University of Miami; and Teri K. Henley, University of Alabama.

Bonnie L. Drewniany

About the Authors

BONNIE L. DREWNIANY is an associate professor in the School of Journalism and Mass Communications, University of South Carolina, Columbia. She has an MBA from Rutgers University, with a concentration in marketing, and a BS from Syracuse University, with a concentration in mass communications.

Before joining the University of South Carolina, she was a visiting professor at Syracuse University's S. I. Newhouse School of Public Communications. She also taught as an adjunct at Parsons School of Design, Rutgers University, and Seton Hall University. Her professional experience includes 10 years with the R. H. Macy Co., where she was advertising copy director for the New Jersey division. She has also freelanced for F. A. O. Schwarz, Fortunoff, and American Express.

Her research interests include the effect of Super Bowl commercials and advertising's portrayal of minorities, women, and older people. Her findings have been published in the *Wall Street Journal* and various academic publications. She serves on the National Advertising Review Board, the American Advertising Federation National Academic Committee, is the education chair of the AAF Third District (representing universities and colleges in North Carolina, South Carolina and Virginia), and is an honorary lifetime board member of AAF of the Midlands. She recently received the Silver Medal Award from AAF of the Midlands, the highest award an advertising chapter can bestow on a member in its community. She spends her summers in Massachusetts.

A. JEROME JEWLER received the 2000 Distinguished Advertising Educator Award presented by the American Advertising Federation. He is a distinguished professor emeritus in the School of Journalism and Mass Communications, University of South Carolina, Columbia, where he began teaching undergraduate and graduate courses in 1972. He is a graduate of the University of Maryland, with a BS in journalism and an MA in American civilization.

He worked as an advertising copywriter before beginning his teaching career. He taught briefly at the University of Tennessee; spent a summer with McCann–Erickson, London, as a visiting professor; spent another summer in research at the Center for Advertising History of the Smithsonian Institution; and spent another summer teaching creative strategy to 19 American students in England.

He has served as codirector for instruction and faculty development for the University of South Carolina college success course and has led workshops on teaching at more than 25 colleges and universities. He, John Gardner, and Betsy Barefoot are the coeditors of *Your College Experience,* a nationally known college success text.

Jewler, who initiated this textbook in 1981 and has turned over the major portion of this work to his dear friend Bonnie, enjoys retirement by introducing school groups to the wonders of history, science, and technology at the South Carolina State Museum and helping patrons at the information desk of the Richland County Public Library. He is currently making plans to publish his memoirs.

CREATIVE STRATEGY IN ADVERTISING

CREATIVITY
UNEXPECTED BUT RELEVANT SELLING MESSAGES

Great advertising is inspired by insights about brands, consumers, and how the two interact. It starts with a problem from the client and ends with a solution for consumers. The problem may be how to make an old, established brand relevant again. Or get a new target to want a brand. Or regain momentum for a brand when the competitors have larger advertising budgets. These were some of the problems that Goodby, Silverstein & Partners (GSP) was asked to solve for Cheetos®.

Throughout the brand's 60-year history, Cheetos had been targeted to kids. Chester Cheetah was introduced in 1986 but the slightly neurotic cat wasn't quite as cool two decades later. Competitive brands Goldfish and Cheez-it were spending twice as much on advertising media. And the clincher? Pepsico/Frito-Lay, the parent company of Cheetos, signed the voluntary Children's Food & Beverage Advertising Initiative in 2007, which restricted advertising to kids under 12 years of age, except for "better for you" products, such as Baked! Cheetos snacks.

Since it could no longer target children, GSP needed to make Cheetos relevant to adults. To get into the adult mind-set, several research methods were used—including focus groups, observational research, and cultural trends studies. The key insight: "Some adults love Cheetos snacks just as intensely as kids. For them, Cheetos is a catalyst for liberating the childlike playfulness and mischief. Chester is the 'jester'—he provides the inspiration to push against constraining adult norms and judgmental behavior."[1]

[1] "Mischievous Fun with Cheetos®," The 2009 ARF David Ogilvy Awards, www.warc.com, accessed July 31, 2009.

Television commercials feature Chester encouraging adults to fight back the way their inner child wants them to do. In one spot, a woman dumps a bag of Cheetos inside the dryer of a woman who has hogged all the machines at a laundromat. The commercials end with "Join Us at the OrangeUnderground .com," the online site that inspires adults to do mischievous pranks using Cheetos snacks. Cheetos also partnered with Comedy Central with its "Pull Some Funny, Make Some Money" April Fool's Day promotion, which invited viewers to film their acts of mischief and post them in the hopes of winning a cash prize and a professional-grade video camera. The pranks had to be benign and harmless, never malicious or hurtful.

The campaign resonates with adults who want to lighten up and play more. Creative director Rick Condos told *Adweek,* "Chester tells you to do exactly what you want to do at that moment, but you hesitate to do because adults don't do that. We target the 12-year-old kid in all of us, but that kid is like Bart Simpson. We don't see him as dark, just representative of the repressed feelings you have in adulthood."[2]

Google searches of "Cheetos" went from 132,000 hits in 2007 to 1,121,000 hits in 2008. And more important, Cheetos's sales increased by 11.3 percent in just one year, nearly double its target goal.

> Creativity Defined

Creative ads make a relevant connection between the brand and its target audience and present a selling idea in an unexpected way. Let's examine components of the definition.

Creative ads make a relevant connection between a brand and its target audience. Creative director Ann Hayden explains, "I'm convinced that people—all people—want to buy from people. Customers want to know who you are, your habits, your values. They want to be able to predict you. They need to trust you. If they connect with you on some kind of human basis, and believe they have something in common with you, they will give you vast permission to sell them things that make them happy."[3]

Creative ads present a selling idea. The method of presenting the selling idea can be rational, emotional, or a combination of both. Because competitors can copy most products and services, emotional selling points are usually more powerful than rational ones.

Creative ads are unexpected. Look at the ad for Stren fishing line in Figure 1-1. The agency could have shown a man reeling in a giant fish. However, it would be so expected that it would blend in with other ads for fishing products. Instead, the close-up of the man's split pants catches you off guard and makes you wonder what the ad is about. Meanwhile, the copy, "The most dependable fishing line in the world," delivers the selling message and helps the visual make sense.

Keep in mind that the unexpected element may be the choice of words, visuals, media, or all three.

---

[2] Barbara Lippert, "Unsavory Characters," *Adweek*, 5 May 2008, pp. 28–29.
[3] From the Saatchi & Saatchi Business Communications website. www.saatchibiz.be, 1999.

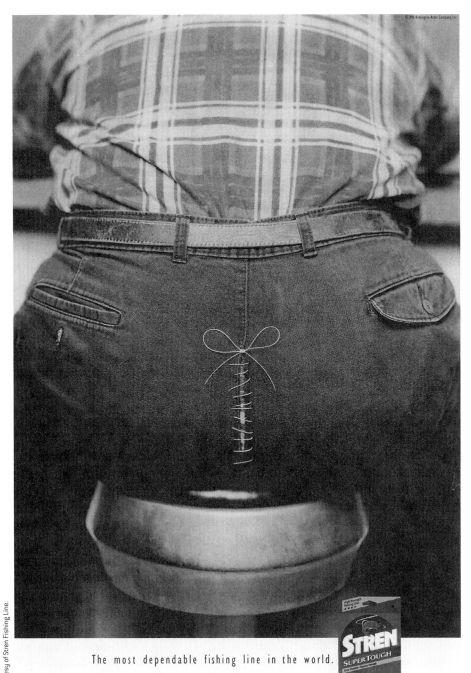

Courtesy of Stren Fishing Line.

The most dependable fishing line in the world.

Figure 1-1
How do you convince customers that your fishing line is incredibly strong? The obvious way would be to show a giant fish that's just been hooked. But that's been done before. This ad from Carmichael Lynch for Stren is unexpected but relevant.

> Media: The New Creative Inspiration

When and where a message runs can be as creative as the words and visuals. Passengers flying into Denver during the 2008 Democratic Primary were greeted by a crop circle made of wheat to promote Papa John's new whole wheat pizza. (To learn more about Papa John's "Pie in the Sky," see the "Briefcase" at the end of Chapter 2.)

Even everyday items have become media vehicles. L'Oréal Paris promoted its Men's Expert line of products by advertising on dry cleaner dress shirt hangers. The cardboard hangers come with a $2 coupon and the following message: "Your shirt doesn't have wrinkles, why should your face?" Continental promoted its new nonstop service between New York and Beijing on Chinese restaurant take-out containers that carry the message, "We deliver all over the world." And the Weather Channel ran the following message on packages of pretzels given to airline passengers: "Trust Us. Don't Open the Window to Check the Weather."

A number of advertisers place messages in restrooms in an attempt to capture people's undivided attention. Greenspon Advertising Southeast took the concept even further and bought ad space above—and inside—men's urinals to promote a hockey team, the Charlotte Checkers. The agency placed Charlotte Checkers–branded hockey pucks inside urinals in 50 bars and restaurants throughout the city. Above the urinals were messages such as, "The disgusting thing is not that we're going to play with that puck. It's that we're going to shove it down Greenville's throat Friday night." Think that's gross? Well, consider this: rumor has it that men stole the hockey pucks from the urinals. Greenspon responded with a mock public service announcement (PSA) featuring Jeff Longo, the president of the Charlotte Checkers. "Recently we placed Charlotte Checkers hockey pucks in various men's urinals around town, thinking that no one will steal a urine-soaked hockey puck." Longo gives listeners the chance to go to the Checkers' website to receive a clean hockey puck, "in an effort to avoid a public health emergency." Did men steal the hockey pucks, or was it just a publicity gimmick? Only the agency and client know for sure.

A word of caution: Just because you *can* run a message nearly everywhere, it doesn't mean you *should*. (Face it. The bottom of a urinal won't work for most brands.) You need to ask if the medium is relevant to the brand and the consumer. Also keep in mind that there are reasons people escape to remote islands that don't have cell service and choose to live in communities that don't have chain restaurants and stores. It's called downtime and quality of life. A major fast-food restaurant was forced to lower its neon sign on a highway in the Berkshires because it ruined the vista of rolling hills. Likewise, a town in the Netherlands fined an advertiser 1,000 euros a day for putting advertising messages on blankets wrapped on sheep. The reason? It violated the town's ban on advertising along the highways.

Even media-saturated cities have their limits. Chicago and San Francisco ordered IBM to pay fines and cleanup costs after its advertising agency spray-painted advertisements on the cities' sidewalks. Nike learned its street decals violated a New York City code that states it is "unlawful to deface any street by painting, printing, or writing thereon, or attaching thereto, in any manner, any advertisement or other printed matter." Right after the Nike faux pas, Microsoft plastered adhesive butterflies on subway entrances, telephone booths, and newspaper-vending machines throughout Manhattan. The transportation department ordered the butterfly decals to go into hibernation. These and other types of government regulations of advertising are discussed in Chapter 13.

It's not just government officials that police messages. Consumers can be the worst critics, as Sony learned when it hired graffiti artists to spray-paint urban buildings with images of kids playing with its PlayStation Portable. The attempt to connect with a hip urban audience backfired in San Francisco as real graffiti was painted on top of Sony's faux graffiti. On one sign someone wrote, "Get out of my city" and added the word "Fony" to the graffiti plus a four-line ditty slamming Sony. In another location, someone spray-painted the graffiti with the commentary, "Advertising directed at your counter-culture."[4]

> Inspiration from Consumers

One way to engage consumers in your advertising campaign is to invite them to create their own ads. Nationwide Insurance invited consumers to tell their versions of how "life comes at you fast" and posted the messages on a giant screen in New York's Times Square. Emerald Nuts invited visitors to devise their own zany story lines based on words starting with the 11 letters that spell Emerald Nuts. Thousands of people tried their hand at the anagram and the winning entry (Enraging Millions England Repainted Antarctica Lavender During Night Using Tiny Swabs) appeared on the Web and in a newspaper ad.

MasterCard invited viewers to create a "Priceless" ad with a commercial that first ran during the Academy Awards. The commercial opens on a man sitting at a desk in the middle of an open field. As he types on an old-fashioned typewriter, the announcer says, "Blank. Nine dollars." A woman on a motorcycle rides into view. "Blank. Sixty dollars." Eventually, the man hops on the back of the bike and they ride down an empty road. "Blank," says the announcer. "Priceless." Seth Stevenson of *Slate* discovered that, at least initially, the site allowed people to enter naughty words in the blanks. He admitted, "I got a juvenile thrill from seeing 'Dildo: $9' superimposed on that high-budget, cinematographically perfect scene of the man in the open field."[5]

General Motors also discovered that consumer-generated ads can be risky. When consumers were invited to post their own commercials for the Chevrolet Tahoe online, some likened the SUV to a gas-guzzler, a contributor to global warming, and a warmonger.

Although it's important that advertisers connect with their consumers, it doesn't mean they should give their detractors free ad space. Nor should it mean anything goes. Consumers are given some limits when they create a Super Bowl commercial for Doritos. Frito-Lay makes sure no posted ads denigrate the brand or send a message not in line with the company's values. The amateurs have done quite well with their Super Bowl ad creations. The 2009 ad, created by two unemployed brothers from Indiana, won the ultimate coup: the number one spot in the coveted *USA Today* poll. As a result of winning the poll, the creative team won $1 million. "Two nobodies from nowhere just walked off with one of the world's top honors," Dave Herbert, one of the creators of the ads told *USA Today.*[6]

Winning one of these creative challenges is a wonderful way to jump-start your advertising career. Another great way to build your portfolio is to enter a creative competition, such as the Student ADDYs (see Figure 1-2). For a list of other creative competitions, check out the box on page 9.

[4] Ryan Singel, "Sony Draws Ire with PSP Graffiti," www.wired.com, 5 December 2005.
[5] Seth Stevenson, "The End of a Played-Out Ad Campaign?" www.slate.com, 5 May 2006.
[6] Bruce Horovitz, "'Two Nobodies from Nowhere' Craft Winning Ad," *USA Today*, 2 February 2009, 4B.

Figure 1-2
Enter your work into the Student ADDY competition and prove to future employers that you're better than all other students vying for the same job.

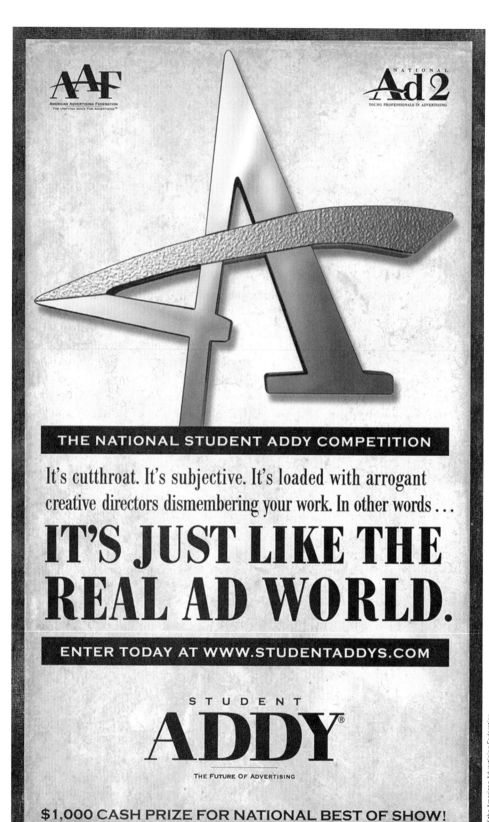

Courtesy of the American Advertising Federation.

Figure 1-2 (continued)

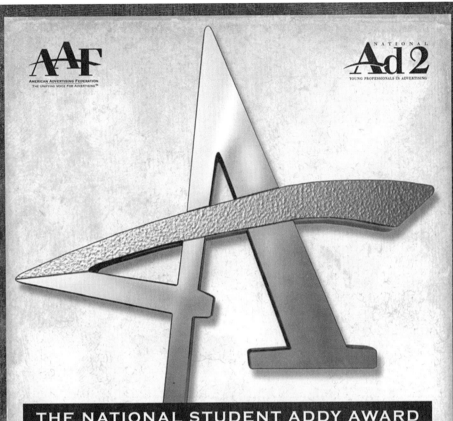

Courtesy of the American Advertising Federation.

Figure 1-2 (continued)

Courtesy of the American Advertising Federation.

CREATIVE COMPETITIONS

Does your work make the cut? There's one way to find out. Have pros judge it against the best work of other students.

Student Competitions

- *ADDY Awards.* Sponsored by the American Advertising Federation; students may enter their work in the local advertising club's annual competition. If it wins, it can go on to compete at the district and national levels for a chance at a cash prize. www.studentaddys.com

- *Andy Student Awards.* Sponsored by the Advertising Club of New York; any student in an accredited institution of higher learning may enter and compete for a $5,000 scholarship and an invitation to the Andy Awards show. www.andyawards.com

- *Art Directors Club Annual Awards Competition.* Students enrolled in undergraduate or graduate programs in advertising, graphic design, photography, illustration, and new media may submit published or unpublished work. Winning work becomes part of a traveling exhibition. www.adcglobal.org/education/competition

- *Clio Student Awards.* Students enrolled in an accredited advertising, film, or design program compete for the opportunity to win a coveted Clio statue. www.clioawards.com

- *D&AD Student Awards.* Winners receive cash prizes and are invited to the annual British Design and Art Direction competition in London. www.dandad.org

- *London International Advertising Awards.* Student work is judged by the world's top creative directors. www.liaawards.com

- *Lürzer's Archive Student of the Year.* Professionals from throughout the world of advertising vote online. The winner gets a trip to an international advertising festival. www.luerzersarchive.us/studentscontest.asp

- *One Show.* Undergraduate and graduate advertising majors create an ad from a brief supplied by the One Club. Winners receive a One Show pencil, cash prizes, and publication in the One Show annual. www.oneclub.com

- *Radio-Mercury Awards.* Students are recognized and rewarded for excellence for their produced radio commercials. www.radiomercuryawards.com

- *Young Guns.* Students may enter individual ads or campaigns of three executions for a cash prize and an opportunity for three-month paid internship with Leo Burnett Worldwide. www.ygaward.com

Team Competitions

- *AAF National Student Advertising Competition.* Student teams develop an integrated marketing communications campaign for a national client. To enter, students must be members of their college's chapter of the American Advertising Federation. Winning schools receive cash prizes, and students gain networking opportunities. www.aaf.org

- *Bateman Competition.* Teams of four or five students develop a public relations campaign for a sponsoring client. Winning schools receive cash prizes, and students gain experience and networking opportunities. Students must be members of their college's chapter of the Public Relations Student Society of America. www.prsa.org

- *DMEF Collegiate Echo Competition.* Teams of up to four students develop a direct marketing plan to solve the challenge presented by a national client. Winning teams go to a major industry conference and receive promotional gifts. www.directworks.org

Publications

- *Archive.* A review that showcases creative work from around the world, including outstanding student work. www.luerzersarchive.us/submission.asp

- *CMYK.* A magazine devoted to student work and judged by pros that invites students to submit advertising, design, photography, and illustrations. www.cmykmag.com

> That's Entertainment, but Is It Advertising?

Rance Crain, president and editorial director of Crain Communications, quoted a letter to the editor from a father: "My 6-1/2-year-old son cut through the mayhem of murderous lizards, a digitally reincarnated Elvis and dancing tomatoes to offer an unwitting, but telling, indictment of Super Bowl ads: 'These commercials are cool. Not like the regular ones where they're trying to sell you something.'"[7]

Like that little boy, most viewers love Super Bowl commercials because of their use of humor, celebrities, and ad critters. Unfortunately, the viewers don't always express their enthusiasm for the commercials at the cash register. Super Bowl commercials are hardly unique in this regard—some of the most popular commercials of all time have been tremendous flops in terms of sales. So does this mean you should avoid humor, celebrities, and ad characters in your ads? No. But it does mean you should use them strategically.

Humor

Consider this TV commercial: An amateur stage production shows two children lost in the forest. The good fairy appears from overhead and starts floating toward them. "Not to fear, little children. I will helpppp. . . ." THUD! She plummets to the stage. Tagline: "Should have used Stren. Stren. The most dependable fishing line in the world." The humor takes us by surprise and shows a situation that we can empathize with. It communicates a relevant, unexpected, and memorable message about the product. It gives us a reason to buy. It works.

Here are some tips on how to use humor in advertising:

- *Know the difference between humor and jokes.* A joke is a one-shot deal. Once you hear the punch line, it's not as funny the second time. And when you hear the same joke a bunch of times, it can become downright tedious. Humor, by contrast, is subtler and often contains nuances that make you want to see and hear it repeatedly. Many humorous commercials become funnier the more times that you see them.

  A comedy club understood the difference between jokes and humor when it created a delightful radio spot that promoted what it was selling: laughter. The spot recorded various types of laughter—the chuckle, the giggle, the cackle, the sputtering burst, the snort, and so on. You could hear the spot repeatedly and laugh each time because the laughter became contagious.

- *Relate to the human experience.* One of the things that made the comedy club spot so amusing was that listeners could identify people they knew who laughed like that. The spot made a relevant human connection.

  Allen Kay—whose advertising agency, Korey Kay & Partners, has won numerous awards for its humorous ads—believes in having a "sense of human." As Kay told *Agency* magazine, "We spell humor h-u-m-a-n. It includes a lot of ironies in life that people recognize and realize and makes them say, 'Yeah, I've been there.'"[8]

---

[7] Remarks by Rance Crain to the Columbia Advertising and Marketing Federation, Columbia, SC, 17 March 1998.

[8] Robyn Griggs, "Grinning in the Dark," *Agency*, Fall 1998, pp. 16–17.

- *Make sure the humor is central to your product message.* Have you ever been so captivated by a commercial that you could repeat almost every detail of it—except the name of the product it was trying to sell? If the product is obscured by the humor, the ad has flopped. To work, humor must be central to the message you're trying to communicate.

- *Understand your audience's sense of humor.* Your ads should reflect the tastes, aspirations, and sensibilities of its intended audience. Just because you and your friends find something hysterical doesn't mean the rest of the world will. People may even be insulted by it. So be sure to test your humor on members of your target audience. Figure 1-3 reflects the sense of humor of its thrill-seeking audience.

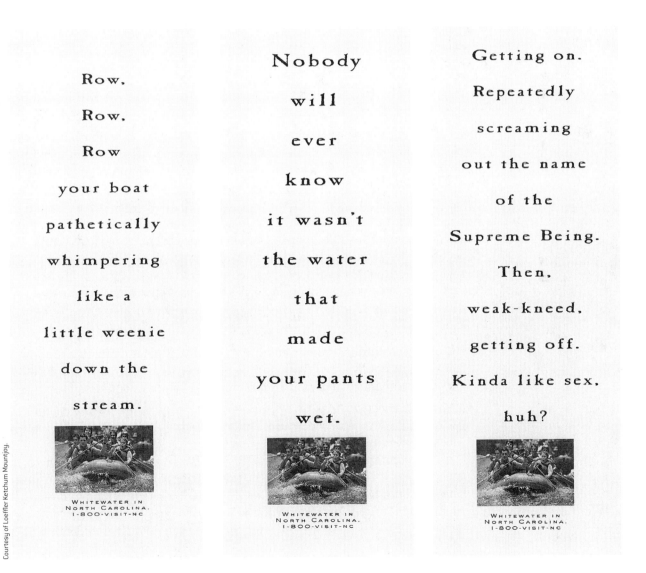

Courtesy of Loefler Ketchum Mountjoy.

Figure 1-3
The joy. The jolts. The jitters. If you've ever gone white-water rafting, you'll agree that these ads capture the experience. And if you haven't tried it, go soon—it'll clear the cobwebs from your brain.

- *Avoid humor that's at the expense of others.* Making fun of ethnic groups, the disabled, and the elderly will likely backfire on you. A car company offended African Americans by running an ad in *Jet* magazine that stated, "Unlike your last boyfriend, it goes to work in the morning." And a discount clothing store offended Jewish people by saying, "Dress British. Think Yiddish."

- *Have fun with your product, but don't make fun of it.* Self-deprecating humor can work if you turn your supposed shortcomings into an advantage. Motel 6 does this brilliantly. The chain doesn't try to hide its lack of amenities but, rather, flaunts it. At Motel 6, you're not going to receive fancy soaps, European chocolates, or fluffy bathrobes. Instead, you'll receive a comfortable room at a comfortable price. See the "Briefcase" section in Chapter 9 for examples of this long-running campaign.

- *Don't assume that your audience is stupid.* Think of it this way: would you rather buy something from someone who apparently views you as an idiot or from someone who seems to appreciate your intelligence?

Celebrity Endorsements

Some of the most popular commercials feature a Who's Who of pop culture. *The Wall Street Journal* credits the late Michael Jackson for helping usher in a new age of celebrity advertising when he signed a $5 million sponsorship deal in 1984 with PepsiCo. Celebrities and musicians had appeared in ads before, but the biggest stars had refrained out of fear of hurting their reputation. "Once-reluctant stars and musicians began to say, 'If the King of Pop can do it, maybe it's OK,'" explained Josh Rabinowitz, senior vice president of music at WPP's Grey New York.[9] Pepsi ads have gone on to feature a Who's Who of pop stars, including Madonna, Michael J. Fox, Ray Charles, Cindy Crawford, and Britney Spears. Other brands have followed Pepsi's success with celebrity endorsers.

There are numerous advantages to using celebrities, including the following:

- *They have stopping power.* Celebrities attract attention and help cut through the clutter of other ads. The "Got Milk?" print campaign makes milk seem cool by showing hundreds of celebrities—from sports figures to political leaders to cartoon characters—sporting milk mustaches.

- *Fans idolize celebrities.* Advertisers hope the admiration for the celebrity will be transferred to the brand. The trick is to make sure the celebrity doesn't overshadow the brand.

   The commercial that won the CBS poll for "Best Super Bowl Commercial of All Time" features a little boy befriending his idol, Pittsburgh Steelers lineman Mean Joe Greene. It opens on Greene hobbling down the players' tunnel, on his way to the locker room. It's quite apparent that the Steelers game wasn't going well and the defensive lineman was through for the day. An awestruck boy meets Greene in the tunnel and

---

[9] Suzanne Vranica, "Jackson Popularized Celebrity Ads," *Wall Street Journal*, 29 June 2009, B5.

asks, "Ya . . . ya need any help?" The mean linebacker snarls back, "Naw." The boy tries to comfort the defeated lineman: "I just want you to know that . . . that you're the greatest." Greene mumbles, "Yeah, sure," trying to ignore the boy. But the boy insists on making Greene feel better, so he asks, "Want my Coke?" Greene waves him off but the boy persists, "Really, you can have it." Reluctantly, Greene accepts the offer and guzzles the 16-ounce bottle of Coke in one gulp. The Coca-Cola jingle starts playing, "A Coke and a smile, makes me feel good, makes me feel nice. . . ." The boy, looking dejected because he thinks he has failed to impress his hero, starts to walk away. Greene stops him and tosses his football jersey to him as a token of his appreciation. The delighted boy utters, "Wow! Thanks, Mean Joe!" and the jingle continues, "That's the way it should be and I'd like the whole world smiling at me. . . . Have a Coke and a smile."

This endearing message, which ran in the 1980 Super Bowl, still resonates with viewers. And it makes the product, not the celebrity, the true star of the ad.

Coca-Cola aired a remake of the Mean Joe Greene spot during the 2009 Super Bowl. The updated version begins just like the original—a Pittsburgh Steeler is limping to the locker room and is stopped by a young boy who tries to console him with a soft drink. Only this time, the limping hero is Troy Polamalu and the soft drink is Coke Zero. After a bit of hesitation, Polamalu accepts the offer and a send-up of the old jingle begins, "A Coke Zero and a Smile. . . ." Just as viewers are convinced this is going to be a scene-for-scene remake of the original ad, two Coke brand managers interrupt the commercial and grab the bottle from the football star: "Coke Zero stole our taste. They are NOT stealing our commercial!" The managers walk away with the Coke Zero but Polamalu tackles them to retrieve the drink. The jingle continues, "Coke Zero adds life. . . ." Then, as a final kicker, Polamalu rips off a brand manager's shirt and tosses it to the boy. Like the original, the product is the true star of the commercial.

- *People are fascinated about the personal lives of celebrities.* Sometimes even the foibles of celebrities can inspire ideas for persuasive messages. Willie Nelson, who got into trouble with the Internal Revenue Service (IRS), appeared in a commercial for H&R Block. In the commercial, he's forced to be the spokesperson for a fictitious shaving cream company as a way to pay off his back taxes. In real life, he released an album to pay his debt. Even if you don't know this little tidbit about the folksinger, the commercial makes sense. More important, there was a relevant connection to the advertiser. The commercial closes with this message: "Don't get bad advice. Let H&R Block double-check your taxes free. We'll find what others miss."

- *Their unique characteristics can help communicate the selling idea.* Seven-foot five-inch basketball star Yao Ming appeared with Verne Troyer ("Mini-Me") in ads promoting Apple's 12- and 17-inch laptops. Yao is shown with the smaller screen, and Verne has the big screen. The two celebrities help further the selling idea—size—in a dramatic way.

- *They're perceived as experts in their fields.* The trick is to make a relevant connection between a celebrity's expertise and the brand being advertised. An athlete is a natural spokesperson for sporting goods but doesn't seem credible when promoting junk food that's high in fat and calories.

Before you think a celebrity is the answer, consider these drawbacks:

- *They're expensive.* Many top athletes, actors, and musicians command contracts in the millions of dollars. Smaller companies shouldn't even dream of spending this type of money, nor should companies trying to promote their low prices. Even large companies should think twice before plopping down millions of dollars for a celebrity, especially in a bad economy. High-priced celebrity endorsers may give consumers, stockholders, and employees the impression that a company is wasting money.

  Conan O'Brien appeared in a Bud Light commercial that parodies celebrity endorsements. The ad opens on Conan's agent trying to convince the talk show host to do a commercial. Conan resists but his agent persists: "It's a ton of money and it's only going to be seen in Sweden." Convinced that "one commercial couldn't hurt," Conan dons bunny ears and a fishnet top in an outrageous ad that is broadcast in Times Square. The commercial-within-a-commercial spoofs the depths that some celebrities will sink to in order to earn some extra cash. As it turns out, Conan didn't accept any payment for his appearance in the ad. Instead Anheuser-Busch gave a donation to one of Conan's charities, the Fresh Air Fund.

- *They're often a quick fix, not a long-term strategy.* Celebrities go in and out of fashion, and as their popularity level shifts, so does their persuasiveness. Look at a *People* magazine from a decade or two ago. How many of the former superstars are still super popular?

  Rapper MC Hammer made it big in the 1980s and spent money as if his star power would last forever. Soon he was out of the limelight and in debt, which prompted an idea for a Nationwide Insurance ad. The commercial opens with Hammer dancing to "U Can't Touch This" in front of a mansion with a gigantic, glittering "H" over the doorway (bling for a mansion). The commercial cuts to "5 minutes later" and shows Hammer sitting in front of his mansion, which has a foreclosure sign. The message: "Life comes at you fast and when it does, Nationwide can help." The self-deprecating humor helps further the message that life is filled with uncertainty. Likewise, a 2009 Super Bowl commercial for Cash4Gold shows Hammer touting, "I can get cash for this gold medallion of me wearing a gold medallion!" In both ads, the has-been celebrity works better than someone who's widely popular.

- *They may lack credibility.* Even though the Federal Trade Commission requires celebrities to actually use the products they endorse (see Chapter 13 for more information), 63 percent of respondents in a study published in *Advertising Age* said that celebrities are "just doing it for the money," and 43 percent believed celebrities "don't even use the product."[10]

---

[10] Dave Vadehra, "Celebs Remain Entertaining, if Not Believable," *Advertising Age*, 2 September 1996, p. 18.

A commercial for Champion sportswear shows images of obnoxious professional basketball players. One dribbles a ball imprinted with the front of a dollar bill. The voice-over inquires, "When did the logo on your shoe become more important than the heart on your sleeve? When did the word 'renegotiate' move from the business page to the sports page? Where have all the champions gone?" The images on the screen change to plain folks playing football and running just for fun. The voice-over continues, "You'll find us in places where the lights don't flash and the only contract you sign is with yourself. We are the champions. . . ."

- *They may endorse so many products that it confuses people.* Tiger Woods got into hot water for bouncing a Titleist golf ball on the wedge of a Titleist golf club while shooting a Nike commercial.

- *They can overshadow the message.* Although a celebrity may draw attention to an ad, some consumers focus their attention on the celebrity and fail to note what's being promoted. In one spot, Yao Ming tries to pay for a souvenir from New York City by writing a check. The cashier responds, "Yo," pointing to a sign that says "no checks." Yao corrects her, "Yao." They go back and forth with the Yo, Yao routine and the spot closes with a brief pitch for Visa's check card. The commercial is a clever spin on the "who's on first" routine. The audience will likely remember Yao's name, but it's not as certain they'll remember which credit card company paid for the ad. The Visa brand name could easily have been made dominant if the cashier had asked the Chinese athlete to show his visa and passport and he presented his Visa check card instead.

- *They may disparage your brand when they think no one's listening.* Executives from Adidas AG weren't amused when they read a blog from their star endorser, Gilbert Arenas. The Washington Wizards guard blogged about a signature Adidas shoe that had not yet been revealed to the public: "I'm sitting there looking at the shoe like 'I hope you guys aren't serious. Because I'm not going to wear this shoe. . . . Nobody is going to wear this shoe.'" He went on to say it reminded him of something a ballerina would wear. An Adidas spokesman told the *Wall Street Journal* that in the end the company benefited from the commentary. Adidas reworked the design and Arenas blogged "I think people are going to like the colors, but they're also going to like the shoe."[11]

- *Bad press about the celebrity can hurt the sponsor.* The Kellogg Co. didn't renew Michael Phelps's contract after a British tabloid published a photo of the Olympic champion smoking pot at a campus party. Nike suspended its contract with NFL star Michael Vick after the NFL star was linked with an illegal dog-fighting ring. Kmart canceled its contract with golfing veteran Fuzzy Zoeller after he joked about Tiger Woods eating fried chicken and collard greens. And O. J. Simpson, once one of the most popular endorsers, probably won't be asked to appear in any commercials in the future.

---

[11] Stephanie Kang, "Companies Try to Score with Athletes Who Blog," *Wall Street Journal*, 4 October 2007, pp. B1–B2.

Some celebrities are able to polish their tarnished images with fans and advertisers alike. However, not everyone is eager to forgive. *Advertising Age's* online edition reported that Michael Vick was in talks to become a spokesman for People for the Ethical Treatment of Animals (PETA) and quoted Dan Shannon, director of youth outreach and campaigns for PETA, as saying: "We want him to discourage people from taking part in dog fighting. I can do it until I'm blue in the face, and it might not convince anybody. Michael Vick sure can. He can say, 'Look, I did it, I was wrong, and it ruined my career.'" A sizeable backlash from enraged readers ensued after *Advertising Age* posted the story online; by the time the printed edition came out three days later, PETA had dropped the idea.[12]

"Having a highly paid, highly visible celebrity endorser is like having an expensive beach home on the Florida coast. It's swell, if you don't mind lying awake all night worrying about approaching storms," says Bob Garfield, ad critic at *Advertising Age*.[13]

At least initially, you should avoid using celebrities in your ads because it's unlikely you'll have that type of budget on your first account. Also, it doesn't show original thinking. Your portfolio should show how you can solve problems creatively, not how a famous personality can do it.

Advertising Trade Characters

Giggling doughboys. Talking dogs. Dancing raisins. All of these whimsical characters have pitched products and ideas over the years. Creative guru Ted Bell notes that characters like the Jolly Green Giant and Colonel Sanders are part of the "fabric" of their companies and that consumers have an emotional attachment to them even after they've been on hiatus. "You see the Colonel, and it's instant recognition, with no explanation necessary. When the old characters reappeared, the new cynical audience seemed to like them. Younger consumers enjoyed them because they were corny and campy; for older viewers, they had nostalgic appeal."[14]

Done right, the character will communicate a selling feature. Snap, Crackle, and Pop reinforce the unique sound that Kellogg's Rice Krispies cereal makes when milk is added to it. The AFLAC duck and the Geico gecko have made their insurance companies seem more approachable and have put their companies' brand names front and center in consumers' minds.

Because they don't age, advertising characters can appeal to different generations of consumers. Smokey Bear, Tony the Tiger, and the Jolly Green Giant are more than 50 years old. The Quaker Oats man has been around since 1887 (his cholesterol level must be great). And to celebrate Mr. Peanut's 90th birthday (and Planters 100th anniversary), ad agency FCB invited consumers to vote for a new look for the famous icon. Ads showed Mr. Peanut in outrageous getups instead of his signature top hat, walking stick, and monocle.

---

[12] Rich Thomaselli, "Can the Public Forgive Vick? Athlete Plots PR Comeback," *Advertising Age*, 4 May 2009, pp. 1, 30.

[13] Bob Garfield, "Champion Forgoes Endorser and Scores a Couple of Points," *Advertising Age*, 14 July 2003, p. 29.

[14] Warren Berger, *Advertising Today* (London: Phaidon Press, 2001), p. 285.

Even the comic strip *Bizarro* had fun with the challenge and showed Mr. Peanut dressed as a rapper.

Perhaps the best thing about animated characters is the control you have over them. Unlike a celebrity, they won't be caught shoplifting, driving under the influence, or saying something stupid in public. But like a celebrity, they can attract a loyal fan base. The parade of advertising icons is one of the most popular features of the annual Advertising Week celebration in New York.

Still, many creative directors find advertising trade characters to be gimmicky and old-fashioned. In some cases, they're right. The trick is to make the character relevant to consumers. This can mean cosmetic surgery and a personality makeover. The old M&M candy characters from the 1950s were cutesy by today's standards. Thanks to a makeover by Vinton Studios and BBDO, the candy characters developed personalities—faults and all. Red is self-absorbed and views himself as the leader of the M&M pack. Yellow is sweet but a bit simple. Green is oh-so-sexy, especially when she wears her white go-go boots. And Blue is cool in his dark shades.

Likewise, the king from Burger King underwent a makeover. The 1970s king was a cheery cartoon character who performed magic tricks with cheesy sidekicks like Sir Shakes-A-Lot and the Wizard of Fries. In 2004 Crispin Porter + Bogusky reintroduced the BK King as a quirky, and some say creepy, character that appeals to young men. Russ Klein, chief global marketing officer of Burger King, told *Adweek* the campaign has "remystified" the brand and has made it a pop culture leader.

Like humor and celebrities, advertising trade characters must be relevant to the consumer and the brand. Also, keep in mind that just because people love your character, it won't necessarily mean they love your brand. Most people loved the singing sock puppet from Pets.com, but few understood why they needed to order pet supplies over the Internet. The loveable sock puppet is now traded on eBay as a collector's item.

> Ethical Issues

How Far Will You Go to Be "Creative"?

Ask yourself these questions about advertising:

- Should profit or prudence prevail as surveys indicate women, Hispanic Americans, and African Americans are prime targets for cigarettes and alcohol when most consumers are consuming less of both?
- Should a commercial for a popular pain reliever reveal that the reason "more hospitals choose our brand" is that it is supplied at a reduced price?
- Should consumers who have no medical background be told to ask physicians about specific brands of prescription drugs?
- Should an automobile maker show a sports car outracing a jet plane in an age when speeding motorists are killed daily?

- Should advertisers cast TV commercials using such imperatives as "she should be blond—or if brunette, not too brunette—and pretty, but not too pretty"; "midwestern in speech, middle-class looking, gentile"; or "if we're using blacks, make them upscale"?
- Is even a mock representation of violence and domination appropriate in commercial speech?
- What about sexual innuendo? If sex sells, should there be limits?

Advertisers can go too far in their attempts to be creative. In some cases, consumers become so outraged they start a boycott. The media may choose not to run an ad they find offensive, as *Elle* magazine did when it ran a blank page instead of running a Benetton ad that showed a man dying of AIDS. And sometimes the ad goes so far that it breaks the law and results in substantial penalties. Chapter 13 addresses legal issues you should consider before crafting your messages.

> The Creative Challenge

Good advertising doesn't come easily. Anyone can dash off an ad in minutes; you see or hear those every day in print, on radio or television, in your mailbox, on billboards, and on the Internet. And anyone can come up with an idea that's rude and offensive. But unless the idea relates to the selling message and to the intended audience, it'll be a flop.

Creative advertising makes a relevant connection with its target audience and presents a selling idea in an unexpected way. The relevance comes from the facts, whereas the unexpected connection is the inspiration of the writer and art director—the added ingredient that gets the message noticed. That's what this book is all about: identifying the advertising problem, gathering the facts, and—through a process of critical and creative thinking—adding your own insight to create a memorable ad that not only commands attention but also delivers the right message to the right audience in a language that audience understands and accepts.

Look at some of the ads in this book. See if you can identify the unexpected element in each ad, and see if it passes the test for relevance. Note whether the idea of entertainment has fused with the factual message so that you now want to read the ad. Did the people who created the ad do everything possible to attract the audience they were seeking? Or did they sacrifice a good idea to a funny punch line or an outrageous statement or image? That is, did the entertainment content intrude on the message or reinforce it?

> Suggested Activities

1. Take inventory of the number of advertising messages you see or hear in a single day. How many did you count, how many do you remember vividly, and what were some of the more unusual places in which you found advertising?

2. Find examples of advertisements that you believe are in bad taste. What could the advertisers have done to eliminate such qualities without diminishing the effect of the selling message?

3. Although some might argue that it's impossible to be creative about ordinary products, advertising professionals will retort, "Boring is no excuse!" Writer James Gorman takes nearly three magazine pages exploring the charm of the lowly pencil. In part, he writes:

> *Remember pencils? Remember the smell of cedar shavings, the pleasure of writing on clean paper with that first, sharp point, the sense of guilt and personal inadequacy that comes from seeing the gnawed and stubby evidence of your own anxiety neurosis next to some obsessive's long, sharp points and untoothed hexagonal pencil bodies?*
>
> *I had forgotten about pencils until recently, when I overdosed on computers and decided I needed a rest cure. Pencils. Do people still use them? Are there living pencil devotees? Or have the laser printer and the felt tip pen conquered all?*[15]

Gorman adds that he called the Pencil Makers Association in Moorestown, New Jersey, and discovered "pencils are doing fine." U.S. companies make about 2 billion pencils each year, he learned. He also discovered pencils got their start in 1564, when a large graphite deposit was uncovered in England. Gradually, folks figured out what to put around the graphite, what to mix it with, and how to cook it to make it stronger and better for writing. Ernest Hemingway and Walt Whitman used pencils, not pens or typewriters (or computers). So did Vladimir Nabokov and Herbert Hoover. Henry Thoreau ran a family pencil-making business. Finally, Gorman learned "you could eat one every day without harming yourself," mainly because the "lead" in a pencil is not lead but graphite.

If Gorman can take three full pages to entertain you about pencils, can you create a single advertisement to provide the pencil with a personality so appealing that readers will clamor for more pencils? Try it.

4. Write a critique of an ad using the following guidelines:

   a. Does the ad gain your attention without confusing you? Does it stand out?

   b. Does the ad show empathy with the target audience? Is the target clearly defined? Is there a sense of involvement—that is, does the ad make you exclaim, "That's me they're talking about"?

   c. Does the ad clearly communicate the key benefits? Is there a reason to consider purchase, whether rational or emotional, overt or implied? If implied, is it clear enough?

---

[15] From James Gorman, "Pencil Facts," *Wigwag*, February 1990.

d. Does the ad use a memorable device to make you remember something important? Is there a line or phrase in the copy that is especially outstanding?

e. Does the ad make you feel positive about the product, the ad, the manufacturer, and yourself?

f. Is there anything about the ad, however small, that might be improved? How could it be improved?

BRIEFCASE

IKEA Thinks Outside (and Inside) the Box

IKEA, the world's leading home furnishings retailer, is found in 36 countries and four continents. From Abu Dhabi to Zurich, nearly every major city has an IKEA store. So it might come as a surprise that New York, one of retailing capitals of the world, didn't have an IKEA store until 2008. Until then New Yorkers had to travel to New Jersey, Long Island, or Connecticut to shop at IKEA.

IKEA turned to Deutsch NY to create a campaign announcing the grand opening of its Brooklyn, New York store. But this couldn't just be a typical grand opening; it had to be a GRAND opening.

Deutsch started by defining the target audience as New York women, specifically New York moms, age 25 to 54. To that broad demographic they added the following insight: "She lives in the most creative city in the world—she is modern, progressive, stylish and smart and she prides herself on expressing her own creativity. This is especially true within her home; she ultimately wants to feel proud about opening the doors to her home, as this is a reflection of her personal taste. She is constantly on the lookout for ways to creatively optimize her living space. Being New York, the sources of inspiration are everywhere and sometimes she feels overwhelmed with the stimulus."

From this insight came the strategic idea: "IKEA is a destination for inspiration." But Deutsch understood that the campaign messages couldn't just *say* inspiration; they had to *be* inspired. After all, the campaign was going to run in the world's most media-saturated city in front of an audience that has seen it all. The messages also needed to communicate the June 18th grand opening as well as several selling points, including affordable prices, multiple transportation options, and home delivery.

So where did Deutsch find inspiration for the campaign? From one of the unique characteristics of IKEA furniture—the fact that it comes flat-packed in cardboard boxes, ready to take home and enjoy.

Deutsch hired artist/architect John Hobbs to create gigantic sculptures of New York City landmarks out of IKEA boxes. Hobbs and his team assembled four sets: the Brooklyn Bridge, Empire State Building, Brooklyn water towers, and the Brooklyn/Lower Manhattan scene that showed the new IKEA store in the foreground. The sets were massive; one measured 96 feet long and 16 feet high. These sculptures were featured in television, print, and out-of-home media and were later displayed on-site at IKEA Brooklyn.

© Inter IKEA Systems B.V. Reprinted with the permission of Inter IKEA Systems B.V.

© Inter IKEA Systems B.V. Reprinted with the permission of Inter IKEA Systems B.V.

A television commercial used stop-motion photography to show people constructing the lower Manhattan skyline out of IKEA boxes. The final box, a replica of the new IKEA Brooklyn store, is placed in the foreground as the announcer says, "IKEA is moving to New York City. Help us unpack June 18th."

A second spot features a replica of the iconic Brooklyn Bridge being constructed out of IKEA flat-packed boxes. Once completed, a delivery truck made of IKEA boxes crosses the bridge and the announcer says, "For the Grand Opening of IKEA Brooklyn, we wanted to do something big. So, taa daa. Help us unpack on June 18th."

Billboards used the ubiquitous IKEA boxes as teasers. Prior to the grand opening, passersby were told, "Do not open until June 18th." After June 18th, the boxes were opened to reveal photos of innovative room settings. Prices for the rooms reinforced the IKEA value proposition.

To give New Yorkers the opportunity to experience the inspired designs IKEA offers, 20-by-20-foot boxes were placed along the high-pedestrian-traffic areas of Union Square, Borough Hall Plaza, the Brooklyn Public Library, and Cadman Plaza. Brand Ambassadors beckoned curious passersby to venture inside the studio size boxes to discover fully decorated IKEA room settings.

© Inter IKEA Systems B.V. Reprinted with permission of Inter IKEA Systems B.V.

© Inter IKEA Systems B.V. Reprinted with permission of Inter IKEA Systems B.V.

Fully decorated room settings also traveled the streets of New York. The ultimate room with a view, a room with glass walls, was transported on the back of a truck to showcase innovative small-space solutions for New Yorkers, whether they live in a brownstone, studio, or railroad flat.

Mass-transit messages highlighted the ease of getting to the Brooklyn store, an important consideration since most New Yorkers don't own a car. A radio spot reinforced the myriad of ways you could get to the store, including a few tongue-in-cheek methods, such as teleportation.

Messages on bus shelters captivated commuters: "Yo! Check this out. It's a box. It's a cardboard box from IKEA. That's right. Admit it. You're awestruck by its corrugated awesomeness. But don't be jealous. You can get your own box. Just go to the new IKEA store in Brooklyn. It's open June 18th. And it's easy to get to. Just hop on a B77 or B61 bus. They drop you off right in front of the store. Mighty convenient. You should give it a shot. Who knows, maybe you could get a box of your very own. Boxes rule!"

Subway signs reinforced how easy it is to get to IKEA Brooklyn: "See this box? It just came home on the subway from the new IKEA store in Brooklyn. A lot of people don't like to touch the handrails on the subway. Which is silly. This box touched the handrails and it's perfectly fine. If this box can do it, so can you. IKEA Brooklyn is open on June 18th. And it's a safe subway ride away. Just take the F, D, M, N, R to the 4th Ave./9th Street station. From there, free shuttle buses run to IKEA every 15 minutes. And if you really don't want to touch the handrails, just use your sleeve."

A message promoting the free water taxi reads: "Look at this! An IKEA box, fresh from the IKEA store in Brooklyn. Right across the East River. Very scenic ride. Didn't have to pay a cent for the privilege, either. You should try it.

Smell that? That's the sweet aroma of home delivery. Smells like convenience. Get a whiff. It's kind of like the feeling you'll get with home delivery from the new IKEA Brooklyn. Just order your furniture when the store opens June 18 and it will arrive flat-packed and ready for assembly the very same day. Just like this box. Think of the possibilities. Think of the smells. You could get a dining table delivered and then get pizza delivered to eat on it. That's living.

IKEA®

Home is the most important place in the world.

It's free for people, too. IKEA Brooklyn is open on June 18th. And it's just a short sail away. Take the free water taxi from Pier 11 in lower Manhattan. It leaves every 15 minutes. And remember to watch for the seagulls. Furniture shoppers make easy targets."

Not only is it easy to get to Brooklyn IKEA, it's also easy to get the purchases home. For those who don't want to schlep the boxes home with them, IKEA offers same-day home delivery. And what better way to tout the virtues of home delivery than on the ultimate home delivery box, a pizza box?

Now that's thinking outside—and inside—the box.

BRANDING
IDENTITY AND IMAGE STRATEGY

By Sue Westcott Alessandri, PhD

Assistant Professor, Suffolk University

Think for a minute about the Apple campaign featuring Justin Long as a Mac and John Hodgman as a PC. Long is portrayed as laid-back, young, and cool, and Hodgman is portrayed as middle-aged, dated, and stodgy. Anyone who has ever experienced either type of computer knows Apple is making a statement about its computers: that they are simple to use, are protected from viruses, and will look great on any desktop. By using Long to portray these attributes—and an opposite person to portray the competition's negative attributes—Apple is reinforcing the personality of its brand. Simply put, Macs are cool.

To help ensure the campaign resonates across the globe, Apple changes the actors and humor to reflect the cultural tastes of different nations. In the U.K., actors from the "Peep Show" play characters that are similar to the roles they play in the British television sitcom. David Mitchell is sensible and stuffy, while Robert Webb is sociable and uninterested in getting a job. In Japan, where it is rude to brag about one's strengths, two local comedians from the troupe "Rahmens" highlight the work/home divide.

The Mac vs. PC campaign has become part of our pop culture. Numerous riffs and takeoffs of the campaign appear on YouTube. Microsoft even responded with its own send-up, starring a Microsoft engineer who resembles Hodgman saying, "Hello, I'm a PC, and I've been made into a stereotype." When covering the 2008 Democratic Primary, the *New York Times* ran a story titled, "Is Obama a Mac and Clinton a PC?"[1]

[1] Noam Cohen, "Is Obama a Mac and Clinton a PC?" *New York Times,* 4 February 2008, p. C3.

> Branding Defined

A brand, much like a person, has a personality, and all of what you know
and think about a brand comes through in this personality in two ways:
through its identity and through its image. A brand's identity is its strategically planned and purposeful presentation of itself to gain a positive image in
the minds of the public. Basically, this is the company or brand's presentation
of itself, including its name, logo, tagline, color palette, architecture, and even
sounds. So everything the brand presents to the public—everything people see
and hear—is part of its identity. You could say that this is like a person: name,
appearance, clothing style, and mannerisms make up someone's identity.

Identity Leads to Image

How the public perceives that identity is another story, which in advertising
is called the image. A brand's image is the public's perception of the company
or brand. Generally, the image is a direct result of the associations people
have with the company or brand identity. If you think about this from a communications perspective, the image is formed every time a consumer sees an
ad, goes into a store where the brand is sold, or has an interaction with the
brand's service staff.

A brand's identity—and subsequent image—form the core of a brand, and
both are considered important when it comes time to advertise the brand. After
all, without an identity, a brand would have no public persona, because its identity is its public face in the marketplace. The identity elements used in advertising serve as shortcuts that help consumers form an image of the brand:

Identity + Image = Reputation

All of the individual identity elements—the name, logo, tagline, colors, and
architecture—taken together are often referred to as the brand's "gestalt,"
which means a whole is more than the sum of its parts. Take Target. From
the ads on television to the décor in the stores, the experience is the same:
a clean, hip, cool experience that elevates the image of discount shopping.
The same is true of Apple—its TV ads, with the white background, match the
clinical white feel of the retail stores, which reflects the clean white of the
company's personal computers. This consistency and symmetry contribute to
the feelings of loyal Mac users: that there is no better computer.

A brand's identity, however, is about more than just visuals. If you begin
to think of a brand's identity as the way it projects itself to the public, and
its image as the way that projection is perceived, then it's easy to take the
next step and say that a brand's identity and image are directly related to the
brand's reputation.

The reputation of the brand is less fleeting than its image and a lot
harder to shape: it is formed over time through the overall impressions of the
brand image. This means an investment in a positive brand identity could pay
off in the form of a positive reputation, which often translates into customer
loyalty. For example, Saatchi & Saatchi has coined the term "Lovemark" to

refer to brands "inspiring loyalty beyond reason."[2] Lovemarks represent those brands, like Mac, that almost defy logic in terms of loyalty.

Just as loyalty can be won, it can also be lost. In some cases, it might even come back. Lacoste, the once-iconic "alligator" brand named for famous tennis star René Lacoste, was introduced in the 1930s and became a pervasive brand among the preppy set. Allegedly the first logo to be displayed on clothing as a design element, the brand was mass marketed and lost its luxury appeal. Eventually, the brand all but faded away. Recently, however, the brand has made a comeback: with a higher price point and a reputation for being among the most expensive tennis shirts on the market. Sales have increased 800 percent since 2002, and you have to wonder if the "firm's emblematic logo" is at the heart of its success.[3]

Although it's not possible for every brand to reach legendary status, it should always be a brand's aspiration. That said, reputation starts with the identity. Given that the reputation of a brand is derived from its image, marketers can at least *indirectly* control the image and the reputation of a brand by *directly* managing the visual identity.

> Brand Identity Elements

Name

A brand's name is one of its most important assets—and one of its most marketable ones. Naming brands has become such a big business that some agencies do nothing *but* name brands. Think about some brand names you like: did you ever think about how they were created? Naming companies may have created some, others might have been created by advertising agencies, and brand owners—maybe even the chief executive—might have created some.

Today, the Nike brand name is so pervasive that you probably don't even think about how perfectly it fits the brand: Nike was the goddess of victory. Would "Dimension 6" have catapulted a sneaker company to the same type of success? That was Nike founder Phil Knight's choice for a name. Legend has it that the Nike name came to an employee in a dream.[4] And who says sleep is unproductive?

A good name breeds success, but even the best name can't shield a company from poor performance. A name is just one part of the brand identity.

Logo

A logo is the visual symbol a brand or company uses to identify itself to consumers. A logo might be simply a graphic element, or it can be a word. The latter is typically called a logotype.

---

[2] Kevin Roberts, *Lovemarks: The Future Beyond Brands* (New York: Powerhouse Books, 2004).

[3] Vivian Manning-Schaffel, "Lacoste: The Alligator's Back in Style," *BusinessWeek,* 13 September 2006. Rumor has it that the alligator logo appeared on shirts as a joke. Rene Lacoste was dubbed "The Alligator" by the American press after a bet he made. Lacoste asked a friend to draw a crocodile, which he then had embroidered onto the blazer he wore on the court.

[4] Karen Post, "Brand Naming," *Fast Company,* 6 June 2005.

Think about Target's red bull's-eye logo. The red and white symbol is an example of a simple logo that realistically reflects the brand's name. Now picture the bull's-eye logo with three bullet holes through it. Does it work the same way? Would the store be as successful with a bullet-riddled logo? Target founders considered the bullet holes in the 1960s, but even then they decided it probably wasn't in the best interest of the brand.[5]

Two strong brands that employ a logotype as their primary identifiers are JetBlue and FedEx®. The origins of JetBlue are somewhat quaint. The team developing the start-up airline had been struggling for a name. The chief executive officer, David Neeleman, wanted the word "blue" either as the airline's name or in the airline's name. Trademarking such a generic term, however, would have been difficult. In discussing the name with Neeleman, the airline's communications person suggested incorporating "blue" into the name. "'I just kept babbling,' she said, 'and I said, "you can call it 'fly blue' or you could call it 'jet blue' or you could . . ." 'Jet Blue,' conjured seemingly from nowhere, was, clearly, what they'd been groping for." Later that evening, the communications person sketched out a simple logotype on a napkin. It was as simple as that.[6]

The FedEx logotype, on the other hand, was designed by Landor Associates. It was designed in 1994 during a corporate name change from Federal Express to FedEx. If you look at it quickly, the purple and orange logo seems simple and straightforward. When you look more closely at the white space between the "e" and the "x," you see clearly an arrow pointing to the right. Landor designed the logo this way, but FedEx chose not to promote the arrow. Instead, finding the arrow, which has been said to connote speed and precision, is a hidden bonus (see Figure 2-1).

Tagline

A tagline is the short phrase typically used with a brand name or logo. It might also be called the brand's slogan or even motto. More than any other identity element, the tagline will change over time. It will change on a number of occasions: when there is a new creative campaign developed, when a new advertising agency is hired, or just when the tagline has outlived its usefulness. Verizon Wireless, for example, has used several taglines in recent years including "Can You Hear Me Now?" "We Never Stop Working For You," and "America's Most Reliable 3G Network."

Some taglines, however, remain—and even become a part of the vernacular. Having a tagline that becomes a part of popular culture can be both positive and negative. In the short term, having a popular and memorable tagline helps people associate the tagline with the brand. That's the positive side. On the negative side, a tagline that has become a part of popular culture is close to becoming a cliché. Over the long term, the tagline becomes less about the

---

[5] Laura Rowley, *On Target: How the World's Hottest Retailer Hit a Bull's Eye* (Hoboken, NJ: John Wiley & Sons, 2003).
[6] Barbara S. Peterson, *Blue Streak: Inside jetBlue, the Upstart that Rocked an Industry* (New York: Penguin Group, 2004).

© 2007 FedEx. FedEx service marks used by permission.

Figure 2-1
The arrow within the
FedEx logo promotes the
brand's promise of speed
and precision.

brand than about being a punch line. If people start quoting the tagline but can't name the brand, it's time to dump the line.

Color Palette

Think about your favorite brand. Is the brand strong enough that you can identify it with just a color? It might seem strange that just a single color can help market a product, but think about your college. It probably has one or two colors that it uses as its primary means of identification, and those colors are worn proudly by athletes, fans, and anyone stopping at the bookstore to buy a T-shirt. In some cases, schools' athletic programs adopt names that include their major color. Syracuse University's official color is orange, and the athletic teams were renamed in 2004. The new name? You guessed it: The Orange.[7]

This isn't simply a collegiate phenomenon, however. Companies have begun to understand the power of having their brands associated with colors. For example, UPS began an advertising campaign in 2002 that asked, "What can brown do for you?"

When you think of Coca-Cola, you probably think of soda, but you probably also think of the color red. The strong associations people have with Coke and the color red are the result of more than 100 years of Coca-Cola cultivating them. Legend has it that Coca-Cola's long-running series of Christmas ads inspired Santa to wear red and white.

In 1994, Coca-Cola's number one competitor, Pepsi, decided it didn't "own" a color the way Coke owned red, unless you counted its heavy use of white on its cans and signage. Instead, Pepsi decided it could build on blue as its color. The company did research and determined blue was a color that "consumers viewed . . . as modern and cool, exciting and dynamic, and a color that communicated refreshment."[8]

---

[7] There are several schools that include their official color in their team names. A few examples include Tulane University Green Wave, Marquette University Golden Eagles, DePaul University Blue Demons, Cornell University Big Red, Duke University Blue Devils, St. John's University Red Storm, University of Alabama Crimson Tide, and Harvard University Crimson.

[8] John A. Quelch, *Pepsi Blue* (Boston, MA: Harvard Business School Publishing, 1998).

Color alone is also a marketable element of identity. For example, Glidden and Home Depot partnered in 2006 to offer "Team Colors," a collection of licensed paint colors that are exact matches to the colors of professional basketball, football, and baseball teams, as well as NASCAR drivers and colleges.

If you still don't believe in the power of color associations—and the marketability of color—think about how it would feel to receive a diamond ring in a red velvet box. And now think about how it might feel to receive a ring in a Tiffany & Co. robin's egg blue box. Tiffany & Co. has developed such a strong brand association for its packaging that empty boxes are regularly sold on auction sites.

Architecture and Interior Design

The next time you enter a company's building or headquarters, think about what the building or office says about the company. Could you tell (without looking at a sign) what the company does? If the answer is "yes," the company or brand is doing a good job projecting its identity onto its architecture and interior design.

Perhaps one of the most prevalent uses of interior design to reflect identity is in the communications industry. Advertising agencies often decorate their offices to reflect what they do. Because advertising is a creative field, it's not unusual to walk into an agency and see theme décor. The interior design of Concept Farm in New York is built around a farm theme. This is carried over from the agency's website.

Finally, some of a company's identity—and its interior design—results from its history. The Leo Burnett agency in Chicago keeps a bowl of apples in every reception area to remind those working there that Burnett was told he would end up selling apples on the street when he opened an advertising agency during the Great Depression.

Sounds

For years, motorcycle company Harley-Davidson had an application pending with the U.S. Patent and Trademark Office to trademark the sound of its "common crankpin V-Twin engine." Harley-Davidson thought its engine's roar was unique enough to distinguish itself from other motorcycles, and the company wanted to make sure no other company was able to copy this unique sound.[9] Although Harley-Davidson eventually withdrew its application, the government has recognized that sounds make up an important part of an organization's identity and may serve as a trademark. (For more information about trademarks, see Chapter 13.)

---

[9] Michael B. Sapherstein, "The Trademark Registrability of the Harley-Davidson Roar: A Multimedia Analysis," *Intellectual Property and Technology Forum,* www.bc.edu/bc_org/avp/law/st_org/iptf/articles/content/1998101101.html, accessed August 10, 2006.

Figure 2-2
Squeeze this toy AFLAC duck and it quacks, "AFLAC...AFLAC...AF-LAAACK," just like in the TV commercials. Profits from the sales of the stuffed toy duck support the AFLAC Cancer and Blood Disorder Center at the Children's Healthcare of Atlanta hospital.

Photo by Debbie Garris.

In 1950, NBC was allowed to register its chimes as a trademark. Still in use today, the musical notes G, E, and C instantly identify the peacock network. Another soundmark you might recognize is the roar of the MGM lion, which you have likely heard at the beginning of movies.[10]

Today there are few sound trademarks, but many companies and brands recognize specific sounds can be an efficient—and memorable—part of their identities. Think of the sounds you hear as you enter a Starbucks—anywhere around the country. Chances are good that you can describe it, even if you don't know the exact musical composition, because the sound has become so closely associated with the store.

A specific example of sound being part of a brand's identity is the "zoom zoom" campaign for Mazda. The sound of the whispered "zoom zoom" has become indelibly linked with the brand, and hearing it makes people think of Mazda.

Another great example is the advertising campaign for the American Family Life Insurance Company. Don't think you know the campaign? Sure you do—it's the AFLAC campaign where the duck quacks "Aflaaaack!" to remind people that they need supplemental insurance. Check out Figure 2-2. If you're like many people, you'll find yourself quacking—not saying—the name of the insurance company.

[10] Ibid.

Developing a Brand's Identity: Doing the Research

As with most advertising projects, a brand's identity is typically developed only after thorough research. Later in this book, you will learn about various types of research methods that advertising agencies use to gain insight about their brand's consumers.

The type of research required to build a brand's identity involves looking at two different audiences: internal and external. The internal audience is generally employees and perhaps other people who have a close connection to the brand. The external audience is made up of customers, shareholders, vendors, the community, and other stakeholders.

For example, recalling the Pepsi example, when Pepsi wanted to learn how consistently its identity elements were being projected to consumers around the world, it hired an agency to perform a visual identity audit. The agency collected 2,000 photographs of Pepsi identity elements (in this case, the name and logo as it was used on signage and on soda cans) from 34 countries. What this collection of elements reflected was startling: there were a number of inconsistencies in the identity elements being used both within some countries and between countries.[11]

> Projecting a Unified Message

Think about how you learn. Most people need to hear, see, or experience something more than once to really understand it. For example, when an ad appears on television, you might not see the entire spot the first time or you may hear the spot while you're doing something else so that you don't actually see the ad. It may take a few times before you can actively process what the ad is trying to achieve. Marketers generally understand this, and most have come to embrace the concept of integrated marketing communications (IMC), which refers to the idea that a brand will communicate most effectively if it sends a unified message through multiple media.

The pioneers of IMC developed the concept based on how consumers process the information they receive. Just as you learn by building on the knowledge you have in memory, rather than starting from scratch each time, marketers now understand information is not replaced but is combined with existing messages stored in memory. What this means for you as an advertising professional is that you need to remember consumers are receiving—and trying to process—not just the messages you create but also those being created by all types of communications professionals. You see, the average consumer doesn't care about differentiating among the various forms of communication: advertising, public relations, promotions, and so on. Rather, consumers tend to view all of a brand's communication as one flow of indistinguishable media.[12] (See Chapter 12 for IMC tactics.)

---

[11] Quelch, Pepsi Blue.
[12] Don Schultz, S. I. Tannenbaum, and R. F. Lauterborn, *Integrated Marketing Communications: Pulling It Together & Making It Work* (Chicago: NTC Business Books, 1993).

In terms of media, brands today have a number of choices when it comes to deciding how to send a message to consumers. Each of these media choices should be viewed as a consumer touchpoint, an opportunity to communicate with the public and reinforce the brand message. Often, individual elements or a group of them will appear in a number of the following media: advertising, websites, product packaging, building interiors and exteriors, signs, clothing and uniforms, stationery, forms, publications, automobiles and other vehicles (including airplanes and blimps), promotions and giveaway items. These are traditional elements, but marketers have begun to use more creative ways to reach people with brand messages, including inserting identity elements into TV shows and films.

Translating an Identity for Different Media—and Cultures

If you've ever traveled to another country, you've probably noticed the existence—some would save pervasiveness—of American brands. Perhaps the brand names and logos were the same as you've seen in the United States, or maybe the brand names were translated into the local country's language or dialect and the logo was different from the one used in the United States. Either way, the decision to standardize (maintain consistent identity elements across countries and cultures) or localize (translate and design identity elements for the local culture) is an important one for marketers.

The decision to standardize or localize includes many considerations, including how consumers in a particular part of the world view the brand and whether the name of the brand will translate effectively. Whatever the decision, it is not made lightly.

> Protecting Brand Identity

One of the best ways to protect the investment in a brand identity is to build support for the identity from the inside out. Employees who truly embrace a brand become brand champions or brand ambassadors, and these employees can typically be counted on to protect the brand's identity. One good way to motivate all employees is to reward employees for spotting infringement or potential infringement of any elements of the identity.

At a minimum, however, all employees should be educated on the importance of brand identity. This education should focus on the importance of consistency day to day. Even minor inconsistencies over a long period can harm the brand's equity—and may result in a diminished brand image.

The law can also be a powerful ally for those responsible for protecting a brand identity. As stated earlier, the brand identity's "owner" is accountable for the integrity of the identity, so every available method should be used to protect it before invoking the protections of both trademark and copyright law. But if the need arises, the law can provide a powerful defense.

An identity is considered intellectual property, and the three areas of the law that protect intellectual property are trademark law, copyright law, and patent law. Trademark law and copyright law are the most relevant in the context of advertising and to issues of identity. (Both are discussed in Chapter 13.)

> The Identity Strategy

Identity strategy includes all processes and decisions made relating to how a brand projects itself in the marketplace. The specific decisions related to identity include choosing a logo, developing a tagline, deciding which color or colors will best identify the firm, and determining whether the brand should have a sound or particular architectural style that will help differentiate it in the marketplace.

A brand's identity is its primary source of identification, but it's also the source of a consumer's associations, which are the links between values and a brand. These can be positive or negative, and the way to help control these associations—this image—is to carefully manage identity strategy.

To help develop or enhance a brand's identity, a company should engage in appropriate research—from perceptual research with consumers (if developing a brand identity) to a brand audit to ensure consistency (if enhancing a brand identity).

Once a strong identity is achieved, brand owners need to protect the identity to ensure its exclusivity. Protection can include preventative measures, such as training employees on the proper use of the identity, or invoking legal means, such as through trademark or copyright law. (For more on this, see Chapter 13.)

> Suggested Activities

1. Think about two brands that compete in the same category, such as Coke and Pepsi or UPS and FedEx. Investigate which is the stronger brand from a market share perspective. In your opinion, how much of the brand's dominance is derived from its identity and its image?

2. Think of your favorite brand and make a list of its identity elements. What is the brand's name? What does the logo look like? Can you remember the tagline used in marketing? Are there specific colors associated with the brand? Does the brand use sound as one of its identity elements?

   a. Now think about the same brand's image: what do you perceive when you see any of the brand's identity elements?

   b. Do you know if the brand generally has a positive, neutral, or negative reputation?

3. Perform a brand identity audit: choose a brand and then gather as many items—or pictures of items—as you can find that include the identity elements. Once you have the items and pictures, spread them out and see if the elements are used consistently or inconsistently. What are the benefits of consistency? What are the problems with inconsistency? If the elements are used inconsistently, what could the brand do to fix the problem?

Now That's a Large Pizza!

"Better ingredients. Better pizza" is more than a catchy slogan. It's the brand promise that Papa John's restaurants deliver every day. Papa John's pizzas are made with fresh-packed tomato sauce from vine-ripened tomatoes, not concentrate. The dough is fresh, never frozen, and is prepared with clear-filtered water. Vegetable toppings are cut fresh everyday. And what's *not* in Papa John's pizzas also adds to the brand promise. Papa John's does not add monosodium glutamate to any pizza topping. It does not use meat fillers in its meat products. And all Papa John's pizzas and side items feature zero trans fats. It's little wonder why for nine years running Papa John's has been rated number one in customer satisfaction among all national pizza chains in the American Customer Satisfaction Index.

In its quest to offer pizza lovers better ingredients, Papa John's became the first national pizza chain to add a 100 percent whole-wheat crust to its menu. Introduced in May 2008 at all 2,700-plus Papa John's restaurants in the United States, the whole-wheat crust is the answer to Americans' desire to eat more whole grains as part of a healthier diet. One large slice of cheese pizza on whole-wheat crust contains fewer calories, two-and-a-half times the fiber, and less sodium when compared to one large slice of cheese pizza on the original Papa John's crust. Containing 40 grams of whole grains per serving—more than 80 percent of an entire day's recommended whole grains intake—the Papa John's whole-wheat crust pizza has earned the official "100% Whole Grain Stamp" from the Whole Grains Council.

Papa John's wanted a big idea to promote its new offering so it turned to famed "earth grains" artist Stan Herd to create a six-acre crop circle depicting its new wheat crust. Herd's all-natural masterpiece, located in a wheat field a mile away from the Denver International Airport, took 600 hours to complete and used red mulch for pepperonis, corn stalks for green peppers, black mulch for black olives, and harvested wheat for cheese. The crop circle also included the Papa John's logo, the words "New 100% Whole-Wheat Crust Pizza," and "America's choice."

Courtesy of Papa John's.

Courtesy of Papa John's International, Inc.

The "pie from the sky" was officially unveiled on August 7, 2008. As a way to celebrate the completion of the crop circle, Papa John's offered its whole-wheat crust pizza for just $8.88 when ordered online at www.papajohns.com on August 7–8.

The timing and location were "part strategy, part serendipity," according to Papa John's PR director Tish Muldoon. The wheat used to make the flour for the crust is grown in Colorado, a fact that the Colorado Department of Commerce was pleased to promote. Denver was also host of the 2008 Democratic National Convention in August, which brought more traffic—and news media—into the already busy Denver International Airport.

The larger-than-life pizza was seen daily by thousands of passengers, right up until the first snowfall. Stories about the crop circle appeared in 314 media outlets, including *The New York Times* and CNN. Gross media impressions exceeded 65 million. Moreover, whole-wheat crust pizza orders accounted for 20 percent of online sales during the promotional push and the offering is now a permanent menu item. So the next time you want a healthier answer to your pizza cravings, be sure to order the whole-wheat crust at Papa John's. And be sure to bring a big appetite.

3

DIVERSITY
TARGETING AN EVER-CHANGING MARKETPLACE

An African American President. A Latina Supreme Court judge. We've recently made great strides in this country on issues of diversity . . . so why is this chapter necessary? The answer is quite apparent if you walk into a typical advertising agency. You'll find that people of color are underrepresented. Men hold the majority of creative director positions. And people over 50 are a rare breed at advertising agencies that want to project a young, hip image.

As you will remember from Chapter 1, effective advertising makes relevant connections with its target audience. To be successful, advertisers must understand, respect, and embrace the diversity of American consumers (see Figure 3-1).

Today, one-third of Americans are people of color.[1] And four states—California, Texas, Hawaii, and New Mexico—are what demographers call "majority-minority" states, meaning that more than half of their population belongs to a group other than non-Hispanic whites.[2]

The buying power of ethnic Americans is growing dramatically. The Selig Center for Economic Growth at the University of Georgia estimates the buying power of African Americans, Asians, and Native Americans in the United States was $1.5 trillion in 2008, more than triple its 1990 level of $454 billion. Selig also reports that these three minority racial groups account for 13.8 percent of the nation's total buying power in 2008, up from 10.6 percent in 1990.[3]

---

[1] Unless otherwise specified, data reported in this chapter are from the 2000 U.S. census.
[2] Brad Edmondson, "America New and Improved," *Advertising Age,* 2 January 2006, p. 31.
[3] Jeffrey M. Humphreys, "The Multicultural Economy 2008," *Georgia Business and Economic Conditions,* Third Quarter 2008, p. 2.

campaignforrealbeauty.com 〜 *Dove*

New Dove Firming.
As tested on real curves.

Courtesy of Unilever USA, Inc.

Figure 3-1
The Dove Campaign for Real Beauty understands that beauty comes in all sizes, ages, and ethnicities.

Ethnic groups dominate the purchases of numerous products and services. Not only that, but white consumers, particularly those aged 12–34, are increasingly influenced by the fashion, dining, entertainment, sports, and music tastes emerging from minority communities.

Figure 3-1 (continued)

☐ wrinkled?
☐ wonderful?

Will society ever accept
old can be beautiful?

Courtesy of Unilever USA, Inc.

> African Americans

African Americans are 39.3 million strong and have an annual purchasing power of $913 billion.[4] From 1990 to 2008, the nation's black population grew by 28.3 percent compared to 22.1 percent for the total population.

[4] Ibid, pp. 3, 10.

Figure 3-1 (continued)

flawed?

flawless?

Does beauty mean looking like everyone else?

Courtesy of Unilever USA, Inc.

The American Community Survey indicates that the median age of blacks is 31.4, compared to 36.4 years for the total population. Furthermore, 29.5 percent of the black population is under 18 years old compared to 24.6 percent of the total population, which may explain why African American consumers increasingly are setting trends for young adults of every race and ethnic background.[5]

[5] Ibid, p. 5.

Figure 3-1 (continued)

Courtesy of Unilever USA, Inc.

Magazine Publishers of America reports that African American teens spend 20 percent more than the average U.S. teen on items such as clothing, casual/leisure shoes, and video game hardware. They also exert more influence on household purchases of cereal, fast food, and personal care products than do average U.S. teens. And they're more brand-loyal when it comes to personal care products, footwear, and food purchases.[6]

The median income for African American households is $29,470, which is considerably less than the $42,228 median income of the population as a whole. Part of this may be attributed to the fact that African Americans lag behind the U.S. average in academic attainment. Just 4.8 percent of the African American population hold advanced degrees, compared with 8.9 percent for the population as a whole. However, the education level is improving. Census data show that the proportion of African Americans who have completed high school or college rose by 7.4 percent from 1997 to 2007, and that gain was the largest reported for any group. If it is true that income follows education, then this market will be even more important to advertisers in the future.

> Hispanic Americans

The nation's 47 million Hispanic Americans represent 15 percent of the U.S. population, making them the nation's largest minority group. The Hispanic population is gaining strength not only in their numbers but also in their spending power. Hispanics' economic clout has risen from $212 billion in 1990 to $951 billion in 2008.[7]

Hispanics originate from many places, including Mexico, Cuba, Puerto Rico, Central and South America, and Europe. The majority live in large cities, particularly Los Angeles, New York City, and Miami, and when it comes to advertising, most prefer to read and hear ads in Spanish. According to Strategy Research, 55 percent of Hispanics prefer to see ads in Spanish, 30 percent would choose English, and 13 percent don't have a preference between the two languages.[8] However, Christy Haubegger, the founder and former publisher of *Latina,* says, "Income is closely correlated with language ability. It's rare to see an affluent household that is Spanish-dependent."[9] Chiqui Cartagena, author of *Latino Boom!,* believes it is wise to advertise in both languages because acculturated Latinos live in two worlds: the English world of work or school and the Spanish world of family and friends[10] (see Figure 3-2).

As a result of the diversity of their roots, Hispanic Americans have varied tastes in food, clothing, and music. Advertisers should pay attention to these cultural subtleties, as Coca-Cola did when it ran three versions of an ad for Hispanics. Each ad featured the Coca-Cola logo and a can of Coke, along with the words *y su comida favorita* ("and your favorite meal"). But the food next to the Coke was changed to reflect different cultural preferences. Tacos were featured for the western Mexican American segment, pork loin for the southeastern Cuban American segment, and *arroz con pollo* ("rice with chicken") for the northeastern Puerto Rican segment.

[6] "African-American/Black Market Profile," Magazine Publishers of America, 2008, p. 11.
[7] Humphreys, "The Multicultural Economy 2008," p. 7.
[8] Laurel Wentz, "Reverse English," *Advertising Age,* 19 November 2001, p. S2.
[9] Laurel Wentz, "Cultural Cross Over," *Advertising Age,* 7 July 2003, p. S2.
[10] Chiqui Cartagena, *Latino Boom!: Everything You Need to Know to Grow Your Business in the U.S. Hispanic Market* (New York: Ballantine, 2005).

Figure 3-2
People from all over the country have stories about loved ones killed by a drunk driver. This urgent plea to stop friends from driving drunk runs in English and Spanish to reach all segments of Hispanic Americans.

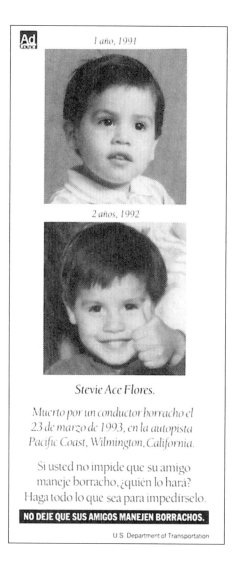

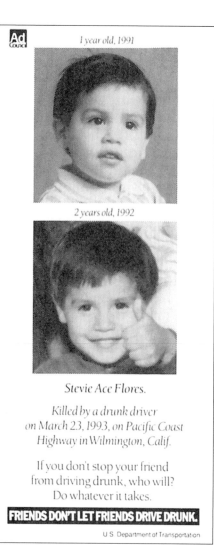

Courtesy of the U.S. Department of Transportation and the Ad Council.

Although it's complex, the Hispanic American market is attractive to advertisers. Hispanics go grocery shopping three times as often as non-Hispanics and spend 43 percent more per household on food than non-Hispanics, according to the Food Marketing Institute. *American Demographics* reports that when compared with the average U.S. household, Hispanics allocate 100 percent more of their budget on apparel for babies, 67 percent more on apparel for girls, 33 percent more on apparel for boys, and 22 percent more on apparel for men. And like African Americans, they spend 91 percent more on rented dwellings than the average American household.[11]

Part of the reason for these expenditures is that Hispanic Americans tend to have larger families, with almost 3.5 people per household compared with

[11] Alison Stein Wellner, "Our True Colors: The Multicultural Market Is Fast Becoming a Multibillion Dollar Marketplace," *American Demographics,* November 2002, p. S9.

the national average of just greater than 2.5.[12] To reach Hispanics successfully, advertisers should recognize the importance placed on the family and tradition. A radio station learned this lesson after it promoted a sweepstakes that offered a prize of two tickets to Disneyland and received a limited response from Hispanics. The reason? Hispanics didn't want to choose which family members should go.

Marketers must also pay close attention to the ages of their target groups. Nearly 70 percent of the Hispanic population is younger than age 35, representing more than $300 billion in purchasing power.[13] As you might expect, age plays a major role in shaping attitudes, styles of dress, and choice of music. But there's an interesting twist: the younger generation of Hispanics is often more in tune with its ancestry than the older generation is. A special *Newsweek* poll reports those older than age 35 are more likely to identify themselves as American, whereas those younger than age 35 are more likely to identify themselves as Hispanic or Latino.

Matias Perel, CEO of interactive agency Latin3, says when approaching second- and third-generation Hispanic youth, "You are going to capture him with an online campaign, not because you speak to him in Spanish, but because you are going to capture his heart—with an action that is relevant to him, relevant to his roots and his ethnicity."[14]

> Asian Americans

Asian Americans, at 14.5 million, represent 4.8 percent of the U.S. population and are one of the fastest-growing segments. The median income for Asian American households is $55,026, which is 28 percent higher than the U.S. average. Asian Americans are also better educated than the overall U.S. population. Nearly half (49.2 percent) of Asian Americans over age 25 have at least a bachelor's degree, compared with 28 percent of the general U.S. population. Furthermore, 17 percent have an advanced degree, compared with the national average of 9 percent.[15]

Perhaps due to their higher-than-average education and income levels, Asian consumers spend more than the average U.S. household on housing, education, vehicles, insurance, and pensions.

Despite the affluence of this market, advertisers have been slow to target Asian Americans because of the complexity of their varied languages and cultures. Many nationalities are included in this minority group, among them Chinese, Japanese, Korean, Filipino, Vietnamese, and Asian Indian. And there's not a common language among them. People of Chinese origin, the largest subgroup, speak dozens of different dialects, with Mandarin, Cantonese, and Taiwanese being the most common. Elliot Kang of Kang & Lee Advertising explains, "If your father is Japanese and your mother is Korean

---

[12] "While U.S. Households Contract, Homes Expand," AmeriStat release, March 2003.
[13] Mireya Navarro, "Advertisers Carve Out a New Segment," www.nytimes.com, 22 May 2003.
[14] Julie Liesse, "The Face of the New General Market," *Advertising Age Special Edition,* 3 March 2008, p. A5.
[15] Wellner, "Our True Colors," p. S2.

and you lived in Taiwan and then your parents got divorced, moved to Los Angeles and your father took up with the Filipino woman next door and married her—well, that's almost like being Asian American."[16]

As you can imagine, horror stories abound about advertisers who have inadvertently alienated this market. Marlene L. Rossman points to a number of such stories. One advertiser wished Chinese Americans a "Year New Happy" rather than a "Happy New Year." Another used Korean models to target the Vietnamese community, oblivious that the two groups rarely look anything alike. And a footwear manufacturer depicted Japanese women performing foot binding; as Rossman observed, this not only stereotyped Japanese people as "shogun" characters but also displayed the company's ignorance about Asian cultures, given that foot binding was practiced exclusively in China.[17]

InterTrend Communications, an agency specializing in the Asian market, offers the following tips on its website. From Japan: It's bad luck to write your name in red ink and good luck to dream about Mt. Fuji. From Vietnam: Never take a picture with only three people in it because it is unlucky for all. From China/Taiwan/Hong Kong: Don't give clocks as gifts to Chinese people because they are a symbol of death, and try to avoid dining with seven dishes because it symbolizes a funeral meal. From Korea: Never shake your foot because it drives out good fortune. Colors and numbers have special meaning. Red means prosperity, happiness, and luck to the Chinese, Japanese, and Vietnamese. White means death and bad fortune to the Vietnamese and Chinese. The number 7 means wealth to the Japanese and luck to Koreans. The number 8 means wealth and luck to the Chinese, which explains why the 2008 Olympics started on 08-08-08.

Although each nationality has distinct cultures and traditions, there are two important commonalities: the importance of family and tradition. In Asian cultures, it is inappropriate to call attention to oneself; therefore, tactful ads targeted at Asian Americans don't show an individual standing out from the crowd or achieving personal gain by using the product. Instead, culturally conscious ads focus on how the family or group benefits. With the importance placed on tradition, "new and improved" claims are far less effective than those that stress a company's or a product's many years of excellence.

> Native Americans

The estimated 2.5 million Native Americans make up less than 1 percent of the nation's population, and nearly 42 percent earn less than $25,000 annually.[18] As a result of its small size and limited spending power, few marketing efforts are aimed at this group.

Although companies don't often target this group in advertising campaigns, they use Native American names and symbolism. For example, Chrysler uses

---

[16] Elliot Kang, "Marketing to a New America Conference," New York City, 22 May 1996.
[17] Marlene L. Rossman, *Multicultural Marketing: Selling to a Diverse America* (New York: American Management Association, 1994).
[18] Wellner, "Our True Colors," p. S18.

the name Cherokee for one of its jeeps, Land O' Lakes butter features a Native American on its package, and fans of the Atlanta Braves buy toy tomahawks to show their team support. Ironically, Crazy Horse malt liquor was named after the Sioux leader who was opposed to alcohol consumption among his people. Needless to say, these images are insulting to Native Americans.

The Selig Center for Economic Growth reports that Native American buying power rose to $61.8 billion in 2008, up from $39.1 billion in 2000. The Selig Center predicts Native American buying clout will reach $84.6 billion in 2013.[19] Furthermore, the 2002 Survey of Business Owners Minority-Owned Business Enterprises, released by the U.S. Census Bureau in 2001, showed that the number of Native American–owned firms increased more than six times faster than the number of U.S. firms and their receipts rose 4.5 times faster than those of all firms.[20]

> Arab Americans

There are 1.25 million Americans with Arab ancestry, according to the 2000 census. As with other ethnic minorities, Arab Americans are extremely diverse, with ethnic roots tracing back to Lebanon, Syria, Egypt, Palestine, Iraq, Morocco, and Jordan. Roughly two-thirds of the Arab American community is Christian. Arab Muslims represent 23 percent of the Arab American population and are the fastest growing segment. Although bilingualism is disappearing in most assimilated groups, nearly half of Arab American households report some Arabic use.

Arab Americans live in every state, but more than two-thirds live in just 10 states. The metropolitan areas of Los Angeles, Detroit, and New York are home to one-third of the population. And 20 percent of the population of Dearborn, Michigan, is Arab American, with more than 40 percent of the public school students of Arab heritage.

Similar to the national average, about 64 percent of Arab American adults are in the labor force, with 5 percent unemployed. More than 70 percent of working Arab Americans hold managerial, professional, technical, sales, or administrative jobs. Medium income for Arab American households in 1999 was $47,000, compared with $42,228 for all households in the United States. Close to 30 percent of Arab Americans have an annual household income of more than $75,000.

As is often the case, high income correlates with a high level of education. More than 40 percent of Arab Americans have a bachelor's degree or higher, compared with 24 percent of Americans at large. Seventeen percent of Arab Americans have a postgraduate degree, nearly twice the American average of 9 percent.

Although advertisers traditionally seek segments of the population that are highly educated and have high incomes, Arab Americans are often ignored in advertising. Even worse, they are often the victims of negative

[19] Humphreys, "The Multicultural Economy 2008," p. 5.
[20] Ibid.

stereotypes. Legal scholar Leti Volpp explains: "September 11 facilitated the consolidation of a new identity category that groups together people who appear Middle Eastern, Arab or Muslim. This consolidation reflects a 'radicalization' wherein members of this group are identified as terrorists and misidentified as citizens."[21]

The terrorist stereotype has infiltrated into advertising messages. Fortunately, some of these messages were prevented from airing. A commercial for an Ohio car dealership called for a "Jihad on the automotive market" and said salespeople would be wearing burqas, a traditional garment in some Muslim nations, and children would receive rubber swords on "fatwa Friday." The radio script said, "Our prices are lower than the evildoer's every day. Just ask the Pope." This spot didn't make it on the air because several radio stations refused to run it.

Likewise, objections from the Arab American Institute put a stop to a billboard that the Missouri Corn Growers Association planned to run to promote ethanol. The objectionable billboard asked, "Who would you rather buy your gas from?" and showed a farmer standing in a cornfield and King Fahd of Saudi Arabia.

In an ad designed by the New York–based Coalition for a Secure Driver's License, a man was wearing a kaffiyeh, a traditional Arab headscarf, and clutching a grenade in one hand and a driver's license in the other. The headline read, "Don't license terrorists." Lamar Advertising, a national billboard firm, refused to run the ad.

Rachel Ray triggered a backlash when she appeared in a commercial for Dunkin' Donuts wearing a scarf that some thought looked like a kaffiyeh. She was chided for wearing a "jihadi chic" garment on some blogs. Dunkin' Donuts dropped the ad.

Rumors spread during the 2008 Presidential election that Barack Obama is Muslim. Former Secretary of State Colin Powell, a Republican, endorsed Obama on NBC's *Meet the Press* and addressed the Muslim "controversy." Powell commented, "Is there something wrong with being a Muslim in this country? No, that's not America. Is there something wrong with some 7-year-old Muslim kid believing that he or she can be President?"[22]

> How to Reach Ethnic Minorities

Savvy advertisers know several methods for reaching ethnic minorities:

- *Feature minorities in starring roles, not just in the background.* In addition to making a positive connection to the ethnic group portrayed, research shows general audiences favorably receive advertisements featuring minorities. Luke Visconti, partner at Diversity, explains, "A white audience will say, 'That's a nice picture of a mother and child' and an

---

[21] Michael Hastings-Black, "To Draw Muslin Customers, Marketers Must Engage Them Instead of Isolate Them," *Advertising Age,* 10 November 2008, p. 16.
[22] *NBC's Meet the Press*, 19 October 2008.

African-American audience will say, 'Ahhh, an African-American mother and African-American child; this product gets me.'"[23]

- *Seek the opinions of people who hail from the culture you are targeting.* However, be aware that traditional research methods may not work. For example, a survey written in English won't achieve results representative of all American households because more than 15 percent of the U.S. population doesn't speak English at home. In addition, many immigrants are uncomfortable giving out information to strangers over the telephone or through the mail.

- *Be sensitive to nuances in language.* It's not enough merely to translate the English copy of a campaign into another language. Perdue found this out the hard way when someone unfamiliar with regional slang translated the line "It takes a tough man to make a tender chicken" into Spanish. The translation came out something like, "It takes a sexually stimulated man to make a chicken affectionate." For some other examples of mistranslations, see the box on page 50.

    Spanish words can have different meanings, depending on national heritage. The word *bichos,* for example, means "bugs" to Mexicans and "a man's private parts" to Puerto Ricans. Imagine you were writing an ad for an insecticide and weren't aware of this subtlety! Also, be aware of different uses of English words because they can mean different things to different groups. For example, sales of Stove Top stuffing improved among African Americans after the company realized this group uses the word "dressing" rather than "stuffing."

    Keep in mind that what may be acceptable to one group of people may be offensive to another group, as Volkswagen learned when it ran billboards for the GTI sports car accompanied by the words "Turbo-Cojones." *Cojones,* which means "testicles" in Spanish, has become a casually used term for boldness or guts in the English vernacular but has never lost its more vulgar connotation in its native language. Volkswagen removed the billboards after receiving complaints.

- *Show the diversity of each group.* Advertisers from a few decades ago were guilty of showing light-skinned African American models in fashion ads and dark-skinned African Americans in ads promoting services. Their botched attempt to be inclusive helped further stereotyping.

- *Learn about their heritage.* It's important to show respect for ethnic holidays, whether it's the Chinese New Year, Kwanzaa, or Cinco de Mayo. It's also important to pay close attention to details and learn about preferences in food, icons, customs, and clothing. For example, McDonald's was praised for a commercial that featured a celebration that looked like a simple birthday party to most viewers but was recognized by Hispanics as the *quinceañera,* the celebration of a girl's coming of age at 15.

[23] Stuart Elliott, "Campaigns for Black Consumers," www.nytimes.com, 13 June 2003.

DIVERSE GOOFS: TRANSLATING AMERICAN ADVERTISING INTO OTHER LANGUAGES

- When Braniff Airlines touted its upholstery by saying "Fly in leather," it came out in Spanish as "Fly naked."
- Coors' slogan "Turn it loose" means "Suffer from diarrhea" in Spanish.
- When Vicks first introduced its cough drops in Germany, they discovered that Germans pronounce "v" as "f," which made their trade name reminiscent of the German word for sexual penetration.
- Puffs tissues learned its lesson in Germany, too. "Puff" in German is a colloquial term for a whorehouse.
- The Chevy Nova never sold well in Spanish-speaking countries, perhaps because "No va" means "It does not go."
- When Pepsi's old campaign, "Come Alive. You're in the Pepsi Generation," was translated into Chinese, it announced that "Pepsi will bring your ancestors back from the grave."
- GM's "body by Fisher" translated, in some languages, into "corpse by Fisher," something you would not want associated with automotive design.
- Coke discovered problems in China when they used Chinese characters that, when pronounced, sounded like "Coca-Cola" but meant "Bite the wax tadpole."

> The 50-Plus Market

Today, 38 percent of American adults are older than age 49, and that group is expected to grow to 47 percent by 2020, according to the U.S. Census Bureau. Furthermore, those in the 50-plus population control 55 percent of the discretionary income in the United States and account for the majority of personal assets—upward of 80 percent of the money in savings and loans and 70 percent of the net worth of U.S. households. The Federal Reserve Board reports family net worth peaks between the ages of 55 and 74 at an average of $500,000.[24]

Some of these older, affluent consumers choose to spend a portion of their wealth on second or third residences, luxury goods, or vacations. According to recent statistics, the 50-plus population purchases 60 percent of all packaged goods, more than half of all new cars, and spend 75 percent more per vacation than consumers under 50.[25] The Travel Industry Association of America estimates that people 55 years and older account for $130 billion in travel spending and 80 percent of luxury travel. "The name of the game is not $59 hotel rooms but $15,000 cruises," Richard M. Copland, president of the American Society of Travel Agents told the *New York Times*.[26]

Despite the wealth and spending power of older Americans, advertisers remain youth obsessed. "For a lot of brands we work with, it's sexier to advertise to the younger consumers who are trendier, much more fashion-forward, very social and very in the public eye," Melissa Pordy, former senior vice president and director for print services at Zenith Media, told *Advertising Age*.[27] Other marketers believe it's important to reach younger consumers

[24] Peter Francese, "Older and Wealthier," *American Demographics,* November 2002, pp. 40–41.
[25] Brent Bouchez, "Engage: Boomers," Mediapost.com, 22 June 2009.
[26] Harriet Edelson, "Appealing to Older Travelers' Wanderlust, and Wallets," www.nytimes.com, 25 May 2003.
[27] Hillary Chura, "Ripe Old Age," *Advertising Age,* 13 May 2002, p. 16.

who aren't yet brand loyal, rather than go after older consumers who are more set in their ways. However, a study conducted by the American Association of Retired Persons (AARP) and Roper ASW found brand loyalty varies more by product category than by age.

The young-obsession may be explained by the hiring practices at ad agencies. The average age of an advertising agency creative person is 28, and nationwide less than 5 percent of agency personnel are over 50.[28]

Ignoring the older market is bad enough, but some advertisers go so far as to insult older people by portraying them as doddering and senile. Fifty-six percent of respondents in an *Adweek* online poll agreed that when seniors appear in advertising it's usually as an unflattering stereotype.[29] A commercial for Midas was pulled after the company received complaints from adults of all ages. In the commercial, an older woman learns about Midas' lifetime guarantee, takes off her shirt, and asks, "What can you do with these?" A commercial for Boost Mobile showed an old man falling off a skateboard. The supertitle on the screen explained the joke, "Boost Mobile. Designed for young people. But it's just more fun showing old people."

Tips to Reach the Older Market

- *Don't think of older people as just one market.* Think about some of the older people you know: grandparents, neighbors, professors, and community leaders. Chances are these people are quite different from one another. They have different political views, different senses of humor, different lifestyles, and so on. Like any group, the older population is composed of people with varied incomes, education levels, ethnic backgrounds, and life experiences. Using one message to reach all these people is about as absurd as saying one message will work for all people aged 18–49.

- *Don't specify age.* Research has shown most older people feel younger than their birth certificate indicates. As financier and statesman Bernard Baruch said, "To me, old age is fifteen years older than I am." Several years ago, an advertising campaign featured the claim "the first shampoo created for hair over 40." It bombed. The problem? Younger people refused to buy a product aimed at older people, and older people didn't want to be reminded they had older hair.

- *Cast models who reflect the way your audience feels.* Use models who portray an upbeat, positive image, not those who reinforce the negative stereotypes of frailty and senility. But don't go to the opposite extreme. Although you may be tempted to show a person in his 80s who bungee jumps, most older people won't identify with this portrayal.

  Also, keep in mind that many older people feel younger than what their birth certificate says. Remember how you identified with the "big" kids when you were younger? Well, the opposite is true as you age. Most

[28] Bouchez, "Engage: Boomers."
[29] Jack Feuer, "Pride and Prejudice," *Adweek,* 28 October 2002, p. 9.

older people see themselves as 10 to 15 years younger than their birth certificate indicates. Therefore, use models who are younger than your target audience. But don't go overboard. Jack Feuer from *Adweek* said, "Stop treating us like middle-aged people who are trying to stay young. Start talking to us like young people who have some wrinkles."[30]

- *Tell the whole story.* Although commercials with fast editing cuts and little copy may appeal to younger audiences, older audiences prefer a narrative style, with a beginning, a middle, and an end. As Grey Advertising summed it up, this generation is MGM, not MTV.

  When writing copy, give facts, not fluff. After years of shopping, older people are not going to be fooled into buying your product simply because you tell them that it's "new" or "the best." After all, these folks remember product flops, and they want facts to back up your claims. Give them a compelling reason to try your product, and they'll be willing to read lengthy copy or listen to a detailed pitch.

- *Set your ad in type at least 12 point to make it more legible.* Ad legend Jerry Della Femina joked about small type on packages to make his point at a creative conference, "I rubbed bath gel into my beard and followed it with shampoo, thinking it was conditioner."[31]

- *Don't remind older people of their vulnerability.* It's a fact of life: arthritis, high blood pressure, heart problems, and other ailments bother more older people than younger people. However, older people know they have aches and pains without being reminded by you. Rather than dwell on the problems, your advertising should show how your product offers solutions.

- *Show older people as they are, happy with themselves.* A poll from Harris Interactive, in conjunction with the Marriott School of Management at Brigham Young University, found that 47 percent of those 65-plus consider themselves "very happy," compared to only 29 percent of those aged 18 to 24.[32]

  Show older people enjoying life, playing with their grandchildren, volunteering their time, starting new hobbies, and learning new things. Advertisements for Fox Hill Village, a retirement community in Massachusetts, used to show smiling retirees on balconies admiring the beautiful landscape. But when the community ran a series of ads featuring Ben Franklin, Clara Barton, Noah Webster, and other individuals who became famous during their later years, inquiries went up 25 percent.

- *Don't call them names.* "Elderspeak," calling older people by terms such as "Sweetie" and "Dear," is belittling. Even the names "grandma" and "grandpa" can get on the nerves of some older people. "I didn't want to be called 'Grandpa.' A grandpa is a stereotype—someone who has white

[30] Jeff Johnson, "Boomer-ocracy," presented to the Columbia Advertising Club, 9 May 2006.
[31] "The Fine Print," *Adweek,* 25 November 2002, p. 34.
[32] Mark Dolliver, "What Makes Most People Happy?" *Adweek,* 12 May 2008, p. 50.

hair, is hunched over and pees involuntarily," said Alan Zweibel, one of the original writers on *Saturday Night Live*.[33]

- *Try an ageless approach.* Lee Lynch, founder of Carmichael Lynch, points to Harley-Davidson's campaign where the rider is faceless, allowing people to project themselves into the image, regardless of age.[34]

> People with Disabilities

About one in five U.S. residents—19 percent—reported some level of disability in 2005, according to the U.S. Census.[35] Once nearly invisible in ads, people with disabilities are starting to have starring roles. McDonald's showed that people with disabilities can work and be productive citizens through a heartwarming commercial narrated by an employee named Mike, who has Down syndrome. Walmart's advertising features employees and customers in wheelchairs, and one of its TV commercials stars an employee with a hearing-impairment signing to a customer.

Although many people praise these ads, some question the motives behind them. Bob Garfield, a critic for *Advertising Age,* states that jumping from not showing people with disabilities to portraying them as superhuman or as tokens does not help them or the advertiser in the long run.

Screenwriter Mark Moss, who ended up in a wheelchair after a diving accident, told the *Boston Globe,* "Advertisers know that using people with disabilities is politically correct and a viable way to catch people's attention. I look at the phenomenon like I do politicians kissing babies. It's good for the babies . . . it's good for the politicians . . . but we can't be blamed for looking at it with cynicism."[36]

As with any consumer segment, advertising must take care in communicating appropriately to the special-needs community, and extra care should be taken so that they do not appear to be taking advantage of the market. Sensitivity is key, according to Nadine Vogel, president of Springboard Consulting, who says that the disability should never define the person. Rather than call someone a "disabled child" or a "Down's Child," the correct language is "a child with special needs" or "a child who has Down syndrome."[37]

As with any target group, it's important to ask group members what they think. For example, a major fast-food chain ran a newspaper ad with the headline "Introducing our new easy-to-read menu," which was printed over a design that looked like Braille. A student appropriately asked, "Why didn't

---

[33] Ann Zimmerman, "A Grandma or Grandpa by Any Other Name is Just as Old," *Wall Street Journal,* 23 January 2009, pp. A1, A4.
[34] Eleftheria Parpis, "Shades of Gray," *Adweek,* 28 October 2002, p. 19.
[35] Robert Bernstein, "Number of Americans with a Disability Reaches 54.4 Million," U.S. Census Bureau News Release, 18 December 2008.
[36] Maggie Farley, "Ads with a Soul Touch Untapped Market," *Boston Globe,* 6 July 1992, p. 10.
[37] Nadine Vogel, "Not Marketing to People with Disabilities? You're Missing Out," *Advertising Age,* 31 July 2006, p. 18.

they actually print the ad in Braille? If they printed it on a heavier stock and inserted it into the paper, then I could keep it for future reference."

Target learned the importance of being sensitive to the needs of the disabled the hard way. The giant retail agreed to pay $6 million in damages to plaintiffs in California who were unable to use its online site. Many links on Target's website were unintelligible to screen-reading software, which converts written words into speech. The issue centered on the Americans With Disabilities Act, which requires retailers and other public places to make accommodations for people with disabilities. Target is working with the National Federation of the Blind to make its site more accessible.[38]

> Gays and Lesbians

The all-knowing U.S. Census Bureau doesn't ask about sexual preference. While same-sex marriage is legal in a few states, not a single one will show up in the 2010 Census. As a result, there are varying opinions on this market's size, but it is estimated to be between 6 and 10 percent of the population.[39] Its annual spending power was estimated to be $614 billion in 2005 and is projected to grow to $708 billion in 2008, according to Witeck-Combs Communications.[40]

Data from gay publications illustrate the importance of the lesbian, gay, bisexual, and transgender market to advertisers. Six in ten readers of gay and lesbian newspapers have household incomes of more than $60,000, and *The Advocate* reports the median household income for its readers is $90,000.[41] Furthermore, Simmons Market Research Bureau notes that this market segment is exceptionally loyal, with 89 percent of those surveyed reporting they would buy products or services that advertised in gay publications. A spokesperson for Hiram Walker & Sons confirmed this, telling *Advertising Age,* "I have a file of letters an inch or two thick from gay consumers thanking us and vowing their loyalty. A straight consumer wouldn't take the time and say thank you for validating us."[42] When the conservative American Family Association launched a boycott of Ford for advertising in gay publications, gay groups advocated a counter "buycott" to reward Ford.[43]

Another plus to advertisers is what Stephanie Blackwood, cofounder of Double Platinum, calls the "*Will & Grace* spillover." She explains, "First, an upscale gay male in New York City or Los Angeles buys a new product. He then influences his urban, educated female friends, who may work in the fields of communications, fashion or the media, to buy that product. These women, in turn, talk to each other about what to buy, where to eat and even what to buy a boyfriend or father, influencing purchase choices. The result:

[38] "Target Settles with Blind Group on Web Access," *Wall Street Journal,* 28 Augusst 2008, p. B4.
[39] Nicci Brown and Margaret Costello, "Surveying an Untapped Market," *Syracuse University Magazine,* Spring 2002, p. 13.
[40] Michael Wilke, "Luxury Goes Gay," presentation by the Commercial Closet, 2006.
[41] Sandra Yin, "Coming Out in Print," *American Demographics,* February 2003, p. 20.
[42] Nancy Coltun Webster, "Playing to Gay Segments Opens Doors to Marketers," *Advertising Age,* 30 May 1994, pp. 5–6.
[43] Erik Sass, "Gay Ad Market Tops $212 Million," www.mediapost.com, 11 May 2006.

What began as a gay-targeted marketing campaign becomes an efficient and affordable way to promote a product in the mainstream."[44]

> Lessons That Apply to All Segments

Whatever group you are targeting, certain basic principles apply, including the following:

- *Look at the whole person, not one demographic characteristic.* To understand your target audience, you must factor in other demographic aspects, as well as psychographic issues such as values, attitudes, personality, and lifestyle. For example, a middle-aged Hispanic American business executive living in the suburbs is likely to have different attitudes from an inner-city Hispanic American youth living below the poverty line or a single Hispanic American working mother who earns minimum wage. Second- or third-generation Americans have views different from those of recent immigrants. African Americans who formed their core values before the 1960s will have one outlook, those who were a part of the civil rights movement will have another, and teenagers will have still another.

- *Avoid stereotypes.* Taco Bell offended Mexican Americans with its border search commercial because it looked like a search for illegal immigrants. Pennsylvania offended Chinese Americans with its state lottery promotion that featured the line "No tickee—no money." Dow Chemical insulted African Americans with a commercial in which a robust black woman exclaimed, "Ooh-wee!" because it was a reminder of the black mammy stereotype.

  Be wary even of "positive" stereotypes. Not all African Americans are great athletes, musicians, or dancers, yet advertising often portrays them this way. Likewise, not all Asian Americans are good at math or science. When figure skater Kristi Yamaguchi won the Olympic gold medal, the *New York Times* printed an anonymous comment: "We are not all math or science wizards or laundry operators or restaurant owners, but skaters, architects, writers. And more. And less." The same holds true for every group you'll ever want to reach in your advertising.

- *Laugh with them, not at them.* Humor does have a place—if it doesn't rely on insulting stereotypes. To test whether your humor might be insulting to some group, consider replacing one of the characters with a person from a different market segment. For example, if you wanted to make sure customers remembered your client's name, you might be tempted to create a humorous commercial featuring an older person who is hard of hearing and needs to have everything repeated, as Country Time Lemonade did. Or you might feature an older woman who keeps forgetting the name and needs to be constantly reminded, as another company did. However, would it be as funny if a young, physically active college student couldn't hear or remember the name? Probably not.

[44] Yin, "Coming Out in Print," p. 19.

Courtesy of Carnival Cruise Lines. All advertisements property of Carnival Cruise Lines.

Figure 3-3
Carnival Cruise Lines realizes people's idea of fun is quite diverse. Although you might view the campaign as a prime example of niche marketing, in reality it expands the target audience each time it asks, "What's your idea of fun?"

What if you replaced the older woman with a college student who was high on drugs? Would it be a fair portrayal of college students? Of course not.

- *Make relevant ties to their special causes.* Consider donating a portion of your sales to causes dear to your audience's hearts, such as AIDS research, the Council on Aging, the Special Olympics, the Rape Crisis Center, the Native American Arts Foundation, the Sickle Cell Disease Foundation, the United Negro College Fund, or ASPIRA, a scholarship fund for Hispanics. However, make it a long-term commitment, not a one-shot deal.

- *Test your ads on a member of the target audience.* You may find an embarrassing mistake in time to correct it before it runs. For example, the Publix grocery chain might have saved itself from the embarrassment of wishing its customers "a quiet, peaceful Yom Kippur" right below an announcement of a sale on center-cut pork chops and fresh pork shoulder picnics if it had double-checked with someone who is Jewish.

- *Show diversity in your ads.* As America becomes more diverse, it's not only the right thing to do but also the smart thing to do. Figure 3-3 is a good example of an ad that reaches a diverse audience.

Courtesy of Carnival Cruise Lines. All advertisements property of Carnival Cruise Lines.

Figure 3-3 (continued)

> Suggested Activities

1. Watch two hours of prime-time television and record the way the groups mentioned in this chapter are portrayed. How many are in starring roles? How many reflect stereotypes? What products are they selling?

2. Compare print ads for fashion, liquor, and travel that appear in general interest magazines (such as *Cosmopolitan, Vogue, Sports Illustrated,* and *Newsweek*) to those that appear in special-interest magazines (such as *Essence* and *Ebony,* which target African Americans; *Latina* and *People en Español,* which targets Hispanic Americans; and *AARP: The Magazine,* which targets older people). Are the ads similar? If not, comment on the differences in visuals and text that appear to reflect different targeted audiences.

3. Choose an ad (such as for toothpaste, soap, or potato chips) and redo the ad to appeal directly to an ethnic minority.

4. Create an ad selling jeans to people older than age 50.

5. Look at automobile ads from recent decades and comment on the changes in the way people from different ethnic groups are portrayed.

How Sweet the Sound

Verizon Wireless worked with Erwin-Penland (EP) to create an experience that literally touched the heart and soul of the African American community. In what could be described as *Gospel Hour* meets *American Idol*, Verizon Wireless launched "How Sweet the Sound," a two-month-long competition to find the best church choir in Memphis, Tennessee, which culminated in a filled-to-the-rafters, let-it-all-out final concert at the FedEx Forum® Arena in October 2007.

The African American market in Memphis, research showed, was extraordinarily involved in their church communities and very engaged with the gospel music emanating from their choirs. And since music is integral to the DNA of Verizon Wireless, with many of their phones doubling as MP3 players with V CAST music and Rhapsody music downloads and custom ring tones, it seemed liked a natural fit.

Church choirs from all over the greater Memphis area were invited to participate, with cash prizes up for grabs. A "pastor pack" was mailed to nearly 2,000 congregations, which included a DVD trailer to help them imagine the possibilities. Truck-side ads and outdoor advertising blanketed the area, along with targeted banners and table tents placed in the mall across the FedEx Forum. Compelling point-of-sale displays appeared in every Memphis-area Verizon Wireless store.

A website was developed where the choirs could enter the competition and upload their audition videos. Visitors to the site could learn about the competition, view audition videos, vote for finalists, and subscribe to an e-mail newsletter. Verizon engaged local media outlets as cosponsors and endorsers of the event, lending credibility and production assistance for the final big show at the FedEx Forum, where more than 11,000 people poured in.

The contest provided a platform for the Memphis community to experience Verizon's many offerings beyond basic cell phone service. Concertgoers were able to use text messaging to vote for their favorite choir. Text-to-screen allowed concertgoers to interact with the large video screens next to the stage at the final event. Mobile videos of the choirs were provided to download through Verizon Wireless's V CAST music service.

Courtesy of Verizon Wireless.

Local TV affiliates gave the event great coverage. DJs from the local gospel station gave on-air endorsements and provided MCs and judges for the final event. They also helped produce a live web cast of the finals.

"How Sweet the Sound" touched the hearts and souls of the African American community and substantially grew both Verizon Wireless sales and market share. As a tribute to its success, "How Sweet the Sound" won the ultimate accolade from the advertising industry: a Gold Effie, which honors marketing communications that contribute to a brand's success.

Due to the overwhelming success of the program, "How Sweet the Sound" expanded to 10 cities across the country in 2008 and 11 cities in 2009. "Working with Erwin-Penland to execute this amazing program has been a remarkable journey," said Robyn Duval, Associate Director, National Advertising for Verizon Wireless. "'How Sweet the Sound' delivers for the brand AND the Verizon Wireless communities it touches, and this Effie Gold Award win is the ideal culmination for the company."

Courtesy of Verizon.

Courtesy of Verizon.

Courtesy of Verizon.

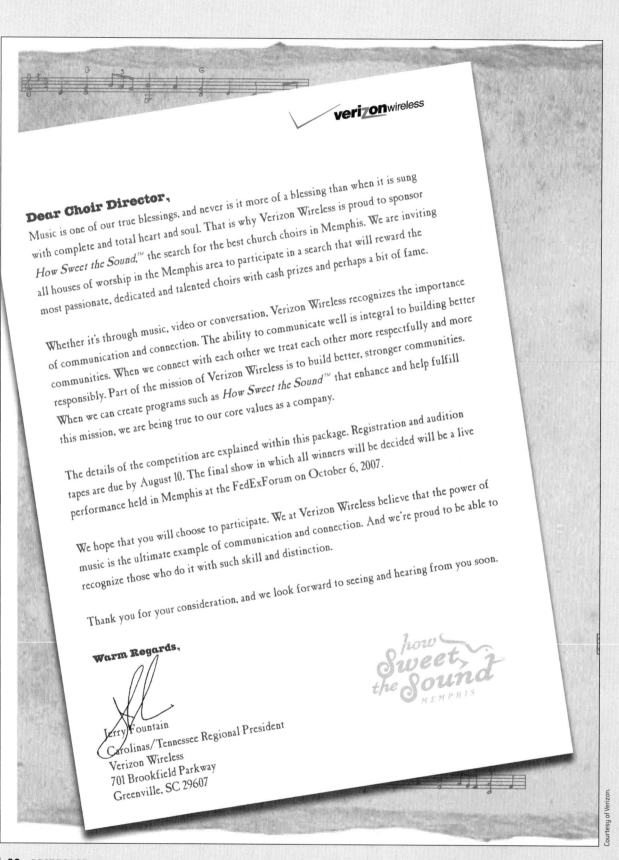

verizonwireless

Dear Choir Director,

Music is one of our true blessings, and never is it more of a blessing than when it is sung with complete and total heart and soul. That is why Verizon Wireless is proud to sponsor *How Sweet the Sound,*™ the search for the best church choirs in Memphis. We are inviting all houses of worship in the Memphis area to participate in a search that will reward the most passionate, dedicated and talented choirs with cash prizes and perhaps a bit of fame.

Whether it's through music, video or conversation, Verizon Wireless recognizes the importance of communication and connection. The ability to communicate well is integral to building better communities. When we connect with each other we treat each other more respectfully and more responsibly. Part of the mission of Verizon Wireless is to build better, stronger communities. When we can create programs such as *How Sweet the Sound*™ that enhance and help fulfill this mission, we are being true to our core values as a company.

The details of the competition are explained within this package. Registration and audition tapes are due by August 10. The final show in which all winners will be decided will be a live performance held in Memphis at the FedExForum on October 6, 2007.

We hope that you will choose to participate. We at Verizon Wireless believe that the power of music is the ultimate example of communication and connection. And we're proud to be able to recognize those who do it with such skill and distinction.

Thank you for your consideration, and we look forward to seeing and hearing from you soon.

Warm Regards,

Jerry Fountain
Carolinas/Tennessee Regional President
Verizon Wireless
701 Brookfield Parkway
Greenville, SC 29607

how
Sweet
the Sound
MEMPHIS

Courtesy of Verizon.

Calling All Memphis Church Choirs

Join us for a moving celebration of music

We are linked, all of us, in pieces of music. And whether the notes are rich like Mississippi mud, or clean like cool rain, this music, those notes - these words - have something to say. Something to sing. And we want to hear it. So bring your old gospel, your country traditional, your up-tempo contemporary, and everything in between to *How Sweet the Sound*™ Memphis. It's time you shared your song.

What brings us together

Communication is an essential part of what ties our community together. Verizon Wireless and our partners want to celebrate the community and people of Memphis with this grass-roots celebration of church music.

What sets you apart

Verizon Wireless is proud to sponsor *How Sweet the Sound,*™ the search for the best church choirs in Memphis. If your baritones sound like sweet caramel or your sopranos like crushed velvet, then you can't miss this unique opportunity to showcase your stuff.

Share your song

We invite you to register and submit your five-minute audition tape showcasing the best of your church choir no later than August 10. This is the tape that will be judged based on technical merit and originality.

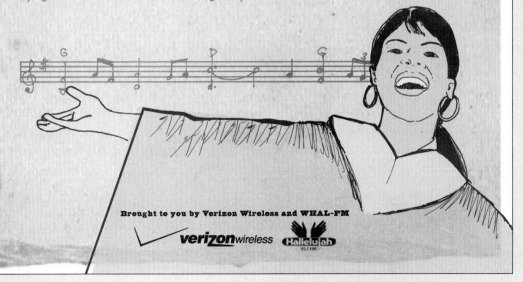

Brought to you by Verizon Wireless and WHAL-FM

verizon wireless   Hallelujah 95.7 FM

Courtesy of Verizon.

Bring the House Down

Create a winning audition tape and submit your registration form

- Audition tape and registration form due by August 10, 2007.
- Audition tapes will be reviewed by a panel of judges who will initially narrow the field to 15. Then of those 15, nine will be chosen to perform onstage at the FedExForum in Memphis Saturday, October 6th.

Requirements for submission

- Passion for faith-based music
- Audition tape (No longer than 5 minutes please)
- Audition tapes must be submitted on Hi-8, MiniDV or VHS

Visit howsweetthesoundmemphis.com for complete contest rules and requirements.

3 Ways to Register

Online

- Log on to howsweetthesoundmemphis.com
- Follow the link at the top of the page labeled "Registration and Audition Tape"
- Complete the form
- Hit submit and follow instructions for mailing in your audition tape
- Print the completed registration and release forms, sign and mail forms and audition tape to *How Sweet the Sound*,™ P.O. Box 8519, Greenville, SC 29604-8519

By mail

- Pick up registration and release forms at a Verizon Wireless Communications Store or WHAL-FM
- Sign and mail the completed forms, along with your audition tape, to *How Sweet the Sound*,™ P.O. Box 8519, Greenville, SC 29604-8519

In Store

Visit your local Memphis area Verizon Wireless Communications Store, where you can leave the completed forms and audition tape with a member of management.

Courtesy of Verizon.

The Winning Sounds

Once the judges have narrowed the choir selections to 15, the general public can log on to howsweetthesoundmemphis.com to vote for their favorite choirs. In addition to being eligible to win an additional $10,000, all 15 will receive $500 just for being named one of the best choirs in Memphis.

That makes the top prize $10,500.

3 category winners will then be chosen in each of three congregation sizes:
- Small: 1 – 500 Congregation Members
- Medium: 501 – 1500 Congregation Members
- Large: 1501 and up Congregation Members

Nine choirs will be chosen altogether to participate in the final event, three from each category. From these nine, there will be three winners, one from each category who will be awarded $5,000 for their choir. There will also be one overall winner who, in addition to a category win of $5,000, will also receive an additional $5,000 for being the overall winner.

Finally, there will be a Memphis Favorite Trophy awarded to the choir who really captures the heart of Memphis.

We are excited to bring such an extraordinary occasion to a community that is so rooted in music. We look forward to your participation and to hearing the best that your choir has to offer.

Brought to you by Verizon Wireless and WHAL-FM

Courtesy of Verizon.

Dates to Sing By

♪ Registration form and audition tape needed by August 10, 2007

♪ Online voting to take place between August 27 and September 7 (to narrow the field from fifteen to nine finalists)

♪ The nine finalist choirs will be notified no later than September 14, 2007

♪ Musical event October 6, 2007 at the FedExForum. Admission is free.

how Sweet the Sound

Courtesy of Verizon.

For More Information

Additional details, entry rules, and judging criteria are available at howsweetthesoundmemphis.com. Or you can speak to a *How Sweet the Sound*™ representative at 800.230.0053, visit one of the Verizon Wireless Communications Stores below or stop by WHAL (95.7FM) 2650 Thousand Oaks Blvd. Suite 4100 Memphis, TN 38118.

Bartlett
8350 Highway 64
Suite 101
Memphis, TN 38133
(901) 759-0515

Collierville
1055 W. Poplar Ave.
Collierville, TN 38017
(901) 854-1067

Hacks Cross
7945 Winchester Rd.
Suite 101
Memphis, TN 38125
(901) 368-6822

Poplar
5323 Poplar Avenue
Memphis, TN 38119
(901) 365-2355

Southaven
6870 Airways Blvd.
Southaven, MS 38671
(662) 349-5665

Union Avenue
1529 Union Avenue
Memphis, TN 38104
(901) 278-2355

Once you've registered and submitted your audition tape, visit howsweetthesoundmemphis.com for updated information and a chance to look at contestant photos, videos and auditions.

Brought to you by Verizon Wireless and WHAL-FM

verizon wireless   Hallelujah 95.7 FM

Courtesy of Verizon.

4

UNCOVERING INSIGHTS
THE BASIS FOR EFFECTIVE CREATIVE WORK

An ad for Chippers Funeral Home in Perth, Australia, features a close-up of an elephant's eye with a tear streaming down. The headline reads, "It is not uncommon to see elephants weep openly at funerals." The copy goes on to describe the "humanity" that elephants extend to dying members of their family. When an elephant dies, the extended family circles it. Slowly, with their heads hanging gloomily, they walk around the body several times before standing still. The bereaved then place branches, leaves, and clumps of grass on the body of their dead relative to form a grave. Occasionally, the elephants also weep.

This poignant ad didn't just write itself. It happened because the agency, Vinten Browning, researched the difficult subjects of death and grieving before writing a single word.

Whether you're trying to understand how people grieve or how people wash their laundry, research is one of the most important stages in advertising.

Thorough searches can help you discover what makes people "tick," uncover new uses for products, learn about new market areas, and spot new trends. By doing a complete job in the research stage, you'll find it's much easier to come up with the big idea and write convincing copy. As advertising legend Ed McCabe shares, "When you are ready to write, it should be automatic, fueled by knowledge so comprehensive that advertising almost writes itself. Only with absolute knowledge of a subject can you hope to transcend the banality of mere facts and experience the freedom of insight."[1]

So where do you start?

> Step 1: State Your Questions

Before you do your research, you need to define the questions or problems you're investigating. For example, who is the most likely prospect for the product? What real or perceived differences make your brand better than a competitor's? How should this be communicated? How do customers perceive the current campaign? By carefully defining your questions, you avoid gathering irrelevant information and wasting time. (See the box below for additional questions you may want answered.)

QUESTIONS THAT MAY LEAD TO THE BIG IDEA

INDUSTRY

Who is the brand leader?

How long have they held that position?

What are the trends in the industry?

Does your brand set the trends or follow them?

Are there any pending issues (legislation, mergers, etc.) that may affect your brand's future?

How does the nation's economic and diplomatic climate affect sales?

Are there any emerging industries that may affect sales in the future?

COMPANY

How long has your company been in business?

What are the high and low points in your company's history?

What is the corporate philosophy?

How has the media covered your company?

How is your company involved in the community?

Is your company known for its product innovations?

Who are the key personnel/managers?

Which company employees have direct contact with customers?

How many brands does your company offer?

How important is your brand to your company?

BRAND

What do current customers feel about your brand?

To what extent does your brand match up with consumers' needs, wants, problems, and interests?

In what ways does your brand exceed consumer expectations?

CONSUMER ANALYSIS

What are the demographic characteristics of the current customers? Competitive customers? Prospects (emerging users)?

What are the geographic characteristics?

What are the psychographics?

When and how often do consumers use the product?

When and how often do consumers buy the product?

How do they use the end product/service?

How do they make the buying decisions?

What information is most important?

Where do they get their information?

Who are your best customers?

COMPETITION

What are competitors doing for the same service/product?

How can we do it better?

What do competitors' previous advertising campaigns look like?

What worked, what didn't?

How do consumers perceive the current campaigns?

---

[1] Warren Berger, *Advertising Today* (London: Phaidon Press, 2001), p. 120.

> Step 2: Dig Through Secondary Sources

Once you have a clear statement of the question, look for answers from information that exists in company records, trade associations, and libraries and on websites.

Company Records

Annual Reports.　In addition to financial data, an annual report contains information about corporate philosophy, the competition, and future goals. However, even bad news in such reports usually has an optimistic slant to it. Therefore, annual reports should be primarily used as a starting point.

Customer Profiles.　If you've ever filled out a product warranty card, entered a sweepstakes, applied for a credit card, or sent for a rebate, you've supplied important information, such as your age, sex, income, education, family size, and living situation (see Figure 4-1). You may also have been asked to state how you learned about the product, where you bought it, and whether you have owned that brand before. Your answers become part of a database that helps marketers know how to reach you and others like you.

Technical Reports.　Granted, much of the information in these reports may sound like gobbledygook to the average reader, but you never know when you'll happen on the perfect line. For instance, Harley Procter uncovered the "99 and 44/100% pure®" claim for Ivory soap from a chemist's report, and David Ogilvy wrote an ad for Rolls Royce using an engineer's statement: "At 60 miles an hour the loudest noise in this new Rolls Royce comes from the electric clock." But don't think you'll see instant results. Ogilvy spent three weeks reading about Rolls Royce before he wrote his classic ad. Procter had to do a little math to arrive at the famous slogan. The chemist reported that the ingredients that did not fall into the category of pure soap equaled 56/100%, hardly a line that would help sell a product for more than 100 years. Figure 4-2 on page 73 shows how facts can make interesting reading.

Websites.　The company's website is a great starting point because it gives an overview of the history of the organization, profiles key employees, highlights its product line, and allows customers to ask questions, download tips, play games, and so on. Also, log on to your competitors' websites and see how they position themselves. Much like an annual report, the website presents the company's best face and is one sided. Therefore, you'll need to do additional digging to uncover insights for your campaign.

One way to obtain a variety of viewpoints is to do a Google search of your brand's name and check out what people are saying. You'll uncover interesting insights from blogs, social networks, consumer comments to websites, wikis, and more. Keep in mind that these sources often represent extreme reactions from people who are in love with a brand as well as people who want a place to vent their frustrations.

PLK®
Multi-Dimensional Intelligence™

IMPORTANT!   IMPORTANT!
Please complete and return within the next 10 days!

1. 1. ☐ Mr.   2. ☐ Mrs.   3. ☐ Ms.   4. ☐ Miss
First Name   Initial   Last Name

Street   Apt. No.

City   State   ZIP Code

Date of purchase
Model number
Serial number
Price paid

Product & Purchase Related Questions Appear Here

11. *Not including yourself,* what is the GENDER and AGE (in years) of children and other adults living in your household?
1. ☐ No one else in household   2. ☐ Child under 1 year

Male Female	Age	Male Female	Age
1. ☐ 2. ☐	|___| years	1. ☐ 2. ☐	|___| years
1. ☐ 2. ☐	|___| years	1. ☐ 2. ☐	|___| years

12. Occupation: *(check all that apply)*   You   Spouse
Professional/Technical .... ☐   1. ☐
Upper Management/Executive .... ☐   2. ☐
Middle Management .... ☐   3. ☐
Sales/Marketing .... ☐   4. ☐
Clerical/Service Worker .... ☐   5. ☐
Tradesman/Machine Operator/Laborer...... ☐   6. ☐

13. Are you or your spouse: You   Spouse
A Homemaker? .... ☐   1. ☐
Retired? .... ☐   2. ☐
A Student? .... ☐   3. ☐
Self Employed/Business Owner? .... ☐   4. ☐
Working from a Home Office? .... ☐   5. ☐
In the Military? .... ☐   6. ☐
A Federal Employee? .... ☐   7. ☐

14. Which group describes your annual family income?
01. ☐ Under $15,000   08. ☐ $45,000-$49,999
02. ☐ $15,000-$19,999   09. ☐ $50,000-$59,999
03. ☐ $20,000-$24,999   10. ☐ $60,000-$74,999
04. ☐ $25,000-$29,999   11. ☐ $75,000-$99,999
05. ☐ $30,000-$34,999   12. ☐ $100,000-$124,999
06. ☐ $35,000-$39,999   13. ☐ $125,000-$149,999
07. ☐ $40,000-$44,999   14. ☐ $150,000 & over

15. Level of education: *(check highest level completed)*
1. ☐ Completed High School
2. ☐ Completed College
3. ☐ Completed Graduate School

16. Which credit cards do you use regularly?
1. ☐ American Express, Diners Club
2. ☐ MasterCard, Visa, Discover
3. ☐ Department Store, Oil Company, etc.
4. ☐ Do not use credit cards

17. For your primary residence, do you:
1. ☐ Own?   2. ☐ Rent?

18. Which of the following do you plan to do within the next 6 or 12 months?

	1-6 Months		7-12 Months
Get Married	☐	1.	☐
Have a Baby	☐	2.	☐
Buy a House	☐	3.	☐
Remodel a Home	☐	4.	☐
Move to a New Residence	☐	5.	☐
Buy a Personal Computer.....	☐	6.	☐
Buy/Lease a New Vehicle.....	☐	7.	☐
Buy/Lease a Used Vehicle	☐	8.	☐

9. Your date of birth: |___| 19 |___|
                      Month   Year

10. Marital status: 1. ☐ Married   2. ☐ Single

> **PLEASE CONTINUE ON BACK!**

Courtesy of the Polk Company.

Figure 4-1
A classic warranty card designed for manufacturers by Polk, one of the nation's leading information gatherers, indicates the scope and nature of data that most consumers are willing to share with companies. The form allows space for product- and purchase-related questions on the left side, but the balance of the questions (usually answered by an overwhelming majority of recipients), covers demographics, lifestyles, shopping habits, and ownership or preferences for pets, computers, Internet services, and large/tall sizes, among other things. Imagine how valuable such information might be, not only to the company whose product the consumer purchased but also to thousands of other companies that use Polk's data services.

Figure 4-1 (continued)

Please send products and
other correspondence to:

First-Class
Postage
Required
Post Office will
not deliver
without proper
postage.

Multi-Dimensional Intelligence™

PO BOX 17XXXX
DENVER CO 80217-XXXX

Standard 7.3

(7/96)

Please fold here.

19. To help us understand our customers' lifestyles, please indicate the interests and activities in which *you* or *your spouse* enjoy participating on a *regular* basis.

01. ☐ Bicycling	21. ☐ Automotive Work	41. ☐ Our Nation's Heritage
02. ☐ Golf	22. ☐ Electronics	42. ☐ Real Estate Investments
03. ☐ Physical Fitness/Exercise	23. ☐ Home Workshop/Do-It-Yourself	43. ☐ Stock/Bond Investments
04. ☐ Running/Jogging	24. ☐ Recreational Vehicles	44. ☐ Mutual Funds
05. ☐ Snow Skiing	25. ☐ Listen to Records/Tapes/CDs	45. ☐ Entering Sweepstakes
06. ☐ Tennis	26. ☐ Avid Book Reading	46. ☐ Casino Gambling
07. ☐ Camping/Hiking	27. ☐ Bible/Devotional Reading	47. ☐ Science Fiction
08. ☐ Fishing	28. ☐ Health/Natural Foods	48. ☐ Wildlife/Environmental Issues
09. ☐ Hunting/Shooting	29. ☐ Photography	49. ☐ Dieting/Weight Control
10. ☐ Power Boating	30. ☐ Home Decorating/Furnishing	50. ☐ Science/New Technology
11. ☐ Horseback Riding	31. ☐ Attending Cultural/Arts Events	51. ☐ Self-Improvement
12. ☐ Sailing	32. ☐ Fashion Clothing	52. ☐ Walking for Health
13. ☐ House Plants	33. ☐ Fine Art/Antiques	53. ☐ Watching Sports on TV
14. ☐ Grandchildren	34. ☐ Foreign Travel	54. ☐ Community/Civic Activities
15. ☐ Needlework/Knitting	35. ☐ Cruise Ship Vacations	55. ☐ Home Video Games
16. ☐ Flower Gardening	36. ☐ Travel in USA	56. ☐ Motorcycles
17. ☐ Vegetable Gardening	37. ☐ Gourmet Cooking/Fine Foods	57. ☐ Watch Cable TV
18. ☐ Sewing	38. ☐ Wines	58. ☐ Home Video Recording
19. ☐ Crafts	39. ☐ Coin/Stamp Collecting	59. ☐ Moneymaking Opportunities
20. ☐ Buy Pre-Recorded Videos	40. ☐ Collectibles/Collections	60. ☐ Current Affairs/Politics

20. Using the numbers in the above list, please indicate your 3 most important activities: |__|__| |__|__| |__|__|

21. Please check all that apply to your household.

01. ☐ Shop by Catalog/Mail	06. ☐ Own a Compact Disc Player	11. ☐ Subscribe to an Online/Internet Service
02. ☐ Member of Frequent Flyer Program	07. ☐ Own a Camcorder	12. ☐ Own an IBM or Compatible Computer
03. ☐ Donate to Charitable Causes	08. ☐ Have a Dog	13. ☐ Own an Apple/Macintosh Computer
04. ☐ Wear Women's Large/Tall Sizes	09. ☐ Have a Cat	14. ☐ Own a CD-ROM
05. ☐ Wear Men's Large/Tall Sizes	10. ☐ Own a Cellular Phone	15. ☐ Speak Spanish at Home

Thanks for taking the time to fill out this questionnaire. Your answers will be used for market research studies and reports. They will also allow you to receive important mailings and special offers from a number of fine companies whose products and services relate directly to the specific interests, hobbies, and other information indicated above. Through this selective program, you will be able to obtain more information about activities in which you are involved and less about those in which you are not. Please check here if, for some reason, you would prefer *not* to participate in this opportunity. ☐

If you have comments or suggestions about our product, please write to:
Customer Service • **XXYZZ Inc.** • **123 Road Ave.** • **Anywhere, USA 12345**

Copyright © 1996 The Polk Company All Rights Reserved

Please seal with tape. Do not staple.

Courtesy of the Polk Company.

Courtesy of Brian Zufall.

ONE GOALIE.

TWO DEFENSEMEN.

THREE FORWARDS.

FOUR HUNDRED FIFTY-SIX STITCHES.

Hockey isn't complicated. There's no high math or complex equations. Just a few basic rules. So after only one game, you'll be an expert. And now you can come see for yourself right here in Columbia. Starting this October you can watch the Columbia Inferno rack up the numbers at the Carolina Coliseum. Call 1-800-4HOCKEY for tickets. Bring a friend, but leave your calculator at home.

THE HEAT IS ON
IN COLUMBIA

Figure 4-2
Facts can be fun, particularly if they have an unexpected twist at the end.

Trade Associations

Name a trade or area of interest, and there's bound to be an association for it, staffed with knowledgeable people. Some of the more offbeat associations include the Flying Funeral Directors of America, the Committee to Abolish Legal-Sized Files, and the International Barbed Wire Collectors Association. There's even an association of associations, the American Society of Association Executives. The following advertising associations provide useful information for its members: The Account Planning Group, the American Association of Advertising Agencies, the American Advertising Federation, the Direct Marketing Association, the Newspaper Association of America, Magazine Publishers of America, and the Radio Advertising Bureau.

Library resources

The following resources will help give you important background information on your client, the industry, and consumers.

- *Business Source Premier* is a great source for full-text articles about companies found in trade publications, business magazines, and scholarly journals. It includes SWOT Analysis, which covers a company's strengths, weaknesses, opportunities, and threats.

- *Compact Disclosure* contains complete Securities and Exchange Commission (SEC) filings for publicly held companies.

- *Communication Abstracts* is arranged by subjects such as advertising, mass communications, journalism, and public communication.

- *County and City Data Book* gives information on states, counties, and cities in the United States on a variety of subjects, including education, labor, income, housing, and retail and wholesale trade.

- *Hoover's* gives industry overviews and detailed listings of companies within industries.

- *InfoTrac Business Index* contains more than 3 million citations, some with complete articles from more than 1,000 business journals and news sources.

- *Lexis-Nexis* provides full-text documents from news, business, legal, and reference publications.

- *Mintel* contains in-depth reports on consumer goods industries for U.S. and overseas markets. Covers competition, consumer demographics, and market share.

- *Standard & Poor's Industry Surveys* provide comprehensive reports analyzing U.S. industries. Each covers trends, current environment, how the industry operates, statistics, and a comparative company analysis.

- *Statistical Abstract of the United States* is considered the "bible" of social, political, industrial, and economic statistical information of the United States. It contains information on everything from the annual retail sales of men's fragrances to the number of eye operations performed in a year.

- *U.S. Census* is updated every 10 years and provides population, ancestry, marital status, education, geographic mobility, occupation, income, and other demographic data. One of the few things it doesn't report, because of the constitutional separation of church and state, is religious data.

Syndicated Market Data

A number of research companies offer paid subscribers a detailed look at the lifestyles and shopping habits of various U.S. markets. Here's a sample:

- *Mediamark Research, Inc.* (often referred to as MRI) provides information on heavy, medium, and light users of various product categories and specific brands and gives the media usage patterns of these groups.

- *Nielsen National Marketing Survey,* available through ACNielsen, provides share-of-market data for products sold in supermarkets, drugstores, and mass merchandisers.

- *Prizm,* available through Claritas, defines every U.S. household in terms of 66 demographically and behaviorally distinct types, or "segments," to help marketers discern those consumers' likes, dislikes, lifestyles, and purchase behaviors.

- *Scarborough Research* surveys 75 markets and provides information about local consumer-shopping patterns, demographics, and lifestyle activities.

- *Simmons National Consumer Survey* is a comprehensive study of the U.S. adult population (18-plus years). It provides information on consumer usage behavior for all major media, more than 450 product categories, and more than 8,000 brands, and it includes in-depth demographics, psychographics, and lifestyle descriptors of the American population. The National Hispanic Consumer Study surveys more than 8,000 Hispanic adults living in the United States as part of the Simmons National Consumer Survey to identify their media habits, product and service preferences, attitudes, and opinions. Refer to the boxes on pages 76–79 to see how to use this important data to uncover insights about your brand and consumers.

- *Survey of Buying Power* ranks zip code areas in special characteristics, such as Asian American population, children younger than 5 years of age, and households in mobile homes. It also gives 5-year projections and percentage of change for population, buying income, and retail spending in all U.S. counties.

- *VALS 2,* developed by SRI, groups consumers into eight categories: (1) *Innovators* are successful, sophisticated, active, take-charge people who have high self-esteem. (2) *Experiencers* are motivated by self-expression. They are young, vital, impulsive, and rebellious and seek variety, excitement, and the offbeat. (3) *Strivers* seek motivation, self-definition, and approval from others. (4) *Thinkers* are mature, satisfied, well-educated professionals. (5) *Achievers* are successful, goal oriented, in control of their lives, and respectful of authority. (6) *Believers* are conservative, have deeply rooted moral codes, and have modest income and education. (7) *Makers* are suspicious of new ideas and unimpressed by physical possessions. (8) *Survivors* live narrowly focused lives and are cautious consumers.

> Step 3: Conduct Primary Research

Once you've exhausted the secondary sources, you will likely find you still have unanswered questions that warrant primary research. Here's where observation, focus groups, surveys, and experiments come in.

FINDING INSIGHT IN A SEA OF NUMBERS

The Simmons National Consumer Survey and the National Hispanic Consumer Study provide agencies, advertisers, and marketers with unmatched insights into the important and influential consumer population. For this example, we are going to look at the different demographics and psychographics of consumers who purchase three different brands of candy bars and compare and contrast them to determine how best to market and advertise to the brand consumer.

	ELEMENTS	A18+	HERSHEY'S ALMOND	SNICKERS	3 MUSKETEERS
Total Sample	Sample	24,438	2,427	3,156	1,550
	(000)	212,488	18,527	30,449	15,230
	Vertical	100%	100%	100%	100%
	Horizontal	100%	8.72%	14%	7.17%
	Index	100	100	100	100
Mean Age[2]	Sample	24,438	2,427	3,156	1,550
⟶	(000)	46	48	44	47
	Vertical	0.02%	0.26%	0.14%	0.31%
	Horizontal	100%	103%	95%	102%
	Index	100	1,186	660	1,429
MALE: GENDER	Sample	10,706	1,001	1,478	663
	(000)	102,474	8,583	15,468	7,086
⟶	Vertical	48%	46%	51%	47%
	Horizontal	100%	8.38%	15%	6.91%
	Index	100	96	105	96
FEMALE: GENDER	Sample	13,732	1,426	1,678	887
	(000)	110,014	9,944	14,980	8,144
⟶	Vertical	52%	54%	49%	53%
	Horizontal	100%	9.04%	14%	7.40%
	Index	100	104	95	103

Look only at mean age (in years, and located in the (000) row) and gender distribution (vertical row shows the percentage of brand users who are male or female). All three brands are similarly situated. In this example, 3 Musketeers consumers have an average age of 47 and are 47 percent male and 53 percent female. But digging deeper into the data enables you to gather further insights to differentiate the brand from others and to thus create more targeted and focused marketing and advertising campaigns.

For example, although the mean age for the three brands is nearly equal, if you look at three age group clusters (18–34, 35–54, and 55+), a picture of differentiation begins to appear. Looking at the index row, you can see that Snickers overindexes among 18–34 at 114 (an index of 100 is average usage, and any number above or below indicate above or below usage). This means that this age group is 14 percent more likely to consume this brand. On the other hand, Hershey's Almond and 3 Musketeers both underindex with this age group but do much better for consumers that are older than 55 years of age, where Snickers underindexes.

	ELEMENTS	A18+	HERSHEY'S ALMOND	SNICKERS	3 MUSKETEERS
18 – 34: AGE	Sample	6,197	645	977	381
	(000)	60,465	4,186	9,911	4,085
	Vertical	28%	23%	33%	27%
	Horizontal	100%	6.92%	16%	6.76%
	Index	100	79 ⟵	(114) ⟶	94
35 – 54: AGE	Sample	9,565	956	1,261	587
	(000)	84,147	7,808	12,528	5,604
	Vertical	40%	42%	41%	37%
	Horizontal	100%	9.28%	15%	6.66%
	Index	100	106	104	93

(continued)

FINDING INSIGHT IN A SEA OF NUMBERS (CONTINUED)

	ELEMENTS	A18+	HERSHEY'S ALMOND	SNICKERS	3 MUSKETEERS
55+: AGE	Sample	8,676	826	918	582
	(000)	67,876	6,533	8,010	5,541
	Vertical	32%	35%	26%	36%
	Horizontal	100%	9.63%	12%	8.16%
	Index	100	(110) →	82	← (114)

The next set of data examines where our candy bar consumers live.

	ELEMENTS	A18+	HERSHEY'S ALMOND	SNICKERS	3 MUSKETEERS
NORTHEAST: CENSUS REGIONS	Sample	4,907	426	511	314
	(000)	40,023	3,125	4,488	2,950
	Vertical	19%	17%	15%	19%
	Horizontal	100%	7.81%	11%	7.37%
	Index	100	90	78	103
MIDWEST: CENSUS REGIONS	Sample	5,019	433	673	292
	(000)	47,597	4,117	7,276	2,858
	Vertical	22%	22%	24%	19%
	Horizontal	100%	8.65%	15%	6.00%
	Index	100	99	107	84
SOUTH: CENSUS REGIONS	Sample	9,062	946	1,223	595
	(000)	77,218	6,633	11,720	6,191
	Vertical	36%	36%	38%	41%
	Horizontal	100%	8.59%	15%	8.02%
	Index	100	99	106	(112)
WEST: CENSUS REGIONS	Sample	5,450	622	749	349
	(000)	47,650	4,652	6,965	3,232
	Vertical	22%	25%	23%	21%
	Horizontal	100%	9.76%	15%	6.78%
	Index	100	(112)	102	95

Census regions are used for simplicity's sake, but even with this expanded area selection, you can see that 3 Musketeers is more popular in the South, Hershey's Almond pops in the West, and Snickers does fairly well in both the Midwest and the South. These data could be used to focus a marketing or advertising campaign, choosing either to make a push in an underutilized region or to reinforce consumer behavior in a region where the brand is already popular.

In continuing to build the brand profile of candy bar consumers, look at race and ethnicity and see how these vary among the brands.

Firsthand Experience

Try it. Taste it. Touch it. Hear it. Smell it. What were your perceptions of the product before you used it? How about now that you've used it? Try the competition. What are the competitors' weaknesses? Your client's strengths? Why would you choose to buy your client's brand?

Firsthand experience gives you important insights that may lead to the big idea. The idea for the memorable line "Two scoops of raisins in a box of

FINDING INSIGHT IN A SEA OF NUMBERS (CONTINUED)

	ELEMENTS	A18+	HERSHEY'S ALMOND	SNICKERS	3 MUSKETEERS
WHITE: RACE	Sample	19,417	1,782	2,371	1,237
	(000)	167,253	13,236	22,195	12,089
	Vertical	79%	71%	73%	79%
	Horizontal	100%	7.91%	13%	7.23%
	Index	100	91	93	101
BLACK OR AFRICAN AMERICAN: RACE	Sample	1,357	136	236	97
	(000)	22,772	2,596	4,558	1,887
	Vertical	11%	14%	15%	12%
	Horizontal	100%	11%	20%	8.28%
	Index	100	131	140	116
ASIAN/PACIFIC ISLANDER: RACE	Sample	516 *	48 *	54 *	18 *
	(000)	8,786	818	1,161	166
	Vertical	4.13%	4.42%	3.81%	1.09%
	Horizontal	100%	9.31%	13%	1.89%
	Index	100	107	92	26
SOME OTHER RACE: RACE	Sample	3,148	461	495	198
	(000)	13,677	1,876	2,535	1,089
	Vertical	6.44%	10%	8.33%	7.15%
	Horizontal	100%	14%	19%	7.96%
	Index	100	157	129	111
YES: RESPNDNT-SPANISH/HISPANIC/LATINO ORIGIN?	Sample	8,435	1,198	1,181	565
	(000)	27,355	3,772	4,312	2,015
	Vertical	13%	20%	14%	13%
	Horizontal	100%	14%	16%	7.37%
	Index	100	158	110	103

* The sample sizes for individual candy bar brands are too small to be statistically useful for the Asian sample; concentrate on the other groups here. White consumers underindex on two of the brands and consume just about the national average for 3 Musketeers. Black consumers, on the other hand, overindex on all three brands, especially Snickers and Hershey's Almond. The consumers who fall under the Other Race category have preferences for Hershey's Almond, but overindex across all three of the selected brands. Finally, in this section, look at the Hispanic customers, who overindex on all three brands, but prefer Hershey's Almond.

For the last profile section on candy bar consumers, look at a set of attitudinal statements that reflect their opinions on certain subjects. Here, we're going to look at some attitudes about media that differentiate the consumers of one brand from the consumers of other brands. These statements are asked on a 5-point Likert scale, including Agree a Lot, Agree a Little, Neither Agree nor Disagree, Disagree a Little, and Disagree a Lot. In this case, Any Agree encompasses the top two box scores for each question.

(continued)

Kellogg's Raisin Bran" came from an art director who emptied a box of the cereal onto his kitchen table and counted the raisins.

However, be careful not to assume that everyone thinks or behaves the same way you do. You may have a more sophisticated understanding of the product, you may have a bias toward your client, or you may not be part of the target market. Therefore, other research methods are essential.

FINDING INSIGHT IN A SEA OF NUMBERS (CONTINUED)

	ELEMENTS	A18+	HERSHEY'S ALMOND	SNICKERS	3 MUSKETEERS
NOTICE ADS IN LOBBIES OF MOVIE THEATERS	Sample	7,343	845	1,046	463
	(000)	64,021	6,408	10,446	4,351
	Vertical	30%	35%	34%	29%
	Horizontal	100%	10%	16%	6.80%
	Index	100	115	114	95
I AM A TV ADDICT	Sample	5,290	580	767	359
	(000)	45,347	4,414	7,504	3,385
	Vertical	21%	24%	25%	22%
	Horizontal	100%	9.73%	17%	7.47%
	Index	100	112	115	104
RADIO IS MY MAIN SOURCE OF ENTERTAINMENT	Sample	4,284	506	589	296
	(000)	33,561	2,987	5,298	2,522
	Vertical	16%	16%	17%	17%
	Horizontal	100%	8.90%	16%	7.51%
	Index	100	102	110	105
CABLE TV TOO MANY CHANN; CAN'T PICK 1	Sample	6,270	704	832	414
	(000)	48,427	4,754	7,224	3,519
	Vertical	23%	26%	24%	23%
	Horizontal	100%	9.82%	15%	7.27%
	Index	100	113	104	101
MORE INCLND TO BUY FROM SPNSR THAN NOT	Sample	4,800	529	632	319
	(000)	40,365	4,046	6,257	3,209
	Vertical	19%	22%	21%	21%
	Horizontal	100%	10%	16%	7.95%
	Index	100	115	108	111

From this, you can see that it would be easier to reach either a Hershey's Almond or a Snickers consumer using an ad in a movie theater lobby, as both of them overindex on this statement. Reaching Snickers consumers is also an option through radio because they indicate that this is more likely to be their main source of entertainment. To reach the 3 Musketeers and Hershey's Almond consumers, you could take advantage of sponsorship opportunities.

Simmons data also track media habits, right down to half-hour periods on television and top magazines for each segment. However, for brevity this information is not included here.

In summary, Simmons data can be used to gain innumerable insights into your brand consumer, creating an efficient targeting profile that can be used across a number of departments and for a variety of marketing, advertising, and branding purposes.

Observation

Go to a store and see how your brand is displayed. Is it gathering dust on the bottom shelf? Do competing brands have in-store signs and displays? Ask a sales associate a few questions about your brand and its competitors. Was the associate knowledgeable? Did the associate speak highly of your brand? Also, observe customers interacting with your brand. How much time do they spend reading your brand's label? Looking at the price? Examining other brands? If you have permission from the store manager, ask the customers why they chose a particular brand, when and how often they usually buy it, and how they use it.

One of the more offbeat methods of observation came from an archaeologist who found that studying people's garbage might uncover hidden truths. Several marketing researchers have adopted this method and discovered some rather interesting things, such as that cat owners read more than dog owners.

Surveys

Surveys, one of the most common primary-research methods, ask current or prospective customers questions about product usage, awareness of ad campaigns, attitudes toward competing brands, and so on. Surveys are conducted online and by mail, telephone, or personal interview.

Whichever method you use to conduct your survey, be certain to test the survey on a small sample to ascertain whether there are leading or ambiguous questions. When a team of advertising students wanted to determine people's awareness level of the American Red Cross slogan "Help Can't Wait," it tested a survey that asked respondents to match five nonprofit organizations to five slogans. Almost all the slogans were correctly matched. But did this mean people knew the "Help Can't Wait" slogan, or was it a fluke? To find out, the students conducted another test, using seven slogans and five organizations. The results were quite different. The fictitious slogan "The Life Blood of America" was matched to the Red Cross by 65 percent of respondents. Why the different results? In the first survey, respondents could guess the correct answer through the process of elimination. The second survey prevented the respondents from covering a genuine lack of awareness.

The structure of your question can also give different results. In the Red Cross example, respondents were given a multiple-choice question, an example of a closed-end question. As you may imagine, the results may be even more dramatic if the students chose to use an open-ended question, asking the respondents to answer in their own words.

In addition to checking for ambiguous and misleading questions, keep the following points in mind when you design a survey:

1. Keep the survey short.
2. Use simple language.
3. Include complete instructions.
4. Put easy-to-answer questions first.
5. Ask general questions before detailed ones.
6. Save potentially embarrassing questions, such as about income, for the end.

Focus Groups

Invite 5 to 10 people who are typical of your target market to discuss their feelings about your product. You'll want their permission to record the session, and you will need a moderator who encourages everyone to speak and who keeps the discussion on track. Because participants are urged to say what's on their minds, important issues may be uncovered.

Remember the Cheetos ad campaign mentioned in Chapter 1? When Goodby, Silverstein & Partners wanted to get into the mindset of adults who eat Cheetos snacks, responses were along these lines: "Look, it's a kids' snack. Sure I eat them, but it's not something I'm exactly proud of." However, when Cheetos were put in front of them, "crunching and finger-licking took over. Orange fingers and smiles were brandished proudly, almost as badges of honor. These adults were looking for permission to not act their age and not conform to expectations of 'adult behavior.' Cheetos snacks let them do that."[2] This insight helped inspire the campaign in which Chester Cheetah helps adults have mischievous fun with Cheetos.

Although focus groups can uncover some interesting attitudes, keep in mind this research method reflects the opinions of only a few people. Some critics wonder about the quality of information that can be gathered from a 2-hour session that involves 10 people, in which each person has 12 minutes to speak. Others wonder about the types of people who willingly give up their personal time in return for a modest incentive. Still others complain that the traditional focus-group setting of a conference room with a two-way mirror is like studying wildlife at a zoo. To determine whether you've uncovered something important, you'll need to back up your focus-group findings with other research methods.

Interviews

One-on-one interviews usually last from 30 minutes to 2 hours and can uncover important insights. To ensure accuracy, ask the participant for permission to record the interview.

Ask a lot of questions and remember this is an interview, not a two-way conversation, so you should do little talking and should refrain from giving personal opinions. Also, always remember that people may not want to reveal the real reasons they do or don't like a product. A mother in England told a market researcher that milk was best for her children but soda pop was terrible. Then he asked what she bought for them, and she replied, "Soda pop. They hate milk." What could you do with this information if you had to sell milk?

Phil Dusenberry, former chairman of BBDO North America, believes that insights come by listening to consumer complaints. "Take the Chunky Soup case. If you asked consumers what they liked about soup, they would serve up the usual pat answers: soup is hearty, soup is nourishing, soup warms you up. The answers we've all heard since soup advertising began. But when we asked consumers to complain about soup, the answers were entirely different: the pieces of meat were too small, the vegetables are skimpy, it doesn't fill me up. The insight here practically jumped onto our plate. From there it was a hop, skip, and a jump to the birth of Chunky, and the perfect answer to what mattered most to the soup customer."[3]

---

[2] "Mischievous Fun with Cheetos®," The 2009 ARF David Ogilvy Awards, www.warc.com, accessed July 31, 2009.
[3] Phil Dusenberry, *Then We Set His Hair on Fire* (New York: Penguin Group, 2005), p. 65.

Ethnography

People are more open when they're in an environment that's familiar to them, rather than a conference room with a two-way mirror. Ethnographic research observes people in their natural surroundings.

Sunbeam sent researchers with video cameras to hang out with the guys around the backyard barbeque grill before introducing a new line of Coleman gas grills. By listening in on the conversations, the team gathered a key insight: A gas grill isn't really a tool that cooks the hamburgers and hot dogs. Rather, "it's the centerpiece of warm family moments worthy of a summer highlights reel." So, rather than promote the Coleman grill in terms of size, BTUs, and accessory options, Sunbeam designed the grill to evoke nostalgia for the warm family experience. The marketing strategy positioned grilling as "a relaxing ritual where the grilling area is the stage." The result: The Coleman Grill did $50 million in sales in its first year, making it one of the most successful launches in Sunbeam's history.[4]

The insight for an advertising campaign for Cesar dog food came by observing small-dog owners pampering their pets like spoiled children. The research revealed that owners want to give the dog the best because the dog is giving them its best. One woman said, "For once in my life, I'm perfect, in the eyes of my dog."[5] The ad campaign gives the dogs a voice. "I promise to go where you go, to be happy to see you, to be woman's best friend," several small dogs promise in a TV spot. "Love them back with Cesar," the announcer recommends and closes with the tag line, "Cesar. It's canine cuisine." A print ad in the entertainment trade publication *Daily Variety* reads: "Your agent says he loves you. Your publicist says she loves you. The studio says they love you. Your dog really does."

To learn how women feel about laundry, a Procter & Gamble research team did something a bit unusual. Rather than talk with women in the laundry room, the research team interviewed women over lunch, took them to the hair salon, and went clothes shopping with them. By changing the venue, the team learned about the role that clothing plays in women's lives. The key insight, that clothing is a part of self-identity and self-expression, led to a new spin on laundry in ads for Tide. In one ad, a very pregnant woman with ice-cream cravings drops her dessert on the one shirt that still fits her. "The More I See You" by Sabina Sciubba sets the tone for the commercial.

Projective Techniques

Consumers may not come right out and tell their true feelings about a brand in a survey, focus group, or interview. Perhaps it's because they don't want to offend you. Perhaps they haven't articulated the reason in their own minds and therefore have a difficult time explaining it. Perhaps they want to avoid appearing irrational or vain. For example, if you ask people why they bought an expensive imported luxury car, you may be given rational explanations

---

[4] Allison Stein Wellner, "Watch Me Now," *American Demographics*, October 2002, pp. S1–S8.
[5] Stuart Elliott, "Campaign Spotlight: Is This Dog's Day the Ides of March?" www.nytimes.com, 5 June 2006.

about the car's safety record and resale value. However, if you ask the participants to describe the type of person who owns the expensive imported luxury car, you may learn it's about showing off or getting even.

Using projective techniques, researchers ask respondents to sketch drawings, tell tales, finish sentences, do word associations, create collages, and match companies with animals, colors, places, and types of music so that they can understand consumers' subconscious attitudes toward products. These techniques sometimes uncover surprising motives for behavior.

Goodby, Silverstein & Partners asked luxury-car owners to draw the way they feel about their cars. Most of the drivers of the BMW, Mercedes, Infiniti, and Lexus drew the outside of the cars. Porsche owners, by contrast, rarely drew the car. Instead, the point of view was from the driver's seat, showing winding roads. This exercise gave the agency the idea to emphasize the fun you'll have while driving a Porsche.

Although projective techniques may uncover information that would be missed with other research methods, it's important to keep in mind that they are expensive to use on a per-respondent basis and require the expertise of trained psychologists.

Experiments

This research method answers questions about cause and effect. Suppose you want to compare the attitudes of a group of people who saw your ad with a group who didn't. Did the people who saw your ad have a more favorable impression of your client? Were they more knowledgeable about the brand? And so on.

Want to uncover opinions about product usage? Give participants your product to use for a week and then ask them to discuss their experiences in a focus group. The planners at Goodby, Silverstein & Partners chose a "deprivation strategy" to understand people's feelings about milk. Participants were asked to go without milk for a week before attending a focus-group session.

At first, the participants didn't think it would be difficult, but the week without milk proved otherwise. The idea for the famous two-word line "Got Milk?" came out of the responses from the focus-group participants who had been deprived of milk for a week.

Online Research

Conducting surveys, interviews, and focus groups online is fast and inexpensive. It also allows you to reach people who would not be willing to travel to a facility for a focus group or may feel uncomfortable giving responses about sensitive issues in person. But there are disadvantages, too. One individual can provide multiple responses to a single survey. Someone not in your target audience can respond; you may think you're interviewing a 20-something single female when in fact you're interviewing a 60-year-old married man. Also, you don't have the advantage of nonverbal cues such as tone of voice, facial expressions, and body language.

Using Multiple Research Methods

Each research method has advantages and disadvantages. Therefore, researchers will often use more than one approach to find the answers to their questions. Kraft, the makers of DiGiorno Pizza, used seven research firms to conduct surveys, focus groups, taste tests, and copy tests to learn the best way to position its brand. Surveys and focus groups found that people wanted a frozen pizza with a fresh-baked taste but so far hadn't found one in the stores. In blind taste tests, DiGiorno scored highest among frozen brands and placed second only to one carryout pizza. With this information, the creative team came up with the theme "It's not delivery. It's DiGiorno."

The ads creatively addressed the research findings, but still a question remained: Were the spots effective? To find out, Kraft ran a quantitative copy test to measure the effectiveness of the spots. Roughly 64 percent of the respondents recalled the spot's main message of "fresh-baked taste," whereas an average commercial scored about 24 percent. The ad also generated strong brand identification, with 52 percent recalling the DiGiorno name. And finally, one other set of figures proved the success of the big idea: Three years after its introduction, it became the second best-selling frozen pizza. Today, it's the top-selling brand.[6]

> Step 4: Interpret the Data

You can collect mountains of data, but it's useless if you don't know how to interpret your findings. For example, your research may uncover some negative opinions about your client. An almost immediate reaction would be to try and change these perceptions. However, this may not be the best move.

For example, Sabena Qualitative Research developed a perceptional map whereby customers evaluated stores on best or worst value and most or least up-to-date in fashions. Talbots was placed in the best value/least up-to-date quadrant. At first glance, you might be tempted to do something to make Talbots seem more up-to-date. The company tried that a number of years ago, introducing flashier colors and more current styles. Guess what?

Sales dropped because the store's customers wanted classics, not the latest fashions. Talbots quickly went back to what it does best, and its loyal customers were happy once again.

> Future Steps in the Process

After the information is gathered, the account executive or planner will prepare a creative brief, also known as a creative strategy statement, to give to the writer and artist. (This will be discussed in detail in Chapter 5.)

---

[6] Sara Eckel and Jennifer Lach, "Intelligence Agents," *American Demographics,* March 1999, p. 58, and Holly Hetager Bradley, "Pizza Pizzazz," www.bakingbusiness.com, 1 April 2005.

The creative team will use this information as inspiration to develop numerous ideas or creative concepts (discussed in Chapter 6).

To ensure that the ideas are on strategy, the agency may do some concept testing with members of the target audience to see their reaction before the ads run. As you can imagine, this can help avoid costly mistakes.

Concept testing can be useful for new product ideas and new approaches for existing products. However, it's far from infallible. The popular AFLAC duck might never have aired if the president of the American Family Life Insurance Company listened to the results of a focus group. Although many participants liked the duck, others found it insulting. Convinced that its idea was a winner, the Kaplan Thaler Group offered to pay for the testing of the commercial by Ipsos-ASI, a worldwide advertising research firm. The result? It earned the highest recall score that the research firm had ever seen in the insurance category. Two years later, 91 percent of all Americans recognized the name AFLAC. And the curious part? One third of the people could not say AFLAC; they had to quack it.[7]

Some top creators of ads warn that the more an advertising idea is tested and manipulated on the basis of consumer research, the more watered down it becomes.[8] Social researcher Hugh Mackay cautions, "If you show someone an ad and get them to talk about it as if they are on some kind of consumer jury, almost certainly what you'll get is a spurious art director's or amateur copywriter's assessment." But Mackay concedes, "If the planner, writer, art director and client are in disagreement or are experiencing doubt, testing ads would be appropriate. But the testing should be as naturalistic as possible and always done in homes. If it's a print ad, don't get a group discussion and hold it up. Give it to them in the context of a magazine or paper, ask them to look at it overnight and come back tomorrow for a chat."[9]

> Common Mistakes in Research

Research is a valuable tool, but it's not foolproof. Here are some common mistakes:

- *Asking the wrong questions.* Before Coca-Cola introduced New Coke in 1985, it conducted numerous focus groups, which showed people preferred the taste of the new soft drink to the old one. The research led the company to change its 100-year-old formula. However, consumers revolted, and Coca-Cola had to reintroduce its old flavor. The problem was that consumers were not told that the original Coca-Cola might be eliminated.

- *Believing everything people tell you.* Account planner Jon Steel points to the problem of people saying the "right" thing: "To hear people talk in focus groups, and indeed to believe the answers they give in larger, more

[7] Linda Kaplan Thaler and Robin Koval, *Bang!* (New York: Doubleday, 2003), pp. 17–28.
[8] Berger, *Advertising Today*, p. 470.
[9] Jim Aitchison, *Cutting Edge Advertising* (Singapore: Prentice Hall, 1999), pp. 29–31.

reliable quantitative surveys, one would think that Americans are the cleanest living, healthiest race on the planet. They all eat well, they work out, and cholesterol levels are universally low."[10]

- *Not testing to see if the data are relevant to your client's problem.* The ad agency for Jell-O found that consumers were interested in lighter desserts, so it positioned Jell-O as a light, tasty dessert that won't fill people up. Sales declined. The problem wasn't that the data were erroneous. It was that the data didn't apply to Jell-O's core consumers, who thought of desserts as the fun part of the meal. Sales increased when the agency repositioned the brand as fun: "Make Jell-O gelatin, and make some fun."

- *Biasing the results.* To be reliable, your research must be repeatable; that is, the same questions or research techniques must produce similar results, regardless of who conducts the study. However, a variety of factors can bias results. For example, with *interviewer bias,* the person interviewing respondents gives cues (smiles, frowns) that suggest one answer is better than another. With *sample bias,* the sample doesn't represent a good cross section of the target audience. Thus, if you wanted to investigate whether teenagers like an advertising campaign, you wouldn't test it on a weekday morning at a shopping mall because the target market would be (or at least should be) in school, not at the local mall. With *source bias,* the source of the research message influences the answer. People aim to please, so they may say only nice things about company XYZ if they know the person asking the questions works for XYZ. With *nonresponse bias,* questions aren't answered because they're too difficult, confusing, personal, and so on.

- *Not studying someone typical of your audience.* Bill Oberlander warns against focus groups: "Anybody who's going to cut out an hour and a half of their time on a Thursday night to go to a very small, fluorescently lit, stale cookied, bad coffee'd room to talk about how they consume mosquito-bite ointment in their lives, I think those people are losers."[11]

> Suggested Activities

1. Select two cities from different parts of the country and prepare a report of their similarities and differences in shopping habits, food preference, income levels, home ownership, number of children in the family, and so on.

2. Observe how your target audience uses the product you're about to advertise. If you're selling golf balls, go to a golf course and watch players in action. If you're selling a detergent, go to a self-service laundry and observe how the people load their machines. If you're selling dog food, watch friends feeding their pets. What did you notice? Were there

---

[10] Jon Steel, *Truth, Lies & Advertising: The Art of Account Planning* (New York: Wiley, 1998), p. 83.
[11] Aitchison, *Cutting Edge Advertising,* p. 26.

any surprises? Any common rituals? What insights can help direct your advertising?

3. Play a game with friends. Choose a product category (such as cars, jeans, or perfume) and write the names of different brands within the product category on index cards (each index card will have a different brand name). Distribute a card to players and ask them to describe their brand as if it were a person, without revealing the brand name. (To get them started, you might give them some questions to answer, such as what would the brand do for a living? Where would it live? What kind of movies would it like? What kind of books? Magazines? TV shows? Who's its best friend? How would it dress? What kind of hairstyle would it have?) Then ask other players to guess the brand that's being described. What did you discover?

4. Choose one of the following categories and use the library and web to assemble as much information as you can about the product category: who uses it, what the industry trends are, what the top brands in the market are, how the product differs from competitors, how the product is used, and where the category is headed in the future.

Adult Personal Care

Toothpaste
Mouthwash
Shampoo
Personal-care soaps
Hand and body cream
Deodorants or antiperspirants
Electric shavers

Remedies

Athlete's foot remedies
Indigestion aids

Household Supplies

Cleaners
Glass cleaners
Fabric softeners
Charcoal
Air freshener sprays

Baked Goods, Snacks, and Desserts

Frozen yogurt
Frozen desserts
Cookies
Crackers

Meat and Prepared Meals

Frozen pizza
Mexican foods
Prepared dinners

Beverages

Instant iced tea
Energy drinks
Bottled water and seltzer

Soup, Fruits, and Vegetables

Canned or jarred soup
Flavored or seasoned rice

Icelandair and Baltimore Washington International Airport Take the Travail Out of Travel

Check out a bunch of airline ads and what do you see? Pictures of smiling flight attendants. Relaxed passengers stretched out in spacious seats. Breathtaking views of exotic destinations. And planes. Lots of planes, all flying high above the clouds. Yikes! So many airline ads look the same.

So how do you break through the monotony? And what do you do when you're a small airline and you're facing new competition? That's the challenge Icelandair gave to Nasuti & Hinkle when SAS airlines started offering direct flights to Scandinavia from Dulles International Airport, a competitive threat to approximately 20 percent of Icelandair's Baltimore Washington International (BWI) airport business.

Nasuti & Hinkle discovered that SAS was planning to spend roughly $1 million on advertising—more than three times what Icelandair had available to spend. Also, Icelandair acknowledged that SAS had a better product in terms of flying time to Scandinavia. But none of this discouraged the Nasuti & Hinkle team members because they had a secret weapon—personal experience.

They knew firsthand what it was like to fly from the various Washington area airports because their agency is located in Silver Spring, Maryland. They decided to concede the immediate Dulles geographic area business and assumed that the Baltimore business was safe. That left what they called the "swing" areas that are roughly equidistant to the two airports—Alexandria and Arlington, Virginia; Bethesda and Silver Spring, Maryland; and Washington, DC.

Executives at Nasuti & Hinkle knew that the weak link in the entire Washington-to-Scandinavia SAS chain was one their traveling target audience knew all too well—the starting point in Washington. At the time, as now, air travel in and out of Dulles is not as easy as it might be. With no parking near the terminal and its system of shuttles to a midfield terminal, just reaching the aircraft is a chore.

Their strategy was simple—Dulles Airport—and the creative work focused on how flying to Scandinavia from BWI on Icelandair is easier and more convenient than from Dulles with all its attendant aggravations. The target audience was primarily composed of Scandinavians who were living in the United States but flew back to Scandinavia for business or to visit.

With special thanks to Woody Hinkle of Nasuti & Hinkle.

Hurry home.

Icelandair to Scandinavia.
From BWI. It's just better.

ICELANDAIR
Europe, UK and Iceland, too.
800.223.5500 • icelandair.com

Courtesy of Icelandic Air and Nasuti & Hinkle.

With a limited budget, Nasuti & Hinkle focused all available media dollars into radio (see the accompanying 60-second radio spot, "People Mover"), Metro subway car cards, and signs on bus backs, staggered to stretch Icelandair's budget as far as possible. With a primarily Scandinavian target audience, agency team members used a Scandinavian look to the signs, enlisting a well-known Swedish cartoonist to create a signature character for Icelandair. Headlines included, "Scandinavians were made for snowmobiles. Not shuttle buses," and "Scandinavia doesn't seem so far away when you leave from BWI." They even ran some messages entirely in Swedish, the dominant language in Scandinavia. Through friends, they found a copywriter in Sweden who translated (and in the case of radio, rewrote) their creative work for a Swedish audience.

Courtesy of Icelandic Air and Nasuti & Hinkle.

After the 2-month effort, Icelandair was able to more than hold onto its market share for flights to Scandinavia. Its market share actually increased a few points despite the arrival of SAS in the marketplace.

"People Mover" (60-second radio spot)

WOMAN: Well, see I *like* those people mover things. The airport buses that take you from the terminal to the other terminal where the plane actually is. I mean I *really* like it. Off balance . . . crowded bus . . . bumping up against all kinds of people! Ahhhh! So now that I can fly to Scandinavia from Dulles I'm . . . wow! When I fly BWI on Icelandair—well, at BWI there's more flights a week than Dulles. But the plane's right at the terminal, and there's a parking garage right there next to it so—no bus! But now I can ride two—one from satellite parking and then—the other one! That's *twice* as many people. Close up!

ANNCR: Icelandair to Scandinavia and Europe from BWI. Garage parking. Convenience. Daily flights. Unless you're some kind of freak, it's just better. Call Icelandair at 800-223-5500 or visit Icelandair.com.

STRATEGY
A ROAD MAP FOR THE CREATIVE TEAM

5

John Lyons talks about strategy as

> *a carefully designed plan to murder the competition. Any premise that lacks a killer instinct is not a strategy. Any premise that doesn't reflect or include a consumer's crying need is not a strategy. Any premise embalmed in stiff, predictable language is not a strategy. Any premise that addresses the whole world, women 3 to 93, is not a strategy. Any premise interchangeable with that of another product is not a strategy. The true test of an advertising strategy is to let another human being read it. If that person can't say yes, that's me, or yes, I need that, or yes, that's my problem—throw it away.*[1]

Strategic planning is the stage between fact gathering and creative execution. Think of it as a road map for the client and creative team—it will map out the direction the advertising campaign should take. But it'll be the job of the creative team to describe the scenery. Strategy is the way you plan to sell the product, not the words and images you use to do so. But mere facts do not a strategy make. To the facts you must add your insight—you must see connections that no one else has noticed.

[1] John Lyons, *Guts: Advertising from the Inside Out* (New York: AMACOM, 1987), p. 124.

> The Creative Brief

Creative briefs summarize the consumer and brand insights that are uncovered during the research stage. Written by account planners, creative briefs give direction and inspiration to the creative team. Done right, the brief will help the copywriter and art director get into the mindset of the target audience. Creative director John Stingley says:

> *In many ways, creating advertising is the same discipline as acting. You must start by mentally discarding your own identity. You have to become the people you are communicating with. Internalize their interests, joys, fears, tastes, even biases. Often it means mentally and emotionally becoming someone you would never in a million years be like yourself.*[2]

In addition to the written creative brief, some planners include clips of TV programs the consumers watch, download music they like, create a scrapbook of their hobbies, make a montage of photos that represent what they do in an average day, and so on to help the creative team get into the mindset of the consumer.

> Writing the Creative Brief

Although it may be tempting to share the reams of data that were uncovered in the research stage, the brief should include only what's relevant to solving the advertising problem. Ideally, it should be approximately one page. Kenneth Roman and Jane Mass argue that if you can't fit the information onto one page, the chances of cramming it all into a 30-second commercial are slight.[3]

Kevin Dundas describes two opposite extremes:

> *The urge to fill that piece of paper with detail, data, fact, and hearsay is unbelievably tempting. I recall a senior planner handing me a brief for sign-off and proudly stating, "Let's see the creatives get out of that one." It was a great piece of strategic thinking, but as a stepping-off point to a creative team it was DOA.*
>
> *Equally, I have had planners shuffle into my office embarrassed to reveal the one-page summation of a mountain of strategizing and positioning work for their brand. "It's too simple and obvious; it is what the brand has always stood for." More than likely this is a good position to take; why challenge or rewrite a position like refreshment or performance or safety? The genius, of course, lies in how the planner has configured or retextured the brand proposition for today's target audience.*[4]

---

[2] The Designers and Art Directors Association (D&AD) of the United Kingdom, *The Copywriter's Bible*, (Switzerland: Roto Vision SA, 1995), p. 162.
[3] Kenneth Roman and Jane Maas, *The New How to Advertise* (New York: St. Martin's Press, 1992), p. 5.
[4] Kevin Dundas, "A Passion for Advertising," *Agency*, Summer 1998, p. 38.

Formats for Creative Briefs

Creative briefs vary from agency to agency. However, nearly every brief will include four things:

1. *Insights about the target audience.* As you write your creative brief, you may begin to describe your target audience in demographic terms including age, sex, marital status, income, occupation, owner or renter, user or nonuser of product category, and so on. But don't stop there. Demographics alone cannot help the creative team understand the person they're trying to reach. More meaningful is a profile of that person's lifestyle, including values, leisure-time activities, attitudes toward work and family, and stresses of everyday life. Jon Steel describes the demographic information as the "skeleton" and the lifestyles and values as the "body and soul."[5]

   Margaret Morrison[6] asks you to consider the difference among the following descriptions:

   - Mothers with children under 12 years old.

   - Mothers, with children under 12 years old, who probably do not prepare many meals from scratch but generally use a variety of packaged goods as the basis for their meals. These moms may be users of products such as jarred spaghetti sauce and packaged dinners; they may also be users of foods purchased from the deli counter of their grocery store. They are also busy and highly involved in the lives of their children.

   - Mothers who consider themselves creative and somewhat adventurous in the kitchen but need to balance their creativity with the demands of the picky eaters in the family.

   Morrison's first example provides little information to the creative team about what motivates the target consumer. The second example provides quite a bit of information but no real inspiration. Morrison notes this description is likely to fit virtually every mother with children younger than 12 years old in the United States. The third example creates a vivid picture in the mind of everyone reading the creative brief. It describes what is different about the mothers who are in the target audience compared with the other mothers who may fit the profile demographically but not psychographically.

   Notice how the ads in Figure 5-1 speak to people who treat their car like a baby.

2. *Insights about how the target interacts with your brand.* Are you targeting users of another brand? Consumers who've never used any brand in your category? Consumers who use a related product but might be persuaded to switch to yours? Is there a way you can position your brand to meet an

---

[5] Jon Steel, *Truth, Lies & Advertising: The Art of Account Planning* (New York: Wiley, 1998).
[6] Margaret A. Morrison, Eric Haley, Kim Bartel Sheenhan, and Ronald E. Taylor, *Using Qualitative Research in Advertising: Strategies, Techniques and Applications* (Thousand Oaks, CA: Sage, 2002), pp. 112–115.

Figure 5-1
Among people who drive expensive cars, a ding is a threat to identity. In four words, "I am my car." These bus-board ads reach drivers while they're in their cars.

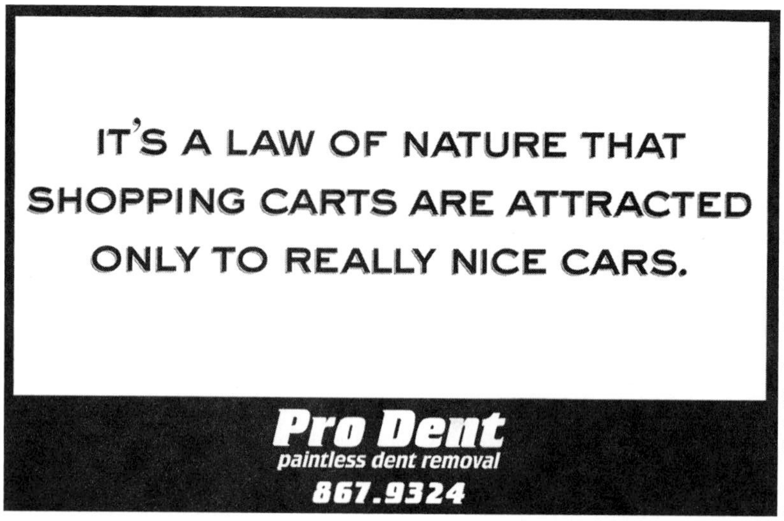
IT'S A LAW OF NATURE THAT
SHOPPING CARTS ARE ATTRACTED
ONLY TO REALLY NICE CARS.
Pro Dent
paintless dent removal
867.9324

Courtesy of SapientNitro, formerly A.K.A Advertising.

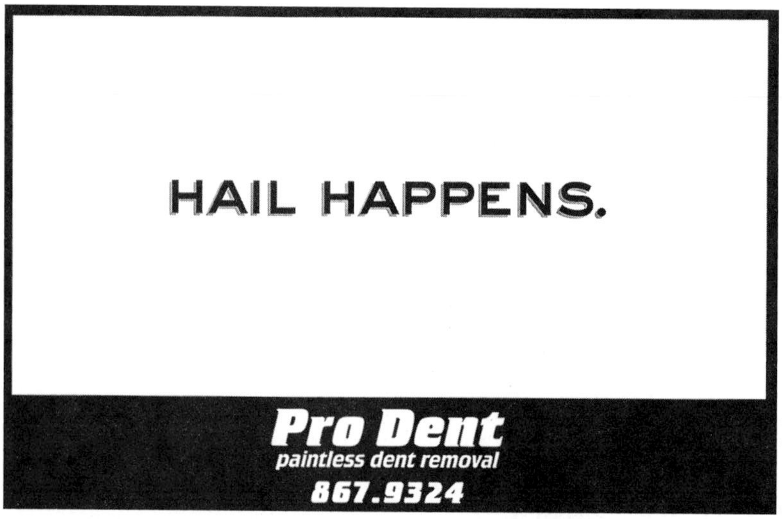
HAIL HAPPENS.
Pro Dent
paintless dent removal
867.9324

Courtesy of SapientNitro, formerly A.K.A Advertising.

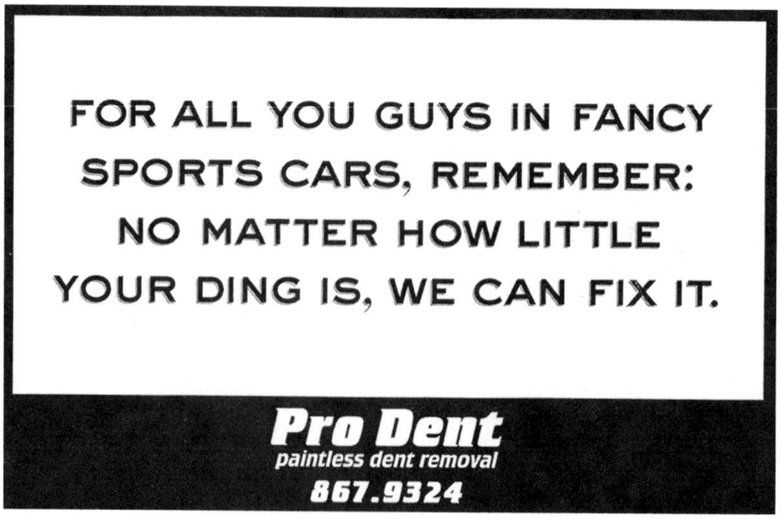
FOR ALL YOU GUYS IN FANCY
SPORTS CARS, REMEMBER:
NO MATTER HOW LITTLE
YOUR DING IS, WE CAN FIX IT.
Pro Dent
paintless dent removal
867.9324

Courtesy of SapientNitro, formerly A.K.A Advertising.

unfulfilled need of a particular market segment? W. Chan Kim and Renee Mauborgne, authors of *Blue Ocean Strategy,* point to Curves as a company that meets the needs of women who don't feel comfortable at most health clubs and who don't have the discipline to exercise at home. By understanding these concerns, Curves created an environment that women can enjoy. In the process, the company made its competitors irrelevant.[7]

Perhaps you're targeting your current customers, urging them to buy your brand more often or simply to remain brand loyal. Or perhaps you're targeting gatekeepers, the people who influence the purchasing decision for your target audience. Ally & Gargano targeted many audiences in its campaign for Federal Express (now FedEx®). As agency president Amil Gargano explained, "We focused on expanding the market with the target moving from management to every department of American business including secretaries, mailroom personnel and trainees. No one was spared."[8]

Likewise, Disney doesn't just target children in its ads. Instead it often shows how people of all ages will enjoy its theme parks. One commercial shows a middle-aged couple talking in bed. The wife says that she fears they're drifting apart because he doesn't talk to her in that "special" way anymore. The husband explains, "But we were younger then. We were in college." She doesn't buy it. To appease her, he cuddles close to her. You expect to hear him whisper sweet nothings in a low, sexy voice. Instead, he warbles like Donald Duck: "I love you. I love you very, very much." She giggles. The title card reads "Magic Happens. Disney." Another Disney spot shows a mother with her daughter and baby boy. They enter a crowded elevator and the daughter tells the strangers about her trip to Disney. She's so enthusiastic about the trip that it sounds as if they just returned, but the mother explains they took the trip a year ago. The daughter tells everyone they got all types of souvenirs from the trip, including her baby brother. The strangers grin. The mother explains, "We all had a good time."

3. *What you want your target audience to know and feel.* Describe how your brand touches one or more human needs: to be popular, to feel attractive and wanted, to obtain material things, to enjoy life through comfort and convenience, to create a happy family situation, to have love and sex, to wield power, to avoid fear, to emulate those you admire, to have new experiences, or to protect and maintain health.

As creative director John Stingley observes, "The basic motivations of people never really change. That's why Shakespeare is still relevant today. Human history pretty much boils down to the influence of love, sex, greed, hunger, and insecurity."[9]

Notice how the ad for Castlewood Builders addresses the insecurities that people have about building a custom home? (See Figure 5-2.)

---

[7] W. Chan Kim and Renee Mauborgne, *Blue Ocean Strategy* (Boston: Harvard Business School Press, 2005).

[8] Bernice Kanner, *The 100 Best TV Commercials . . . and Why They Worked* (New York: Times Books, 1999), p. 35.

[9] D&AD, *The Copywriter's Bible,* p. 163.

Figure 5-2

Building a dream home can be a colossal nightmare if you have the wrong builder. Woody Hinkle of Nasuti + Hinkle Creative Thinking explains, "We wanted to address the fears and concerns that people have about building a home—fears and concerns that are either because friends have told them horror stories (which people seem to wear like a badge of honor sometimes) or because they don't know what to do and fear the unknown."

As you write your brief, explore the emotional and rational rewards of using your product or service. Cheese, for example,[10] offers the following rewards:

- *In-use rewards:* Is convenient (practical), offers a new taste (sensory), earns the gratitude of the family (social), and contributes to the belief that you're a good cook (ego satisfaction).

- *Results-of-use rewards:* Helps build strong bones (practical), makes you feel better (sensory), makes you look good to others (social), and contributes to the belief that you're a good parent (ego satisfaction).

- *Incidental-to-use rewards:* Provides low-cost nutrition (practical), makes no mess (sensory), adds variety to party refreshments (social), and makes you feel like a smart shopper (ego satisfaction).

Which benefits do you think are the most important to mothers of young children? To college students? To professionals? To people living on Social Security?

[10] Adapted from a presentation by Doug Walker at the University of South Carolina, 17 October 1999.

Keep in mind that rational benefits are easy for competitors to copy so try for an emotional appeal. "Women don't buy lipstick, they buy hope," Revlon founder Charles Revson once told his staff. Likewise, Porsche sports cars aren't about moving from point A to point B; they're about power and status and one-upmanship. Consider this comment from a Porsche owner: "There's nothing practical about it. I live in the United States where the law says I have to drive fifty-five miles an hour. It doesn't have room for my kids and my luggage. And that's exactly why I love it."[11] Notice how this consumer insight is reflected in the following headline for Porsche:

> Too fast
>
> Doesn't blend in
>
> People will talk

4. *Key insight (the big idea).* Bill Bernbach once said, "At the heart of an effective creative philosophy is the belief that nothing is as powerful as an insight into human nature, what compulsions drive a man, what instincts dominate his action, even though his language so often can camouflage what really motivates him."[12]

    For example, farming is more than a job or even a profession. It is a way of life. Farmers will tell you they farm because they love working outdoors, because they relish being their own boss, because they can raise their families in a good environment, and because they get deep satisfaction from making things grow, from being a part of "God's miracle."

    At the same time, farmers are businesspeople. Managing millions of dollars in assets and making a profit is no easy task. So, in addition to loving the life they lead, farmers are intensely interested in practical solutions to problems associated with farming. What this all boils down to is that farmers are "spiritual pragmatists." And it was this insight that became the basis of the print campaign shown in Figure 5-3.

McCann Erickson's Role-Playing Approach

The McCann Erickson agency suggests that you climb inside the head of your consumer by acting as if you were that person, writing your responses to the first six questions here in the consumer's "voice" and the final question in your own voice.

1. *Who is my target?* Give brief lifestyle/attitudinal descriptions. Include some demographics, but this is not as important for most products. Are they users, heavy users, nonusers, users of competitive brands? What is the relationship to other product/service usage?

2. *Where am I now in the mind of this person?* They don't know us. They know us, but don't use us. They prefer another brand because. . . . They don't understand what we can do. They don't use us enough. And so on.

---

[11] Jim Aitchison, *Cutting Edge Advertising* (Singapore: Prentice Hall, 1999), p. 45.
[12] Merry Baskin, "What Is Account Planning?" Account Planning Group, www.apg.org.uk.

There are no **atheists out here.**

A close crack of lightning can really put the fear of God into you. But so can the sight of waterhemp. Just a few plants, and by next year a whole field could be ruined. But Canopy® XL from DuPont takes some of that worry away. It's the only herbicide I know that gives me both burndown and residual control of tough weeds like waterhemp and nightshade—all the way to harvest. That saves me costly unplanned trips. Plus, I'm free to make the choices that are best for my fields—and free to plant whatever soybeans I want. It may not be Heaven. But it's close.

GET YIELD-PRESERVING
RESIDUAL PROTECTION
AGAINST WATERHEMP
AND NIGHTSHADE.

DUPONT
Canopy® XL
soybean herbicide

Call toll free 1-888-6-DUPONT. Or visit us at www.dupont.com/ag/us Read and follow the label.

Courtesy of DuPont and Saatchi & Saatchi.

"I didn't get into this business because I loved having people tell me what to do."

I know my fields better than anybody else. And I know that no one herbicide, not even Roundup¹, can get every weed out there. So next year, I'm going with that new program, Authority² followed by DuPont Synchrony® STS®. I'll get in early before that first flush gets out of hand. And I've still got more time at post, just in case bad weather sets in. For me, residual control of waterhemp and nightshade is a must. I also like using high-yielding STS® beans. I get the benefits of using a herbicide-tolerant seed without tech fees or hassles. It's all about having choices. Good choices.

THE HIGH-YIELDING,
HERBICIDE-TOLERANT
SYSTEM WITH SERIOUS
CONTROL OF
WATERHEMP AND
NIGHTSHADE.

DUPONT
Authority followed by Synchrony® STS®
soybean herbicide program

Call toll free 1-888-6-DUPONT. Or visit us at www.dupont.com/ag/us Read and follow the label.

Courtesy of DuPont and Saatchi & Saatchi.

Figure 5-3
DuPont thinks of farmers as spiritual pragmatists. By sharing the farmers' values and positioning DuPont agricultural products as an extension of them, this campaign seeks to promote the DuPont brand through trust and empathy.

The seasons. The weather. Interest rates. Prices.
Everything
changes.
Except what you're doing it for.

Living a life that's reserved for a very few. Doing what's right. That's why I farm. I'm always looking for flexible, new solutions. Like DuPont Basis Gold®. I can use it in a one-pass, total post, or as part of a two-pass program following a preemergence product like new LeadOff™ corn herbicide from DuPont. Either way, Basis Gold® controls emerged weeds and grasses even if it doesn't rain. And when it does, the residual protects me all the way to harvest. Plus, Basis Gold® can be used on virtually any corn, so I can plant whatever works best on my land. I like having these choices—especially the option to do it my way.

IN ANY KIND OF WEATHER, ON ANY KIND OF CORN, IT CONTROLS MY GRASS AND BROADLEAF WEEDS.

DUPONT
Basis Gold®
corn herbicide

Call toll free 1-888-6-DUPONT. Or visit us at www.dupont.com/ag/us Read and follow the label.

Courtesy of DuPont and Saatchi & Saatchi.

Figure 5-3 (continued)

3. *Where is my competition in the mind of this person?* Use the same approach as above, but concentrate on competing brands.

4. *Where would I like to be in the mind of this person?* Product is positioned as. . . . Product is the best choice because. . . . Now they know the product will. . . .

5. *What is the consumer promise, the "big idea"?* State the major focus of your campaign. Not a slogan or tagline at this stage, but a concise idea that sums up what the campaign should be about.

6. *What is the supporting evidence?* Build benefit after benefit in support of your big idea, which you stated in item 5.

7. *What is the tone of voice for the advertising?* Decide on the appropriate tone—warm, family values, startling, hi-tech, sobering fact, mild guilt, humor, and so on.

Writing partially in the first person to arrive at a strategy for reaching parents, the initial thinking for Bell Helmets (see Figure 5-4) probably went something like this:

1. *Who is our target?* "Hi. I'm Lena Emoto. I work full time as an accountant, and my husband, Ray, is a mechanical engineer. We have two growing children: Michelle, 9, and Bobby, 12. And are they busy kids! Dropping in at their friends' houses practically every day. Biking up to the corner convenience store to buy a slush drink. I'm lucky that they can take care

DOES YOUR KID HAVE HUNDRED DOLLAR FEET AND A TEN DOLLAR HEAD?

Ah, kids today. Always going around with expensive sneakers and cheap bike helmets like they do. Hey, wait a second. That's your fault. Or is it?

Maybe it's more a statement of society. Sneakers are status. Helmets, well they're just some dumb safety thing moms— and in some cases, lawmakers —make kids wear. Or maybe it's simply a result of the little bugger wearing you down for the fancy shoes. Either way, let's get this straight. You don't want your kid wearing a cheesy helmet. You want your kid wearing a Bell helmet.

If you spent more money on your kids' bike helmets than you did on their sneakers, don't read another word of this ad. We thought so.

Because nobody makes a better helmet than us. It's been that way for 40 years or so. We pioneered the field of helmet safety— first with race car helmets, now with bike helmets, too. We developed our own safety tests, which we conducted in our own lab. And still do. Understandably, no other company has sold nearly as many helmets. And no other company is chosen by more race car drivers and pro cyclists. Many of whom have had the misfortune of proving firsthand how good our helmets are. With any luck, something your kid will never do.

COURAGE FOR YOUR HEAD. (BELL HELMETS)

Courtesy of Bell Sports, Inc.

A HELMET THOUGHTFULLY DESIGNED BY ENGINEERS, CRAFTSMEN AND DEAD GUYS.

You know what our designers contributed. It's sitting down there in the form of that Fusion In-Mold, SandBlast™ finish 16-vent Psycho Pro, featuring our Full Nelson™ fit system (named after a particularly snug wrestling hold).

You can probably guess what our engineers and craftsmen contributed. For forty years, they have been pioneering helmet structure and safety by tenaciously developing their own unique crash and burn tests (and standards)

No hallucinogens were used in the designing of our new Pro Series. (As far as we know.)

Product Development Engineer, Tom Stone

Industrial Designer, Michele Saward

in their own unique research facility. Then there's the dead guys. They seem to require a bit more of an explanation. Their contribution has been more along the lines of a spongy grayish thing called a brain. You see, to figure out what happens in a real accident, we need to determine what happens to the brain. Crash test dummies don't have brains. So, we used cadavers to test how the G-forces of an impact effect the old cerebellum. We worked with brain surgeons from the

VP of Research & Development, John Doe

St. Louis Medical Center, running crash tests with electrodes hooked up to the brains of, well, dead guys. Of course, no one else does this sort of thing.

Anyway, we've learned a lot.

For starters, no other helmets on the market are better than ours. Which is probably why no company has sold nearly as many helmets. And why 22 out of the top 33 IndyCar drivers and hundreds (too many to count, in fact) of professional cyclists prefer Bell.

As well as most dead guys.

COURAGE FOR YOUR HEAD. (BELL HELMETS)

Courtesy of Bell Sports, Inc.

Figure 5-4
Bell Helmets wants parents to know that their children's safety is worth a few extra dollars.

of themselves after school and that their bikes allow them some mobility. But I sometimes worry about that. After all, the streets can be dangerous. Thank goodness I've convinced them to wear helmets, even though they originally fought me on it."

2. *Where are we now in the mind of this person?* "Sure, there are lots of brands of helmets. I didn't spend much on theirs because they all looked pretty much alike to me. They also looked like they'd protect their heads in case they fell or hit something. So while we almost shelled out big bucks for a higher-priced brand, Ray's car needed a major repair job, and with all we spent for school supplies and clothing, we decided it wasn't necessary to buy an expensive helmet just for riding in the neighborhood."

3. *Where is our competition in the mind of this person?* "As I said, most brands look about the same. We found two great-looking helmets for about thirteen bucks each. So far, they've been OK. Why spend more than you need? Clothes and shoes cost enough as it is."

4. *Where would we like to be in the mind of this person?* "At first I thought it was dumb to spend more on a bicycle helmet. Then I heard about Bell helmets, how they make them with such care, how they test them, how they're practically indestructible, and how they've saved the lives of professional and amateur racers."

5. *What is the consumer promise, the "big idea"?* "They say Bell helmets are thoroughly tested for safety. So when my kids wear one, they can enjoy biking, and I don't have to worry so much about them getting a bad head injury."

6. *What is the supporting evidence?* "Bell pioneered the field of helmet safety. They're first with racecar helmets and now with bike helmets, too. They invented their own safety tests, which they still conduct in their own labs. They sell more helmets than any other company, and Bell is the helmet of choice for more racecar drivers and pro cyclists than any other brand. I discovered that by reading their ad."

7. *What is the tone of voice for the advertising?* Make parents think about spending money on a helmet in terms of safety, not status. Use humor to make a sobering statement.

The Deutsch Approach

Deutsch answers the following questions to inspire the creative team:

1. Why are we communicating? What is the assignment?
2. Who are we talking to?
3. What's the problem and opportunity?
4. What should our communication do? How will it do this?
5. What is the strategic idea?
6. How will we support this idea?
7. What are the mandatories, the must-do's?

8. What are the creative considerations?

9. What are the deliverables? Where will the messages run?

The Creative Brief that inspired the IKEA Brooklyn campaign, featured in the Briefcase in Chapter 1, looked like the following:

Why are we communicating? Capture the attention of the Brooklyn PMA and drive traffic to the June 18th Grand Opening.

Who are we talking to? New York women, specifically New York moms, age 25 to 54. She lives in the most creative city in the world—she is modern, progressive, stylish, and smart and she prides herself on expressing her own creativity. This is especially true within her home; she ultimately wants to feel proud about opening the doors to her home, as this is a reflection of her personal taste. She is constantly on the lookout for ways to creatively optimize her living space. Being New York, the sources of inspiration are everywhere and sometimes she feels overwhelmed with the stimulus.

What's the Problem and Opportunity? IKEA has products for every room of the home that inspire creativity and the expression of personal style. Currently, NY women don't know, don't believe, or have forgotten how IKEA can provide this creative inspiration, all in one place. On June 18th, IKEA will be opening its fourth store in the NY market—IKEA Brooklyn. With IKEA's latest introduction to the NY market, now is the time to reintroduce NY Moms to the "value" of IKEA.

What should our communication do? How will it do this? Demonstrate how IKEA can inspire creativity in NY homes.

What is the strategic idea? IKEA is a destination for inspiration.

How will we support this idea?

- The IKEA value/concept: Beautifully designed for your creative sensibilities, functional products for the way you really live, all at a low price.

- An inspirational destination: Room settings designed for the way NYers really live—railroads, brownstones, and studios.

- It's easy to get here: Multiple transportation options.

- Home Delivery: Your purchases will be waiting for you when you arrive.

What are the mandatories, the must-do's? Communicate the grand opening date.

Creative Considerations: Inspiration . . . be it, don't just say it.

What are the deliverables? Out-of-home (billboards, transit, wild postings), newspaper, radio, guerilla, TV, projection media, mobile messaging.

> Linking Strategy with the Thinking/Feeling and High-/Low-Importance Scales

Advertising agency Foote, Cone & Belding has created a strategy model based on two basic facts: (1) Some purchasing decisions are based more on logic, whereas others are based more on emotions; and (2) some purchasing decisions may involve extensive deliberation, whereas others are made with

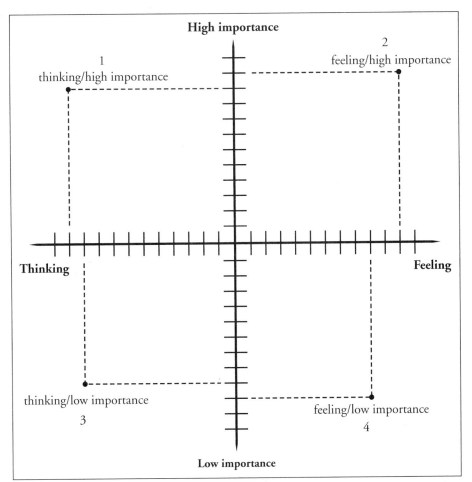

High importance

1
thinking/high importance

2
feeling/high importance

Thinking

Feeling

thinking/low importance
3

feeling/low importance
4

Low importance

Figure 5-5
The Foote, Cone & Belding strategy-planning model ranks consumer purchasing decisions in terms of high versus low importance and thinking versus feeling.

little or no thought. Visualize this model as a grid with four quadrants (see Figure 5-5).

- *Quadrant 1: Thinking/High Importance.* Also called the informative model, this approach assumes that the consumer needs a great deal of information because of the importance of the product and logical issues concerning it. Many campaigns for automobiles, digital cameras, computers, and home entertainment systems fit this category. Long copy, specific information, and perhaps a demonstration might be used to reinforce the selling argument.

- *Quadrant 2: Feeling/High Importance.* Also called the affective model, this approach views the consumer as an individual who relies less on specific information and more on attitudes and feelings about the product because the purchase decision is related to self-esteem. Products for which this strategy works include jewelry, cosmetics, fashion apparel, and motorcycles. Image advertising, which communicates with dramatic visuals and emotional statements as opposed to logic, is the rule of thumb here.

- *Quadrant 3: Thinking/Low Importance.* Also called the habit-formation model, this approach views the consumer as someone who makes purchasing decisions with minimal thought. Simply inducing a trial purchase, as with a coupon, may generate subsequent purchases more readily than pounding home undifferentiated points in the copy. Campaigns for food and household cleaning products often use this approach; the messages always remind the consumer to choose the brand.

- *Quadrant 4: Feeling/Low Importance.* Also called the self-satisfaction model, this approach sees the consumer as a reactor. It is reserved for products that satisfy personal tastes, such as smoking and consumption of alcoholic beverages, and that make the user feel "special" when using the brand in front of peers. Messages are designed primarily to draw attention to the brand.

Note that because consumers buy a variety of goods and services, they may fit any of the four quadrant profiles, depending on the specific purchasing decision.

> Checklist for Creative Briefs

- Does your brief have the potential for relevant and unexpected connections that can build a relationship between the brand and the prospect?
- Did you place the brand at the appropriate point on the thinking/feeling and high-low-importance scales?
- Does your brief address one or more human needs?
- Did you include emotional benefits as well as rational ones? Can the product and its advertising support these benefits?
- Did you consider what strategies competitors are using, as well as what they may have missed?
- Does your brief address the target market in a tone appropriate to this market?
- Does your brief contain enough information to give the creative team members direction but not so much information that it overwhelms them?

> Suggested Activities

1. Review the creative brief formats from McCann Erickson and Deutsch. Using the format that you think gives the creative team the most insight, write a creative brief for a product, service, or organization of your choosing or as assigned by your instructor.
2. Collect several advertisements for a single product, service, or organization. How much of the original strategy can you infer from what each ad says and how it says it? Is the target audience evident? What is the problem, and what is the ad's approach to solving it? Which human needs are addressed? If you were in the target market for this ad, would you believe what it says? Why or why not? Strategically, what might be another way to approach the problem?
3. Using this same campaign or another, do an Internet search for the product or service. What differences do you note in the strategic approach?

BRIEFCASE

Eat Mor Chikin or These Cows Are Goners!

Chick-fil-A is a quick-service restaurant chain with more than 1,000 units and more than $1.2 billion in sales. From 1963 to the 1980s, Chick-fil-A grew to become America's dominant mall-based restaurant chain on the strength of its signature chicken sandwich. As mass merchandisers began to erode mall traffic in the 1980s, Chick-fil-A management moved the chain's expansion strategy out of the mall and onto the street with freestanding units.

Chick-fil-A now competes in one of the economy's largest and most competitive segments—fast-food restaurants. Chick-fil-A is outnumbered in store count by up to 15 to 1 and is outspent in the media by up to 20 to 1 by the likes of McDonald's, Burger King, and Wendy's. Industrywide, flat pricing and rapid store growth have held average same-store sales increases to a modest 1 to 2 percent for several years. Also, deep discounting has been the dominant marketing message in the fast-food industry.

In 1995, Chick-fil-A hired the Richards Group to develop a campaign that would clearly position Chick-fil-A as the preferred alternative to hamburgers in the fast-food restaurant marketplace. To arrive at the best approach, the Richards Group used its Spherical Branding process, in which it defines the client's business, the brand's positioning and personality, and the desired affiliation.

The Spherical Branding process revealed significant differences between Chick-fil-A customers and traditional fast-food customers. Chick-fil-A customers were older, better educated, wealthier, more white collar, and skewed female. They came to Chick-fil-A for a unique, better-tasting chicken sandwich.

Research confirmed that Chick-fil-A was rich with positive associations. The great-tasting chicken sandwich was the strongest association. Also, customers associated Chick-fil-A with a clean, comfortable restaurant environment; well-run operations; accurate service; friendly, clean-cut employees; and strong values. Customers described the brand's personality as upscale, successful, healthy, intelligent, clean-cut, and wholesome. Sounds perfect, right?

Courtesy of Chick-fil-A.

Well, a bit too perfect. The Richards Group discovered other personality traits included status driven, finicky, uptight, self-absorbed, and boring.

Clearly, Chick-fil-A was seen as the premium chicken sandwich in the quick-service restaurant category. The Richards Group, however, understood that talking about "quality" products was not unique or motivating. It might even add to the negative characteristics of being uptight and finicky.

After thorough consumer research and an extensive review of the fast-food restaurant category, the Richards Group developed the following brand positioning for Chick-fil-A: to choosy people in a hurry, Chick-fil-A is the premium fast-food restaurant brand that consistently serves America's best-loved chicken sandwiches.

"Calling All Cows" :60 radio

SFX:	OPEN ON SFX [SOUND EFFECT] OF DIAL TONE. THEN WE HEAR NUMBERS BEING DIALED, BUT THE TONE IS SLIGHTLY OFF AS IF THE NUMBERS AREN'T BEING PRESSED PROPERLY. THIS GOES ON FOR A FEW SECONDS AND IS FOLLOWED BY AN OFF-THE-HOOK SFX.
ANNCR:	The cows are calling . . .
SFX:	WE HEAR A SORT OF COW GRUMBLING OR MOO AND THEN MORE EFFORT IN MISDIALING THE PHONE.
ANNCR:	The cows are trying to call you on the phone to tell you to eat more chicken.
SFX:	DISGRUNTLED MOO. MISDIAL, MISDIAL, MISDIAL.
ANNCR:	Unfortunately, cows have hooves. So not only is the receiver hard to pick up, but the little numbers are nearly impossible to dial.
SFX:	POORLY DIALED NUMBERS AND COW SFX CONTINUE UNDER . . .
ANNCR:	Oh, how stubborn cows can be. You see, they want you to know about Chick-fil-A. Chick-fil-A invented the chicken sandwich over 30 years ago. Made a special way, it's more tender, juicier, better. The cows want you to eat more chicken.
SFX:	DIAL TONE.
ANNCR:	The cows also want to tell you to quit puttin' bells around their necks, but that's a whole other story. Chick-fil-A. We didn't invent the chicken, just the chicken sandwich.
SFX:	ROTARY DIAL SOUND FOLLOWED BY A MORE SATISFIED MOO SOUND.

"The B-Word" :60 radio

ANNCR: And now the Chick-fil-A update. The BCC—the Bovine Communications Committee, sister agency of the FCC—has banned the use of a number of words on commercial airwaves. First and foremost is (BEEP). The cows call it the "B" word—ends in "F," two "E's" in the middle.

This particular word, the cows claim, is corrupting the minds and bodies of America. Phrases like (BEEP) jerky, (BEEP)-cake, (BEEP) stroganoff, "Where's the (BEEP)," "One-hundred percent, pure, Grade-A Angus (BEEP)" are now punishable with time in a pig trough and random electric cattle prodding. An acceptable substitute is the "C" word, a.k.a. chicken. Saying (BEEP) in private is still legal, but the cows don't recommend it. Should you find yourself saying (BEEP), thinking about (BEEP), or craving (BEEP), head to Chick-fil-A. There you can purge your wrongdoings by thinking wholesome thoughts and eating wholesome things. Like the Chick-fil-A Original Chicken Sandwich.

It features a tender, all-white breast of chicken cooked a special way to seal in the juices, then placed atop a hot, buttered bun with two crucial pickles. I've got no (BEEP) with that. Chick-fil-A. We didn't invent the chicken. Just the chicken sandwich.

The target of choosy people in a hurry encompasses those who, regardless of their demographics, are more choosy about the food they eat, the restaurant they eat in, the employees who serve them, and the healthfulness of the food. They are choosier people about most aspects of their lives.

From the consumer perspective, Chick-fil-A is fast food. The frame of reference as a premium fast-food restaurant acknowledges that consumers consider Chick-fil-A among the most respected, highest-quality fast-food restaurants.

Chicken sandwiches are the dominant signature products and the most compelling reason for choosing Chick-fil-A. "Consistently serves America's best-loved chicken sandwiches" is a specific and vivid reason to choose Chick-fil-A.

Chick-fil-A's brand personality had to be easy to connect to emotionally. The Richards Group determined that Chick-fil-A's brand personality should be:

Caring. Genuine. Clean-cut. Dependable. Unexpectedly fun.

Caring to capture the community and people orientation of the company and its principled and giving culture. *Genuine* to capture the sense of an organization that is authentic, classic, and comfortable with itself and that puts substance over style. *Clean-cut* to capture the wholesome and healthy quality of the nature of the people. *Dependable* to characterize people who have their act together and have some stability in their lives. They are people who you would consider good neighbors. *Unexpectedly fun* to leave room for the company to not take itself too seriously, to be lighthearted and creative.

The Richards Group wanted people to feel the following brand affiliation when they choose to eat at Chick-fil-A:

> *People who eat at Chick-fil-A see themselves as a little more discerning. "Chick-fil-A is a little more expensive, but it's worth it." They also see Chick-fil-A as a place for active, family-focused folks who appreciate Chick-fil-A's strong values.*

With the Spherical branding process complete, the Richards Group realized it needed to create a campaign that would leverage the premium product and enhance the personality of the brand. The creative solution, "Eat Mor Chikin," features cows trying to persuade consumers to eat more Chick-fil-A chicken.

The campaign rolled out initially in 1995 as a three-dimensional billboard in which cows appear to be writing "Eat Mor Chikin" on the sign. This board is used when Chick-fil-A opens in a new market to welcome new customers. As a market matures, the cows begin to rotate other boards into the mix. Sometimes the cows are used outdoors to promote specific items,

Courtesy of Chick-fil-A.

like breakfast, with boards such as "Eat Mor Chikin or Weer Toast." They aren't particular, however, about how humans eat chicken, just that they do. So sometimes they encourage the general consumption of chicken by tying their message to current events with boards like the "Vote Chikin" board that ran during an election year. A fully integrated campaign was added in 1996, which included outdoor billboards, television, radio, freestanding inserts, direct mail, costumed mascots, and apparel and novelty items.

The campaign has won numerous awards in the Cannes, ADDY, OBIE, and other creative competitions. In 2009, the campaign won its second Effie Award, which is given to campaigns that meet or exceed advertising objectives, and is based on planning, market research, media, creative, and account management.

The "Eat Mor Chikin" Cows have also won the accolades of the toughest advertising critics: consumers. In 2007, the Cows were recognized as one of America's most popular advertising icons in a public vote sponsored by Advertising Week. The Cows are permanently featured in New York's Madison Avenue Advertising Walk of Fame.

In the process, the traffic-stopping cows have convinced a lot of people to "eat mor chikin." Since 1996, Chick-fil-A's unaided brand awareness has grown more than 80 percent. During that same period, sales have increased 120 percent. In January 2009, Chick-fil-A reported its 16th year of double-digit sales growth. That's a lot "mor chikin" than before the cows and the Richards Group came on the scene. Now if only we can convince the cows to use spell check.

6

IDEAS
THE CURRENCY OF THE 21ST CENTURY

Roy Spence, founder of Austin-based GSD&M, says that ideas are "the currency of the 21st century," but observes, "the market is ad rich and idea poor."[1]

> How Do You Come Up with the Big Idea?

Some writers and artists say their ideas come to them while they're taking a hot bath or a long walk. Others get ideas in the shower or while driving. And still others get ideas through free association with a colleague. Terence Poltrack describes the process of coming up with the big idea as

> *one man, one style. For every idea out there, there's a way to get to it. Ask advertising's creative thinkers about their personal road maps to The Answer, and you confront a mix of fear and bravado, chilly logic and warm emotion. The process is one part reason, one part heart, and one (big) part pure, simple intuition.*[2]

[1] Bill Meyers, "He's in the Idea Business," *USA Today,* 29 April 1999, p. B1.
[2] Terence Poltrack, "Stalking the Big Idea," *Agency,* May/June 1991, p. 26.

James Webb Young, a former creative vice president at J. Walter Thompson, described a five-step process in his book *A Technique for Producing Ideas:*[3]

1. *Immersion.* Even the pros don't write the magic line the first time. Engross yourself in background research. Visit the client. Watch consumers interact with your brand. And so on.

2. *Digestion.* Play with the information. Look at it from different angles. Make lists of features. Draw doodles. Write down phrases. Exercise your mind. This chapter will give you some creative exercises that may help spark an idea.

3. *Incubation.* Put the advertising assignment aside. Go for a walk. See a movie. Shoot some hoops. Do whatever will relax your mind. Young likened this step to the way Sherlock Holmes solved mysteries. In the middle of a case, Holmes would drag Watson off to a concert. This habit was irritating to the literal-minded Watson, but it always helped Holmes crack the case.

4. *Illumination.* Once your brain has been allowed to relax after being loaded with information, it will spurt out an idea. It can happen anywhere, any time. Be ready to write the idea down because, as quickly as an idea pops into your head, it can pop out of it. Forever. It doesn't matter if the idea is captured on a scrap of paper, a cocktail napkin, or in the dust on your car's dashboard, just as long as you record it somehow.

   Creative director Ann Hayden was having a difficult time coming up with the right approach for a Roche commercial. She knew the commercial needed to convince patients to discuss their weight with their doctors. But every idea she came up with seemed trite. Finally, the big idea came to her when she was having dinner at a restaurant and noticed the couple at the next table had a baby with them. That's it! Babies. One of the first things that happens when a baby is born is that he or she is weighed. This inspired a commercial that opens on a baby and dissolves into a grown woman who is overweight. The announcer says, "We're all born into this world small, within 3 to 4 pounds of each other. Then life happens. And we can end up weighing more than is healthy for us. Fortunately, today there are some truly different prescription options that can help. Doctors have been weighing you since you were born. Isn't it time you talked about it?"[4]

5. *Reality testing.* Ask yourself, is the idea good? Does it solve the problem? Is it on strategy? As you gather ideas, put them inside an envelope or folder and don't look at them right away. If you evaluate early on, you may settle for an idea that's just so-so or you may never allow a gem of an idea to develop.

   Be sure to test your idea on others. You may be so close to the idea that you don't see potential problems, so show it to others and listen to their feedback. Ogilvy & Mather tells its account people to ask the following questions when evaluating creative work: Is it on strategy? What did you get from the advertising? Was that net impression a good

---

[3] James Webb Young, *A Technique for Producing Ideas,* 3rd ed. (Chicago: Crain Books, 1975).
[4] Adapted from a lecture given by Ann Hayden at the University of South Carolina, 13 May 2000.

or bad one? Why? Did you remember to react to this ad as a consumer, not as an advertising person? Does the ad address the right group of people? Is the tone consistent with the strategy? Is it a good execution? Is the promise visualized effectively? How? Is the brand name up front enough? Is the core selling idea clear? Does the execution lend itself to a total campaign? If so, what might be some other executions? Does something make you stop, look, listen quickly? What is it?

> There's a Big Idea in the Creative Brief

The creative brief you learned to write in the last chapter serves as a road map for your idea-generation process. For instance, the brief for Kellogg's NutriGrain breakfast bars told the Leo Burnett creative team that consumers want to eat the right thing. They know healthy food will make them look and feel good, but they're tempted by junk food that goes straight to their hips and thighs. Using the insights from the brief, the creative team members realized that they weren't just selling a breakfast bar; they were selling self-respect. The tagline, "Respect yourself in the morning," summed up the big idea. To develop ideas for individual ads in the campaign, the team jotted down words, phrases, and images of what consumers are—and should be—eating. One ad shows a humongous donut wrapped around someone's waist, and another shows giant sticky buns stuck on a woman's rear end. In keeping with the strategy, billboards are placed next to donut shops and fast-food restaurants.

> Turn an Idea into a Campaign Theme

It's rare that you will be asked to come up with an idea for a single ad. Most often, you'll be asked to come up with an idea that has "legs"—one that can run over time as a campaign. Some of the most famous and successful campaigns have been running for decades. So before you settle on an idea for a single ad, ask yourself, what will the next ad be like? And the one after that? And the one a year from now? And 5 or 10 years from now? Does the idea stand the test of time? That is, can you create a campaign for it?

Bud Light ads center on the concept that guys will go to great extremes to protect their favorite brand of beer. This big idea has been developed into numerous award-winning commercials. In one, a skydiver is reluctant to jump out of a plane. To inspire him to jump, the instructor drops a six-pack of Bud Light out of the plane's door. To the audience's surprise, the pilot jumps out of the plane to retrieve the beer. Another Bud Light commercial shows two young guys in an apartment. One of them is concerned that their friends will drink all their beer. Not to worry: the other guy has installed a magic fridge. With the pull of a lever, the kitchen wall revolves and the refrigerator is replaced with a kitchen table and chairs. Pure genius! The only problem is on the other side of the wall is another apartment filled with guys who rejoice when the refrigerator appears. As if they are worshiping an idol, the men bow down and chant, "Magic fridge."

Notice the similarities in the two Bud Light ads. Although the scenarios are different, they come back to the same big idea. A campaign is a series of ads that reflect the same big idea and have a similar theme and attitude. Often the individual ads will have the same look, in which the art director specifies the size and location of the visual and logo, the size and font of the type, and so on. Also, often the copy in each ad follows the same structure, from the length of the headline down to the last line of copy. Although your campaign doesn't have to be this structured, there should be some constants. Unless there's a very good reason for changing it, use the same type font, and copy and design style.

Campaign ideas transcend different media. Peek back at the Chick-fil-A "Briefcase" section found in Chapter 5, and you'll see how the big idea—cows pleading for people to "eat mor chikin"—works for outdoor billboards, television, and radio. In each case, the cows appear to be creating the ads. Go to chick-fil-a.com and you'll get to see a "familee" slideshow, view TV "commershals", order a "calindar," and "git" cow stuff.

At times, you'll be asked to develop multiple campaigns to reach different target audiences. For example, Loeffler Ketchum Mountjoy created numerous campaigns to convince a variety of people to visit North Carolina. Its research showed some people want to "veg out" and leave their worries behind when they go on vacation. Others want to discover new things while they're visiting new places. And a third group, filmmakers, need to know why one location is better than another to shoot a movie. These wonderful campaigns for North Carolina are found in Chapter 7. Study these ads and you'll see how they appeal to different audiences.

> From One Big Idea to Hundreds of Ideas

Once you develop your big idea, you'll need to come up with an infinite number of ideas for individual ads that support the campaign theme. It's not easy. To help the brainstorming process, apply the following questions to your advertising problem.

Where Will Your Ad Run?

DiGiorno Rising Crust Pizza reinforced its message "It's not delivery. It's DiGiorno." by placing ads in yellow-page directories next to ads from take-out pizza restaurants. The headline asked, "Looking for a pizza that bakes up fresh like pizzeria pizza? Look in your freezer." The copy led users to an 800 number for a coupon worth $1.50 off their next purchase.

Minute Maid bought the back page of each section of the *New York Times* to introduce its Premium Choice juice. The ad in the Business section included a coupon, along with some financial advice: "This might be the only sure thing you'll ever find in the business section." The ad in the Metropolitan section played off the numerous New Yorkers who become snowbirds when they retire: "Today, the Metropolitan section also has important news

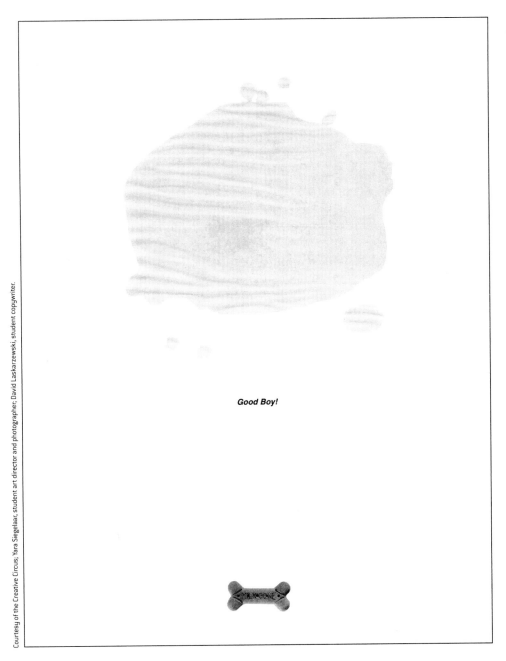

Good Boy!

Courtesy of the Creative Circus; Yara Siegelaar, student art director and photographer; David Laskarzewski, student copywriter.

Figure 6-1
What's that giant spot doing on this newspaper ad? If you're a dog owner, you know. Good boy! And good use of media to generate a creative idea.

from New York's sixth borough, Florida." Students from the Creative Circus showed how newspaper ads are the perfect medium to reach dog owners (see Figure 6-1).

Don't just stick to traditional media to run your message. Think creatively, as Kirshenbaum, Bond & Partners did when it stenciled the sidewalks of New York with the message "From here, it looks like you could use some new underwear. Bamboo Lingerie." Crispin Porter + Bogusky also used unconventional media to describe what it's like to be homeless. Ads for the Miami Rescue Mission ran on shopping carts, bus shelters, park benches, and trash dumpsters. Each had the following copy: "When you're homeless, you see the world differently. To help call 571-2273." What made the ads so powerful was how the headlines and media choices related to the overall message: The ad on the park benches was headlined "Bed." The message on the dumpsters read "Kitchen." The poster inside the bus shelter was labeled "House." The sign on the grocery carts described it as a "Closet."

What's the Context of Your Message?

What will the members of your target audience be doing when they see or hear your ad? A Clorox coupon insert appeared inside boxed DVD sets of *Mad Men* Season Two, the pop culture phenomenon about the advertising world of the sixties, where sex and booze were the norm.[5] The connection? One side of the insert featured a lipstick-stained collar with the message, "Getting ad guys out of hot water for generations."

Noxzema bought ad space in women's restrooms throughout Manhattan. The ads grabbed your attention because they were printed in reverse—you needed a mirror to read them. Appropriately, the ads were hung in frames on the walls across the mirrors so that, when a woman checked her makeup in the mirror, she was greeted with messages such as these:

"Look as good as the woman your date is hitting on."

"Did someone miss her beauty sleep?"

"He must really love you for your inner beauty."

Here are other clever messages that make a relevant connection to what consumers are doing when they see the message:

"Ref, you need glasses."
    (Outdoor board for an optician, placed at a sports stadium)

"Hello to all our readers in high office."
    (Message for *The Economist* magazine, painted on the roof of a bus)

"20 ounce soda. 6 inch pothole."
    (Message for Tide, placed on the exterior of a bus)

What's the Timing of Your Ad?

When will your ad run? Is the timing significant to your target audience? For example, Pepto-Bismol ran an ad in April issues of magazines. How does the month of April relate to queasy stomachs? April 15 is tax day, a day that can make some taxpayers sick to their stomachs. That's why Pepto-Bismol ran a full-page copy of a 1040 form, with a corner rolled up to reveal a bottle of Pepto-Bismol.

Wild Turkey Kentucky Straight Bourbon Whiskey made an unexpected but relevant suggestion for people who were expecting company for the

---

[5] There's some debate from industry pros whether the show accurately portrays what really went on at ad agencies in the sixties.

holidays: "This Thanksgiving serve Turkey before dinner." Vicks' NyQuil ran an ad during the holiday season, when many people seem to catch colds, with this message: "Silent night." And Saatchi & Saatchi used holidays as a source of inspiration for Tide laundry detergent ads:

"The only way to wear white after Labor Day."
(Ran on Labor Day)

"It takes a wee bit more than luck to get green beer out of your clothes."
(Ran on St. Patrick's Day)

"Removes alien goo, fake blood and, oh yeah, chocolate."
(Ran on Halloween)

Don't just rely on major holidays as a source of inspiration. Look up some of the more offbeat holidays and see if you can make a relevant connection to your brand. Chick-fil-A gives free meals to customers who visit their restaurants on July 10, Cow Appreciation Day. To get the free meal, customers must come dressed as a cow from head to hoof. A complimentary entrée is given to customers who are a bit more timid and come partially dressed in cow attire, such as a cow-spotted scarf, purse, hat, or other accessory. Chick-fil-A even has a special website dedicated to the occasion, cowappreciationday.com, to share cow costume tips as well as downloadable cow spots, masks, and other bovine-themed accessories for customers to use to create their costumes.

What's in the News?

Did something major just happen? Is something about to happen? Ads that tap into current events reflect what's on people's minds and make your brand seem timely. This approach is great if you have the resources to constantly change your ads.

America's Dairy Farmers and Milk Processors often tap into major events such as sporting events, elections, and TV shows. For instance, on Super Bowl Monday, you'll see the winning quarterback sporting a milk mustache. Two versions of the ad are shot in advance, just in case the outcome isn't what everyone expects.

Several companies found inspiration from the 2008 Presidential election. Convenience store chain 7-Eleven ran a presidential coffee cup poll, which gave coffee drinkers their choice of a red 20-ounce cup for John McCain or a blue 20-ounce cup for Barack Obama. Pepsi's redesigned logo, which some say resembled Obama's logo, was incorporated into slogans "Yes You Can," "Optimismmmm," and "Hope." Pedigree ran an ad addressed to President-elect Obama that read, in part, "We'd love to help you fulfill your first campaign promise. We are thrilled that you are celebrating your victory by adopting a dog into your family. We think you'll find that shelter dogs are among the most loyal, loving and special dogs in the world. And no dog is more in need of a little hope." For another example of how a brand embraced the election, turn to the IKEA Briefcase found in Chapter 12.

Can You Borrow from the Pages of History?

McCann Erickson's Singapore office studied old ads from the Simmons Bedding Company and discovered a brochure from the 1930s that featured a testimonial from Eleanor Roosevelt. This inspired an idea that won gold at the One Show. The headline read:

> For President Roosevelt,
>
> a day at the office
>
> involved sending 750,000 men
>
> into a minefield.
>
> Ever wondered how he
>
> slept at night?

What Are the Negatives about Your Brand?

What negative thoughts do your potential customers have about your client? What negative thoughts do you have about your client? Don't try to cover up a negative—embrace it. After all, what's negative to one person can be positive to another. A copywriter at Macy's was faced with the challenge of selling orange luggage. It was just plain ugly. What could she do? She could omit that it was orange. After all, she wasn't taking mail and phone orders, so she didn't have to mention color. And, because the newspaper ad was going to run in black and white, no one would know the difference, right? Wrong. Customers would know the minute they came to the store. They would be furious, and the store could lose valued customers. So she wrote something along these lines: "Does your luggage get lost at the airline terminals? We've got the perfect luggage for you!" The luggage sold out because she turned a negative into a selling advantage, and she told the truth.

Notice how the students at the Creative Circus turned the small size of the Audi TT into an advantage (see Figure 6-2).

What If Your Product Were Something Else?

Make an analogy. If your product were an animal, would it be a finicky cat, a loveable mutt, or a graceful swan? If it were a tree, would it be a giant redwood or a bonsai? How about if it was a person? Would it be young? Old? Carefree? Uptight? *Good Housekeeping* magazine touted the virtues of its Seal of Approval to advertisers: "The seal is like your therapist: It assures you everything will be alright." Pier House Resort and Caribbean Spa likened itself to a woman sipping iced champagne at sunset (see Figure 6-4).

An MTV campaign promoted the use of condoms by using an analogy to other types of safety equipment. In one spot, a roller coaster attendant tries to put a safety belt on the young man who protests, "I want to be free. I want to feel everything. I just want to make this time special." The attendant reluctantly agrees, "All right, just this once." The roller coaster takes off, a scream

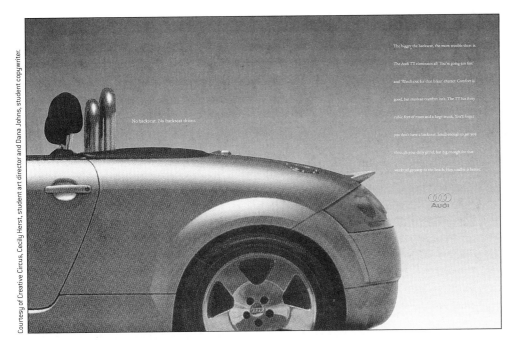

Courtesy of Creative Circus, Cecily Herst, student art director and Dana Johns, student copywriter.

Figure 6-2
Copy reads: "No backseat. No backseat driver. The bigger the backseat, the more trouble there is. The Audi TT eliminates all 'You're going too fast' and 'Watch out for the biker' chatter. Comfort is good but minivan comfort isn't. The TT has forty cubic feet of room and a large trunk. You'll forget you don't have a backseat. Small enough to get you through your daily grind, but big enough for that weekend getaway to the beach. Hey, smaller is better."

Courtesy of the Creative Circus; Cecily Herbst, student art director; Dana Johns, students copywriter.

Copy reads: "Lots of elbow room. If you hang one out the window. Just enough. No more. We at Audi purposely spent more time on the TT's design than contemplating how many bags of groceries you're hauling. Shouldn't luxurious, yet sporty cars be small? How else could a TT weave in and out of traffic while others sit in their SUV's and stare?"

is heard, and the young man's seat is empty when the roller coaster returns. Another spot shows a young man swimming in shark-infested waters without a shark cage, and a third shows him climbing a mountain without a harness. The spots end with the message "Stop making excuses. Always use protection"; viewers are directed to a toll-free number and website for more information about AIDS prevention.

What Is Your Target Audience Reading and Watching?

Books, movies, games, and TV programs can serve as inspiration. It can be the highbrow variety or the pop culture variety. Just make sure it's relevant to your target audience.

FedEx® did its own version of the movie *Castaway* in a commercial that shows a FedEx employee delivering a package that he has protected the entire time he was marooned on a deserted island. He asks the grateful recipient what's in the package and discovers it contains a satellite phone, GPS locator, fishing rod, water purifier, and some seeds. "Silly things" to the recipient, but the very things that could have helped the FedEx employee escape the island or at least could have made his stay more enjoyable. Movie buffs appreciated finding out what was in the mysterious package, which Tom Hanks protected the entire time he was on the island. The commercial also resonated with people who had never seen the movie because the abbreviated version made sense on its own.

Keep in mind that you can't just "borrow" footage from movies. FedEx obtained permission from Twentieth Century Fox and Dreamworks, which wasn't hard, given the package delivery company's cooperation in the making of the movie. While FedEx did not pay for product placement in the movie, they did supply trucks, airplanes, uniforms, and packages.[6] (See Chapter 12 for information on product placement.)

What Does the Product Look Like?

Try dipping a french fry in some ketchup. See anything special? Saatchi & Saatchi's Singapore office saw a matchstick that led to an ad for Burger King's "fiery fries." Meanwhile, fast-food rival McDonald's golden arches have appeared in ads as the straps on a backpack, the ears on an Easter bunny, and the body of a car.

In an effort to influence behavior, Allstate Insurance illustrated how drinking and driving don't mix. No, it didn't show a car wreck. Instead, it invented a "killer cocktail"—a martini with a car key jabbing the olive as if it were a toothpick. To make its brand welcome in any home, American Standard put a friendly face on its bathroom fixtures (Figure 6-3).

Where Is the Brand Made and Sold?

Pace Picante Sauce promoted its authentic Tex-Mex heritage by poking fun at other brands that were "made in New York City!" Meanwhile, a billboard for Zamboli's Italian restaurant (located in South Carolina) told drivers the mileage to the closest great Italian food:

Great Italian Food Ahead

Rome 4,574 Mi. Venice 4,634 Mi. Zamboli's Next Right

What regions of the country (or the world) will see your ad? Can you customize it? Some ads have fun with regional accents. An ad promoting a

---

[6] David Barton, "Packagetour." *The Sacramento Bee*, 22 December 2000, p. D1.

© 1993 American Standard Brands.

Figure 6-3
What does your product look like? Is there an idea in the shape of your product? In this case, the bathroom fixture looks like a friendly face.

concert by a Southern choir read, "Hallaluy'all." An ad in a tourist magazine invited people to visit "The Boston Museum of Fine Ahht."

IKEA customizes its messages to reflect the distinctive personalities of the regions where its stores are located. To create buzz about the opening of its Tampa, FL store, IKEA created giant messages in bottles. Four 10-foot bottles were completely furnished with IKEA merchandise and displayed at the St. Petersburg Pier. More than 6,000 mini bottles with an IKEA message were given to curious passersby. (See the Briefcases found in Chapters 1 and 12 for other big ideas from IKEA.)

Is There an Ideal Spokesperson or Spokes-character?

As Chapter 1 states, the right spokesperson or advertising trade character can help you break through the clutter and make a relevant connection with your target audience. When Goodby, Silverstein & Partners found that 65 percent of Cheetos were eaten by adults as a guilty pleasure, they put a little mischief in Chester Cheetah, which has been the brand's spokes-character since 1986. One commercial, set in an outdoor café, features an obnoxious woman screaming on a cell phone: "I must be on the ugly side of town because everyone here is like, gross!" Chester points to a roof that's covered with pigeons, giving a fellow diner the idea to toss some Cheetos under the obnoxious woman's feet. Dozens of pigeons swarm the woman, giving her a real reason to think she's on the gross side of town.

Is There an Idea in the Brand's Name?

Most people never heard of supplemental life insurance until the spunky AFLAC duck came along in 1999. Brand-name recognition quickly rose to more than 90 percent as the duck quacked, "Af-laccck!"[7] Now that brand recognition has been achieved, the new "Aflacts" campaign messages focus on what Aflac does. A series of ads feature the famous duck holding informative signs that explain Aflac is insurance for daily living; it pays cash benefits to help with daily expenses, such as groceries, childcare, and rent. The tagline, "We've got you under our wing," reinforces the brand promise.

What's the Opposite of What You're Trying to Say?

If you're trying to say that something's comfortable, show something that's uncomfortable. If you're trying to sell something big, show a tiny detail. Likewise, if you want to sell peace, show the tragic outcome of war. A famous political commercial featured an adorable girl counting the petals on a daisy. When her count is about to reach 10, the visual motion freezes, and you hear a countdown in a man's voice. As the countdown proceeds, the camera zooms in on the girl's face until you're looking into the pupil of her eye. You see black for a tiny fraction of a second. When the countdown reaches zero, a nuclear mushroom cloud appears in the girl's black pupil and you hear Lyndon Johnson: "These are the stakes, to make a world in which all God's children can live, or to go into the darkness. Either we must love each other or we must die." The screen goes to black with white type, "on November 3rd, Vote for President Johnson." The commercial ran only once, but some say it demolished Barry Goldwater's chances of winning the 1964 election.

> Guidelines for Brainstorming

- *Don't think you must come up with the big idea all by yourself.* Steve Hayden, one of the creators of the famous 1984 commercial that launched Apple's Macintosh computer, puts it all in perspective: "It's better to own 20% of a great idea than 100% of a so-so idea."[8]

    A great visual idea can come from a writer. The perfect headline can come from an artist. And, as shown earlier, creative solutions can come from media experts. You may want to work independently at first and

---

[7] Stuart Elliott, "This Duck Means Business," www.nytimes.com, 11 February 2003.
[8] Laurence Minsky and Emily Thornton Calvo, *How to Succeed in Advertising When All You Have Is Talent* (Lincolnwood, IL: NTC Business Books, 1995), p. 99.

Courtesy of Nasuti & Hinkle Creative.

Figure 6-4
This analogy helps vacationers understand that Pier House Resort and Caribbean Spa isn't just a destination. It's a state of mind. Now consider doing your own analogy. What if Pier House was a man? A piece of artwork? A drink? A car?

then bounce ideas off your creative partner. You may want to start out by doing free association with one or two colleagues. Perhaps you want to brainstorm with a group of 6 to 12 people. When you brainstorm in a group, be sure to designate a leader who will keep the session going and record the ideas. Also, be sure that every person participates and that no idea is considered stupid. After the session, there will be time to sort quality from quantity.

- *Start a swipe file.* Fill a folder or file cabinet or wallpaper an entire room with work you consider outstanding. You shouldn't "swipe" ideas, but you can use them as a springboard. The legendary Leo Burnett used to rip out ads that struck him as being effective communications. About twice a year, he'd riffle through that file—not with the idea of copying anything, but in the hope that it would trigger an idea that could apply to something else he was doing. Burnett also kept a folder of phrases he liked.

> *Whenever I hear a phrase in conversation or any place which strikes me as being particularly apt in expressing an idea or bringing it to life or accentuating the smell of it, the looks of it or anything else—or expressing any kind of an idea—I scribble it down and stick it in there.*[9]

[9] Denis Higgins, Conversations with William Bernbach, Leo Burnett, George Gribbin, David Ogilvy, Rosser Reeves (Lincolnwood, IL: NTC Business Books, 1989), p. 47.

Burnett made that comment back in the 1960s, but the advice is still appropriate today.

- *Pay attention to life's experiences.* The best ads create an emotional connection with consumers. Take note of situations that move you because there's a good chance these same scenarios will trigger an emotional response with your audience. Art director Steve Bougdano was moved when he witnessed a troop of soldiers receiving a standing ovation at an airport terminal. He remembered this when Anheuser-Busch asked its agencies to develop a commercial paying tribute to the soldiers fighting in Iraq. This poignant commercial went on to receive numerous awards.

- *Exercise your creative mind regularly.* Hang out with creative people, whether in your field or a different one. Go to the zoo. Visit a museum. See a play. Do something you've never done before. And be sure to pay attention to the nuances of everyday life. Creative director Jim Riswold admits,

  > *I have never had an original thought in my career. Everything I have ever done has been borrowed, reformulated, regurgitated, turned upside down or inside out, played back at a different speed, and sometimes just plain stolen from either popular culture, music, history, art, literature, the back of cereal boxes, Hegelianism, an athlete's life, a bedtime story my grandmother once read me—whatever. Anything and everything is fair game when it comes to stimulus.*[10]

- *Give yourself some down time.* You need to give your mind a break; otherwise, you'll overload on stimuli. Try spending some time alone. Try turning off the television, radio, and e-mail for a week. You'll find that removing the extra "noise" is the equivalent of meditation. Also, write in a journal every day to keep your ideas flowing. Don't think of it as creative writing; think of it as "brain dumping." The idea is to put two to three pages of your thoughts on paper daily.

- *Come up with a lot of ideas.* The more ideas, the better. Luke Sullivan, an award-winning copywriter, warns, "As a creative person, you will discover your brain has a built-in tendency to want to reach closure, even rush to it. . . . But in order to get to a great idea, which is usually about the 500th one to come along, you'll need to resist the temptation to give in to the anxiety and sign off on the first passable idea that shows up."[11]

Consider these two sets of instructions:

1. Come up with a good idea that will solve the problem of declining student enrollment at XYZ University. Your name and idea will be forwarded to the president of the university.

2. Come up with as many ideas as possible to help solve the problem of declining student enrollment at XYZ University. Jot down as many ideas as possible. Try to come up with at least 25 ideas. Don't judge the merits of your ideas. Write every idea you have.

---

[10] Warren Berger, *Advertising Today* (London: Phaidon Press, 2001), p. 157.
[11] Luke Sullivan, *Hey Whipple, Squeeze This: A Guide to Creating Great Ads* (New York: Wiley, 1998), p. 72.

What would happen if you received the first set of instructions? You'd probably freeze up because you'd place unnecessary pressure on yourself. You'd second-guess the thoughts that came into your head and would automatically dismiss any that you felt weren't good. The idea you finally put on paper would most likely be a safe approach because you knew others—including the president of the university—would be evaluating it.

Now what would happen if you received the second set of instructions? You'd probably come up with some dumb ideas. But you'd also probably come up with some good ones. You might even come up with a great idea. Idea 23 might be the winner. But if you only came up with one idea, idea 23 would never occur to you. And who knows what would happen if you came up with 100 ideas or more!

Keep the second set of instructions in mind in the idea-generation stage. Give yourself total freedom to come up with bad ideas. Who knows? Those bad ideas may spark great ideas when someone else hears them. And if the idea is a real dud, you can always drop it later in the process.

> Using Criticism to Improve Your Ideas

A critical part of the creative process involves working in teams and checking your work by asking others to react to it. First, other people can see your idea with a clear and unbiased mind. Second, if your evaluators know advertising, chances are that they can judge your work both as consumers and as professionals. The key to a good critique is objectivity. This means you evaluate the work, not the person. Look for positive things, and then question things that may not seem clear or strong or that simply don't work for you.

Here are some additional pointers to help you make your criticism palatable to others:[12]

- *Make "I" statements.* Own your criticism by saying, "I'm confused by this sentence," not "You confused me."

- *Be clear and specific, commenting on the work, not the person.* Instead of "Why do you always make the same mistake?" try "This should be written as two separate sentences. Do you remember doing that before?"

- *Never say, "This is great, but . . ."* Eliminate the threatening "but" and get to the point: "I think the opening is fine. Here in the middle, I don't know if you're stressing the right benefits."

- *Control your emotions and speak in a normal tone of voice.*

- *Show some empathy and understanding.* "I wonder if the directions for this assignment seemed unclear."

- *Offer practical suggestions.* Without suggestions on how the work might be improved, criticism is generally useless. Surprisingly, students seem to have a greater knack for offering suggestions to their peers than for

[12] Courtesy of Dr. Serge Piccinin, director of the Teaching Centre at the University of Ottawa.

figuring out how to fix their own work. Try it; pair up with someone in your class and trade suggestions for improvement.

- *Be honest.* If you don't like something, explain why. But begin with a positive comment, end on a positive note, and sandwich the negative comment between the two. This helps the recipient be more accepting of what you have to say.

Here are some guidelines for nonverbal behaviors for receiving or offering criticism:

- *Make eye contact with the person.* Looking away diminishes the power of the communication.
- *Show your interest through a warm and expressive tone of voice.*
- *Use facial expressions that are consistent with your message.* Don't grin as you address deficiencies, and don't frown as you offer compliments.
- *Don't slouch or slump.* This is important because these postures suggest that either you're uncomfortable with what you have to say or you're not honoring the evaluator's effort.
- *Stand or sit an appropriate distance from the other person.* Either you both stand or you both sit.
- *Choose an appropriate time and place for this discussion.* As the recipient of the critique, you have both rights and obligations in this process. First, you have the right to ask for a later meeting if the time or place chosen is inconvenient or uncomfortable. And you have the right to terminate the critique if it is delivered in an offensive manner.

> Suggested Activities

1. Think of unconventional media to convince people to stop smoking, to drink responsibly, and to recycle. Now develop messages for each of these issues.

2. Create an ad that uses a headline and visual to communicate a selling point in an unexpected way. Next, create an ad that uses just a headline. Finally, create an ad that lets the visual stand on its own. Which approach works best? Why?

3. Develop 20 advertising ideas for a pawnshop. Here's some background information:

   - Pawnshops date back to ancient times.
   - Queen Isabella of Spain pawned her jewelry to finance Columbus on his voyage to America.
   - The three gold balls in front of a pawnshop are derived from symbols used by Italian merchants.

- Pawnshops are the forerunners of modern banks. The pawnbroker loans money on personal property that customers supply. The customer is issued a ticket, which is a contract stating the amount of the loan, the service charge, and the specific time the pawnbroker will hold the property. The process takes only a few minutes.

- All pawnbrokers are regulated by law, so the customers know they're not being "taken."

- Pawnshops offer values. Because pawnbrokers deal with people from all walks of life, they can offer for sale an array of merchandise—televisions, diamond rings, power tools, exercise equipment, and more—at lower prices than just about any other place.

- All classes of people borrow and buy from pawnbrokers.

4. Let your imagination run rampant, relax, and write a whimsical paper on any or all of the following fantasy situations:

   - If it rained all day, how would my life be different?

   - If I had unlimited income, how would my life be different?

   - If I lived on an island in the Pacific, how would my life be different?

   - If the sun never set, how would my life be different?

   - If 50 degrees were the temperature constantly and forever, how would my life be different?

5. Using the scenarios listed in the previous activity, develop ideas for new products that will make the most of the situations.

6. Create a game to see how creative you and your friends are. On one set of index cards, list various products and services (for example, cough medicine, facial tissues, soft drinks, canned soup, sports car, bath towels, and lamps). On another set of cards, describe various sounds on paper (for example, man snoring, buzz, creak, cricket chirp, scream, siren, and running water). Without looking, draw one card from each stack. Use the sound you have drawn as the basis for a radio commercial to sell the product or service you have drawn. Act it out.

7. Look at the two campaigns for food banks shown in Figures 6-5 and 6-6. Which campaign do you think is stronger? Why? Now come up with new ideas that will motivate people to donate to food banks.

8. Make an inventory of your "creative resources" and seek new worlds to conquer. First, make a list of your favorite films, entertainers, music, fiction and nonfiction books, magazines, live plays and musicals, live concert performances, TV programs, and leisure activities. Share these with classmates and your professor. Now make a concerted effort to add something different to that list. If you watch TV sitcoms, spend an hour or more watching a nature program, a ballet performance, or a historical documentary. If you like country music, try a symphony. What did you learn about yourself as a result of this exercise?

Figure 6-5
You probably heard of reading messages in tea leaves. Now you can read social messages in alphabet soup. Public donations to the Food Bank of Central New York increased 70 percent as a result of this campaign.

Courtesy of (MRA) Mark Russell & Associates, Inc.

Figure 6-5 (continued)

Courtesy of (MRA) Mark Russell & Associates, Inc.

Figure 6-6
All too often people think bad things happen elsewhere. These ads helped wake up residents of Greenville, South Carolina, to the reality that hunger is right in their backyards.

Courtesy of Project Host.

Figure 6-6 (continued)

Courtesy of Project Host.

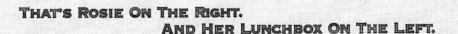

THAT'S ROSIE ON THE RIGHT.
AND HER LUNCHBOX ON THE LEFT.

This is not Calcutta. Or Rwanda. Or Haiti. This is your backyard. This is Greenville. And every night, hundreds, if not thousands of your neighbors go to sleep hungry. But many who might otherwise be hungry aren't, because of a place called Project Host. Project Host is a soup kitchen in downtown Greenville that served over 63,000 meals to the needy last year. Every weekday, Project Host offers homemade soup, a sandwich, fruit, and a beverage to those in our community who, for one reason or another, can't quite make it on their own right now. We don't ask why. We don't criticize. We don't judge. We simply feed. And if you'd like to help, we, and the host of hungry people we provide for would be eternally grateful.

PROJECT HOST
Soup · Kitchen

864–235–3403

Please send donations to:
PROJECT HOST
P.O. Box 345
Greenville, SC 29602

The Cows Are Singing, "California Here I Come!"

Warm weather. Gorgeous scenery. A relaxed attitude. The very things that make California such a great place to live helped inspire the big idea behind the award-winning campaign from Deutsch LA for the California Milk Advisory Board (CMAB). The premise is simple: Great milk comes from Happy Cows, and Happy Cows come from California.

Introduced in 2000, the Happy Cows campaign has received numerous accolades from the CMAB for raising awareness for California dairy products and the Real California Milk and Real California Cheese seals. Over the years, consumers have gotten to love the quirky personalities of the Happy Cows. There's Diane, who likes ocean breezes and singing. But Mondays just aren't her thing. Janice is into sunshine and fresh air, but finds alarm clocks to be a bit too alarming. Sadie prefers naps and rainbows. Just don't ask her to do any math.

As you can imagine, cows from around the globe were vying for the opportunity to join Diane, Sadie, and Janice in sunny California. It was a daunting task to select which of the many California-wannabes was most deserving of the illustrious Happy Cow title so Deutsch LA and CMAB invited consumers to view the bovine auditions and cast their votes online.

"It just seemed like the next logical step in a totally illogical world. If the cows are happier in California, then it just seemed to make sense that cows from everywhere else would be clamoring to come here," said Eric Hirshberg, President, Chief Creative Officer for Deutsch LA. "The reality show audition tape format is something everyone can relate to. From American Idol to online dating services, people are used to seeing other people pitch themselves like this. Why would our fictitious bovine friends be any different?"

The series of auditions ran between October 2008 and December 2009. The integrated TV and web campaign showcased 10 new TV spots that featured wannabe Happy Cows from all over the world. There's the super-spunky teenager named Alicia, out to prove to her friends and her taunting brother that she can make it as a California babe. Cajun Jenn hails from the heart of the Bayou and is eager to break out from under her stage mom's overpowering presence.

Across the pond, there's Shelby, the English bovine who boasts a royal bloodline. This bon vivant (bovine vivant?) is well versed in proper teatime

Courtesy of California Milk Advisory Board and Deutsch, Inc.

etiquette and was voted most likely to rule a very small country. Soo, who hails from South Korea, has dreamed of living in America and has been studying the glorious food, palm trees, and sunshine of California. She did her audition in her native tongue—fortunately CMAB had a translator for those of us who aren't fluent in Korean!

Kirsten did her audition tape in the midst of a Canadian blizzard, while the Swiss-born Anna yodeled on the edge of a mountain to win the hearts—and votes—of her fans. Cheerleader Lisa performed a little skit to win some votes (she's bound to learn how to spell California one of these days!)

A few bovine contestants already had experience in the spotlight. April, who's from "where the buffalo roam," has won a bunch of singing competitions at local and state fairs. Singing is also Kathy's passion. In fact, Kathy's mom said she was born singing! And then there's the diva Destynee who works as an actor and model on the east coast. Perhaps you caught her in the off-Broadway hit "Mammalia Mia" or saw her on the widely acclaimed after-school special "Udder Catastrophe."

Consumers could interact with the campaign and vote online for their favorite contestant at RealCaliforniaMilk.com from October 13, 2008 to December 31, 2009. Like the TV commercials, the website had attitude. As the site loaded, a message appeared on the barn door: "Because of our laid-back California lifestyle, this site may take a few moments to load." Once loaded, the barn door opened, revealing Happy Cows watching a TV set. As you navigated through the page, you could overhear the Happy Cows commenting about the contestants: "Do you think she dyes her spots?" "Oh, that's original. Everyone likes an accent," and "The bulls are going to love her!"

Each Happy Cow contestant had her own photo and audition tape. Consumers could also see bloopers and outtakes to help make up their minds. Once they voted, the rankings were revealed. And if you didn't like the ranking of your favorite bovine, you could always vote again or encourage your Facebook friends to vote . . . often.

"Audition series is a perfect example of taking consumer interaction and taking it to the next level" said Michael Freeman, Vice President, Advertising, for California Milk Advisory Board. "Imagine motivating consumers enough to elicit over one million votes for fictitious cows. We were very impressed with the results." Freeman added, "The voting strategically allowed us to drive consumers to our website where we could then tell a deeper story about the lives and practices of our Real California Dairy families."

The aspiring Happy Cow with the most votes was announced in January 2010. And the winner? Kirsten, who captured more than 50 percent of the votes. Everyone's happy to get her out of the frigid Canadian weather.

SHELBY

FROM:
England

HOBBIES:
Playing Marco Polo in the fog, creating new blends of afternoon tea.

BIO: I'm one of the few cows in the neighbourhood to have had a proper education. In boarding school I was voted most likely to rule a very small country. I come from a prestigious bloodline. My great-great-great-great-great grandmother was somewhat romantically involved with livestock from the royal pasture, so I'm told. Each member of my family has at least one distinguishing pattern or spot. Mum's is a teapot. Father's, a waffle iron. I have many. I won't list them off since you can see them clearly here.

Great milk comes from Happy Cows.

Vote at RealCaliforniaMilk.com

Courtesy of California Milk Advisory Board and Deutsch, Inc.

Courtesy of California Milk Advisory Board and Deutsch, Inc.

안녕하세요!
Pick SOO
she's got Seoul
RealCaliforniaMilk.com

SOO

FROM: South Korea

HOBBIES: 축구, 노래방, 공부, 서핑 배우기

Translated by Real California Milk -- Soccer, Karaoke, Studying, Want to learn surfing.

BIO: 저는 아주 어릴적부터 아름다운 미국서의 생활을 꿈꿔왔습니다. 저뿐만이 아니라 저희 가족들은 여러 세대에 걸쳐 이런 꿈을 가져왔습니다. 너무나도 아름답고 훌륭한 집을 보유하고 있는 미국이라는 나라에 대해 열의를 가지고 공부해왔으며, 캘리포니아의 해변에서 희망이라는 파도를 타는 것에 대한 상상을 해왔습니다. 아자~~아자~~~화이팅!!!

Translated by Real California Milk -- Since my earliest childhood memories, I remember dreaming of a wonderful life lived in America. For many generations, my ancestors have also dreamed of this spectacular country. I've been studying very hard the glorious food, palm trees and sunshine that make up your wonderful state. And my deepest fantasies involve me surfing the waves of opportunity along the sandy beaches of hope in California.

Great milk comes from Happy Cows.

REAL CALIFORNIA CHEESE

REAL CALIFORNIA MILK

Vote at RealCaliforniaMilk.com

Courtesy of California Milk Advisory Board and Deutsch, Inc.

7

WORDS ON PAPER
CONNECTING TO CONSUMERS' HEARTS AND MINDS

Stephen King admits he doesn't so much create his stories as unearth them. Likewise, mystery writer James Lee Burke never sees more than two or perhaps three scenes ahead in a story. For him, the creative process is more one of discovery than one of creation. Ernie Schenck, columnist for *Communication Arts,* thinks that there's a lesson in this for advertising copywriters:

> *I've got a theory on why we don't see as many long copy print ads anymore. And it's got nothing to do with shrinking attention spans or MTV or video games. I think it's because we've lost touch with our inner storyteller. We think the concept is the story. Nail the big idea. Funky headline. Hip layout. Few lines of mandatories at the bottom and thank you, thank you very much.*[1]

Schenck suggests that advertising copywriters spend less effort manufacturing a brand and more effort helping it simply reveal itself:

> *Yes, there are points we have to make. Information we need to impart. But how we get there, how we weave the story, this is something you can't plot out. You just start writing, conscious of the stuff that needs to find its way into the copy, but letting it form on the page almost on its own. Instead of consciously writing, you are unconsciously writing. The story tells itself.*[2]

[1] Ernie Schenck, "Mummies, Lost Arks and Long Copy Ads," *Communication Arts,* March/April 2003, pp. 134–136.
[2] Ibid.

Courtesy of Loeffler Ketchum Mountjoy.

Figure 7-1
Copy reads: "Why sugarcoat it? There is an undertone—the slightest whiff—of danger about the place. Of course, that's what gives the Outer Banks its seductive, otherworldly appeal. These islands were, after all, the favorite hideaways of some of history's most feared pirates: Blackbeard and Stede Bonnet. Today, the same qualities that drew those fugitives from justice attract a different breed of runaways: vacationers. Qualities like its remoteness. Its unapologetic plainness and simplicity. Its stark contrast to the bland tranquility of the cities. It's an edge of the world type of place. A place where the sand dunes grow taller than four-story buildings. Where dignified old lighthouses shine beacons atop the restless waters. And over 2,000 shipwrecks lie below them. The Outer Banks. Spare. Romantic. Unhip. Stunning. Part beauty. Part beast. We'll be expecting you."

Look at an advertising campaign for North Carolina tourism as an example of great writing (see Figure 7-1). Notice how the writer was able to weave information about North Carolina's history and topography into the ads. But you didn't sense that you were reading a fact sheet, did you? Instead, you were reading a story about a destination that now beckons you. The copy in each ad is more than 125 words long, but you probably didn't even notice the length because it was so engaging.

Your goal is to write in such an engaging way that the readers will give you their undivided attention. The message you write may be a line or two, or it may be hundreds of words long. In some cases, the right visual can do most of the talking. The next chapter addresses the design process, but for now what's important to remember is that *how* an ad looks and *what* an ad says can contribute equally to the effectiveness of the message.

Courtesy of Loeffler Ketchum Mountjoy.

Figure 7-1 (continued)

Copy reads: "In the beginning, they were both part of the prehistoric continent called Pangaea. Today, a living link still remains: the North Carolina Zoo in Asheboro, America's first natural habitat zoo. Here, during the course of a day, you and your children can watch antelopes and birds gather as they do on the African veldt. Observe endangered white rhinos feeding in a natural grassland habitat. Laugh at the antics of a family of lowland gorillas. And the age-old bond between the two lands continues to flourish in other ways. For example, a rare female wattled crane born in captivity here was recently flown back to her native South Africa to breed and help replenish their dwindling population. Strolling the grounds, you get a sense of the fragile interrelatedness of things. But that's as it should be. You see, long ago, we learned a valuable lesson: It's not just animals who benefit from staying connected with the past. Human beings do, too."

> Headlines Help Form Good First Impressions

Be honest. You don't usually pick up a magazine or newspaper and say, "I can't wait to see the ads." You probably just skim the ads unless something stands out from the clutter and captures your attention. It's the job of the copywriter and art director to create headlines that turn skimmers into readers.

Functions of Headlines

- *Capture the attention of your target audience.* Imagine that you're reading a food magazine filled with delicious recipes. You have a ravenous appetite when suddenly you read, "Start your next meal with Clorox bleach." The advertisement shows a fish with an eerie stare. It's disgusting.

You don't want to look, but you can't help yourself. You read on and learn that Clorox bleach can sanitize your kitchen and prevent salmonella. You've lost your appetite, and you want to start cleaning. The ad has done its job.

- *Select your audience.* You need to make certain the right people are reading your ads. Leo Burnett, founder of one of the most famous ad agencies in the world, had this to say:

  > *Best attention comes from the entirely natural interests of the reader, built around the results of the product advertised. Being different from others is not an asset if the others are right. An ad may get attention and fail completely in getting anything else. An able show window designer once said, "The thing to avoid is drawing a crowd. The hard thing is to catch the eye of every possible customer and keep the others walking past." It is better to attract the serious attention of possible buyers than, through an exaggerated and clever headline, to attract other possible readers who won't be interested in the message anyway.*[3]

- *Lure readers into the body copy.* A good headline will make you think, "This is interesting. I want to know more." For example, who could resist wanting to know "What not to do in bed"? (Interested? Read on to find the answer later in this chapter.)

- *Communicate a benefit.* Tell readers what your product will do for them. Will it make them look better? Help them get ahead in their jobs? Make their children smarter? Protect their home? Your job as a writer is to take the benefit and bring it to life. Here's how Chevrolet told customers that its S-10 model could go fast:

WITH 190 HORSEPOWER, THERE'S A REASON WE PUT SCOTCHGARD™ ON THE SEATS.

- *Reinforce the brand name.* Have you ever loved an ad but been unable to remember the name of the product? It's fine to entertain readers, but don't sacrifice getting the product name across for the sake of creativity.

  The award-winning campaign for Absolut vodka is a wonderful example of how a brand name can be used creatively. Here are two examples:

ABSOLUT L.A.
(Visual: Swimming pool in the shape of an Absolut bottle)

ABSOLUT NANTUCKET
(Visual: Boardwalk in the shape of an Absolut bottle)

- *Make an emotional connection to the customer.* Most people are suspicious of advertising claims. Therefore, you must make your message

---

[3] Leo Burnett, from a memorandum to his creative staff, 13 November 1947. Reprinted in *Communications of an Advertising Man: Selections from Speeches, Articles, and Miscellaneous Writings of Leo Burnett* (Chicago: Leo Burnett Company, 1961). For private distribution only. Used with permission.

believable. Avis won a spot in people's hearts with the line "We're #2. We try harder." This is more convincing than boasting, "We're one of the nation's leading car rental companies."

- *Enhance a visual.* If a picture is worth a thousand words, a picture and a headline are worth thousands more. Together, a headline and a visual create synergy, whereby the whole is greater than the sum of its parts.

  For example, how do you show that a portable vacuum cleaner is powerful? One solution is to run the warning "Be careful where you point it." This is a boring statement until you see the picture of a man's toupee flying toward the nozzle of the vacuum. Now that's picking up a rug!

Types of Headlines

Direct Benefit.   Offer readers a reason to use the product. For example, Shore's Fishing Lures boasts:

IT'S LIKE TOSSING A TWINKIE
INTO A WEIGHT WATCHER'S MEETING.

Reverse Benefit.   Imply that consumers will be worse off without the advertised product or service. Alternatively, you can imply, "You'll be sorry if you go with the competition." If you use a reverse benefit, make sure you don't give your competition free advertising. Also, be careful that you don't make any remarks about your competition that aren't true.

The ads for Icelandair's BWI flights, shown in the "Briefcase" in Chapter 4, are great examples of a reverse benefit. Here are some other examples:

No wonder they call it high fashion.
To dream up some of those prices you'd have to be high.
(Ad for Daffy's clothing discounter)

I NEVER READ THE ECONOMIST.
—MANAGEMENT TRAINEE. AGED 42.
(Ad for *The Economist* magazine)

Factual.   People love to read interesting pieces of trivia. The following headline gives an interesting fact:

It takes 12 miles of cotton
to make a Lands' End® pinpoint oxford.
And that's just the beginning

The Lands' End copy goes on to explain that the shirt is tailored with 69 sewing steps and the buttonholes are edged with 120 lock stitches. How much will readers remember? If they recall only that Lands' End cares about the quality of its clothing, they got the message.

Selective.   To attract a specific audience, address it in the headline. Sometimes, the audience is directly identified. For example, a headline for Allstate

Insurance asks, "Do you own a small business?" Other times, the tone and the choice of words and visual will identify your audience:

Michelin. Because so much is riding on your tires.

(Ad shows a baby sitting next to a tire)

Curiosity.   Tempt your readers with just enough information to make them want to read more. "Ever wonder why most people make love in the dark?" entices readers to continue, especially when the only visual is a black rectangle where the picture should be. The ad, for a workout program, talks about getting in shape.

Although curiosity headlines can pull readers into the copy, they should be designed to arouse interest, not to confuse. An impatient reader who turns the page after reading an incomplete thought will miss your message.

News.   Just as you want to know what's new with friends and family, you want to know what's new to eat, to wear, and to see. Many advertising experts believe that the word "new" is one of the most powerful in a copywriter's vocabulary. Other powerful words include "introducing," "now," "finally," "at last," "today," "presenting," and "first." Here's an example:

LIFE IN THE SOUTH
JUST GOT A LITTLE SWEETER.

(Ad for Kellogg's Raisin Bran in *Southern Living* magazine)

Command.   Order readers to do something. For years, Nike told sports fans, "Just do it." In the process, this simple phrase convinced people to just buy it (Nike, that is). Other persuasive command headlines include the following:

Hire us to paint your house and you won't need this newspaper.

(Ad with paint blotches on it for Merriam Park Painting)

Rekindle your love affair with New York.

(Ad for New York City)

Imagine filling out a job application and running out of room where it says "experience."

(Ad for U.S. Army that ran in college newspapers)

Question.   A question piques curiosity and involves readers in the ad. A question headline should make readers want to stop, think, and read your ad for the answer, so be careful not to make the answer too obvious. Here are questions that grab attention and make people want to read on:

IF YOU WERE TWO YEARS OLD, COULD YOU TELL THE DIFFERENCE?

(Visual: Plastic jug of milk and gallon of bleach)

How do you deal with an enemy
that has no government, no
money trail and no qualms about
killing women and children?

This first line of body copy that followed the preceding headline likely surprised many readers. It read: "The enemy is Mother Nature." The ad asked readers to urge Congress to support legislation that uses insurance premiums—not tax dollars—to protect Americans from future natural catastrophes like hurricanes and earthquakes. The ad ran on the 1-year anniversary of Hurricane Katrina, one of the deadliest hurricanes in U.S. history.

Repetition.   Some lines are worth repeating to hammer home the message.
An ad for McGraw-Hill magazines uses repetition to communicate the power of advertising:

I DON'T KNOW WHO YOU ARE.
I DON'T KNOW YOUR COMPANY.
I DON'T KNOW WHAT YOUR COMPANY STANDS FOR.
I DON'T KNOW YOUR COMPANY'S CUSTOMERS.
I DON'T KNOW YOUR COMPANY'S RECORD.
I DON'T KNOW YOUR COMPANY'S REPUTATION.
NOW—WHAT WAS IT YOU WANTED TO SELL ME?

Word Play.   Writers love to play with words, twisting them in a way that gives special meaning. Done right, word play can attract readers' attention and make them pause a few moments to process the message. For instance, McDonald's took a common phrase, "Want fries with that?" and turned it into a clever headline for its Monopoly game promotion: "Want cash with that?"

The word play in Gold's Gym ads (see Figure 7-2) is unexpected and relevant, and it communicates a selling idea. This regional campaign was named "Best Gold's Gym Advertising Worldwide" by the company.

Be careful not to become so caught up in the play that you forget that you're selling a product. Make sure the word play helps further your message and isn't clever for the sake of entertainment. Beware, also, of overdosing on puns. Your readers won't appreciate it, nor will creative directors when you're showing your portfolio.

Metaphors, Similes, and Analogies.   One way to describe your product is to make a connection to another commonly known image. A metaphor takes the characteristics of one thing and associates it with something different.

An ad for Books-A-Million tells book lovers

Think of us as an amusement park for readers.

©2001 Gold's Gym

Small Ass For Sale

For more info, call or come by any of our Columbia area locations.

508 Evelyn Dr	275-2 Harbison Blvd	9940 Two Notch Rd #108	619 N Lake Dr
803-798-1000	803-749-9700	803-419-0222	803-359-6100

GOLD'S GYM.

Courtesy of Gold's Gym.

Figure 7-2
The idea for this campaign came straight from the mouths of consumers who want to get back in shape and lose their big rear ends and potbellies.

A simile states that one thing is "like" something else. For example, to dramatize the odor problem of litter boxes, an ad for Kitty Litter Brand shows a skunk in a litter box. The headline reads

SOMETIMES YOUR CAT CAN SEEM
LIKE A WHOLE DIFFERENT ANIMAL.

An analogy compares two things on the basis of a similar feature. For example, an ad for Lubriderm lotion shows an alligator to communicate rough,

Figure 7-2 (continued)

Courtesy of Gold's Gym.

scaly skin. The headline implies the lotion will smooth and soften dry, flaky skin. It reads

SEE YOU LATER, ALLIGATOR.

Parallel Construction. Repeat the structure of a phrase or sentence to emphasize a point. Outward Bound uses the technique to communicate their experience (See Figure 7-3).

Courtesy of Loeffler Ketchum Mountjoy.

Figure 7-3
These knots capture the Outward Bound experience: butterfly knot, fisherman's knot, your stomach.

Rhyme.   Use the repetition of sound to make a point. Avoid the temptation to make a rhyme unless it helps stress a selling point, as in this example:

SAIL BY MAIL.

(Ad for Royal Caribbean inviting the reader to write for a brochure)

> Body Copy Tells the Rest of the Story

Whereas the headline piques the readers' attention, the body copy completes the story. Remember the headline "What not to do in bed"? As promised, here's the answer:

> You can read.
>
> You can rest.
>
> You can sleep.
>
> You can make phone calls.
>
> You can eat breakfast.
>
> You can watch television.

You can listen to music.

You can exercise.

You can snore.

You can even eat crackers—provided you're alone.

And, yes, you can snuggle.

But don't ever light up a cigarette when you're in bed.

Because if you doze off just once, all your dreams can go up in smoke.

Although R. J. Reynolds could have run a public service ad with the simple headline "Don't smoke in bed," the combination of an intriguing headline and interesting copy involves readers and makes it more likely that they'll remember the message.

Approaches to Writing Body Copy

The Standard Approach.   Most ads start with a lead-in paragraph that bridges the headline and the rest of the copy. Like the headline, this paragraph should pique readers' curiosity and make them want to continue reading. The interior paragraphs stress benefits as they elaborate on the selling premise. The closing paragraph ties the ad together and often invites the reader to consider the product.

An ad for Columbia Sportswear (see Figure 7-4) follows a standard approach, although there's nothing standard about the ad—or the company or its chairperson, for that matter. The headline grabs your attention: "She snaps necks and hacks off arms." You read on and learn in the first paragraph that "My Mother, Columbia Sportswear's chairman, will stop at nothing to get what she wants—superior outerwear." In the next few sentences, you learn about the demands of Mother, the "vociferous chairman"; in the process, you learn about the construction of a Columbia Sportswear parka. The copy closes with "All in all, it's easy to see why not just any parka can survive Mother's rather pointed demands."

Copy as Story.   Narrative copy reads like a piece of fiction because it sets a scene and presents characters who become involved in some action.

Dialog Copy.   You know the routine "I said. She said." Although you usually find this format in radio and television, it works in print, too. However, make certain that your dialog sounds realistic by reading your copy out loud. The ad for eggs shown in Figure 7-5 is a fun example, even if the conversation is a bit one sided.

Bulleted Copy or Listings.   An ad for the Massachusetts Society for the Prevention of Cruelty to Animals was headlined "Get the best of everything. Adopt a mutt." The picture shows an adorable mutt looking straight into the reader's eyes, and bulleted copy addresses the advantages of adopting a mutt: "The smarts of a Lassie. The spots of a Dalmatian. The bark of a Shepherd. The friendliness of a Beagle. The heart of a St. Bernard. The paws of a Great Dane."

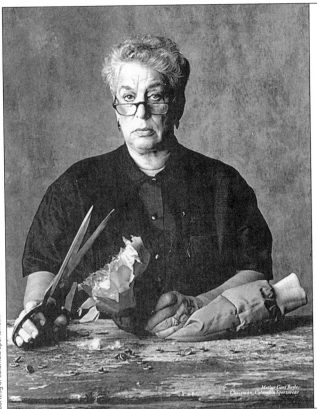

Courtesy of Columbia Sportswear.

"SHE SNAPS NECKS AND HACKS OFF ARMS."

—By Tim Boyle, President, Columbia Sportswear

My Mother, Columbia Sportswear's chairman, will stop at nothing to get what she wants—superior outerwear.

In fact, the mountains around Portland, Oregon, frequently echo her sharply barked commands. "When I say a snap closed neck and storm front, that's what I expect to see!" Or, as she hacks away at an inappropriately attached sleeve, "All seams are to be double sewn!"

What, you may ask, is the end result of having such a, uh, vociferous chairman? The Columbia Interchange System," for one. It lets you brave multiple weather conditions with one jacket by matching a zip-in, zip-out liner to a weatherproof shell. They may be worn separately, or together. Take our Ponderosa Parka™ pictured here. The outer shell is 100% Technicloth II™—a soft blend of cotton and nylon woven into a durable rib fabric, oiled to keep water out. To hold warmth in, the bomber-style Zap Fleece™ liner is quilted with Thermoloft™ insulation.

All in all, it's easy to see why not just any parka can survive Mother's rather pointed demands.

Columbia Sportswear Company

6600 N. Baltimore, Portland, Oregon 97203. For the dealer nearest you in the U.S. and Canada, call 1-800-MA-BOYLE.

Mother Gert Boyle, Chairman, Columbia Sportswear

Figure 7-4
Truly, there is nothing standard about this ad. The headline might make you curious, but nothing about it will confuse you, mainly because the headline bears a direct relationship to the product. Remember the difference; it's an important one.

Poetic Copy. Norwegian Cruise Lines used poetic images to sell its fantasy adventures:

It's different out here.
I will put first things last.
I will study a sunset.
I will be naked more.
I will discover a color.
I will memorize clouds.
I will be amphibious.
I will eat a mango.
I will get a really good tan.

> Mandatories: Writing the Small Print

Mandatories are statements required to appear in your ads and are usually found in the small print along the bottom or side of an ad. Sometimes law requires these statements. For example, bank ads state "Equal Opportunity

Figure 7-5
This innovative ad uses personification to convince readers that it's OK to eat eggs again.

At first you said you loved me, you told me I was the only one. You always had me around. But then you turned, because rumors were flying around that I wasn't good for you anymore.

And now you want me back. You've changed your mind and realized I was the one after all.

And you think just because you said that I'll come crawling back to you? Well, I've got news for you mister, You're going to have to do better than that."

"I'll wait for your skillet to get hot."

"Well..., ok."

Eggs

They're more forgiving than you think.

Courtesy of Julie Eyerman.

Lender." Other times the statements are something the client insists on including, such as store hours, a slogan, or an affiliation with an organization. It's your job as a writer to ensure that your copy contains these small but important words.

> Answers to Common Questions about Writing Copy

Is It OK to Break the Rules?

Some people believe advertising has destroyed the dignity of our language. They are appalled when they read sentences such as, "Winston tastes good like a cigarette should." Cringe when they read incomplete sentences (like this one). And wince when a sentence starts with a conjunction. Others argue that advertising must sound like people talking, so it's OK to break the rules. However, most people agree that, before you break the rules, you'd better know them. See the box on the bottom of this page for some copy mistakes.

Here are some headlines that break the rules intentionally:

I QUIT SKOOL WHEN I WERE SIXTEEN.

(A convincing message to stay in school)

I HAS A DREAM.

(Ad sponsored by Atlanta's Black Professionals asking people to speak out against Ebonics)

What's the Best Headline Length?

Unless you're writing to a specific layout with a predetermined character count, there is no "best" length. One of the most famous headlines for a car was one simple word, "Lemon." This unexpected headline for Volkswagen motivated people to read the copy, which explained the auto manufacturer's rigorous quality standards. In contrast, another famous headline for a car contained 18 words: "At 60 miles an hour, the loudest noise in the new Rolls Royce comes from the electric clock."

Sometimes you'll find you don't need a headline—the visual can stand alone. A Volkswagen ad spoke volumes about the car's gas mileage without a single word of copy. A cartoon illustration of a man holding a gas nozzle to his head resonated with consumers fed up with the high prices at the pump.

COPY MISTAKES

You must proofread your copy. While Spell-check is a big help, it can't find every type of error. Here are some mistakes from the classifieds:

"For sale: an antique desk suitable for lady with thick legs and large drawers."

"Four-poster bed, 101 years old. Perfect for antique lover."

"Now is your chance to have your ears pierced and get an extra pair to take home, too."

"Wanted: 50 girls for stripping machine operators in factory."

"Tired of cleaning yourself? Let me do it."

"Used cars: Why go elsewhere to be cheated? Come here first!"

Church bulletins have their share of gaffes. Here are a few of our favorites:

"Thursday, at 5 P.M., there will be a meeting of the Little Mothers Club. All those wishing to become little mothers, please meet the pastor in his study."

"The ladies of the church have cast off clothing of every kind and they may be seen in the basement on Friday afternoon."

"This being Easter Sunday, we will ask Mrs. Johnson to come forward and lay an egg on the alter."

But don't think it's just small-town classifieds and church bulletins that make mistakes. Consider the following:

A Mercedes-Benz accessories ad begins, "Her trademark has always been making art out of the everyday. First, she was taken with fruits and vegetables. Next, she was inspired by popcorn, footballs and sharks. Then one day, Nicole Miller was struck by a Mercedes-Benz."

Bruce Hardwood Floors insulted a few grandmothers with the line "Solid oak, just like your grandmothers."

Which Is Better, Long or Short Copy?

Certain product categories, such as perfume and fashion, are sold primarily on the basis of image, so brief copy, along with a striking visual, is probably the best answer. Other products, such as cars and computers, require quite a bit of thought before the buyer takes the plunge; therefore, they warrant longer copy with specific details about the various features.

However, even these rules are successfully broken occasionally. Volkswagen ads often contain only a few lines of copy. Lands' End fills the page with details about its clothing.

The best advice is to write as much as you need to accomplish your advertising objectives. You may find you don't need any copy. The right visual and logo may be all you need. The North Carolina tourism ads shown in Figure 7-1 on pages 139 and 140 use long copy to capture the interest of people who want to go on an adventure, but there's almost no copy in the North Carolina tourism ads that target those who need a vacation to escape from the pressures of work (see Figure 7-6).

Courtesy of Loeffler Ketchum Mountjoy.

Figure 7-6

The lack of headline or body copy in these ads is perfect for vacationers who just want to "veg out." Notice how different they are from the ads shown in Figure 7-1, which are targeting different groups of visitors.

Does a Brand Need a Slogan?

A good slogan captures the essence of a brand in a few words. Here are a few that work:

"It's not delivery. It's DiGiorno."
(For DiGiorno frozen pizza)

"Every Kiss Begins with Kay"
(For Kay Jewelers)

"Have You Met Life Today?"
(For MetLife Insurance)

"Hey. You Never Know."
(For New York State Lottery)

"We Answer to a Higher Authority."
(For Hebrew National Hotdogs)

"Don't Mess with Texas."
(Started as a slogan for the antilitter campaign; became a rallying call for the state)

Unfortunately, many slogans say little and are indistinguishable from those used by other brands. For years Macy's slogan said, "We're a part of your life." Meanwhile, Sears boasted, "There's more for your life at Sears." And General Electric claimed, "We bring good things to life." Each of these slogans could have worked for a hospital, a real estate agent, a bank, a health food store, a veterinarian, or any number of products and services.

Like the previous examples, too many slogans do little more than add clutter to an ad. Still, many clients will insist on having a slogan, almost as if they're not getting their money's worth from their ad agency if they don't have one. As a writer, you can do two things: talk the client out of one, or write one that means something to their customers.

Steve Cone[4] offers four guidelines that will increase the chances of a slogan standing the test of time:

1. You are different. Say so.
2. Have real attitude; bypass wishy-washy phrases.
3. Be everywhere. For a line to make a lasting impression, it must appear at all customer touch points.
4. Recognize it's an art. The best lines come from individual flashes of inspiration.

Allen Adamson, Landor & Associates' managing director, says it's vital to weave the message through all the communications and the very brand DNA itself. "It has to be the right promise, with the brand living up to it, expressed in a sticky, unexpected way. And then you have to spend money and stay with

[4] Steve Cone, "Help Taglines Regain Lost Glory," *Advertising Age*, 14 April 2008, p. 42.

it for the long haul." Adamson points to GE's "Imagination at Work" as a line that works because it's the mission of the company.[5]

How Should Copy Be Formatted?

Figure 7-7 shows a suggested copy format for print ads. "Slug" the ad in the upper-left corner with the name of the company, size, and medium (full page, magazine) and a working title in quotes. Identify the visual idea, headline, copy, logo, and baseline, plus other elements when used. Double-space so that it's easy to read, easy to revise, and easy to sell. Figure 7-8 shows how the finished ad looks.

> Guidelines for Writing Effective Copy

The following guidelines will help improve your copy, whether you're writing for print, broadcast, direct mail, or news media. Keep these rules in mind as you read future chapters.

1. *Love your product.* Have you ever dreaded taking a required course and then loved it because the professor was so interesting? The professor's love of the subject made you want to go to class and learn more about the topic. It's your job to have a similar passion about your product so that your target audience will want to learn about your brand and then go out and buy it.

   Before you begin writing copy, it's important to put advertising in perspective. You're not writing a letter to your mom who will still love you even if you run on a bit. You're not writing an essay for a professor who is paid to read your work or, conversely, a textbook that students are required to read. You're not even writing a story for readers who have bought a newspaper or magazine to catch up on the news. You're writing for people who view advertising as an intrusion. Therefore, you must be interesting. Perhaps David Ogilvy said it best when he wrote that there are no dull products, just dull writers.

2. *Don't try to do everything in one ad.* You should develop one theme and follow it through. To illustrate the point, creative director Stavros Cosmopulos slammed a piece of cardboard against 100 sharp nails. The cardboard remained intact because the nails formed a solid mass, preventing them from penetrating the cardboard. He then slammed a piece of cardboard against a single nail and bam! It broke through, proving that one single point is more powerful than many.

3. *Write to one individual.* Have you ever noticed how annoyed some people become when you read over their shoulder? That's because reading is an intimate activity, one that exists between the writer and the reader.

[5] T. L. Stanley, "Taglines Lose Their Starring Role in Ads," www.Brandweek.com, 26 November 2007.

COLONIAL SUPPLMENTAL INSURANCE

Two-page spread

"Adorable kids."

VISUAL: Close-up of two adorable kids in the back seat of a car

HEADLINE: On Tuesday, she'll begin ballet and he'll begin chemotherapy.

COPY:

How will you pay for what your health insurance won't? How will you pay the deductibles? The travel expenses to see specialists? The everyday life things? Especially if you're forced to miss work and miss paychecks. Colonial Supplemental Insurance offers affordable cancer, critical illness, disability, accident, and life coverage that can help ease the burden of unforeseen expenses. And, most importantly, provide you with peace of mind. Find out more at www.coloniallife.com.

LOGO: COLONIAL SUPPLEMENTAL INSURANCE

BASELINE: for what happens next

MANDATORIES: (none)

Courtesy of Colonial Supplemental Insurance.

Figure 7-7
In this sample copy draft, note the use of a working title, double-spacing, and adequate margins on all sides. To see how this translates into an ad, see Figure 7-8.

Courtesy of Colonial Supplemental Insurance.

Figure 7-8
This moving ad makes it clear why you need supplemental insurance. Sales of Colonial Supplemental Insurance increased 40 percent in advertised markets. To read the text of the ad, see Figure 7-7.

When people read your copy, they should feel as if you're talking directly to them, not to a vague demographic profile. Use the word "you" liberally and stick to singular nouns and verbs when possible.

4. *Translate business-speak into human-speak.* Many clients know their products so well that they begin to talk in jargon, which will be lost on the average reader. Your job is to listen, ask questions, and translate the jargon into tangible benefits that your readers will understand. Edward T. Thompson of *Reader's Digest* poked fun at a scientist who wrote, "The biota exhibited a one hundred percent mortality response," instead of simply saying, "All the fish died."

    Political consultant Frank Luntz points to the power of a single word. For years politicians and lawyers tried to eliminate the estate tax but the public wouldn't support it. But when it was repositioned as a "death tax," it achieved the support of 75 percent of the American people. The difference? "Estate tax" sounds like something just for wealthy people. "Death tax" sounds like it's for everyone.

5. *Avoid catchall phrases.* Avoid saying things like "quality craftsmanship," "caring service," or "inspired design." Check out the ads in Figure 7-9. Notice how Taylor communicates that its guitars are expertly crafted without ever saying "expertly crafted"?

Figure 7-9
Most guitar ads feature musicians in contorted positions or are filled with technical jargon. Taylor Guitar ads follow a different strategy. They state, "Taylor Guitars—handcrafted from the finest materials to give the sweetest sound." The copywriter could have run the strategy statement as a headline. But, like all talented artists, he brought it to a new level.

Copy reads: "To make a good guitar, you've got to devote a lot of time and attention to it. But then, we haven't been doing much of anything else for the last few years. Write us at 1940 Gillespie Way, El Cajon, CA 92020 to find a dealer near you."

Courtesy of Taylor Guitars and Vitro Agency.

Figure 7-9 (continued)

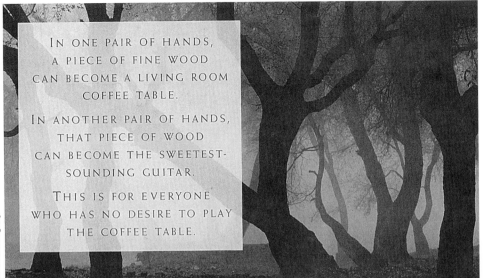

Courtesy of Taylor Guitars and Vitro Agency.

Copy reads: "Some trees become pencils. Some trees become paper that becomes guitar magazines. Some trees become shoe trees. Some trees become Taylor guitars. Some trees have all the luck. Write us: 1940 Gillespie Way, El Cajon, CA 92020."

Courtesy of Taylor Guitars and Vitro Agency.

Copy reads: "There are trees. And then, there are trees. There are guitars. And then, there are Taylor guitars. It's that simple. And that difficult. Write us at 1940 Gillespie Way, El Cajon, CA 92020 to find out the difference."

Steve McKee[6] lists five words that should never be used in an ad because they are overused and meaningless:

- *Quality.* What does quality mean? If a product's worth buying, it's a quality product.
- *Value.* This is in the eye of the beholder. Lexus and Hyundai both are good values depending on the purchase context.
- *Service.* Have you ever heard of a company that promises bad service?
- *Caring.* If your competitors didn't care about customers, they wouldn't remain in business.
- *Integrity.* Every company needs to have integrity if it wants to keep customers (and stay in business).

6. *Be specific.* Avoid vague generalities such as "Save on a vast collection of beautiful tops in a variety of colors." What does this mean? Are they T-shirts? Turtlenecks? Scoop necks? Do they have long sleeves? Short sleeves? Cap sleeves? Are they tailored? Frilly? Sporty? Are they pastels? Brights? Neutrals? Just what is a "vast" collection? And exactly how much will you save?

7. *Don't brag.* Few people are going to care how proud you are of your product or how long you've been in business unless you can translate that information into a specific consumer benefit. Instead of bragging about your product's features, tell your readers what your product will do for them. For example, compare the following sentences:

"We are proud to announce our new flight schedule to New York."

"Now you can fly to New York five times a day."

Did you notice how the second sentence turns the airline's feature (the new schedule) into a traveler's advantage? The second sentence also gives more information in fewer words. That's good writing.

8. *Use the present tense and active voice whenever possible.* The present tense communicates a sense of immediacy, and the active voice enlivens your copy. For example, "We try harder" sounds better than "We have tried harder."

9. *Use transitions to connect different thoughts and establish a relationship between them.* Here are some words that bridge thoughts:

So	On the other hand
Therefore	Furthermore
However	First
In addition	Second
In fact	But

---

[6] Steve McKee, "Five Words to Never Use in an Ad," www.businessweek.com, 25 September 2006.

10. *Avoid clichés.* Describe your product in a new, refreshing way; don't resort to overused clichés such as these:

Age-old secret	Out of this world
A win–win situation	Sharp as a tack
Early birds	Sleep like a baby (or log)
More bang for the buck	State of the art
Hustle and bustle	Talk of the town
World class	It's not rocket science (or brain surgery)
Pushing the envelope	Knock your socks off

Radio copywriter Steven Lang created the following spoof to demonstrate how ridiculous clichés and vague generalities can be:

> *Spring has sprung at the Cliché Factory. They've got all the names you know and love at everyday low, low prices for all your needs. There's a huge selection of savings throughout the store. Their friendly qualified factory-trained technicians will meet or beat any offer. But wait there's more. Prices have been slashed to the bone. So next time you're in the mood for fantastic unbelievable super savings, check out the friendly folks down at the Cliché Factory. And of course, don't miss out because they service what they sell. Conveniently located for your shopping convenience. Check them out.*

11. *Vary the length and structure of sentences.* To highlight the importance of this, the International Newspaper Promotion Association printed the following statement in its *Copy Service* newsletter: "The simple sentence starts with a subject. Then the simple sentence has an object. The simple sentence ends with a period. The simple sentence gets boring as hell after you've read three or four of them. And you just did!" Doug Williams demonstrates this by writing the same message two ways. Read the following paragraphs. Which one do you think is more engaging?

> *The ear demands variety, so listen as I vary the sentence length, and create music that sings with a pleasant rhythm and harmony. I use short sentences, medium sentences and sometimes when I am certain the reader is rested, I will engage him in sentences of considerable length. These sentences burn with energy and build with the impetus of a crescendo. They have a roll of the drums and a crash of a cymbal. They have the kind of sound that urges a reader to listen because this is important.*
>
> *The ear demands variety. Now listen: I vary the sentence length, and create music. Music. The writing sings. It has a pleasant rhythm, a harmony. I use short sentences. And I use sentences of medium length. And sometimes when I am certain the reader is rested, I will engage him in sentences of considerable length—a sentence that burns with energy and builds with all the fire and impetus of a crescendo,*

the roll of the drums, the crash of a cymbal. Sounds that say, Listen to this. It's important.[7]

12. *Make the strange familiar, the familiar strange.* Explain something complex in simple terms. Or take something simple and describe it in colorful language. Here's how the writer described the size of the Biltmore Estate:

THE DRIVEWAY IS MEASURED IN MILES.

THE FLOORPLAN IS MEASURED IN ACRES.

13. *Write "out loud."* Use spoken language, not the written language you use in the typical term paper. Imagine that your customer is sitting in front of you and you're talking to her. If you have a hard time doing this, try recording your conversation. Zap the "uhs," "ums," and "ya knows," and you should have some convincing copy.

14. *Use contractions.* Don't be afraid of using words like "don't," "couldn't," "haven't," or "it's."[8] After all, it's the way people speak.

15. *Pay attention to every word you write.* In his book *The Pursuit of Wow!*, Tom Peters tells how thrilled he was when he noticed that the expiration date on a fresh fruit drink read, "Enjoy by March 12." He wrote, "Why fuss over 'Enjoy by' instead of the normal 'Expires on'? Simple. It's the very essence of humanness, of connecting with the customer—and a strong indicator of superior service and quality. 'Enjoy by' brought a smile to my face and an 'ahhh' to my lips."[9]

16. *Test your copy.* Be sure to read it out loud. If you find yourself cringing or saying "That sounds stupid," ditch it and start again. Once you have copy you like, test it again on someone who represents your target audience.

17. *Revise your work.* Edit. Edit. Edit. Author Truman Capote once said of the revision process, "I know my book is done when the publisher grabs it out of my hands."

18. *Proofread your final version.* One wrong letter can make a world of difference. Tickets to a recent Boston Pops concert were printed as "Boston Poops." Oops! A college brochure boasted about its "pubic relations" program, a rather embarrassing public relations error. For other humorous examples, check out the "Copy Mistakes" box on page 151.

    How can you avoid mistakes such as these? Spell check is a start, but it isn't where you should stop. After all, spell check would miss the previous mistakes. So what should you do? Some people read their copy backward to spot errors. Others set the copy in wider or larger font so that phrases are broken up. And others find mistakes by setting the copy aside for a few days before proofing it. Still in doubt? Ask someone else to proofread your work.

---

[7] From a lecture titled "Mass Media Writing," given at the University of South Carolina, March 1998.
[8] Be careful not to make the common mistake of confusing "its," a possessive, and "it's," a contraction for "it is" or "it has."
[9] Tom Peters, *The Pursuit of Wow!* (New York: Vintage Books, 1994), p. 10.

Don't just proof the words in a vacuum—proof the copy with the art. Does the copy make sense with what's shown? In October 2000, a North Carolina billboard read "Gore 2000" and showed a picture of George W. Bush. This boo-boo was covered by CNN, *Good Morning America, USA Today,* and *The Wall Street Journal.* Three days later, the real sponsor—a job listing service—was revealed when a banner went up across the ad that said, "Proofreader wanted: 123hire.com." The billboard, which cost about $5,000, gave the client national exposure. Boone/Oakley, the agency that created the sign, won some new accounts as the result of the media hype. Although the art–copy mishap was intentional, it's not always that way.

> Checklist for Writing Copy

- Does your message reflect the strategy?
- Does your message make an emotional connection to the reader?
- Is the tone of the ad appropriate for the product and target?
- Does your headline stop, intrigue, and involve the reader?
- Does your headline encourage readership of body copy?
- Does your headline offer a promise or benefit relevant to the selling idea?
- Does your headline work with the visual to create synergy?
- Does your body copy contain readable paragraphs and conversational language?
- Does your copy sound like a conversation between the writer and the reader?
- Do you present selling points in a nonboastful way?
- Does your message end with an urge to action, a summary of the main idea, or an open-ended statement designed to provoke readers to complete the thought?
- Will customers connect your message to the brand name?

> Suggested Activities

1. Go through several recent magazines and cut out advertisements that contain headlines and visuals that fall into at least 6 of the 15 types listed in this chapter (news, benefit, selective, factual, metaphor, and so on). If the same headline accomplishes several things, list them all. As you complete your search, also note why some ads attract you and others do not. To accompany your ad collection, write a brief paper on their positive and negative qualities.

2. Using the creative brief that you developed in Chapter 5, write two pieces of print copy with headlines. Describe any visuals you plan to use and include a rough layout of the ad with your copy. Note: To do the layout,

draw a rectangle on a standard sheet of paper, roughly letter in your headline in the size you think it should be, sketch your visual (stick figures are fine), use lines to indicate where copy goes, and place a logo somewhere near the bottom. Don't spend more than a few minutes on the layout. Instead, focus on the idea for the visual and the copy that will accompany it.

3. Present the ad you created in the previous activity to the class as if you were presenting it to the client. How will you explain your strategy or your ad concept?

4. Find a national ad that has what you think is effective copy. State why you chose it and what you believe to be outstanding about it. How does it meet the criteria for creativity presented in Chapter 1?

5. With a classmate, work out a series of ads for a local business. Begin by gathering information about your "client" and then brainstorm before you try your ideas on each other. Once you've agreed on a solution, develop and present a series of at least three ads.

North Carolina Plays a Starring Role

*F*orrest Gump was filmed in North Carolina. So was *Last of the Mohicans, The Hunt for Red October, Divine Secrets of the Ya-Ya Sisterhood, Teenage Nina Turtles, Dawson's Creek,* and hundreds of other movies and TV shows. In fact, North Carolina is one of the top filmmaking states in the United States, ranked behind only California and New York.

Since 1980, North Carolina's Film Office has recruited more than 800 major films and television productions, generating more than $7 billion in production revenue. In 2005 alone, the film industry spent more than $300 million in North Carolina making movies, television shows, and commercials.

Why are filmmakers interested in North Carolina? For starters, it offers an impressive array of locations, from pristine beaches to tropical swamps to panoramic vistas from atop the Blue Ridge Mountains. More than a million acres of national and state forestlands provide vast unspoiled areas for filming wilderness scenes. Locations in the state's cities and towns feature authentic Colonial, antebellum, modern high-tech, and middle-American architecture.

Another plus is that North Carolina has a generally mild climate, plus the advantage of distinctive spring, summer, fall, and winter seasons. It also has a well-established production infrastructure, which includes a world-class crew base of more than 2,000 seasoned film professionals, 8 full-service studio complexes, more than 30 soundstages, 400 support service companies, and 5 regional film commissions. And there's some truth to the legendary Southern hospitality—the crews are very friendly and accommodating. Overall, there are fewer day-to-day hassles than what filmmakers may experience elsewhere.

The advertising campaign created by Loeffler Ketchum Mountjoy speaks the language of filmmakers and producers and offers convincing reasons to shoot on location in North Carolina. The body copy for the ads follows:

Courtesy of Loeffler Ketchum Mountjoy.

Courtesy of Loeffler Ketchum Mountjoy.

YOU WON'T HAVE TO YELL "QUIET ON THE SET!"

Fade up. Killer location. Something's got to be wrong with this picture. Everything's going too easy. Crew's too bleeping nice. Cut to face of location scout. She whispers, "Wait'll you see the other 5 locations." Dailies roll in. Boffo. You're already thinking sequel. You dial (919) 733-9900 to set it up. You show rough cut. Everybody applauds. Even clueless studio executives. (This worries you slightly.) You remember why you got into films in the first place. Life is good. The end.

North Carolina Film Commission

Copy reads: YOU WON'T HAVE TO YELL "QUIET ON THE SET!" Fade up. Killer location. Something's got to be wrong with this picture. Everything's going too easy. Crew's too bleeping nice. Cut to face of location scout. She whispers, "Wait'll you see the other five locations." Dailies roll in. Boffo. You're already thinking sequel. You dial (919) 733-9900 to set it up. You show rough cut. Everybody applauds. Even clueless studio executives. (This worries you slightly.) You remember why you got into films in the first place. Life is good. The end.

IF THE SCRIPT ISN'T EXACTLY OSCAR BAIT, AT LEAST THE CINEMATOGRAPHY CAN BE.

Fade up. Location to die for. Cameraman needs a cigarette after every shot. Dissolve to scene of your footage arriving in Hollywood. Small crowds gather to marvel over it. Execs are suddenly calling you "that genius who can make anything look great." Cut to Academy Awards. You're rubbing elbows with Meryl, Quentin, Whoopi. And the winner is...you! You start thanking all the little people. Your speech runs too long. The network cuts to a kitty litter commercial. Is this a great business or what? The end.

North Carolina Film Commission

Courtesy of Loeffler Ketchum Mountjoy.

Copy reads: IF THE SCRIPT ISN'T EXACTLY OSCAR BAIT, AT LEAST THE CINEMATOGRAPHY CAN BE. Fade up. Location to die for. Cameraman needs a cigarette after every shot. Dissolve to scene of your footage arriving in Hollywood. Small crowds gather to marvel over it. Execs are suddenly calling you "that genius who can make anything look great." Cut to Academy Awards. You're rubbing elbows with Meryl, Quentin, Whoopi. And the winner is . . . you! You start thanking all the little people. Your speech runs too long. The network cuts to a kitty litter commercial. Is this a great business or what? The end.

Courtesy of Loeffler Ketchum Mountjoy.

THERE'S ONLY ONE PROBLEM WITH SHOOTING IN THOSE FAMOUS BIG CITIES. SOMEBODY MIGHT SHOOT BACK.

Fade up. Gritty urban location. You'd swear by the look that you're somewhere in Brooklyn. Southside Chicago. L.A. But the feel is entirely different. People are friendly. Cooperative. Even government officials. No traffic nightmares. No sea of red tape to wade through. You're having a blast on the shoot. You're getting really good craft service. When you yell "Cut" nobody knifes you. It's the way things should be. You're able to concentrate on your art instead of a lot of moronic distractions. Get your acceptance speech ready. The end.

North Carolina Film Commission

Copy reads: THERE'S ONLY ONE PROBLEM WITH SHOOTING IN THOSE FAMOUS BIG CITIES. SOMEBODY MIGHT SHOOT BACK. Fade up. Gritty urban location. You'd swear by the look that you're somewhere in Brooklyn. Southside Chicago. L.A. But the feel is entirely different. People are friendly. Cooperative. Even government officials. No traffic nightmares. No sea of red tape to wade through. You're having a blast on the shoot. You're getting really good craft service. When you yell "Cut" nobody knifes you. It's the way things should be. You're able to concentrate on your art instead of a lot of moronic distractions. Get your acceptance speech ready. The end.

LAYOUTS
DESIGNING TO COMMUNICATE
By Ronald J. Allman, Associate Professor,
Indiana University Southeast

Advertising is a team sport. The copywriter and art director begin by exchanging ideas on content and approach and then proceed to working out the problems. The design idea may come from the writer, and the headline may come from the art director. Such teamwork implies that each partner has some understanding of and appreciation for the other's talent. We may not all be great artists, but we should be able to understand the principles involved in arriving at a graphic solution.

Designing is like writing. You have to put your imagination to work to produce vibrant headlines and powerful text, just as you do when you come up with a traffic-stopping visual. You're thinking visually, whether you know it or not, when you attempt to find the right words to explain product benefits. So when you start to think about how you want the campaign to look, imagine that someone else will be doing the finished artwork and dig in—just start sketching. It's OK if it's rough. As you will see, the processes for these two endeavors are also similar. Each consists of finding a solution to a problem, and each begins with ideas.

> Functions of Design

In designing your advertisement, keep its purpose foremost in your mind. Remember that an ad must communicate quickly and effectively (see Figure 8-1). The prettiest ad is worthless unless what you want to convey

Courtesy of the Creative Circus [Julie Eyerman and Brad Mislow].

Rubbermaid

TRASH CANS

Figure 8-1
Why waste unnecessary words describing a product's attributes? Sometimes a picture *is* worth a thousand words.

to your audience is clear, understandable, and useful to them. Good design makes your message easier to understand. In other words, your design needs to relay as much information as possible to the audience in the shortest time possible. A thoughtful design helps you accomplish this.

Your design must attract your target audience. Thousands of media messages are competing for consumers' attention. A well-designed ad grabs their attention, at least momentarily. Because you have their attention only briefly, your design must help them remember the message. Good design not only commands attention but also holds it. If your audience is quickly bored with your ad, you're not going to communicate much of anything.

Design enables you to organize ideas. Carefully placed information breaks the facts into digestible messages—some visual, others textual; some large, others small. This helps product facts stick in consumers' minds. Good design makes information easier to remember.

Good design emphasizes the most compelling information. Where you place information in the ad, how large you make that information, and how you display it in relation to other elements in the ad can strengthen or diminish its importance.

> Design Principles

As you design your ad, you need to consider the following principles: *balance, contrast, harmony, proportion,* and *movement.*

Balance

Balance can be symmetrical or asymmetrical (see Figure 8-2). When both sides of an advertisement are equal, the design is symmetrical. So, if there is a picture on the left, symmetrical balance requires that there be a picture on the right that is similar in size, shape, and placement. Think of two children on a seesaw—if they are the same size and you place them the same distance apart, they will balance each other.

Figure 8-2
Asymmetrical balance is the dominant choice in advertising because it allows one point of the design to "take over" and attract the eye to the rest of the ad. To achieve asymmetrical balance, just be certain that there's a difference top to bottom or right to left in the ad, all the while arranging elements so that the ad doesn't appear lopsided. Symmetrical balance suggests a static quality; asymmetrical balance suggests dynamism. Which is appropriate for your ad?

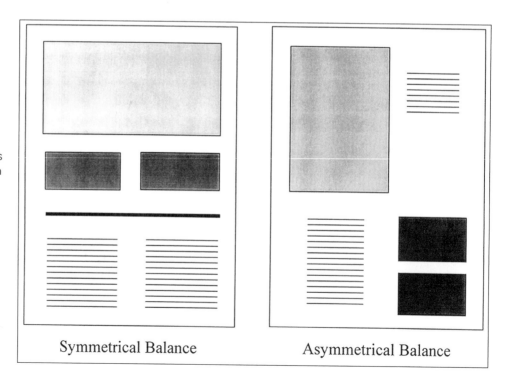

Symmetrical Balance   Asymmetrical Balance

Asymmetrical balance depends on the weight of the items on a page. Imagine the seesaw again, only this time with a larger child on one end and a smaller child on the other end. To balance the seesaw, the larger child moves closer to the center, the smaller child moves farther from the center, or more small children join the smaller child. Although symmetrical balance is fine, it can also be static—something advertisers usually wish to avoid. So we see more ads with asymmetrical balance because the advertisers are striving for a dynamic look.

Knowing what is "heavier" or "lighter" in a layout takes some practice, but you probably already have an intuitive feel for the concept of weight. A darker item is heavier than a lighter item. A bigger item is heavier than a smaller item. Thick is heavier than thin. It is when you combine layout elements that their weights become less clear. Photos and headlines are usually seen as heavier than text or logos. Text usually is the lightest item on a page.

Imagine the pieces of your design as little weights on a page. To balance this design asymmetrically, you must arrange the pieces in such a way that the balance is in the center of the page. You need to balance not only left with right but also top with bottom. A bottom-heavy design will tempt the reader to turn the page. A top-heavy design will discourage the reader from reading the rest of the ad.

Contrast

We encounter contrast everywhere. A white circle stands out among black squares and thus attracts and keeps our attention. But contrast is not limited to color or shape. Contrast can be effectively used in type size, slant, font, and weight. Texture—in both images and text—is another way to use contrast. A feather on a piece of sandpaper will stand out even if the feather and sandpaper are similar colors. Too much contrast, however, and your design can lose its cohesiveness.

Harmony

Harmony is the opposite of contrast. Using text that is all one font, even if the sizes are different, produces a harmonious layout. Harmony lets the viewer know that all elements are related. Using harmonious shades of one color brings a design together. Harmony, like contrast, can also be found in texture, direction, and weight. But remember, if things become too harmonious, people tend to become bored.

Proportion

We like things to be in proportion If your layout violates the rules of proportion, your consumer may reject the whole advertisement. The "perfect" proportion is a 2-to-3 proportion, known as a golden mean. Most photographs are designed to adhere to the golden mean. The Greeks used this proportion when they built the Parthenon.

Figure 8-3
This ad uses repetition to make an important point. Copy reads: "In America, an estimated 15.3 million new cases of STDs are reported each year. And that's just the people who'll admit it. It's a chain reaction; when you have sex with someone without a condom, they're dumping their entire sexual history on you. Literally. It's like a human subway for crabs. Assuming you don't want them to 'hop on board,' why not use a condom? Don't let her past mistake with 'Toothless Mike' become your current itch."

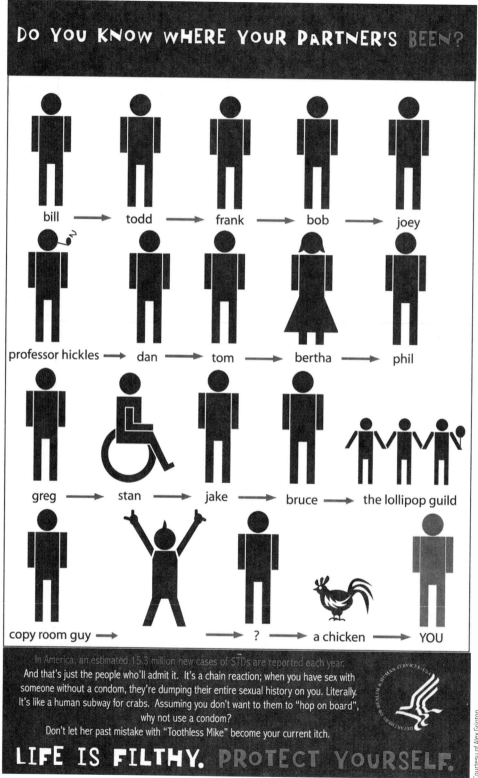

Courtesy of Alex Grinton.

Movement

Most Americans have a natural tendency to start at the upper-left corner of the page and move in a diagonal Z motion to the lower-right corner of the page. With this Z movement in mind, try not to place important elements, such as your logo, in the lower-left corner.

Rhythm is another way to create movement and direct the reader's eyes where you want them to go. Repetition creates rhythm. Photos placed horizontally across the page move the viewer's eyes across the page. But make sure that you place important information at the end of this movement. If you don't, it's likely that the reader will turn the page. Notice how Figure 8-3 uses rhythm to make its point.

The eyes and hands of the models shown in your ad can also direct the reader's eye movement. If your model is looking in the direction of the copy or logo, so will your reader. But if your model's eyes are looking off the page, so will your reader's eyes.

> Gestalt Theory

"Gestalt" comes from the German word that means form or shape. Put simply, gestalt is the idea that the whole is greater than the sum of its parts. Although the parts can be—and should be—observed and analyzed on their own, the whole of a design should strike you first. When you first see a painting, you take it in as a whole. Only later do you look at the individual parts. Similarly, designers use to their advantage the mind's tendency to group things together and see them as a whole (see Figure 8-4).

If objects are similar and are near one another, we mentally close the distance between them and see them as whole. Imagine a flock of geese flying overhead—we first see the wedge shape they form rather than the individual birds. When flowers are arranged a certain way, they can spell out words— we see the words, not the individual flowers. Our eyes are drawn more to groups than to things spaced widely apart. Because we are drawn to such patterns, we respond to them in predictable ways.

Conversely, when an item is dissimilar to the objects around it, it commands attention. At a baseball game, the person in a rainbow-colored wig is definitely going to stand out. When a car is going the wrong way on a one-way street, we notice it at once (thank goodness). People notice and react to items that stand out.

> Negative, or "White," Space

You can think of your layout as the "package" for your idea. How you use white space in your layout can determine how effective your package will be. By "white space" we mean blank, or negative, space. Always leave some white space on the outside of your layout. Allow white space to invade the

Figure 8-4
Gestalt principles remind us that elements of design should be integrated so that the design, not the elements, is the first thing the viewer observes. Design principles such as contrast, harmony, rhythm, and proportion are other ways to focus attention, hold various elements together, and present elements in ways that please the eye.

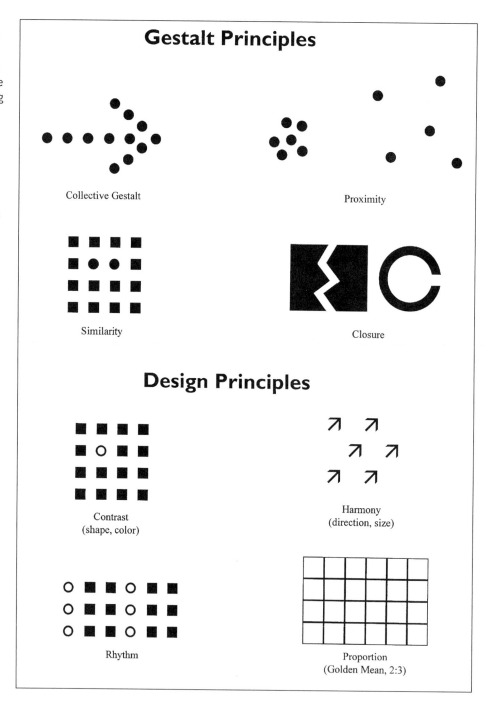

center of your layout, and you are guaranteed to have a scattered, incohesive design.

However, there is more to white space than simply including it on the outside of an ad. Use lots of white space, a great expanse of white space, and what's the result? Often, it's a feeling of exclusivity. Look at an ad from Tiffany & Co. and you'll see how white space puts the item being advertised in the spotlight and adds a sense of elegance to the ad. This can be great for an upscale target audience but probably isn't appropriate for bargain hunters.

White space can make a big statement. A public service ad that ran in the *Boston Globe* warned parents about the dangers that may lurk in Halloween candy. Three-quarters of the page appeared to be blank. A headline that ran along the bottom of the page read, "If you missed it on this empty page, imagine how easy it is to miss it in your kid's Halloween candy." The combination of the empty space and headline grabs readers' attention and makes them examine the ad. Taking a closer look, readers spot a pin in the upper-left corner of the ad.

> The Five Rs of Design

You're ready to start designing an ad. How do you begin? Where do you go from there? All designers use the same process. They may have different names for it, but they all use it. We like to call this process the five Rs: *research, roughs, revise, ready*, and *run*.

Research

You've been asked to design an ad for Acme Flakes. So where do you start? Remember Chapter 4. That's right—you start with research. You first need to know what Acme Flakes are. Are they soap flakes, instant potato flakes, or corn flakes? Or is it simply a cute name for an advertising design company?

You find out all you can about the product, company, or service. Would you approach the design of an ad for Ben & Jerry's Ice Cream differently than you would for Breyer's Ice Cream? They both sell the same product—premium ice cream—but everything about the two companies and their products is different. They offer different flavors, have different public images, attract different buyers, and are packaged in different ways. The more you know about your client, the more appropriate your design will be.

Not only do you need to research the product, company, or service, but you must also know your target audience and your competition. How do your competitors advertise? What do their ads look like? What do you offer that they don't? How can you design an ad that will lure consumers from their product to yours? What is your target audience like? What do they read? What kind of design catches their attention? Once again, the more research you do, the easier your designing job will be.

Another type of research is less project specific but still vital. This involves your swipe file, a collection of advertisements and visuals (photos, illustrations, and the like) that you think are interesting, attractive, or just different. Ideas are not copyrighted. Good designers appreciate good design, so make a copy of a good idea for later reference. Who knows? It may be just the stimulus you need next week. What's important is to borrow the idea, not the ad itself. A swipe file is a great place to start when you need ideas.

It's also a good way to see what sorts of designs, typefaces, and visuals are being used; what they look like; and how they work in layouts.

Roughs

Once you've completed your research, you're ready to start sketching. These early sketches are just rough versions. The important thing is to put your ideas on paper. There are as many ways to do roughs as there are people doing them. Whichever way works best for you, the idea behind the rough is the same. You want to sketch every idea you have about what your finished ad might look like. Don't be afraid—some of these ideas will be goofy. The best designs often start this way. What is important is that you put your ideas on paper before you forget them.

Many designers like to create little roughs called thumbnails. Thumbnails are useful because you can sketch an idea quickly, without much detail; then you have your concept in miniature form. There is no need for great artistic skill here. You just want to give yourself a lot of options. How do you create a thumbnail? Like this: Using a soft-lead pencil or a fine-to-medium black marker or rollerball pen, draw a number of small horizontal rectangles (about 2 inches wide by 3 inches deep) to represent the general shape of a magazine page. Don't try to draw a straight line, just freehand. Place your ideas for headlines and visuals within each rectangle. Scribble the words of the headline in the space and use shapes and simple stick figures to represent the visuals. Indicate body copy with a series of lines and place a rough logo at the bottom, probably in the right-hand corner. Congratulations! You have just done your first thumbnail rough, the beginning stage of every print layout. As you place other headlines in other rectangles, you'll probably think of still more ideas for words and pictures. Good! Don't stop until you've exhausted your topic, even if some of the ideas seem bizarre or ridiculous.

Revise

Once you have your roughs, take a look at your ideas and pick the ones you like best. Let your knowledge of your client and of your target consumer guide you in deciding which ideas will work. Don't become too attached to one idea yet. Develop several ideas. Start making more elaborate sketches and then revise them. And remember that revising is never a one-way street.

You can always go back and do more roughs or more research. You may get lucky and have a couple of ideas that you can develop, but don't be afraid to backtrack if you become stuck.

The revision stage is often a good time to seek initial feedback from your client. But remember: Although your client is in business, that business likely isn't design. The client may not have the background to visualize your big idea from a thumbnail rough, so make certain your ideas are finished enough for him or her to visualize the product. Also, listen carefully to the client's feedback because he or she has to be happy with your efforts thus far.

Seek feedback from other designers, too. They might see ideas or mistakes that you've missed. Just remember that this is your design, not theirs. Keep revising until you create a couple of versions you're happy with. Then choose one and base your campaign on it.

Ready

Once you have an ad with the copy and design elements in place, it's time to prepare a finished layout for your client's approval. Using a computer, you can produce a presentation ad that is nearly as finished as what will be submitted for publication.

After doing scores of thumbnails and choosing the one that best solves the advertising problem, it's time to use the rough to create the final layout.

This layout should be actual size. Because most magazines use the following dimensions, this is a good size to start with:

Trim size: 8 inches by 11 inches

Nonbleed and type area: 7 inches by 10¼ inches

Bleed: 8¼ inches by 11¼ inches

The trim size represents the finished size of the page after the magazine has been printed, bound, and trimmed. Your layout should be drawn to this size if you're designing a full-page ad. Be aware, however, that magazine sizes do vary, so always check the mechanical specifications for each magazine you plan to use. A bleed ad is one that runs all the way to the trim on at least one side. A nonbleed ad is contained within the nonbleed page limits, with a margin surrounding it on all sides. Whether your ad is designed for bleed or not, you should keep all type within the nonbleed limits. In setting type too close to the trim, you run the risk of having a letter or two trimmed off. You might want to draw the nonbleed limit as a second frame within the frame you draw to establish the trim. This will remind you to keep all type within the inner frame, or nonbleed area.

Run

This last step is really not the designer's problem. The advertisement you created is run in the media chosen by the agency or client. What you need to do is to make sure that the printed advertisement is properly prepared for each publication in which it is to run.

> Selecting Type

If you spend any time around designers, you'll hear them talk about type in descriptive, affectionate terms and with good reason. Different fonts have different personalities. Zapf Chancery is an elegant but still a legible font. Helvetica is a workhorse as far as fonts go, but it's rather boring and plain.

Type Categories

Serif Type	*Sans Serif Type*	*Script*	*Novelty*
Times Roman	Helvetica	*Brush Script*	Comic Sans
Garamond	Gill Sans	*Lucia*	**CRACKLING**
Goudy	**Impact**	*Elegant*	**CRYPT**
Bodoni	Eras		**Saint Francis**

Cursive
Coronet
Zapf Chancery

Text Letter
Old English
Lombardic

Figure 8-5

Literally thousands of type fonts are at your disposal on computers. Unless you're a type expert, however, be wary of using most of them. Generally, stick to the serif and sans serif fonts, which contrast with each other nicely. Or use one font for all type in your ad, using a larger size and perhaps a bolder face for the headline and other display lines than the one used for the body copy. Script and cursive, although lovely on invitations, should be used cautiously because they're harder to read. For the same reason, avoid novelty and text letter fonts unless the concept calls for something unconventional. The body copy for this book is Centennial.

Gill Sans has the flair that Helvetica is missing. As Paul Silverman put it, "These days, even the Shakespeare of Madison Avenue would be defeated by lousy typography. Typography supplies color and mood, much as the voice does in spoken language."[1]

Type can be divided into six groups: serif, sans serif, script, cursive, text letter, and novelty (see Figure 8-5). Letters in a serif font have little horizontal strokes at the tops and bottoms of the letter. These serifs help draw the eye along a line of type. Most body text is in a serif font for this reason. The most common serif font is Times Roman. Other serif fonts are Palatino, Goudy, Bookman, Caslon, Bodoni, and Garamond.

Letters without serifs are called sans serif fonts. Sans serif fonts have a more modern and geometric look than serif fonts. Sans serif fonts can be distinctive in headlines and logos. They are clean-looking fonts that communicate a sense of simplicity. Some common sans serif fonts are Helvetica, Futura, Gill Sans, Avant Garde, and Optima.

Fonts designed to look like handwriting are either script or cursive fonts. The difference between script and cursive fonts depends on whether the letters connect. If they connect, it's a script font; if they don't, it's a cursive font. These fonts add a sense of formality and elegance, so they are popular for invitations and announcements. But their use in advertising is limited, perhaps because of their delicacy and because they can be difficult to read.

[1] The Designers and Art Directors Association of the United Kingdom, *The Copywriter's Bible* (Switzerland: Roto Vision, 1995), p. 151.

Park Avenue, Mistral, and Brush Script are common script fonts; Zapf Chancery, Freestyle Script, and Reporter No. 2 are popular cursive fonts.

If the font was created to look like the hand-drawn letters of monks and scribes, it's a text letter font. These fonts, also known as black letter fonts, are hard to read and usable only in certain situations, such as diplomas and newspaper nameplates. The most common text letter font is Old English.

Novelty fonts are those that don't easily fit into the other categories because they are unusual or unconventional. Fonts that make type look like stenciled letters or Old West "wanted" posters are novelty fonts. Novelty fonts are good for display headlines and logos when you need flair. Some of the more commonly used novelty fonts are Hobo, American Typewriter, and Stencil. Text letter fonts are sometimes considered novelty fonts.

When choosing a font, keep in mind the message you want to convey. A headline that says "Welcome to the Electronic Age" in a script font sends a mixed message. A long paragraph in Old English would be tedious to read.

You may want to set your headline in a customized font that reflects the theme of your ad. For instance, the Food Bank of Central New York set the word "food" in music notes and symbols in an ad that ran in the local symphony program (see Figure 8-6). Creative approaches such as these work great in headlines with a few words but would be difficult to read if they were set in a long paragraph of body copy. Keep in mind that readability must always come first.

Type is measured in points. There are 72 points to an inch. Body text is usually between 10 and 12 points. Type larger than 18 points is considered display type and is usually used for headlines. For advertisements, it's wise to consider 10 as the minimal point size, and 12-point type may be more legible in some fonts.

The space between lines of type is known as leading and is also measured in points. If you have 10-point type and want 2 points of space between the lines, you will specify 12 points of leading. In this case, to tell a designer what size type and leading you are using, you would say, "10 on 12." When you want the same font size and leading, specify "set solid." For legibility, however, it's usually wise to have at least 2 points of leading between lines.

The space between letters is known as letter spacing. If you adjust the spacing between two letters, you are kerning the letters. For display lines such as headlines, subheads, and baselines, this is useful with certain letters that can be moved closer together because of their shapes, such as "AV," "To," "AW," and "Te." If you adjust the spacing between all letters, you are adjusting the type's tracking.

You can line up paragraphs of type in four ways (see Figure 8-7). If you want all your text lined up vertically on the left side, specify flush left. If you want it lined up only on the right side, specify flush right. If both sides are lined up, your text is justified. And you can always center your type. Most advertisements are set flush left, ragged right. This is easier on the reader because the eye goes back to a consistent starting point and the ragged right allows some "air" in the text, especially between columns if you use more than one column.

Figure 8-6
This ad ran in a program for the Syracuse Symphony and reminded concertgoers to help the less fortunate.

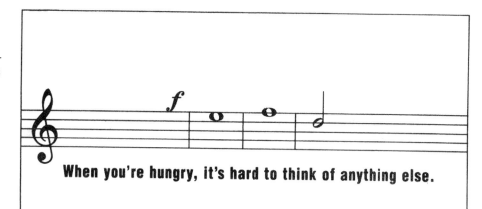

When you're hungry, it's hard to think of anything else.

Think about this: Every night thousands of families right here in Central New York go to bed hungry. But every $1 you donate helps us get $14 worth of nutritious food on their plates. Which is sure to put a song in their hearts. Please help us help them.
(315) 437-1899   www.foodbankcny.org

WE WORK FOR FOOD

Courtesy of (MRA) Mark Russell & Associates, Inc.

At times, you will want to wrap your type around an object or have it form a design to help further your message (see Figure 8-8).

> Basic Ad Layouts

If you can't decide how to lay out your ad and your swipe file is no help, try some of these basic advertising layouts: frame, circus, grid, color field, silhouette, copy heavy, type specimen, picture window, band, axial, or Mondrian.

Type Alignment

Flush Left	*Centered*	*Flush Right*	*Justified*

Dolor in hendrerit in vulputate velit esse molestie consequat, vel illum dolore eu feugiat nulla facilisis at vero eros et accumsan et iusto odio dignissim qui blandit praesent luptatum zzril delenit augue duis dolore te feugait nulla facilisi. Soluta nobis eleifend option congue nihil imperdiet doming id quod mazim placerat facer possim assum. Lorem ipsum dolor sit amet, consectetuer adipiscing elit, sed diam nonummy nibh euismod tincidunt ut laoreet.
Soluta nobis eleifend option congue nihil

imperdiet doming id quod mazim placerat facer possim assum. Lorem ipsum dolor sit. Sit amet, consectetuer hendrerit in vulputate velit. Hendrereit in vulputate velit aliquip exea lorem ipsum minim. Ut hendrerit in vulputate velit aliquip ex ea commodo minim hendrerit i vulputate velit veniam: Sed diam nonummy nibh tincidunt ut laoreet. Dolor in hendrerit in vulputate velit esse molestie consequat, vel illum dolore eu feugiat nulla facilisis at vero eros et accumsan et iusto odio dignissim qui blandit

praesent luptatum zzril delenit augue duis dolore te feugait nulla facilisi. Soluta nobis eleifend option congue nihil imperdiet doming id quod mazim placerat facer possim assum. Lorem ipsum dolor sit amet, consectetuer adipiscing elit, sed diam nonummy nibh euismod tincidunt ut laoreet. Soluta nobis eleifend option congue nihil imperdiet doming id quod mazim placerat facer possim assum. Lorem ipsum dolor sit. Sit amet, consectetuer hendrerit in vulputate velit:

Hendrereit in vulputate velit aliquip exea lorem ipsum minim.
Ut hendrerit in vulputate velit aliquip ex ea commodo minim hendrerit i vulputate velit veniam: Sed diam nonummy nibh tincidunt ut laoreet.
Dolor in hendrerit in vulputate velit esse molestie consequat, vel illum dolore eu feugiat nulla.
Facilisis at vero eros et accumsan et iusto odio dignissim qui blandit praesent luptatum zzril delenit augue duis dolore te feugait nulla facilisi.
Soluta nobis eleifend option congue nihil imperdiet

Figure 8-7

Most ads today have body copy set flush left, ragged right, as in the first column here. The ragged-right column provides "breathing space" between columns of type. Centered type must fit logically into the rest of the layout. Flush right might be used to offset a visual silhouette to the left of the type column. Justified type, although common in books, creates a formal look that also allows little white space between columns.

(The thumbnail sketches in Figure 8-9 will give you an idea of how each looks.) Bear in mind that your ad concept affects the design choice, not the other way around.

> Inviting Readership

You have many options at your disposal for luring readers, including the following:

- *Don't set type wider than 39 characters.* Any wider and you discourage readership. Instead, break the space into two or more columns of equal width. The larger the type, the wider it can be set.
- *Avoid setting copy in less than 10-point type.* Smaller type is hard to read.
- *Break up long copy blocks with subheads.* Careful paragraphing will also help you avoid the "gray mass" look.

As a kid, you never acted out the sounds of an automatic transmission.

① "Air shifting" through imaginary gears prepared you for the ② moment when you would have a car like this. The new Lincoln LS. ③ With a close-ratio five-speed gearbox and lively DOHC V-6, it's ④ not make-believe anymore. Visit www.lincolnvehicles.com or call ⑤ toll-free 877 2DriveLS (237-4835).

⊕ LINCOLN LS
LINCOLN. AMERICAN LUXURY.

Courtesy of Lincoln Mercury.

Figure 8-8
Notice how the ad copy is placed in a way that mimics a motorist shifting from first gear to overdrive.

Courtesy of Anthony Sundlin.

Figure 8-9
These thumbnail sketches show 11 approaches to selling wineglasses.

- *Avoid setting body copy in reverse (white on black).* This tends to cut down readership. Headlines may be reversed for impact, provided the type is large and bold enough.

- *Take care when you print copy over tonal matter, such as photographs.* If you must do this, be certain there is enough contrast to make the type legible.

- *Use lowercase when possible.* It tends to be more legible than all-capital letters, especially in smaller type sizes.

- *Either capitalize the entire headline or capitalize only the first word of a sentence and any proper noun.*

- *End the headline with punctuation.* Use a period or a question mark at the end of headlines that are complete sentences. Save the exclamation point for the rare occasion when it is warranted.

- *Align all copy elements to avoid a jumbled look.* This is easily done in an axial layout by aligning them on a common axis.

- *Use normal punctuation throughout.* Avoid leaders (. . .), which look sloppy and uninviting.

- *Use italics sparingly.* They are good for occasional emphasis, but overuse of italics makes copy look pale and weak, just the opposite of what is intended.

> Creating the Finished Ad: Computers and Design

An advertising designer might use three types of computer applications:

- *Photo manipulation software.* Software such as Adobe Photoshop is mainly used for making changes to photographs and other images on the computer, but it can also be used to create images and text. Because these applications can manipulate images, you can create interesting, eye-catching text and visuals.

- *Illustration software.* If you are looking for more control over image creation and special effects with text, an illustration program might be your design tool of choice. Software such as Adobe Illustrator and Macromedia Freehand allows you to create any type of image or text you can imagine. These applications are less friendly to images already created, such as scanned images, but if you are creating directly from your imagination, this type of software is best suited to your needs.

- *Desktop publishing software.* Perhaps the most useful application for advertising design is desktop publishing software, such as Adobe InDesign, QuarkXPress, or Adobe PageMaker. These programs were written specifically for designers who create pages for publication.

> Designing Outdoor and Transit Ads

Outdoor advertising is a true test of creativity because you need to communicate your entire selling message in an instant. This is one time when the rule "write as much as you need" doesn't apply. It's also not the time to experiment with complicated layouts. Your message must be bold and clear because people will have mere seconds to read and understand the billboard when they're cruising down the interstate and little more on a city thoroughfare.

Here's how to achieve an optimal reaction to your outdoor messages:

- *Keep the graphics simple.* One large headline with one major visual is the rule. Some boards are all type, with no visual. Others are all visual, with just a logo.
- *Make the type bold and big.* Remember, it must be read quickly.
- *Keep the word count to no more than eight words, fewer if possible.*
- *Make the brand or company name prominent.* If it's not in the main headline, use a logo big enough to be noticed.
- *Consider using your campaign theme or tagline as the headline.* This way, your outdoor ad also reminds viewers of the rest of your campaign.

In preparing your outdoor layout, follow the same procedures as for other print layouts. Standard outdoor posters (paper pasted to existing structures) are scaled to a proportion of 1 to 2¼. Outdoor bulletins, painted on boards, are usually scaled to a proportion of 1 to 3½. This translates to a 4- by 9-inch layout for the poster and a 4- by 14-inch layout for the painted bulletin.

Transit advertising appears on the inside and outside of public transportation vehicles, as well as in bus, rail, subway, and air terminals. Like outdoor advertising, it works best when the message is short. It differs from outdoor ads in that the audience can spend more time with the message. For this reason, many transit ads include "take one" cards or other literature attached to the ad.

> Answers to Common Questions about Design

Must You Show the Product?

Many clients want to have their product shown in their ads. However, as Guido Heffels says, "We are not paid to put a product in an ad, but in the consumer's mind."[2] It's not necessary to show a product that's been around for

---

[2] Jim Aitchison, *Cutting Edge Advertising* (Singapore: Prentice Hall, 1999), p. 65.

years because consumers know what it looks like. However, if the packaging changes, you'll want not only to show it but also to make a big deal about it in your ads. The same is true with new products.

Must You Show a Logo?

In most cases, you'll want to include a logo, but there are exceptions even to this rule. For instance, there's no need to show a logo if you show the product that has a clear logo on the package. Well-established brands may even get away with showing only part of the logo if the design is clearly embedded in consumers' minds.

Must Every Ad in the Campaign Look the Same?

No. As mentioned in Chapter 6, ads in a campaign should have a common attitude, but there's no need for them to look as if they came from the same mold. Still, most ads in a campaign will share a similar typeface, color scheme, and logo treatment.

Is Color More Effective Than Black and White?

According to Andy Grunberg, who writes on photography for the *New York Times,*

> *Color has become transparent. It represents reality so well that it sometimes seems to be reality itself. We take color advertising for granted.*
>
> *Black-and-white photography, on the other hand, suggests the realm of the imagination. Once the essence of documentary believability, black and white has become the color of fantasy.*[3]

Still, Grunberg acknowledges that most customers want to see fashion, food, and home furnishings in their true colors.

What about Photography versus Illustrations?

Like color images, photographs seem more real and are more widely used in advertising. Illustrations, on the other hand, lend themselves to the imagination of the viewer.

Should You Study the Look of Your Competitors' Ads?

Absolutely! Line a wall with your competitors' ads. Study them. And then do something different to stand out and make a memorable statement about your brand. For instance, the ads for Chick-fil-A shown in Chapter 5 look nothing like ads from other fast-food restaurants. Likewise, the ads for

---

[3] Andy Grunberg, "Selling You on Black and White," *Metropolitan Home,* June 1989, p. 42.

Icelandair shown in Chapter 4 look nothing like other airline ads. Both campaigns break through the clutter and make consumers take notice.

> Suggested Activities

1. Find a black-and-white ad that presents strong possibilities for rearrangement; perhaps it can even be improved. Don't choose an ad with a simple picture window, in which the only possible change will be to transpose the picture and the headline. Challenge yourself. After looking long and hard at the original ad, sketch some thumbnails. How many ways can you rearrange this ad? Choose your best arrangement.

   Now, tape the original ad to your drawing board. Draw the border on your layout paper, making certain it corresponds to the size of the original ad. Using your thumbnail as a guide, start moving your layout paper around to trace the various components from the original. Shade in dark values with the side of your No. 2 pencil. Compare the new ad to the original. What do you think?

2. Collect several ads that you think are effective and set the headlines in three other typefaces from samples you've collected. Lay the new type over the old. What effect does the change in type style have on the advertisement?

3. Take one of your ads and enlarge and reduce elements to form a new design. Compare your design to the original.

4. Find eight ads with different typefaces and defend or criticize the choices. Does the personality of the type fit the image of the ad? Does it work with the visuals? Does the type overpower everything else and undermine the effectiveness of the ad?

BRIEFCASE

Why Weight?

The Chernoff Newman agency was asked to create a campaign to drive traffic to weight-loss seminars held at Palmetto Health Baptist in Columbia, South Carolina. Creative Director Heather Price explains:

One of the biggest roadblocks to people coming to a weight loss seminar is that they don't want to take the first step to living a healthier life. Therefore we renamed the seminar "Why Weight?" in an effort to drive home the message that the time is now. We then solicited success stories of patients who went through surgery at Palmetto Health Baptist, lost weight, and are now living healthy lifestyles.

We've found that using real people allows others to identify with their situation—and gives them the hope that there is an answer to real, sustained weight loss. Our participants in the Palmetto Health ads were selected by the hospital. As weight-loss success stories, they were very excited to share their stories and encourage others to take the necessary steps to lose weight.

Larry Moseley and Christie Carper became the campaign stars, with their stories tied intrinsically to the one thing that anyone who is overweight can relate to: wearing flattering, off-the-rack clothing. Both ads featured clothing labels that defined not only the success of our heroes' surgeries, but also the outcome of it: being back in clothes that you can find in any store at the mall. We were even able to update Christie's information when she called and told us she lost 20 more pounds by adding a sale tag to her original label. Other success stories were added to the campaign series.

Prior to this campaign, the hospital was showcasing the typical "hold your pants up to see just how big you were" creative. When researching the psychology around a morbidly obese person we found that walking into a store and purchasing clothing in the mall was what was considered a huge milestone. So instead of presenting the person who lost the weight, we decided to show the article of clothing that was coveted.

One of the first ads featured a pair of jeans. We made someone at the office go take off their jeans so we could scan them for the mock-up ad that

Courtesy of Palmetto Health Baptist and Chernoff Newman. Special thanks to Heather Price for supplying the insights for the campaign and briefcase.

Christie Carper M

100% SATISFIED
WITH LAP-BAND®
SURGERY
LOST 80 LBS
60 INCHES
FEELS GREAT

Courtesy of Palmetto Health and Chernoff Newman.

Why Weight?

As a Bariatric Surgery Center of Excellence, Palmetto Health Baptist offers Why Weight?, a free seminar where we discuss weight loss surgery and its risks and health benefits. While there, a team of professionals along with Dr. Dalton Prickett or Dr. James Tribble will determine whether you're a candidate for gastric bypass or an adjustable gastric band. Call today to find out more.

PALMETTO HEALTH BAPTIST

Weight Management Center
PalmettoHealth.org/BariatricServices • 376-5982

Why Weight?

As a Bariatric Surgery Center of Excellence, Palmetto Health Baptist offers Why Weight?, a free seminar where we discuss weight loss surgery and its risks and health benefits. While there, a team of professionals along with Dr. Dalton Prickett or Dr. James Tribble will determine whether you're a candidate for gastric bypass or an adjustable gastric band. Call today to find out more.

PALMETTO HEALTH BAPTIST

Weight Management Center
PalmettoHealth.org/BariatricServices • 376-5982

Courtesy of Palmetto Health and Chernoff Newman.

Courtesy of Palmetto Health and Chernoff Newman.

LARRY MOSELEY

COLUMBIA, SC

WEIGHT LOSS SURGERY : CURED DIABETES
FROM 19 MEDS TO 1 : FEELS GREAT

LOST 204 LBS   W38   L30

Why Weight?

As a Bariatric Surgery Center of Excellence, Palmetto Health Baptist offers
Why Weight?, a free seminar where we **discuss we**ight loss surgery and
its risks and health benefits. While there, a team of professionals along with
Dr. Dalton Prickett or Dr. James Tribble will determine whether you're
a candidate for gastric bypass or an adjustable gastric band. Call today
to find out more.

PALMETTO HEALTH
BAPTIST

Weight Management Center
PalmettoHealth.org/BariatricServices • 376-5982

we presented to the client!!! In deciding to produce the artwork for our campaign all in-house, we really had to take a close look at the trademarks that so many jeans companies have on their denim. I never thought I would look at men's jeans so closely! We examined different pocket styles, stitching and created our very own label so that we would not infringe on any copyright. It was a bear but in the end, it paid off.

The campaign began in upscale magazines like *Southern Living* and was expanded into a newspaper and poster series. The hospital's website features the stars of the ads who share their personal stories of how their lives have improved after surgery.

The campaign results are outstanding. In the first month, we added more than 20 people to the seminar from the previous year. The next month, attendance almost doubled. Since then attendance is up by more than 20 percent. Many individuals who attend the seminars take the next step of meeting one-on-one with the Weight Management staff and, ultimately, schedule surgery.

RADIO
CAN YOU SEE WHAT I'M SAYING?

Radio is everywhere—at home, in cars, at places of business. Radio reaches everyone, from teens to seniors. There's a format for every listener and for every advertiser: alternative, blues, business, classical, country, hip-hop/rap, jazz, Latin, pop, oldies, R&B/soul, reggae, religion, rock, sports, and talk. You name it, radio has it.

> Why Advertise on Radio?

Advertisers love radio because it's a great way to take a small budget and do big things with it. Exciting things. Creative things. Funny things. Production budgets are tiny compared with those for television, as is the cost of airtime. Radio is a great stand-alone medium and a great support for other media.

And what do writers love about this medium? One calls writing for radio a unique adventure that transcends the limitations and the costliness of the camera lens and the shooting schedule. Another likes being involved in every stage—writing, casting, selecting sound effects, directing, and editing. Others say radio is "a lot sexier than sex" and must touch our hearts to work effectively. And seasoned radio writers will remind you that radio is a visual medium, in which the audience members see whatever the writer makes them see. The better the writer knows radio, the more the audience will see.

> The Theater of the Mind

Radio has been called, appropriately, "the theater of the mind" because radio writers have to deliver visual impressions through their choice of words, voices, sounds, and music—not pictures. For example, a commercial for Aztec suntan lotion uses a character called the Aztec Sun God, who speaks as if he's just earned an Ivy League degree. (Nothing like unexpected connections to hold interest, remember?) As he converses with a store manager, he mentions that most customers won't recognize him in his suit and wingtip shoes. Then he begins to strip down to his bronzed body as the store manager expresses understandable anxiety. That's not only funny and involving, but it also reinforces the point of the spot: Aztec suntan lotion can make your body look like a sun god's body.

> Guidelines for Writing Effective Radio Spots

- *Write for the ear, not the eye.* Remember, radio is unique. Your eyes don't see the message; your mind does. Don't just run the soundtrack from a TV commercial on the radio. Don't read a print ad into a microphone and expect it to work as a radio commercial. Some copy that works in print sounds dreadful when read aloud. For example, a radio commercial sent a powerful message about the problem of child abuse. The sound of an abused child's blood-curdling scream sent chills down listeners' spines. But the mood was blown when the announcer read the tagline in an upbeat voice; "Kids. You can't beat them." Although the line may have worked as part of the logo in a print ad, it was far too cute when read aloud.

  As you start to write your commercial, think of the voice or voices that will work best for your message. Imagine sounds and music or no sounds and no music. Begin with something relevant yet unexpected to gain the listener's attention. End with something as memorable to drive home your point.

- *Keep it simple.* Radio is a wonderful medium for building brand awareness. But it's not so good for spewing out a long list of benefits or making complex arguments. In 60 or 30 seconds, you can't expect listeners to remember a series of facts. They can't go back and reread what interests them as they can in a print ad or on the Internet. As you start to conceive your radio commercial, think about the one big idea you need to communicate and then take this idea and play it for all it's worth for the length of the commercial.

  IKEA ran a radio spot to let New Yorkers know how easy it is to get to its new Brooklyn store. The one idea, that it's easy to get to the store, required a listing of the myriad of modes of transportation. A few offbeat methods were intertwined to keep the spot interesting.

ANNCR: IKEA is opening in Brooklyn June 18, and it's important you know how to get there.

There's the subway. The free NY water taxis. The free IKEA shuttle buses. The B61 bus. The B77 bus.

You could walk, run, crawl, hop on one leg, take a hot air balloon, a submarine, even a rickshaw.

And don't forget teleportation—very efficient, very now.

There are so many ways to get to IKEA Brooklyn, you don't even need a car, plus they have same day home delivery.

So visit IKEA-USA.com/Brooklyn for complete and realistic directions.

IKEA. Home is the most important place in the world.

- *Grab the listener's attention in the first few seconds.* Keep in mind that radio is often playing in the background as people are doing a myriad of things including homework, exercising, and driving. It's vital that you capture their attention right away and make them want to listen to what you have to say. This can be done a variety of ways. Try asking an intriguing question. Consider using an attention-grabbing sound effect that sets the stage. You may even consider whispering.

- *Use sound effects to paint scenery in your listeners' minds.* Consider how you would "show" the ad's location on a radio spot. You could simply have the announcer (ANNCR) say, "Here on a busy street . . ." or you could use sounds to present the location: stalled traffic with a few well-chosen taxi driver groans or muffled car horns thrown in for good measure.

    Sound effects (SFX) should further the message, not be the ends in themselves. They shouldn't attempt to duplicate reality; calling for footstep sounds serves little purpose unless it helps make the point.

    Unexpected sounds may be more compelling. One public service announcement on child abuse uses the violent sound of doors slamming as the narrator talks about how some people hide such abuse behind closed doors. A spot urging older people to remain active uses a constant background sound of rocking chairs squeaking on a wooden porch as the narrator tells listeners to do quite the opposite.

    The Minnesota Zoo created an award-winning radio commercial that sounds like a car dealer ad. The spot opens with an announcer stating that the world's fastest animals have inspired the names of some of the world's fastest cars. The sound effects of the Ford Mustang, Volkswagen Rabbit, and the Jaguar speeding by are interspersed by the announcer stating how many seconds it takes each of the cars to go from 0 to 45 mph. Then, in an unexpected twist, the announcer acknowledges that even the world's fastest cars can't catch the world's fastest animal, the cheetah. The sound of a jet roars and the announcer makes the final pitch: "Catch the cheetahs if you can, now through Labor Day at the Minnesota Zoo." This clever spot, which encouraged fathers to take their children to the zoo, probably wouldn't have been as effective with the target audience if it had used the more expected sounds of animals growling, chirping, and snorting.

Another award-winning commercial captured the attention of its target audience by pretending to be for something entirely different. The spot opens with an announcer talking about the "one gift that will ignite the fire and passion in the hearts of your loved ones. Diamonds." The music and announcer's voice resemble that of a typical diamond commercial. But this isn't a typical diamond spot at all. The announcer is talking about baseball diamonds and the pitch is for National season tickets.

Keep the rules of creativity in mind as you choose your sound effects. Don't use unexpected sounds just for the sake of doing something different. The sound effects must be relevant to your message and presented in a way that doesn't confuse your audience. Remember, most people are doing other things when they listen to radio.

- *Identify your sound effects.* Unless you do, you may confuse listeners. For example, what does "s-s-s-s-s-s" sound like to you? To some, it may sound like bacon sizzling in a pan. To others, it may remind them of rain falling in a tropical forest. Others may think it's the hissing of a snake or the sound of air being let out of a balloon. Let the context of the spot remind listeners of what they're hearing or even have someone voice an explanation. ("Another day in the rain forest, where the waters feed lush tropical plants.")

- *Avoid annoying sound effects.* A loud siren may grab your listeners' attention, but it'll likely distract them from your message. If they're driving, they may lower the volume of their radio and look around to learn where the sound is coming from. Once they realize it's "just" a commercial, they'll become annoyed, which is the last thing you want. Also avoid other offensive sounds, such as a dripping faucet, a fly buzzing in your ear, or fingernails scratching a chalkboard. After all, you want to keep the audience listening to you, not searching for another station.

- *Use music as a sound effect.* Music can enhance a mood or take your mind to exotic destinations. A brokerage house created an image of financial power with the same sounds of kettledrums Prokofiev used in his classic symphony *Peter and the Wolf* to conjure up hunters. Another commercial depicted a German neighborhood by playing a few bars of oompah band music.

Be certain that the music you select adds to your message. Never plug music in for its own sake. If the tune has a life of its own, it may detract from what you're trying to say. And remember not all music is readily available for advertising purposes. Even a recording of a classic such as the *1812 Overture* must be cleared because the performing orchestra will own a copyright to its rendition. Obtaining commercial rights to copyrighted music and music performances can be extremely costly, and such rights usually have to be renewed annually. Some music isn't available at any price because some musicians refuse to allow their art to be part of a commercial endeavor.

Consider finding music in the public domain, which doesn't have a copyright, or using original music that you have commissioned especially for your campaign. Several music companies offer public domain (PD) music for a small fee, and most radio stations have libraries of public domain selections for the convenience of their advertisers.

- *Consider using no sound effects.* A distinctive voice, and a powerful message delivered straightforwardly, can be extremely powerful. People love to hear a good story. If it can stand alone, be conservative in your use of other sounds. Ant-Stop Orthene Fire-Ant Killer from Ortho used an announcer with a serious voice to deliver a series of entertaining and persuasive messages. Here are the opening lines of one of the commercials:

    > ANNCR: Fire ants are not loveable. People do not want fire ant plush toys.
    > They aren't cuddly; they don't do little tricks. They just bite you and leave red, stinging welts that make you want to cry.
    > That's why they have to die.

    While it may sound cruel to want any living creature to die, you'd understand if a fire ant ever bit you. These tiny ants really do "leave red, stinging welts that make you want to cry!"

- *Describe the voice or voices that can best command the attention of your audience.* Help cast the spot by describing the type of person who should say your words: skeptical young woman, trustworthy older woman, genius child, conservative Vermonter, gushy Southern belle, thickheaded caveman. Be sure to offer directions on the script in parentheses as to delivery: for example, angry, sarcastic, dopey, heavy British accent, or snobbish.

    Ads for the National Thoroughbred Racing Association use the voice of a racetrack announcer to describe activities that are a lot less thrilling than a day at the races. This campaign, created by DeVito/Verdi, won the triple crown of advertising in 2006: It took home the gold at the Clio Awards, won the top prize at the Radio Mercury Awards, and received a Gold Lion at the International Advertising Festival in Cannes. One spot begins:

    > RACETRACK
    > ANNCR: And they're off.
    > Out of the gate is Wine, Cheese and Shakespeare in the Park.
    > And Act One is off to an excruciatingly slow start.

- *Tailor your commercial to time, place, and a specific audience.* If it's running in morning drive time, remember that most people tuned in may be on their way to work. If it runs in Milwaukee, tailor it for Milwaukee. Talk breakfast at 8 a.m. or offer a commuter taxi service during rush hour.

- *Repeat the name of your client.* You can't show the product's package or product logo as you can in print and television. Instead, you need to incorporate it into your overall message. As a general rule, try to state your client's name at least three times. The trick is to do it without being obnoxious. Mnemonic devices, such as a unique voice, music, or sound effect, are great ways to put the brand's name in the listener's mind. An award-winning campaign for Bud Light opens the same way each time:

SFX:	MUSIC UP.
ANNCR:	Bud Light presents: Real Men of Genius.
SINGER:	Real Men of Genius!
ANNCR:	Today we salute you . . . Mr. _____

The music, the announcer's voice, and the phrase "Real Men of Genius" serve as cues that this is another hilarious commercial for Bud Light that celebrates an average guy and all his idiosyncrasies. Some of the Men of Genius include Mr. Jean Shorts Inventor, Mr. Way Too Much Cologne Wearer, Mr. Highway Line Painter, and Mr. Really, Really Bad Dancer. The Real Men of Genius ads, created by DDB Chicago, are pure genius because they capture the imagination of their audience. One person may visualize "Mr. Way Too Much Cologne Wearer" as their favorite uncle, while another person may visualize him as an obnoxious former boyfriend. Now that's theater of the mind!

- *Avoid numbers.* Few people are sitting next to the radio with a pen and pad in hand, just waiting for you to give them an important number. So avoid numbers if you can. If you have to give a phone number, spell it out as a word. It's much easier to remember the American Red Cross's phone number as "1-800-HELP-NOW" than it is to remember a bunch of numbers. And if you need to include a street address, put it in terms your listeners can visualize. Instead of "17349 Main Street," say, "On the corner of Main and Green Streets" or "On Main Street, across from City Hall."

Sometimes there's no bypassing mentioning a number. If you must include a number, then you'll need to find a clever way to repeat it to make it memorable. The public radio station in Albany, New York, sets its phone number (1-800-323-9262) to the tune of Stephen Foster's "Camp Town Races" so that listeners will remember the number when they go to the phone to make a pledge during the fund drive. The last four digits (9-2-6-2) are repeated numerous times because the prefix and first three digits of a phone number are easier to remember and therefore don't need to be repeated as often.

As with most rules, there are exceptions to the rule about avoiding numbers in radio. A powerful radio spot for Mothers Against Drunk Driving (MADD) lists a dozen statistics facing the "lucky" survivors of drunk driving accidents. One in four marriages breaks up from the strain, two out of three dreams are nightmares, and five of six letters are bills. The listeners may not remember the specific statistics listed in this public service announcement (PSA), but they will remember one very important point: Don't drink and drive.

- *Be aware of time considerations.* Too much copy works against you by forcing performers to rush through your lines with little time for those pauses and special inflections that add color, clarity, and depth to the spoken word. And too little copy will give dead airspace. As a general rule, about two words per second is a good place to start when writing your script. But the best way to time a commercial is to set a stopwatch and read your spot aloud, pacing it the way you want it recorded and acting out the sound effects and music. Also be sure to time your spot for the personality of your brand. A spot for a used-car dealer will likely be read fast to instill a sense of urgency, whereas a spot for an expensive restaurant will be read more slowly to reflect the elegant dining experience.

- *Make your copy easy to read.* Specify pronunciations in parentheses after the word appears. For example, "Nutella (NEW-TELL-AH)" will ensure that the announcer won't mispronounce the brand as "NUT-ELL-A." Do the same with local pronunciations. Huger Street is pronounced "YOU-GEE" in Columbia, South Carolina, not "HUE-GER" or "HUG-ER," as outsiders are prone to say.

  Also, avoid tongue twisters and stilted language. Alliterative phrases—red roosters rarely run recklessly—may look fine in print but can cause even a pro to stumble over the words.

- *Present your commercial idea to the client on a CD if possible.* Dialog, timing, vocal quirks, and sound effects come alive when you can hear them. And most recording studios will produce a "demo" at a reduced cost if you promise to let them produce the approved script. If you can't put it on a CD for presentation, have a person or people on hand who can act out voices and sounds and indicate music.

- *Love the medium.* Radio is the true test of a copywriter. Unlike other media, which use visuals to capture people's attention, it's your writing that will make or break a radio spot. Your choice of words, music, and sound effects will paint vivid scenery in the minds of your listeners.

  Visit the Radio Advertising Bureau (www.rab.com) and the Radio Ranch (www.radio-ranch.com) to listen to award-winning commercials for inspiration. Notice how these commercials engage the listener. Also listen to Garrison Keillor's A Prairie Home Companion, which is broadcast on public radio. Clips from the show are found at http://prairiehome.publicradio.com. Pay particular attention to his signature piece, "The News from Lake Wobegon," as well as his "commercials" for Powdermilk Biscuits (a product of Keillor's imagination).

> Approaches to Radio Commercials

However you structure your radio script, remember to begin with an attention-grabbing opening. The lead-in must lure the listener into hearing what follows. Generally, it's a good idea to have an announcer drive home the key selling idea at the end. Think of the announcer as the voice of the advertiser; character voices in the rest of the spot should sound like genuine people or exaggerations of them.

One Voice

Make the voice interesting and relevant. Make the words exceptional. You might add music or sounds, or you might choose to let the voice "speak for itself."

The Ant-Stop Orthene Fire Ant Killer commercial, which you read a few pages ago, is an example of one-voice exposition, in which the announcer speaks directly to the listener. Another approach is one-voice internal dialog, which sounds like we're listening in on someone's private thoughts. Here are the opening lines of a commercial that uses one-voice internal dialog:

SFX:	SOUND OF WRITING.
WOMAN:	Dear Tom. I completely understand why you stood me up last night. You're too good for me. How could I ever expect to hang on to a guy like you?

The commercial goes on to describe what a loser Tom is. As the internal dialog continues, we learn Tom's former girlfriend is writing in lipstick on his windshield. The announcer finishes the spot with a pitch for Unocal 76, which gives customers the use of squeegees and soapy water.

Dialog

Two people talking. Sounds simple, doesn't it? But be careful. Some product categories don't lend themselves to a dialog format. When's the last time you chatted with someone about toilet paper or canned vegetables? It's likely that the dialog you create for such products will sound stilted and phony.

It's also easy to fall into the trap of having an expert talking to a naïf. The naïf says dumb things like, "Why isn't my uniform as white as yours?" and the expert responds with something along these lines: "Brand X detergent has a water-soluble bleaching agent that seeps through dirt to render fabrics brighter than ever!" The commercial closes with the naïf asking, "Gee, where can I buy Brand X detergent?" How do you make the dialog sound real while still sending a selling message? Use the dialog to set the stage, and let the announcer do the selling.

Multivoice

A number of voices speak, not to one another but to the listener. A commercial for AIDS awareness used a variety of voices to make young people aware of the number of misconceptions about the disease and its victims.

For this spot, college students were asked to speak candidly about their chances of contracting AIDS. The producers edited small sound bites from each of the participants:

VOICE 1:	It can't happen to me. . . .
VOICE 2:	There's no way he's got it.

VOICE 3:	You can't get it from a girl. . . .
VOICE 4:	Isn't there already a cure?
VOICE 5:	I know she doesn't have it. . . .
VOICE 6:	I just want to have fun.
VOICE 7:	But I'm not gay.
VOICE 8:	I hope it doesn't happen to me.

A message about AIDS was read by an announcer and appeared within the commercial.

Dramatization

A dramatization uses the structure of a play, with a beginning, a conflict, and a resolution. You can use sound effects and several voices to act out the story, or you can use a narrator to tell the entire story.

Sound Device

With this approach, a sound or sounds are used repeatedly or intermittently to make the main point. For example, in one ad you can hear someone trying to start a car. The engine goes, "EEEERRRRR . . . EEEERRRRR . . . EEEER-RRRR." As the person continues to try to start the car, it sounds weaker and weaker. "Eeeerrrrr . . . eeeerrrrr . . . eeeerrrrr." The sound of military taps fades in as the sound of the engine fades out. The battery finally dies. A voice-over announces that Sears is having a sale on DieHard batteries.

Sometimes music is used as the big idea for a commercial. For example, one spot opens to the sound of a man singing in the shower. His voice is dreadful—but he keeps singing and singing. You can't imagine what's going on until an announcer interrupts and asks, "Think this has gone on long enough? So do we. Take shorter showers and save water."

Vignette

A vignette is a series of short situations linked by a repeated device (for example, announcer line, musical bridge, or sound effect). After the first vignette makes the point, the ensuing situations need not be as long. An announcer usually wraps up the spot near the end, followed by a quick closing vignette. To illustrate, here's a portion of the commercial for George Schlatter's Comedy Club:

ANNCR:	Number 17. The chuckle.
SFX:	MAN CHUCKLING.
ANNCR:	Number 22. The giggle.
SFX:	WOMAN GIGGLING.
ANNCR:	Number 56. The snort.
SFX:	WOMAN SNORTING WHILE LAUGHING.
ANNCR:	Number 61. The nasal burst.
SFX:	MAN LAUGHING THROUGH HIS NOSE.

Interviews

With this approach, someone is interviewing someone or groups of people, somewhere—on a busy street, at the North Pole, in outer space. In one spot, the interview takes place under a house, where the interviewer talks to two termites as they casually chew up the wood subflooring.

Jingles

David Ogilvy said, "When you have nothing to say, sing it." Not everyone agrees with that, however. A catchy jingle can make a lasting impression in our minds. For example, there's a good chance you can sing the lyrics to "Oh, I wish I were an Oscar Mayer wiener . . ." and "Hot dogs, Armour hot dogs, what kind of kids eat Armour hot dogs?" Most copywriters are not lyricists or composers, so you'll probably want a professional songwriter to develop the jingle. But you'll need to supply the songwriter with your key selling point and the attitude you want to convey (upbeat, sexy, whimsical, and so on).

> Live versus Produced

Most national radio spots and a growing number of local spots are recorded in a digital format, ready to be aired. But some commercials are sent in script form and are either read live or recorded for airplay by a staff announcer. Other advertisers don't even furnish a script; instead, they send a fact sheet describing the major selling points and benefits of their product, service, or place of business. Which should you choose? Here's a general guide to what works and when.

- *Use a fact sheet when the radio station has a popular on-air personality.* Number the facts in descending order of importance, and you may get more than your paid minute's worth if the personality is having fun chatting about your product or place. A donut shop did just that. The shop sent a dozen donuts each morning to a local announcer who was known to love his food. Each morning, the announcer would lovingly describe every bite and rhapsodize on the flavor, texture, and so on. The spots ran during morning drive time, when people are most likely to buy donuts. The campaign was a tremendous success.

- *Only read a script live if you're using straight copy with no sound effects, music, or multiple speaking parts.* A problem with this approach is that many radio personalities are flippant by nature and can have too much fun being cynical or sarcastic with live copy. Therefore, use this approach primarily when you must make last-minute changes to your advertising: a store announcing an extended sale or a promotion that changes daily.

- *Use a live-recorded commercial when you want to be able to update copy regularly.* The advertiser records a musical introduction. At some point, the music "fades under" or is reduced in volume so that a local announcer can read copy over the music. At the end, the music swells to its conclusion, usually with a recorded closing line. Because the middle of the spot contains this "hole," this format is called a "live donut." While the music provides continuity for the entire campaign, the scripted inserts keep the ad up-to-date. The inserts must be timed so that they fit the hole in the music.

• *Use a produced commercial when your script calls for multiple speaking parts, sound effects, music, or any combination of these and when you want assurance that the quality of the spot will never waver.* You can imagine why many advertisers prefer this approach. Like a print ad that arrives ready to run, the produced radio commercial allows little room for human error once it leaves the advertiser. Some produced commercials allow a 5-second space at the end for the local announcer to voice a local tag (where to buy a product, when it goes on sale).

Most local radio stations provide basic production for free, but you may prefer to use a production house that specializes in a particular style. During production, the writer should be present to review and approve script adjustments and to work with the production staff on ways to enhance the spot. Some of the best commercials result from last-minute ideas in the studio. That's fine, as long as the essential message and strategy remain unchanged. For example, the slogan for Motel 6 came about through a fortuitous accident. After Tom Bodett finished his folksy monolog, there was still a smidgen of time left on the tape, so he ad-libbed, "We'll leave the light on for you."

> Radio Script Format

Like all copy, a radio script begins with a tag in the upper-left corner (see Figure 9-1). In this instance, you should indicate on the second line, after the timing, whether the spot is a fact sheet, is live announcer copy, or will be produced.

Because radio scripts typically go through many revisions before being produced, many writers also indicate the date the script was written or the script revision number to ensure that everyone is working with the same version.

All radio copy should be double-spaced to facilitate reading and should leave room for notes and alterations during production.

The designation for a sound effect is SFX. This is capitalized and underscored, along with the entire sound-effect direction, to alert the producer to the effect and its position within the script. For the same reason, all effects are entered on a separate line. If the effect should come in the middle of a line of dialog, use ellipses (. . .) to break from the first part of the line, drop to a new line for the SFX, and then continue the dialog on the following line with additional ellipses at the beginning to indicate resumption of the dialog.

Courtesy of Kathy Van Nostrand Leland.

Figure 9-1

Here's what an actual radio script looks like. This one also provides a wonderful example of how sounds can be used to bring an idea to life. Notice how the sound effects are capitalized and underscored for quick identification. Also notice how the spot wraps with a restatement of the theme line.

RENT.NET "Vampires" :60 Radio

SFX	<u>COFFIN CREAKS OPEN. SPOOKY MUSIC BEGINS TO PLAY, THEN FADES UNDER.</u>
VAMPIRE 1:	Hey! What are ya doing?! You know we can't go out in the daylight! Vampire Code 6!
VAMPIRE 2:	Relax! I'm just trying to find us a new apartment . . . Maybe a *nicer* one?!
SFX:	<u>DRIPPING FAUCET</u>
VAMPIRE 1:	I'm tellin' ya—this is the only place where the landlady would meet us *after dark!*
VAMPIRE 2	(sarcastically): Yeah! Crazy ol' bat!
VAMPIRE 1	(nervously): But anyway, you can't do this NOW! I mean, how you gonna get a newspaper out there in the sunlight! You can't go out there, man!
VAMPIRE 2:	Relax! I'm using rent.net!
SFX:	<u>MODEM DIALING IN</u>
VAMPIRE 1:	What?!
VAMPIRE 2	(exasperated): Have you been living in a cave? Rent.net! It's the most comprehensive rental guide on the net! We can search for an apartment right here online by city, number of bedrooms—we can even choose our price range and view photos and check out the apartment's amenities!
VAMPIRE 1:	Oh! Hey—do a search for a place that allows pets—you know those juicy little, uh, I mean cute little puppies!
VAMPIRE 2	(typing): You're sick man, really sick . . .
VAMPIRE 1:	Hey a vampire's gotta eat!
ANNCR:	Rent.net—the easiest way to find a new apartment in any city. Find your new home without leaving the . . . <u>(SFX: CREEPY APARTMENT NOISES)</u> . . . *comfort* of yours.

Names of speakers should be typed in capital letters. Note the abbreviation for announcer is ANNCR. Directions to the speaker should be typed in upper- and lowercase and enclosed in parentheses after the speaker's name. Dialog should be typed in upper- and lowercase.

Music is simply another type of sound effect and should be treated as such. If a commercial is to begin with music, which is then to fade under the speakers (play softly in the background), a direction might read like this:

SFX:	<u>HARP INSTRUMENTAL AND FADE UNDER.</u>
TIM:	I wanted to impress my girlfriend so I took her to this snooty restaurant. Everything was going great until . . .

If the music is to disappear at some point, you should indicate this through another sound-effect cue:

SFX:	MUSIC OUT.
TIM:	She told me she wanted to date my brother because he liked the same things she did. Greasy hamburgers . . . fries . . . not foie gras and caviar.
SFX:	FORK DROPS ON PLATE.

Often, especially if your commercial consists of a conversation between two or more people, you may want to wrap up the message by bringing in an authoritative announcer at the end. This is a good way to bring your audience back to earth (especially if you've been treating the subject with humor) and to reinforce what you want remembered about your message.

> Checklist for Radio Copy

- Is there one major premise?
- Is the structure appropriate for the message?
- Are voices, music, and sounds described clearly?
- If you used copyrighted music, is it essential, affordable, and available?
- Do music or sound effects help support the selling message?
- Is there sufficient time for comfortable, believable delivery of the lines?
- Is there time for all sound effects and musical bridges?
- Does the commercial time correctly?
- Is brand recognition achieved through mention of the brand, music, or sounds that trigger awareness?

Radio is fun and challenging. As with all advertising copy, it isn't always easy to find the best solution. But when you hear your commercial in finished form, you'll know if it's right. A well-written, well-produced radio spot can have a tremendous effect on its target audience.

> Suggested Activities

1. Using the campaign theme from your print ads, write a radio commercial for the same product or service. Write it as if it were to be produced. Note as you are doing this that merely paraphrasing the text from a print ad may not work because of the essential differences between the media. What sort of voices will work best for your message? What will be the appropriate tone? These are but a few of the new issues you need to consider.

2. Visit a local business and interview the person in charge. Devise a creative strategy for this business, indicating how radio might be used. Cover approaches, target audience, mood, and expected results. Then write two or three radio spots based on your strategy and tie them together using a specific theme or device.

3. Listen to a different radio station every day for the next week. Make mental notes of the types of commercials you hear on each station. What did you learn?

4. Practice your editing skills. Take a print ad from this book and use the information to create a 30-second radio commercial.

Tom Bodett Sells Affordability and Comfort for Motel 6

Motel 6 helped define the budget motel sector when it opened its first property in Santa Barbara, California, in 1962. Its "no-frills" concept offered a cheap alternative to the pricey full-service hotels that then dominated the market. However, in 1980 occupancy rates for Motel 6 began to decline at an average of nearly 2 percentage points per year. Finally, in 1986, with no end to the decline in sight, the company set out to overhaul its business. It turned for help to the Richards Group to reverse the occupancy decline, boost revenue, and regain share.

Richards Group representatives nosed around the properties, talked to a few customers, and found a partial reason for the decline—the product itself. It was woefully out of step with the modern traveler. There were no phones in the rooms. There were televisions, but you had to pay to watch. The Richards Group recommended putting advertising on hold (imagine an agency saying that) and fixing these problems. Motel 6 agreed, and it was done.

Meanwhile, the Richards Group continued its dialog with consumers, and a curious thing happened. In focus groups with people who had stayed at Motel 6, no one mentioned the brand when they were asked where they had stayed. Only after probing did someone finally step forward and admit having stayed at Motel 6; then everyone in the group acknowledged a stay.

Why had they held back? Simply because they feared being perceived as cheap for selecting Motel 6. What they really felt was that they were frugal, even virtuous. And they were proud of it.

Pride in frugality. There it was. So simple, but so hidden from view. This insight became the foundation of the Richards Group Spherical brand-development process, where positioning, personality, and affiliation are written in stone. The positioning statement became: "To frugal people, Motel 6 is the comfortable place to stay that's always the lowest price of any national chain." The personality for the brand was defined as follows: "Honest. Simple. Friendly and fun. Humble. Unpretentious. Good-humored and commonsensical." And affiliation was described as follows: "People who stay at Motel 6 are solid citizens with enough common sense not to throw away their hard-earned money. Regardless of how much money they make, they take pride in finding ways to save a buck."

Courtesy of Motel 6 and the Richards Group.

From that day forward, these brand strategies have driven more than the communication of Motel 6; they have driven critical business strategies. Spherical branding drives price. The lowest price is unassailable territory for Motel 6. Only one can be the lowest. Motel 6 adjusts its price market by market, but it is always the lowest price of any national chain. It also drives renovation strategy because of the promise of a clean, comfortable room. Motel 6 spent $600 million from 1993 to 1998 in renovations to make certain this promise is not an empty one.

Spherical branding also drives the communication strategy. Tom Bodett, an obscure carpenter from Homer, Alaska, and occasional commentator on National Public Radio, became the poster boy for frugality. Bodett took the new Motel 6 to the airwaves in 1987, granting permission to stay at Motel 6 and even to brag about your "smart choice."

Spherical branding paid an enormous media dividend, too. As one sage said, no one ever arrives at Motel 6 by air. They are in their car, which led the agency to radio. So while the competition went head-to-head in television, Motel 6 underspent and outflanked them.

Today, no matter where you run into Motel 6, from listening to its commercials to walking into the lobby, you sense the same message, the same personality. Try it. Call Motel 6 and listen to the on-hold message. Check out its Click 6 Web bargains. Or better yet, stay there and enjoy a wake-up call.

The Richards Group has won numerous awards for its work. *Advertising Age* magazine picked the Motel 6 campaign as one of the 100 best of the 20th century. In 2009, Motel 6 won the grand prize from the Radio Mercury Awards for the "DVD" radio spot. Perhaps the most meaningful award is the dramatic rise in Motel 6 revenues, which are now more than three times their 1986 level.

Here is a small sample of how Bodett and the Richards Group work their magic to create an honest, good-humored, and commonsensical personality for Motel 6:

Motel 6 "DVD" :60 radio

TOM:	Hi. Tom Bodett for Motel 6 here, with a DVD edition of my latest commercial. It's basically the same as my other commercials, just with one of those fancy 'Director Commentary' features. Anyway . . . for a clean, comfortable room for the lowest price of any national chain, Motel 6 is the only place to . . . (Fades under)
DIRECTOR:	Okay, well, what I was going for in this scene was a sense of childlike innocence, with a subtext of man's eternal struggle against ennui and stuff. I think I got it.
TOM:	(Fades up) . . . plus free local calls, and most locations . . . (dips under)
DIRECTOR:	Funny story here—I planned to use a swing and tilt camera for that line, but our budget was cut. So I improvised with a shoebox and two pounds of bacon.
TOM:	It's like I always say . . .

DIRECTOR:	Love that.
TOM:	. . . life is a bowl of cherries . . .
DIRECTOR	Hate that.
TOM:	. . . and happiness is friendly, courteous service.
DIRECTOR:	Producers made me say that.
TOM:	I'm Tom Bodett for Motel 6, and we'll leave the light on for you.
DIRECTOR:	I was going to go for a darker ending, something about not leaving the light on, but it didn't test well. . . .

Motel 6 "Pets" :60 radio

| TOM: | Hi, Tom Bodett here. I've always wondered what exactly dogs are dreaming about when they're moving their paws and grunting in their sleep. Some say that the dream state lets the soul slip free of its earthbound shell to resume a past life. That maybe Buster harbors the reincarnated spirit of Constantine the Eleventh, last of the Byzantine emperors, who each night gallops once again through the rubble, tears of rage falling from one eye, tears of sorrow from the other, as the ancient walls are breached. Personally, I'm betting dogs are just dreaming about table scraps or chasing the neighbor's cat. Something to contemplate as you watch your dog's paws twitch in your room at Motel 6, where they have the lowest price of any national chain, and where pets are always welcome. I'm Tom Bodett for Motel 6, and we'll leave the light on for you and your best friend Buster . . . the Eleventh. |
| ANNCR: | Motel 6. An Accor Hotel. |

Motel 6 "Business Talk" :60 radio

| TOM: | Hi, Tom Bodett for Motel 6, with a word for business travelers.
Seems business has its own language these days, full of buzzwords.
Like the word "buzzword" or "net-net." And after a day spent white-boarding a matrix of action items and deliverables, it's nice to know that you can always outsource your accommodation needs to the nearest Motel 6. You'll get a clean, comfortable room for the lowest price, net-net, of any national chain. Plus data-ports and free local calls in case you tabled your discussion and need to reconvene offline. So you can think of Motel 6 as your total business travel solution provider, vis-à-vis cost-effective lodging alternatives for Q-1 through Q-4. I think. Just call 1-800-4-MOTEL-6 or visit motel6.com. I'm Tom Bodett for Motel 6, and we'll maintain the lighting device in its current state of illumination for you. |
| ANNCR: | Motel 6. An Accor Hotel. |

10

TELEVISION
THE POWER OF SIGHT, SOUND, AND MOTION

In Alfred Hitchcock's classic 1959 thriller *North by Northwest,* there's a 14-minute scene that's a self-contained movie within a movie. Using the barest amount of dialog, the 14 minutes elapse with a story made unmistakably clear through the careful actions, sounds, camera angles, and editing of the legendary director. It goes something like this:

1. We open on an extreme long shot, aerial view, of the middle of nowhere: a dusty crossroads on the prairie. A bus rolls into the frame, stops, deposits a passenger, and drives off.

2. We cut to a medium shot of our hero, Thornhill, who has just left the bus. In the previous scene, we learned he was to travel to this spot alone and wait for a man named Kaplan. He looks around.

3. Through a succession of crosscuts between Thornhill and point-of-view shots showing what he's seeing, we realize his frustration that no one is in sight.

4. We cut back and forth as he watches, then we see what he's watching: cars whizzing by. No Kaplan.

5. Soon he looks toward the camera. We cut to what he sees: a long shot of a car just coming out of a dirt road onto the main highway across from where he's standing.

6. The car drops off a man and heads back where it came from.

7. Thornhill stares at the man.

8. The man halfheartedly stares at Thornhill.

9. Thornhill begins crossing the road toward the man as the camera dolly moves to parallel his movement.

10. We cut to what Thornhill sees as he crosses: The camera moves closer and closer to the stranger.

Once Thornhill discovers the man isn't Kaplan, he's left alone again as the man boards an arriving bus. The rest of the scene takes us through a harrowing episode in which a crop-dusting airplane begins firing shots and spraying insecticide at Thornhill. The scene culminates in a fiery crash when the out-of-control plane smashes into an oil truck.

What does all this have to do with writing TV commercials? Everything. Although the scene runs for about 14 minutes and your commercial will probably run no more than 30 seconds, one thing both have in common is the use of film "language" to tell a story. Rent *North by Northwest* and watch the scene (watch the whole film; it's terrific) after reading the visual description at the beginning of this chapter. You'll begin to see why the director chose those shots and how they are connected to one another to heighten the effect of the story. In a commercial, you can do the same.

> Combining Sight, Sound, and Motion

Kevin Roberts, worldwide CEO of Saatchi & Saatchi Ideas Company, coined a new word, "sisomo," which captures the powerful effect of combining sight, sound, and motion on the screen. Roberts believes sisomo is the way to engage people as they watch messages, whether on a traditional TV set, a giant stadium screen, or a 1-inch cell phone screen.

Keep sight, sound, and motion in mind as you develop your ideas for commercials. If you have a static visual, you probably have an idea for a print ad, not a TV spot. And if your idea requires a lot of copy, you probably have the makings of a radio spot or print ad. As you begin to work on ideas for television, George Felton suggests you ask yourself, "What part of [the] product story moves? What motion is inherent in my client's product? Does it go around like a can opener, splash through water like a bike, squirt like a tube of toothpaste, what?"[1]

The visual of beer being poured into a glass is typical imagery for a beer commercial. But a Super Bowl XL commercial for Budweiser made it captivating by showing football fans holding up stadium cards to form the imagery of a bottle of Budweiser and an empty glass. As the football fans hold their cards on cue, the beer is poured from the bottle, which is on one side of the stadium, and into the glass, on the opposite side. The fans hold up new cards and the beer "disappears" from the glass, as if someone is drinking it. When the glass finally empties, the stadium crowd gives a satisfied, "AHHHH!" The idea for "The Wave" was something that the DDB Chicago creative team, Steve Bougdanos and Patrick Knoll, thought of 8 years earlier. However, the

[1] George Felton, *Advertising Concept and Copy* (New York: W. W. Norton, 2006), p. 111.

computer graphics weren't advanced enough to make it look real. The lesson? Hang on to your good ideas.

Stories are natural ways to give your commercial movement. Here's how the Bougdanos–Knoll team told a story titled "American Dream." The commercial opens on a paddock as a Clydesdale colt frolics with two fully grown Clydesdales. After a few moments, the commercial dissolves to a long shot of the interior of the barn and we watch the colt trot inside. The camera follows the colt as he explores the barn. The commercial then dissolves to a medium shot of the Budweiser wagon, which looks almost like a sacred object as a beam of sunlight shines on it. Next we see a close-up of the colt looking at a photo of the Clydesdale team pulling the legendary wagon. As the colt nuzzles the framed photo, we see his reflection superimposed on the image of the Clydesdale team. The camera follows the colt as he walks away. Then, as if through the eyes of the colt, the camera zooms inside the opening of a harness. The colt slips his head inside the harness, which is gigantic on him. Next we see the determination of the colt as he tries to pull the wagon. The commercial dissolves to a long shot of adult Clydesdales, who are watching from outside the barn door. It dissolves back to a close-up of one of the wagon wheels, which begins to move a few inches at first, and then effortlessly. As the wagon moves across the screen we see two adult Clydesdales are pushing it from behind. Cut to a man holding a Dalmatian, who has witnessed the whole thing. The man says to the dog, "I won't tell if you don't." Dissolve to a frame of the Budweiser logo and message, "Please drink responsibly." The "American Dream" was just 30 seconds long and had only six spoken words, but it told a big story through masterful writing, filming, and direction.

Another spot you probably recognize from the Bougdanos-Knoll team is Bud Light's "Magic Fridge" commercial, in which a young, 20-something guy tries to hide his refrigerator that's packed with Bud Light by pulling a lever to make the refrigerator revolve to the other side of the wall. The punch line? The refrigerator revolves to the neighboring apartment, which is filled with other 20-something guys who worship the "Magic Fridge."

The approaches to "The Wave," "American Dream," and "Magic Fridge" are different from one another, but each relies on striking visuals and movement to engage the audience. Notice, too, how there's no mistaking the brand in any of these commercials.

> Preparing to Write Ads for Television

For the copywriter–art director team, it's especially important to remember this: Although the bag of computer-generated, interactive, digital tricks is growing almost daily, be careful. If it furthers the strategy, use it. If it doesn't, don't. When you have no more than 30 seconds to make an impression, strategy is where the TV commercial begins.

Watching TV Commercials with a Critical Eye and Ear

If you think about it, you'll probably realize that the commercials you remember are uncommon. What makes you forget most commercials, and what makes you remember those rare gems? Sit down in front of the television and start watching commercials. Watch at least 10. For each commercial, jot down answers to the following questions:

1. What was the single central message or idea?
2. What was the value of the opening shot with respect to that idea?
3. Did you become involved with the commercial? If so, at what point did it happen?
4. To what extent did the pictures, as opposed to the words, tell the story?
5. Were the words redundant, or did they add something? What did they add?
6. Were interesting, exciting, complicated, beautiful visuals on screen long enough for complete understanding or appreciation? Were dull, static visuals on too long? How would you make them better?
7. Was the story an irrelevant attention getter, or was the product an integral part of the story?
8. Did you enjoy the story? Did you believe it or find some other value in it? Or was it unrelated to the product and just there to make you watch?
9. Afterward, could you say why you should care about the product or service in a sentence?

Getting Your Idea on Paper

As you write your commercial, keep in mind the criteria for creativity. Your commercial should be unexpected, relevant, and persuasive. Here are some tips.

- *Start by brainstorming how your idea can be communicated visually.* What's the key visual element that will attract—and keep—the viewer's attention? Is there a way to make that visual idea move? What sounds will enhance that visual? A commercial for Diet Pepsi MAX needed to communicate that it gives people a boost. To bring this idea to life, agency BBDO NY showed visuals of people nodding off at inopportune times and then waking up after they drink the caffeine and ginseng-infused soft drink.
- *Now take that idea and write a narrative.* The Diet Pepsi Max narrative went along these lines, "Throughout this spot, groups of people are falling asleep, but then their heads snap back up—just like when you nod off on a plane. The rest of the people are alert and are drinking Diet Pepsi Max. It's all set to Haddaway's 'What is Love?' We open on a couple of ranchers in the midst of a herd of cattle. They are both nodding off. Cut to a packed elevator. The doors open and a group of people nod off in unison.

> The other people are alert and have Diet Pepsi Max. Cut to a platform of a commuter rail. . . ."

- *Once you're happy with the scenario, put it in script form.* Everything on the left side is video, or what we will see. Everything on the right side is audio, or what we will hear. (See Figure 10-1, and the instructions for writing a script later in this chapter.)

Bell Helmets "Reason" :30 TV

1. (GRAINY FOOTAGE THROUGHOUT) LS CAR CRASHING ON TRACK.	SFX: SOFT WHISTLING THROUGHOUT. NO OTHER NOISES.
2. LS GUY WEARING HELMET FLIPPING OFF BIKE.	
3. TITLE (WHITE ON BLACK): "HUMANS ARE THE ONLY SPECIES"	
4. LS GUY IN HELMET FLYING THROUGH THE AIR AS HE LEAVES BIKE.	
5. TITLE (WHITE ON BLACK): "WITH THE ABILITY TO REASON"	
6. LS SHOTS OF VARIOUS OTHER CRASH SITUATIONS.	
7. TITLE (WHITE ON BLACK): "AND SOMETIMES"	
8. GUY CRASHES BIKE FLIPPING OVER IN MIDAIR IN THE PROCESS.	
9. TITLE (WHITE ON BLACK): "THEY EVEN USE IT."	
10. CUT TO FULL SCREEN BELL HELMETS LOGO.	ANNCR (VO): Bell Helmets.
11. CUT TO REVOLVING "BRAIN." HELMET WRAPS AROUND IT.	SFX: WHOOSH OF HELMET COVERING HEAD, CHIN STRAP LOCKING TIGHT
12. CUT TO TITLE: "COURAGE FOR YOUR HEAD."	ANNCR (VO): Courage for your head.

Courtesy of Bell Sports, Inc.

Figure 10-1

Note that it's more what you see than what you hear in this script. And rightly so. This is television, where most good commercial ideas begin with the pictures, adding words and sounds to fortify the visual images. Each number on the left moves the visual story forward—title shots included. The audio on the right simply calls for a soft, easy whistling, which makes a surprising contrast to the mayhem on the screen. At the all-important close, the theme line literally wraps things up with a startling graphic along with sounds that bring the whole idea of "courage for your head" to a memorable finale.

- *Read the script aloud.* Check for timing, clarity, and continuity. Do the words and pictures follow a logical sequence? Check for product identity. Is the product buried by needless overproduction or story exposition? Are there any scenes that will be difficult or too cost prohibitive to shoot? Have you kept your story to one major point?

  One of the scenes in the Diet Pepsi Max narrative depicted a crowd at a Star Trek convention nodding off. Rather than pay for the rights to use Star Trek imagery, the script was revised to show a convention without any brand references.

- *Revise. Revise. Revise.* How well does the opening shot command the attention of the viewer? How much does the opening relate to the main idea of the message? How well does the closing reinforce the main idea and drive home the point? How much time is spent on the product? How visual is the idea? Try telling the story in pictures only, leaving out the words, and see whether it still makes sense.

  The original script for the Diet Pepsi Max commercial opened on a couple of ranchers. Since this was going to air during the Super Bowl, it was much more relevant to open on Joe Buck and Troy Aikman in the commentator's booth and show Buck nodding off as Aikman talks to football fans.

- *Finalize.* Once you have a script, prepare your storyboard (see Figure 10-2 for an example).

> Formats for TV Commercials

As with other types of advertising, the best way to begin thinking about a TV commercial is to immerse yourself in facts and ideas about the product. Only then do you start writing. If nothing happens, these suggestions can jump-start the process:

Demonstration Television. A demonstration can show what the product can do better than any other visual. Here are some examples:

- *Product in use:* A man swipes shoe polish on his handkerchief and cleans it by shaking it in a cocktail shaker filled with ice and a bit of brand X laundry detergent.
- *Before and after:* A guy who looks to be about 100 years old shampoos some coloring into his hair. Presto! He's 35. (OK, we admit we're exaggerating a bit, but you get the idea.)
- *Side by side:* Two identical battery-operated toys are entertaining the viewer. One of the toys dies, and the toy with brand X batteries keeps working.

Product as Star. A bulldog sizes up a Mini automobile. After the stare down, the dog circles to the rear of the car and starts sniffing the tailpipe. Graphic: "Let's get acquainted." Tagline: "Mini. Let's motor."

Figure 10-2
The Chick-fil-A cows convinced many people to "eat mor chikin" by painting messages on billboards (see Chapter 5). Now they're creating their own TV commercials!

CLIENT: CHICK-FIL-A
JOB: :30 TV
TITLE: "OVERHEAD"

Video		Audio
OPEN ON A SHOT OF A GIANT PAIR OF BOOTS. TYPE THAT SAYS "LEATHER BOOT-O-RAMA" SPINS ONTO SCREEN OVER IMAGE. CUT TO STATIC.		TWANGY MUSIC UNDER VO: The finest leather boots are at Big Bob's... SFX: (STATIC AND TV EMERGENCY SOUNDS INTERRUPT VO.)
CUT TO "COW TV" CARD. MORE STATIC.		SFX: (BARNYARD SOUNDS. COWS MOOING. CHICKENS SQUAWKING. COW HOOVES MOVING TRANSPARENCIES ON OVERHEAD PROJECTOR.)
CUT TO INTERIOR OF BARN. OVERHEAD PROJECTOR IS PROJECTING HEADLINE ON BARN WALL. IT SAYS "KNOW YER FOOD GROOPS."		
THAT CARD IS REMOVED AND REPLACED BY ANOTHER THAT READS, "FIG. 1 FOOD PYRUMID". UNDER THE HEADING IS A TRIANGLE THAT HAS A DRAWING OF A CHICKEN WITH THE WORD "CHIKIN" UNDER IT.		

Courtesy of Chick-fil-A.

Vignette. Several brief episodes are threaded together to repeatedly drive home the same point. Each episode usually involves different people at different places, but they all say something relevant to the product story. For example, a spot for ESPN shows people watching television and shouting instructions at their TV sets. "Get out of the crease!" a woman screams. "Basketball 101," says a man. "Tackle somebody!" yells another fan. Tagline: "Without sports, there'd be no one to coach."

Slice of Life. The star of the commercial has a problem, and brand X is the solution. A Swedish commercial shows beautiful people at a wedding. The bride and groom walk up a staircase and wave goodbye to their wedding

Figure 10-2 (continued)

Courtesy of Chick-fil-A.

COW HOOVES SLIDE THE IMAGE UP TO REVEAL THE WORD "DESSURT" UNDER "CHIKIN".

COW THEN WALKS IN FRONT OF PROJECTOR AND KNOCKS IT OVER.

SFX: (SOUND OF COW KNOCKING OVER THE PROJECTOR THEN STATIC.)

PICTURE COMES BACK UP. IT IS THE OVERHEAD PROJECTOR AGAIN. A COW IS SITTING ON GROUND JUST UNDER THE PROJECTION ON THE WALL. THE WORDS "EAT MOR CHIKIN" ARE PROJECTED ON THE WALL.

SFX: (BARN NOISES. COWS MOOING. CHICKENS SQUAWKING.)

CUT TO ANIMATED CHICK-FIL-A LOGO

SFX: (RUBBER BAND SOUNDS AS LOGO ANIMATES ONTO SCREEN.)

guests. The guests wave back, and some blow kisses. The groom lifts the bride to carry her over the threshold and . . . THUD! The bride's head hits the doorway as the groom tries to carry her through, and he drops her. The camera cuts to a close-up of two pills being plopped into water. The groom drinks the remedy, and a voice-over says, "Headaches can suddenly appear. Treo gives quick and effective relief."

Presenters.   Someone looks into the camera and tells you why you should buy the product. It could be an expert, such as a nurse who recommends a certain brand of painkiller. Or it could be someone associated with the company, such as a CEO. Or a celebrity may look cool using your product (or any product, for that matter—see Chapter 1 for guidelines on using celebrities). Or the presenter could be an animated or animal character, such as the M&M characters or the Chick-fil-A cows.

Testimonials. "I use this product. So should you." Testimonials must be true and must be based on real experiences of real people. Professional golfer Nancy Lopez seems credible when she endorses Synvisc, a treatment for osteoarthritis (knee pain).

Stories. Think of commercials as 30-second TV shows. For example, in one ad, a boy spots an attractive girl in class. He passes her a note that reads, "I love you. Do you love me?" There are two boxes ("Yes" and "No") for her to check off her answer. The girl looks at him, scribbles her answer, and passes the note back. He opens it. The answer is no! He hangs his head. When he looks up, he spots another cute girl. He erases the no and passes her the note. The tagline appears on the screen: "You're never too young to start recycling. Weyerhaeuser."

> Camera Shots, Camera Moves, and Transitions

Camera Shots

How many shots should you use in 30 seconds? It all depends on the story you want to tell and the best way to tell it. Each shot, however, should fulfill a specific need. Here are the basic shots to know.

Extreme Close-up (ECU). In this shot, you move as close as you can and still show what needs showing: part of a face, a detail on a product. The ECU permits a bigger-than-life glimpse that can be used to dramatic advantage to further your story.

Close-up (CU). In this shot, a face fills the screen, or a product stands tall, commanding your attention. Early moviemakers such as D. W. Griffith invented this way of magnifying the emotional communication of the moving image, partly to compensate for the absence of sound. It's still a powerful way to provide visual emphasis. The CU contains no distractions; it shows only what you want the viewer to see. When we're this close, however, we rarely know where the action is taking place. So the choice of a CU or a wider shot depends on the purpose of the shot.

Medium Shot (MS). A typical MS shows two people, from the waist up, engaged in dialog (also called a 2-shot, because it covers two people). In this shot, one can identify location to some degree, making it an ideal compromise in framing action. When a CU reveals too little and a long shot is too broad, the answer usually lies somewhere between.

Long Shot (LS). Also known as an establishing shot, the LS broadly covers an area, revealing instantly where we are—flying in the clouds, working in the kitchen, exercising in the gym. Use an LS to open a commercial if your audience needs to know where it's taking place from the start. Or start with a CU to purposely hide the location until later. Again, it depends on the story you want to tell.

Camera Moves

Zoom In/Out (Dolly In/Out).   This involves a movement toward or from the subject. In a zoom, the lens revolves to bring the image closer or to move it farther away. In a dolly, the camera moves forward or backward.

A zoom is limited by the range of the lens, whereas a dolly is limited only by the imagination. Use either term in your script or storyboard and allow the director to make the final decision.

Pan R/L (Truck R/L).   This involves a movement to the right or left. In a pan, the camera turns to one side or the other or follows a moving object as it travels across the screen. In a trucking shot, the camera rolls sideways to follow or keep alongside the action—creating quite a different perspective than that of the pan.

Tilt U/D (Boom or Crane Shot).   In a tilt, the camera "looks" up or down—like a vertical version of the pan. In a boom or crane shot, the entire camera and cinematographer are hydraulically raised or lowered while film or tape rolls. A famous boom shot is *Gone With the Wind*'s dramatic pullback as Scarlett O'Hara wanders aimlessly through rows of wounded soldiers at the Atlanta train depot. The camera finds her, swoops majestically upward to suggest her insignificance amid the thousands of casualties, and then comes to rest on a tattered Confederate flag. How many words do you think would be necessary to adequately relate what this single shot communicates?

Transitions

Like camera moves, transitions carry you from one point of action to another but usually in less time. When you have only 30 seconds, timing is critical.

Cut.   The cut is the most basic transition and one you should rely on. A cut is an instantaneous change from one shot to another—for example, from a CU to an MS. One second we're seeing a CU, and then suddenly we "cut" to an MS. It's essential that the two shots make visual sense when run together and that they carry the action forward with purpose.

Dissolve.   The dissolve is a softer transition in which the first image gradually becomes more transparent as a second image, exactly behind the first, becomes more opaque. Stopping mid-dissolve results in a shot in which neither image is dominant. A dissolve can suggest the passage of time, freeing the writer to skip chunks of time in a sequence to focus on the most important elements. You don't want to watch a woman washing her hair for 5 minutes (impossible in 30 seconds), so you dissolve from her shampooing to her putting the final touches on her hairstyle. You can also use dissolves throughout a commercial to create a softer mood or to connect a series of shots unrelated in time and space yet important in the telling of the story. (See the discussion of compilation cutting later in this chapter.)

Fade. A fade is a dissolve that goes or comes from an image or title to black or white. This is the legendary "fade to black."

> Editing for Continuity

Editing, which should begin with the writing of the commercial script, can accomplish a number of things. It can condense time, extend time, or jumble time. To condense time, you might show a man unable to sleep at night, dissolve to him sleeping soundly, and then dissolve to the reason his sleep habits are better—the product. To extend time, you might show a speeding train approaching a car, cut to the driver's frenzied expression, cut back to the train, cut back to the driver attempting to move out of the way, back to the train, and so on. Trains move fast, and people in the path of trains don't linger, but extending the action makes the sequence more dramatic and involving to viewers. To jumble time, you might cut from present to past in a flashback or even "flash forward" to an imagined scene in the future.

Methods of Cutting

Compilation Cutting. In this type of editing, the storytelling depends on the narration, usually voiced over the action, and each shot merely illustrates what is being said. The shots may be somewhat unrelated to one another, may occur in different places, or may consist of a series of different people or objects shot in similar fashion.

Continuity Cutting. Here, the storytelling depends on matching consecutive scenes without a narrator to explain what is happening. Action flows from one shot to the next. Various angles and cutaways may not even be part of the previous shot. For example, a conversation between two people may consist of a medium shot, several close-ups of each speaker, another 2-shot, and a cutaway to something happening elsewhere in the building that is related to the action within the room.

Crosscutting. Crosscutting combines two or more parallel actions in an alternating pattern. The actions may occur at the same time but in different places—as when we see a farmer driving a tractor, cut to his wife preparing dinner, cut back to the farmer, and cut again to the wife. The actions may also occur at different times in different places—as when scenes of a man enjoying a vigorous shower are intercut with shots of the same man at various times during the day to suggest that using the right soap helps him feel fresh for hours.

Crosscutting may also be used to suggest details of an action that occurs at one time in one place. For example, he runs toward her, she runs toward him, again he runs toward her, again she runs toward him, until—at last—we see both of them in one shot about to run into each other's arms. Their embrace is somehow more personal to us precisely because we've been watching their longing gazes for most of the commercial.

In one beer commercial, crosscutting makes us as thirsty as the man in the story. A bartender reaches for a frosty mug. A man leaves his office. The bartender begins to draw a draft. The man steps out of his building onto a busy street. The bartender has the mug almost topped off. The man walks down the street. The mug is filled. The man enters the bar. The bartender slides the draft down the polished bar top. The man reaches out and catches it just in time.

Point of View

Subjective versus Objective.   Although you won't always have to specify point of view, doing so often helps others understand your idea. Essentially, point of view is either objective or subjective. In the objective point of view (objective camera), the camera records the action from the viewpoint of an observer not involved in the action. Those on camera never look directly into the lens because this would destroy the objective relationship between them and the viewer.

In the subjective point of view (subjective camera), the camera involves the viewer in the action by representing the point of view of a person in the scene. An actor rages at the camera; we know he's angry, not with us but at the guy who just punched him out in the previous shot. The camera itself becomes the punch-happy guy. In an experiment in subjective camera, a late 1940s feature film used this point of view exclusively. The main character was rarely seen, unless he happened to walk by a mirror. Punches were thrown at the camera and were usually followed by a blackout. A hand would reach from the camera to grab someone. The film was probably too odd for most tastes, but it did show the power of subjective camera.

Camera Angle.   An eye-level camera angle presents a view as seen by most of us. A high-angle shot, looking down on the action, may be chosen because (1) it's the best way to say we're on, say, a football field; (2) it's a way to see something you couldn't see yourself, such as overhead shots of dance formations; or (3) it adds a psychological dimension to the story (looking down on something means we think little of it, whereas looking up means we are in awe of it). Low-angle shots can add importance to a product. High-angle shots can make competitors seem somehow diminished.

> Music and Sound Effects

What would the movie *Jaws* be without the repetition of the two-note motif that speeds up, letting the audience know danger is lurking even though they're seeing a tranquil beach scene? What would *Psycho* be like without its soundtrack? Or *Star Wars?* Or any movie or TV show, for that matter? The same is true for TV commercials. Music and sound effects add meaning and texture to the story being told on the screen.

Music

To illustrate the great taste of Pepsi, a commercial features a Coca-Cola delivery guy stocking a convenience store cooler. After he fills the cooler with Coca-Cola cans, he looks around to see if anyone's watching, then sneaks a can of Pepsi from the nearby Pepsi cooler. As he grabs the can, hundreds of cans come tumbling out of the case, prompting a crowd to gather around to see what the commotion is all about. Hank Williams' "Cheatin' Heart" plays throughout. Here, a popular song helps narrate the story perfectly.

Sometimes you'll need to create music for your commercial. A spot for Cheer laundry detergent opens on a couple talking to one another on the telephone. After the woman tells her boyfriend when her flight arrives, she asks, "Hey, do you ever wear that black sweater I gave you?" He gives the perfect response, "Like every time I miss you." She's delighted: "It must be gray by now." He answers, dutifully, "So gray." She has an idea: "Wear it tonight." He's dismayed. "Tonight?" As soon as he hangs up, he removes the sweater from the gift box and washes and rewashes it in an attempt to make it gray. As the action is taking place, we hear the lyrics, "Always thinking about you, 'cause a love like this won't fade away. . . ." Meantime, it turns out that the man is washing the sweater in Cheer, which "helps keep black from fading." The doorbell rings. As he heads to answer the door, the words "Dirt goes. Color stays. (Even black.)" are superimposed on the screen.

People loved the music and began asking for copies of it. One woman even wanted to play it at her wedding. But there was a slight problem; there was no such song. The lyrics were originally a grand total of about 16 seconds and were written by a Leo Burnett copywriter just for the commercial. When Procter & Gamble, the parent company of Cheer, started receiving e-mails and phone calls requesting the song, they asked the writer and production house to create a 4-minute version. With the full version of the song on hand, Procter & Gamble produced an e-mail message with an embedded MP3 file that consumers could download or burn to a CD. The commercial was supplemented with words superimposed on the screen directing them to the Cheer website to hear the full song. Copies of the CD were also sent to radio stations, and within weeks there were 580 broadcasts on stations with an estimated reach of 4 million listeners.[2]

As the Cheer commercial illustrates, music can help put viewers in a right state of mind. It can make them feel romantic, relaxed, filled with fear. Sometimes playing music with opposite emotions can make your message even more effective. For example, a powerful commercial that addresses the problem of spousal abuse shows images of battered women while the song "Stand by Your Man" plays in the background. The irony of the song helps illustrate the absurdity of staying with an abusive partner.

Music can also help your brand stick in consumers' minds.

---

[2] Adapted from Stuart Elliott, "Procter & Gamble's Hit Song," *New York Times,* 3 March 2003.

Sound Effects

Sound effects can help reinforce your message and help paint the scenery. A Pepsi commercial opens with a mysterious mechanical sound. It turns out that a guy, desperate for a Pepsi, keeps trying to feed his dollar into a vending machine that keeps sucking in the money, then spitting it right back out. The guy keeps trying, from dawn until dusk, as Ricky Nelson's "Lonesome Town" plays, adding another layer of ambiance to the commercial.

Voice-over

A voice-over (VO), where someone speaks but isn't seen, can give the final sales pitch or help narrate the entire spot. A classic commercial for Dawn dish detergent shows an oil-covered duck being washed at a wildlife-rescue center as a woman narrates the story: "If this bird could talk, she'd tell you how Dawn saved her life."

A voice-over can emphasize the message that appears on the screen by reading it aloud exactly as it appears on the screen. Note that "SUPER" indicates words to be superimposed over the action on the screen and "TITLE" indicates words to appear on the screen against a solid background.

A recent commercial for Dawn dish detergent doesn't use a voice-over at all. Words superimposed on the screen tell of Dawn's wildlife rescue efforts as Joe Purdy's "Wash Away" plays throughout. The commercial closes with a message on how viewers can help save wildlife.

> Getting It on Paper: The TV Script

Here's how the TV script guides readers through the idea.

Everything on the left side is video, or what we will see. Everything on the right side is audio, or what we will hear. The audio and video are aligned so that we know how they relate to each other. Scenes are numbered down the left side of the page to guide us through the action. The words of the titles appear exactly as they will in the finished commercial.

As in radio, use SFX to denote music and other sounds. Underline all SFX directions for clarity. Specify VO before dialog when the words are to be "voiced over" as opposed to spoken on camera. VO lines are usually recorded after footage is shot. They can also help others understand your concept in script or storyboard form.

> Making It Clear: The TV Storyboard

A storyboard gives more detail than a script and helps the client, producer, director, and postproduction crew understand the spot more clearly. Pictures of key scenes help tell the story from beginning to end. Notice in Figure 10-2 (pp. 214 and 215) that the major scenes are in the center, with video instructions on the left, and audio on the right. Some agencies prefer to format storyboards with scenes on the left and audio and video instructions on the right. Others follow a format where the audio appears under each frame.

> TV Production

Once the client approves a commercial for production, the agency normally seeks competitive bids from a number of sources. A copy of the storyboard is sent as the basis for the bid, along with production notes that cover all aspects of the commercial not specified in the storyboard. Production notes describe in detail casting preferences, wardrobe considerations, sets to be built, special effects needed, specific sizes and packages of the product to be photographed, and other aspects of production. It's also a good idea to discuss the strategy of the campaign with the production house to further clarify the purpose of the commercial.

Once the agency accepts a bid, production begins. Most commercials take several working days to shoot. Before actual shooting, agency personnel, along with the commercial director, audition actors for parts, agree on locations, and work with crews to locate props, products, and other necessities.

Creative magic can happen during the production stage. A great idea may come from an aside that the actor makes or a suggestion that the director makes. For instance, the personality for the persnickety duck that quacks "Aflaaaack!" evolved during the shoot of the first commercial. The commercial features two coworkers on a lunch break discussing what would happen if they were hurt and had to miss work. Like all the commercials that followed, the duck keeps repeating the name of AFLAC, a brand of supplemental insurance.

What wasn't written into the AFLAC script or storyboard was the personality of the duck. It was the director, Tom Rouston, who gave the duck his spunky attitude. Rouston suggested that one of the workers absentmindedly throw a crumb at the duck and have the duck defiantly kick a crumb back at them. Linda Kaplan Thaler and Robin Koval, agency heads of the Kaplan Thaler Group, recount the moment of inspiration in their book, *Bang!*[3]

> *The minute we heard it, we knew that we had the pivotal moment of the campaign. Right there, with the duck's defiant kick, his entire personality was formed, and the critical leverage point of the advertising was crystallized: The duck has an important piece of information that he wants to share and he's furious that no one's listening. It turned the duck from a sweet, feathered mascot to a gutsy critter with attitude. The ending rounded out the duck's personality and gave the campaign a bit of edgy humor. It also became the guidepost for what every other (AFLAC) commercial has to have: a moment when the duck groans, kicks, squawks in ornery frustration.*

[3] Linda Kaplan Thaler and Robin Koval, *Bang! Getting Your Message Heard in a Noisy World* (New York: Doubleday, 2005), p. 192.

After the shoot comes the postproduction work of screening dailies or rushes (all takes from production), choosing the best takes, and editing them down to the required time frame.

> Checklist for Television

- Did you think pictures first and add the words later?
- Did you choose a format that best expresses what you want to say?
- Did you rely on the entertainment value of your commercial to sell the product?
- Did you ask if the opening shot will command attention?
- Did you check to see that the product is afforded enough visibility, in terms of time and closeness to the camera?
- Did you ask if you could move closer to the action to make the action more involving?
- Did you use supertitles to help viewers remember important points and, especially, the product name and the campaign theme?
- Did you choose words that add to the picture's meaning, not that mean the same thing as the picture?
- Did you make certain that important words are related to the pictures that they've been chosen to represent?
- Did you choose music or sound effects that enhance the message?

> Suggested Activities

1. Watch at least five commercials on television this week and take notes on the following:
   a. Was the product shown prominently the first time it was mentioned?
   b. Was the product featured visually in or near the final shot?
   c. Did the first shot grab your attention? How?
   d. Was the first shot related to the product story? How?
   e. Which shot was most memorable? Why?
   f. How did you feel about the product as a result of the commercial? Did it change your feelings? How and why?
2. Write a TV commercial. Begin with a scenario, progress to a script, and present it to the class in storyboard form. Use your classmates' suggestions to make revisions.

Hoping to Connect with Someone a Bit on the Wild Side?

Riverbanks is a 170-acre Zoo & Garden along the scenic Lower Saluda River in the Midlands region of South Carolina. Since opening day on April 25, 1974, Riverbanks' mission has been to foster an appreciation and concern for nature. Each area of the Zoo offers a combination of animal exhibits, graphics, enrichment programs, and special feedings to make each visit enjoyable and informative.

One visit to Riverbanks Zoo and you'll see why this is one of the most popular attractions in South Carolina. The Zoo houses more than 2,000 animals in natural habitat exhibits. You don't just see the animals. You bond with them. Their close proximity allows for you to connect with them. And that connection is something that the zoo's advertising agency, Chernoff Newman (CN), wanted to showcase in its campaign.

CN's research revealed that animals, much like humans, have certain characteristics and behaviors. Creative Director Heather Price explains, "We knew that these animals were on display, waiting every day to show people what they had to offer. So we also took into consideration that our creative needed to pique the interest of our target audience, as well as educate them on something they might not have known about an animal."

"Our 'personals' approach allowed us to do both: we showcased something unique to the animal (like how a giraffe has not only long legs but also a big heart) as well as something unique about the zoo (you can feed the giraffes here). And we did it in the form of a personal ad. Because it made more sense

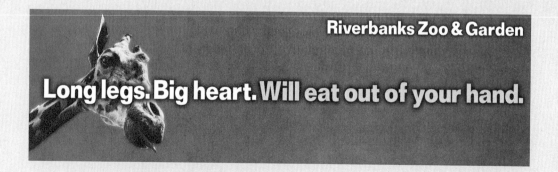

Courtesy of Riverbanks Zoo and Garden and Chernoff Newman. Special thanks to Heather Price for supplying the insights for the campaign and briefcase.

to us to have the animals ask for a visit rather than the zoo itself. We really wanted to utilize our advertising as the first form of animal encounter."

The personals campaign began with outdoor billboards. Price explains that the popularity of the outdoor campaign inspired CN to explore television, "which posed a big question—how do we showcase an animal filling out a personals ad??? And how do we do it with animals who are wild? We thought we'd keep the television nice and clean, which would allow the animal and his or her entry into the personals site take front and center stage. We worked with a production company that specializes in CG effects and 'built' a white room set with a lone computer station. We then took still photographs of each animal and our animator worked to take these stills and turn them into living and moving animals. It truly was amazing to watch."

Courtesy of Riverbanks Zoo and Garden and Chernoff Newman. Special thanks to Heather Price for supplying the insights for the campaign and briefcase.

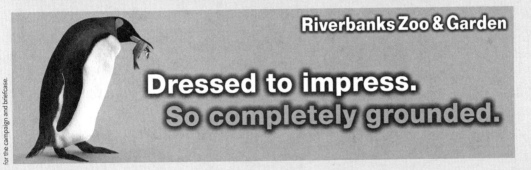

The commercials cut back and forth between an animal "typing" and the screen of the fictitious "SuperLuvyDovey.com" site.

Each animal was given a :15 spot that was used to bump on the frays of commercial breaks—so that you'd see one :15 spot at the top of the break and one :15 at the close of the break.

The media buy began and so did the entry into the gates! In 2008, the Zoo had 950,000 visitors, thanks in large part to the "personals" campaign.

Intellectual seeks communication.

Grey hair a plus.

Courtesy of Riverbanks Zoo and Garden and Chernoff Newman. Special thanks to Heather Price for supplying the insights for the campaign and briefcase.

 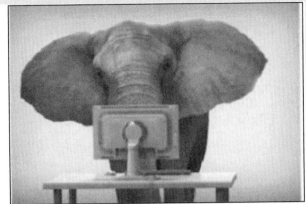

Courtesy of Riverbanks Zoo and Garden and Chernoff Newman. Special thanks to Heather Price for supplying the insights for the campaign and briefcase.

Smart veggie-lovin' big girl. Looking for fun.

RIVERBANKS ZOO AND GARDEN

Courtesy of Riverbanks Zoo and Garden and Chernoff Newman. Special thanks to Heather Price for supplying the insights for the campaign and briefcase.

DIRECT MARKETING
THE CONVENIENCE OF SHOPPING AT HOME

11

A Lands' End ad cuts to the chase: "Like, who has time to shop anymore? Maybe shopping at the mall was fun once. But not these days. You're too busy working, chauffeuring the kids around, doing a thousand other things. You simply can't afford the time to shop, can you?"

> Direct Marketing: An Old Idea Improved Through Technology

Direct marketing has been a healthy and active industry for more than 150 years. Started about the same time that the U.S. Postal Service established coast-to-coast delivery in 1847, early purveyors of direct-response advertising, called mail order in those days, were Sears, Roebuck & Company and the Montgomery Ward Company. Back then, people ordered everything from fashion to farm equipment through catalogs that were inches thick. While the gigantic catalogs may have gone by the wayside, the concept of buying merchandise without ever stepping foot in a store is more popular than ever, thanks to the Internet, cell phones, and other digital media. E-commerce researcher Esther Swilley predicts online shopping will borrow from the virtual world. "Your avatar could move through the store and pick up items. You could even have it put on a shirt and look at it in the mirror before ordering."[1]

[1] "K-State Marketing Professor Says Online Shopping in Future Likely to Look Something Like Second Life," *State News Service*, 19 February 2009.

> Advantages of Direct Marketing over Other Forms of Advertising

Direct marketing has several distinct advantages over other forms of advertising, including the following:

- *Immediate results.* Whereas the goal of advertising is to build brand awareness or to create demand for a new product category, direct marketing is structured to sell now. Urgency is the key component.

- *Two-way communication.* Unlike traditional advertising, where the message is from the advertiser to the consumer, direct marketing has two-way communication: from prospect to advertiser and back to the prospect.

  Papa John's gives customers a variety of ordering options. In 2001, the third largest pizza chain started online ordering. Six years later, it led the industry in introducing text-message ordering. Customers register on www.papajohns.com to save their favorite orders, payment, and delivery information. Then they text FAV1, FAV2, or others to 4PAPA. Papa John's confirms the order and delivers. A flash demo on the website offers a step-by-step tutorial on how to text-message an order. But is text messaging any faster than ordering by phone? To get the answer, they pitted the *Guinness Book of World Records'* fastest talker and fastest texter against each other in an ordering challenge at the Mall of America in Minneapolis. So who won? Morgan Pozgar, the LG National Texting Champion.

- *Pinpointing of prospects.* Advertisers can accurately locate their best prospects by buying names from a number of databases—trades with other companies, motor vehicle records, warranty card data from their own files, birth announcements, lists of college students, subscribers to selected magazines, and so on. Buy fat-free salad dressing and yogurt at the checkout, and a scanner labels you as a prospect for exercise equipment or fitness magazines. Buy a new car, and you hear periodically from the manufacturer asking you to complete a satisfaction questionnaire and reminding you it's time for servicing. Purchase a new home, and a lawn-care service mails you a "welcome to the neighborhood" offer for a trial weeding and feeding. Many of these targeted messages are welcomed by consumers. However, privacy on the Internet is a growing concern as companies monitor the sites you visit, without you even knowing it.

- *Personalized messages.* Specialists in writing direct-marketing copy say that the key to success is the element of one-to-one human contact. Emily Soell explains, "As direct marketers, we need to show we understand the prospect's problem and his or her dream. We must know the prospect's perceptions of the client company before we can address that prospect in a way that will be meaningful."[2]

  The design and tone of the message can be easily personalized. To get the attention of tech executives, copier giant Ricoh created mock book

---

[2] Shira Linden, "Emily Soell Delights HVDMA with Wit and Wisdom," www.hudsonvalleydma.com, 5 November 2003.

covers with titles like *Still Doing Business in a Black & White World?* The prospect's name appeared as the author and inside the cover was a blank journal. A few weeks later, Ricoh sent fictional press clippings about the prospects' "book signings." This campaign yielded an unprecedented 18 percent response rate.[3]

Buy a book from Amazon.com and you'll receive periodic e-mails telling you of similar books that might interest you. Log onto the Amazon site and you'll be welcomed by name and receive some suggestions for ordering.

- *More consumer involvement.* Want consumers to smell, taste, or feel your product? Include a product sample in your direct mail package. Want a television commercial to have legs? Invite consumers to go online and import photos of themselves in the commercial.

> Direct Mail : The Next Best Thing to a Door-to-Door Salesperson

The direct mail industry has been hurt by rising costs in paper and delivery services as well as changes in consumer behavior. Many people prefer the instant gratification of ordering online, rather than waiting for a catalog to arrive at their homes. And many have environmental concerns about the use of paper and ink. As a result, the direct mail industry is seeing a decline. The Direct Marketing Association originally predicted that direct mail volume would only fall 1 percent in 2009, but later revised that estimate to as much as 10 percent.[4]

Despite this, don't discount direct mail as a viable medium. Would you rather receive a Valentine's Day message via e-mail or a greeting card that was signed by the person you're dating? If you're like most people, you'll prefer the card. Likewise, employers consistently say that the person who mails a thank you card after a job interview is viewed more favorably than those who send an e-mail.

Direct mail can also be the perfect way to distribute product samples. To demonstrate that it can remove stains in one wash, Breeze Exel mailed product samples wrapped in a tee shirt. As predicted, the tee shirt got filthy after being shipped. If the recipients wanted their shirt to look new, all they had to do was wash it once with the product sample.

The Three Musts for Successful Direct Mail

- *The List.* As the most important element of a direct campaign, the list should be narrowed to prime prospects for the product or service. The cost of outgoing and incoming messages and telephone calls constitutes the largest single expense of a direct-marketing campaign. Toss out names that don't fit the target profile and won't offer the chance of a response.

[3] Elaine Appleton Grant, "Hard Copy: Copier Giant Ricoh Wooed Scores of Tech Execs with a Personalized Campaign Designed to Appeal to Their Egos," *Delivermagazine.com*, November 2008.
[4] Todd Wasserman, "Direct Mail May Fall 10% This Year," www.Adweek.com, 13 August 2009.

- *The Message.* Copywriters estimate that they have only seconds to grab a consumer's attention with direct mail. Make it oversized. Print a message in boldface type on the front. Laser-print the recipient's name into the message on the envelope. Customize the shape of your mailer—make it in the shape of a hula doll, sports car, or hamburger. To encourage groups to book meetings at Hershey Resorts, a package resembling a suitcase with stickers of various travel destinations was sent to meeting planners using FedEx®. A closer look reveals that all the stickers relate to the many facets of Hershey Resorts—the spa, golf course, hotel, and lodge. Inside the package were treats from the Chocolate Spa, a golf ball, a ballpoint pen, and, of course, a Hershey's chocolate bar. A brochure explained the benefits of booking meetings at Hershey Resorts (see Figure 11-1).

  Inside the envelope, most offers contain a personalized letter, a brochure, and a response card. Stickers for yes or no responses may be used to involve the consumer further.

  The letter carries the letterhead of the company and a salutation in keeping with the list: "Dear Music Lover," "Dear Traveler," or simply, "Dear Friend." To grab attention, the letter digresses from a personal letter by adding a message in large boldface type before the salutation, a message linking the lure on the envelope to the letter that follows.

  Make the letter easy to read by using short, indented paragraphs. As you write the letter, use the word "you" liberally and include a signature at the end that looks handwritten. Underscore key selling points or put them in boldface, but do it sparingly—if everything is bold, then nothing will stand out. Use the postscript (P.S.), one of the most widely read portions of direct response, to give an incentive to act now.

- *The Offer.* The mailing always asks for a response, often in the form of a limited-time offer. This may be as simple as coupons offering reduced prices if you buy before the expiration date, merchandise at a reduced price for a limited time, or a chance to participate in a contest should you buy something now. To raise the odds for a response, use a prepaid business-reply card or envelope, a toll-free number, and web address. The recipient must be told how to respond in the letter in the brochure and especially on the order blank or catalog page. Here, repetition makes sense because the average direct mail reader just skims the mailing. A significant number of prospects will read only the response coupon, ignoring the letter and brochure, because they know they will find a short summary of the entire offer there.

Designing the Direct Mail Package

Want to try your hand at this? Perhaps the most common—and least expensive—design for direct marketing is the mailer designed on standard 8½- by 11-inch paper and folded into thirds. And this is where you begin. Fold a piece of paper this size and rough in the design for each panel. In preparing your rough, you may wish to use the front panel for a teaser headline, with or without a visual. Consider continuing the message on the right-hand

Figure 11-1

Hershey Resorts captured the undivided attention of conference planners with this elaborate mailer, which was sent by FedEx and hand-delivered during meetings. The "briefcases" were created in the spirit of the golden age of travel, with "luggage labels" that reflect the facets of Hershey Resorts. Inside were items that represent the benefits of Hershey—an item from the Chocolate Spa, a golf ball bearing a logo, a ballpoint pen, and a chocolate bar.

©2002 Hershey Entertainment & Resort Company. HERSHEY'S KISS® the comical configuration with attached plume and trademarks used under license and Nasuti & Hinkle Creative.

panel—or "flap"—which is where the eye generally looks next. The left-hand panel will become part of the inside once the flap is lifted, so whatever you place there must work with the flap opened or closed. It's not always necessary to put something major on the back because this has the lowest readership, but you should at least include a logo and perhaps an accompanying tagline.

Prepare your letter and envelope and voilà—you have a direct mailer.

> Catalogs: Bringing the Retail Store into the Home and Office

Catalog advertising has come a long way since the early days of Sears, Roebuck & Company. Some tightening is evident in sales, and a number of marginal catalogs have fallen by the wayside, yet catalog sales have emerged as a major contender in the battle for the retail dollar. Figure 11-2 shows how Lands' End, one of the leading catalog companies, connects with its customers.

Figure 11-2
Selling through direct-response catalogs, Lands' End publicizes its goods through print ads such as this. Even the typeface used in the ads mirrors that used in the catalogs, but the similarities hardly end there. Consider the personal tone of the copy in this ad, as well as in the catalogs themselves, a style partly responsible for the overwhelming success of this company.

The Lands' End charm is nowhere more self-disparaging than in this headline. Here, the writer compares the misplaced apostrophe in the company name ("a boo-boo from the early days") to the quality control that "was (obviously) a little skimpy" in the early days of the company but that resulted in the company's unconditional guarantee of quality.

Courtesy of Land's End.

Successful catalogs follow the trend of all successful direct advertising today: they target specific groups of buyers. There are catalogs for movie lovers, music lovers, cat lovers, and dog lovers. Catalogs for new parents, older travelers, gift givers, and designer collections.

And the list goes on. One of the most spectacular catalogs is the Neiman Marcus holiday catalog, which contains everything money can buy. Gifts in the 2008 catalog included a collection of every top 100 record from 1955 to 1990 for $275,000; an opportunity to play with the Harlem Globetrotters for $110,000; and a life-size sculpture of you and your loved one made in Lego bricks for $60,000.

In addition to being persuasive and interesting, catalog copy must anticipate questions and provide all the answers. Prospects who can't examine a knit shirt in person must know it's 100 percent washable cotton and comes in 16 colors and four sizes. And if the sizes happen to run large, then the copy should tell shoppers that, too.

> You've Got E-mail

Internet direct mail is an inexpensive and easy way to reach loyal customers, the same reasons not-so-legitimate companies cram the Internet with spam. So how does a legitimate company encourage people to read its messages? Here are some tips:

- Clearly identify your company in the FROM line.
- Give your reader a reason to open the e-mail in the SUBJECT line. Think of your SUBJECT line the same way as you think of the message on the outside of your envelope in a traditional direct mail package.
- Summarize your offer in the opening paragraph.
- Include a link to your company's website to give more details and offer ordering information.
- Include an opt-out statement so that you reach the people who want to hear from you and avoid annoying others with unwanted e-mail.

> The Internet: The Ultimate Direct Marketing Experience[5]

The Internet is such a part of our daily routine that it's hard to imagine life without it. Likewise, it's hard to imagine any company trying to do business without it. Web traffic and search results are increasingly regarded as measures of marketing success, according to MediaPost.[6] When Procter & Gamble advertised Tide to Go on the Super Bowl, it had more than 30,000 unique visitors to mytalkingstain.com by the end of the evening. The spot also received more than 100,000 views on YouTube that day and received more

---

[5] The authors thank Jim Speelmon, Digital Consultant, for sharing his insights.
[6] Jack Loechner, "URLs Boost Magazine Ad Response," www.mediapost.com, accessed July 22, 2009.

LIST OF LISTS

To demonstrate the vast amount of data available from list sellers, here is a sample breakdown by lifestyles and demographic data available from a typical organization. Lists are not free. Generally, the more names on the list, the higher the cost. List buyers may request that lists be narrowed by merging demographic characteristics with lifestyle and geographic data in virtually any combination to help the advertiser pinpoint the best potential market for the mailing.

LIFESTYES

Affluent/Good Life

Community activities
Charities/Volunteer activities
Cultural/Arts events
Fine art/Antiques
Gourmet cooking
Own vacation home
Shop by catalog

Stock/Bond investments
Travel for business
Travel for pleasure
Foreign travel
Frequent flyers
Wine purchasers

Community/Civic

Current affairs/ Politics
Military veteran

Donate to charitable causes
Wildlife/Environmental issues

Domestic

Automotive work
Bible reading
Book reading
Fashion clothing by size
Gourmet cooking

Grandchildren
Home decorating
Own cat/Own dog
Own microwave

Entertainment

Buy prerecorded videos
Cable TV subscriber
Casino gambling
Home video games
Watch sports on TV

Home video recording videos
Own DVD
Stereo/Tapes/CDs
Own CD player

High-Tech

Personal/Home computers
Use PC/Use Macintosh
New technology
Photography
Science fiction

Hobbies

Automotive work
Camping and hiking
Coin/Stamp collecting
Crossword puzzles
Do-it-yourself repairs

Fishing
Gardening
Gourmet cooking
Needlework

Self-Improvement

Dieting/Weight control
Exercise: walking for health
Health/Natural foods
Health improvement

Sports

Bicycling
Boating/Sailing
Fishing
Golf

Hunting/Shooting
Motorcycling
Snow skiing
Tennis

DEMOGRAPHICS

Gender: Male/Female (Mrs., Ms., or Miss)

Location: State, County, Zip Code

Age: 18–24, 25–34, 35–44, 45–54, 55–64, 65–74, 75+ (Year of birth available)

Home: Own or Rent

Marital Status: Married or Unmarried

Household Income: Increments from Under $15,000 to $100,000+

Occupation

Professional/Technical
Upper management
Middle management
Sales and Marketing
Clerical
Working women (Spouse's occupation available)

Craftsman/ Blue-collar
Student
Homemaker
Retired
Self-employed business

Credit Cards: Travel/Entertainment, Bank, Other

Children at Home: Exact ages of children from infant to 18 by selection; gender also available

Religion/Ethnicity: Asian, Catholic, Hispanic, Jewish, Protestant

Education: Some high school, finished high school, technical school, some college, completed college, some graduate school, completed graduate school

Other Available Information

Motor vehicle registration
Census data
Your own company's consumer database
Competitive-purchase information (from other list sources)

than 1.5 million views in a month. Part of this was the clever commercial, which shows a man whose voice is muzzled by the talking stain on his shirt. But Procter & Gamble didn't just run a clever commercial; they created an interactive experience. Mytalkingstain.com allowed viewers to watch the TV ad, film a spoof, and "be the stain" with their own face and voice.

> The Interactive Team

When you design ads for the Internet, your team is a bit larger than one for traditional advertising. You still need an art director and a copywriter, but you need a couple of other people as well. You'll need a programmer for technical expertise. You don't want the technology to overwhelm your creative thinking, but at some point you'll need to know whether your ideas are technically feasible. You'll also want to have a producer on hand. Internet sites and banner ads can be like jigsaw puzzles, and it's not unusual to have 10 or 15 people working on a project. The producer makes sure that everyone is on the same "page" and keeps track of the many details involved in completing the project.

> Designing for the Internet: A Four-Stage Process

Whether it's a 100-page Internet site or an advertising banner, there is a method to the madness of Internet design. Much of the Internet design process is similar to that for print and television. The Internet is not as different as you might think.

Stage 1: Planning

Suppose someone asked you to build a house. How would you start? Would you dash off to a building supply store for bricks, lumber, and plumbing supplies? Install the heating system and then build the walls? Shingle the roof before you poured the foundation? Probably not. You would likely start by asking some questions. How big will the house be? How many bedrooms will there be? Will the dining room be formal or just an extension of the kitchen? Will there be one bathroom or two? If you didn't ask questions, then you wouldn't know what to build or how to build it.

Designing for the Internet is a lot like building a house. One of the first things you need to do is put your idea down on paper. Look at the high-level site map shown in Figure 11-3. Just as a blueprint tells a construction manager how many rooms the house will have, where the doors and windows will go, and so on, the site map helps a creative team decide how many pages will be needed and how people will move through them. The map helps them make better decisions about how the site will look and work.

Figure 11-3
This high-level site map provides an overview of the different sections planned for this Internet site. The universal navigation options identified at the top of the map would appear on every page. From the home page, major content sections are identified, giving the creative team a better understanding of the amount of information they have to work with.

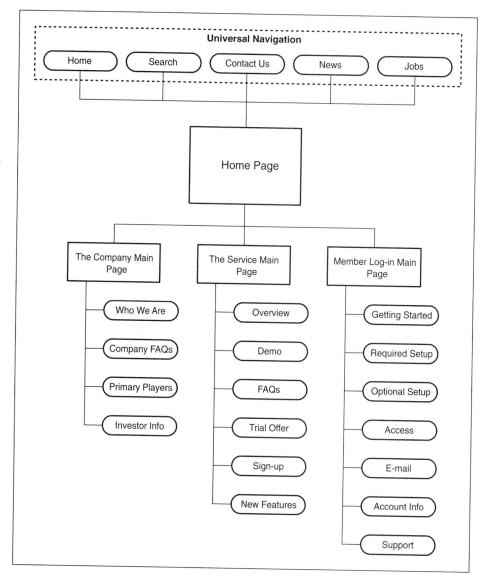

Understanding how people will move through a website is important. Your design approach will vary depending on how many options people have to select from. Look at the detailed site map shown in Figure 11-4.

This version outlines specific details for the sections of the "Service Main Page." Not only does the site map identify the different pieces of content, but it also makes recommendations for using technology. The Demo tab under The Service Main Page leads to an indicator for Flash. When developing concepts for this section, the creative team members will know that they need to design a demo using Macromedia Flash. They also will know that the content window will need to be big enough to play the Flash movie. The demo will have a storyboard and script of its own.

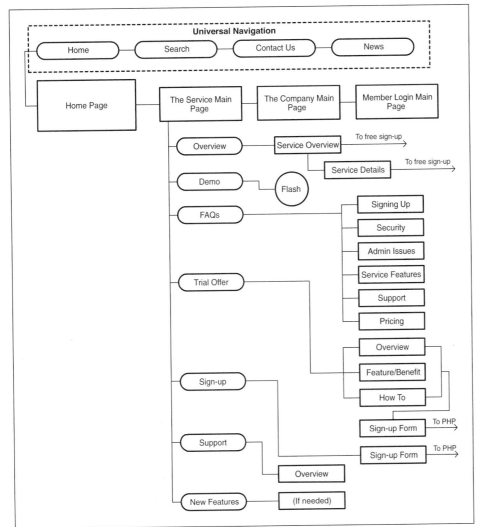

Figure 11-4
The detailed site map provides the particulars about how the pages will work. In this example, boxes with rounded corners identify primary navigation options and rectangular boxes identify specific pages.

Stage 2: Concepts

Once you have an approved site map, you're ready to start developing design concepts. Because of the way Internet sites are built, you have to develop concepts for both the content and the page template. Think of it as developing the "look and feel" (page template) of a magazine first and then coming up with this month's editorial material (content).

Some art directors prefer to create their concepts, or roughs, as a simple sketch. Others prefer to use a computer with illustration or design software. Whatever your preference, the idea is the same: you start by putting together a rough version of your design. This is not the time to be precise. It's more important to capture the basic concept than it is to come up with a completed design.

You might find it helpful to start with your page template, deciding where you want to place constant elements like logos and navigation features. This helps you determine how much space you have for the actual content. Don't worry about whether your initial ideas are possible. At this stage, you want to give yourself plenty of options. Don't let the technology limit your thinking.

Remember that you're looking for interaction, not just a reaction. In traditional advertising, your ad is often considered successful if you stimulate a reaction in your audience. Janine Carlson, marketing director at ESI International points out the greater challenge facing online marketers: "You can't be satisfied with getting a reaction. You have to spark an interaction. One is simply a split-second exchange with your audience. The other opens the door for an ongoing relationship. And that should be the goal for anyone working in advertising or marketing."

Here are some guidelines to keep in mind as you start developing your rough concepts.

- *Make sure your design works across a series of pages.* Internet sites usually have more than one page, and not every page functions the same way. That means that your design for the page template has to be flexible. Some pages might have graphic headlines, text, and supporting images. Other pages might include a Flash movie, a submit form, or some other kind of Internet technology. Your template has to accommodate all these elements. It's usually easiest to start with your most complicated page. Figure 11-5 illustrates how a design works on both the home page and a secondary page.

- *Keep some parts of the template constant.* When you design a page template, it's important to remember that some design elements won't change as you move from one page to the next. For example, you want to keep navigation elements in the same area on each page so that people can find them. Logos are another design element that should stay in one place. Consistency makes your site easier to access and follow. Identifying the location of your constant elements first helps you determine how much space you have left over for everything else.

- *Keep the most important elements in first view.* There is no limit to how long an Internet page can be, but there is a limit to how much of the page a person will see at one time. A person's first view of an Internet page depends on the screen resolution, or size, of the website. Your template design should put the most important elements at the top so that they're easy for people to find.

- *Pay attention to navigation.* Think of navigation as the highway system for your website, helping people to quickly reach the information they're looking for. Just like a real highway system, the navigational highway uses both primary and secondary systems. Primary navigation provides access to the major sections of content on a website. Secondary navigation helps users move around within a specific content section. Some sites also include universal navigation. These navigational options apply to all users on all pages. Examples of universal navigation include a Home option for returning to the home page, a Search option for accessing a site's search capability, and a Contact Us option for sending an e-mail or finding a phone number or address.

Home page

Secondary page

Figure 11-5

This home page design uses a navigation-focused approach, providing visitors with an overview of the information that they can find on the site. The goal of this home page is to quickly move users to the page that best meets their needs. The secondary page provides specific information about the company's services. Notice that there are not huge design differences between the home page and the secondary page. Although they are not exactly the same, the art director for this site continued the initial theme to the lower-level pages, keeping brand and navigation elements in the same location on each page. The result is a consistent and attractive page that is easy to navigate.

Remember that technology will never be a good substitute for solid strategic planning. Just because you can make a logo spin doesn't mean that doing so is a good idea. Julie Johnson, executive producer for Web design firm Elusive Little Fish, advises creative teams to strive for elegant simplicity, noting that too often the message becomes lost in the technology. Movement for the sake of movement doesn't do anything to make your message more memorable or effective. It can, however, be incredibly distracting.

Stage 3: Refining the Design

Now it's time to start making decisions about your design and ironing out the details. An important part of development is comparing your concepts to the site map. You need to make sure that the final design works well on all pages of your site. Sometimes, you find the right design quickly. Other times, you don't and find yourself back at the drawing board looking for a better idea.

You'll likely revise your design more than once before you finalize it. The more complex your project, the more likely the need for revisions. When you're designing a complex website, it's a good idea to do a functional proof of the concept before you progress too far into the project. You'll need your programmer for this. With your help, the programmer can mock up a section of the site and make sure that your design is technically feasible.

As you move through the development process and refine your design, you'll probably end up adding pages. Make sure that you consider the effect this will have on the rest of the site. A web page is useful only if people can find it, and introducing new pages at the end of the development phase can cause problems with the rest of the site.

Writing Copy for the Internet

The development phase is also the stage at which the copywriter starts working. If you start writing too early in the process, you won't know how the pages work and your copy won't make sense. By waiting until you're further along in the design process, you save yourself from having to do a lot of rewriting.

Writing copy for the Internet is different from writing for print. Why? Because people don't read on the Internet. They scan. According to usability expert Jakob Nielsen, principal partner of the Nielsen Norman Group, people rarely read web pages word for word. Instead, they scan the page, picking out individual words and sentences. This means that, when you write copy for the Internet, you need to adjust your style to match how people read online.

- *Use highlighted keywords.* Adding visual emphasis to important words helps catch the scanning eye of the reader. Using boldface or italics is an effective way of highlighting keywords. If you have more detail related to a specific word, turning it into a hyperlink not only catches the reader's eye but also provides easy access to additional information on a subsequent page. However, use highlights sparingly. If every other word is a link or is boldfaced, the reader will ignore them and move on.

- *Make sure your subheads are meaningful and not just clever.* Subheads are a lot like highway signs. Just as motorists use highway signs to find their way through an unfamiliar city, readers on the Internet use subheads to find their way through your site. If your subheads aren't instructive, people will abandon your site and go somewhere else.

- *Aim for one idea per paragraph.* Having a single idea makes it easier to get your point across. Readers will skip over any additional ideas if they're not captivated by the first few words in the paragraph. In traditional advertising, you shouldn't try to say everything in one ad. On the Internet, you should avoid trying to say it all in one paragraph.

- *Present complex ideas with bulleted lists.* Sometimes, a single idea will have multiple parts, making it difficult to get the main idea across quickly and easily. A bulleted list is a great way of organizing complex ideas and presenting the major points. Another benefit is that the specific bulleted items can be turned into hyperlinks so that additional details are just a mouse click away.

- *Write your copy using an inverted pyramid style.* Start with the conclusion and then add the details. If people have to read the entire paragraph to grasp your main point, they won't. Putting the conclusion or benefit up front makes it easy for readers to determine whether they're interested in this information.

- *Use half as many words (or less) as you would with conventional writing.* Reading on a computer screen is a different experience from reading on paper. Studies show that people read about 25 percent slower on a computer than they do when they read from paper. Cutting the length of your copy helps compensate for the slower reading time. Another problem is that reading from a computer screen is hard on the eyes. Think about the last time you spent a lot of time reading from your computer screen. It probably didn't take long before your eyes felt dry and tired. By writing concise copy and tightly focusing your ideas, you can make your point before your reader is worn out.

Stage 4: Production

The final stage in designing an Internet site is putting together all the pieces. With the help of the producer and the programmer, you'll assemble the text, images, and various other parts of the site into the finished product. The programmer will address technological issues such as screen resolutions, operating systems, browsers, and plugins. After production is finished, the website is ready for the public. This last step doesn't require you to do anything except move the fully programmed website to the host server.

> Banner Ads

Many people on the Internet consider banners annoying and go out of their way to ignore them. With the right approach, however, banners can be an effective means of advertising. Consider the following story of a banner that doubled traffic to the destination Internet site:

> *You're browsing an online store looking for a Christmas gift for your best friend. You can't help but notice the banner at the top of the Web page: "Need CASH for the holidays?" The banner animates to the second frame: "Sell last year's gifts." Finally comes the call to action: "Online auctions everyday." You click on the banner and go to an online auction, where you buy the perfect gift for your friend.*

Why was this banner so effective? First, it asked a question. It's more difficult to ignore a question than a statement because even a stupid question makes you pause and think about it. In this case, the use of a question was even more effective because many readers identified with the subject. Who hasn't needed extra cash for the holidays?

Second, it used humor. You certainly don't expect the second frame of this banner. Most of us have probably wished we could sell last year's presents. We just wouldn't say that out loud.

Third, it took a different approach. This banner's objective was to funnel traffic to an online auction. Most banner ads about online auctions focus on the "buy." This banner focused on the "sell," setting this auction apart from the competition and creating an intriguing invitation for both buyers and sellers.

Guidelines for Creating Banner Ads

Sometimes the simplest ideas turn out to be the most effective. Here are some guidelines that will help make your banner ads more effective.

- *Keep it short and simple.* People usually don't visit a website to see banner ads, and they probably won't take the time to notice a complex message. You have only a few seconds to catch people's attention before they move to the next page and away from your banner. That's not much time to grab their attention. Short and simple messages have a stronger focus and are more likely to result in a click-through. As a general rule, each frame of a banner ad should have at most seven words.

- *Animate three times and then stop.* If you've spent much time on the Internet, you've probably noticed that constantly animating banners are annoying. Even if the site doesn't have an animation limit, it's a good idea to use one. After all, you don't want people's reactions to your ad to be negative.

- *End with the logo or the name.* If someone doesn't click on your banner, they might at least notice the name of your company. Although it's not the best response that you could hope for, it's better than nothing. Banner ads may not be the best tool for creating awareness about a brand, but every impression helps.

> Ethical Aspects of Direct Marketing

Although direct marketing represents the ultimate way to establish a relationship with a prospect, its detractors say that computer technology has caused an unprecedented invasion of privacy. Marketers can not only amass data on your age, name, and address but also easily find out what your buying habits are and what your favorite charities are. Every time you pay with a credit card or check, every time you fill out the lifestyle section of a product warranty card or do any number of seemingly innocuous things, you are most likely contributing to a database. Your age, weight, and hair color come from driver's license records, your political leanings from your contributions, and the due date of your baby from the gift registry at the maternity store where you shop.

Behavioral targeting, in which an ad network places a cookie onto your computer and watches which sites you go to, is growing. According to Forrester Research, 24 percent of advertisers used behavioral targeting in 2008, up from 16 percent the year before. Jeff Berman explains, "If you want to focus on 25–40-year-old mom Nascar fans who love romantic comedies and live in 12 specific zip codes, we can do that." The Big Brother nature of this data gathering can backfire as Facebook learned with its Beacon program, which uses cookies to telegraph what Facebook users were up to on member sites among their friends. Initially enrollment was automatic and the opt-out box disappeared after a few seconds. By the end of its first month, 50,000 Facebook members had signed a petition objecting to it, so the social network changed Beacon from an opt-out to an opt-in service.[7]

Privacy issues aren't the only concern with the Internet. Signs plastered on the Hunter College campus promised a $500 reward for the return of Heidi Cee's Coach handbag. Tear-off tabs listed Cee's phone number, blog, MySpace page, and Facebook profile. The blog received more than 15,000 hits shortly after the posters went up. A few days later, Cee blogged that a student returned the bag. The next day she blogged that the bag was "Effing counterfeit" and that she was researching the world of counterfeit goods. The problem? Cee never lost her Coach handbag because Cee doesn't exist. It was a class project that was part of a college outreach campaign by the International AntiCounterfeiting Coalition. Sheldon Rampton, research director at the Center for Media & Democracy, was struck by "the delicious irony of a campaign against counterfeiting creating a counterfeit student."[8] For the record: Facebook's terms of use state the site is for "personal non-commercial use only" and users agree not to "impersonate any person or entity, or to falsely or otherwise represent yourself."[9]

Burger King gave free Whoppers to anyone who severed 10 friends on Facebook and boasted of ending 234,000 friendships. Facebook suspended the "Whopper Sacrifice" program because Burger King was sending

---

[7] Becky Ebenkamp, "Behavioral Targeting: A Tricky Issue for Marketers," www.Brandweek.com. 21 October 2008.
[8] Andrew Adam Newman, "The True Story of a Bogus Blog," *Adweek*, 5 May 2008, p. 25.
[9] Ibid.

notifications to the castoffs letting them know they'd been dropped for a bite of a burger. Burger King dropped the campaign, rather than tweak it to fit Facebook's policy.[10]

As you develop ideas for direct marketing, ask yourself this: Would you like to be the recipient of the message or data tracking effort? How about if the recipient were your mother or younger sister? If the answer is no, then it's not a good idea.

> Suggested Activities

1. To demonstrate how much you can learn from databases, assume that you are the target consumer for your product and fill out the form in Figure 4-1 on page 71. Then answer the following questions: For what products or services might this consumer be a good prospect? What clues, if any, suggest a basis for the relationship you might build with this person? What sort of offer or merchandise would appeal to this person? How would you work with this information to create an integrated marketing campaign?

2. Keeping the "List of Lists" shown in the box on page 236 in mind, collect several direct mail packages from friends and family. Choose one to analyze, paying particular attention to the following questions:

   How well does the message on the envelope motivate the targeted audience to open it and read farther? Inside the mailing, how strong is the relationship between the envelope message and the opening of the letter? How is the letter put together? If a headline begins the letter, does it succeed in persuading the reader to read on? How does the salutation address the audience targeted? How are color, indented phrases or paragraphs, and subheadings used to break up the letter? What types of information are highlighted by such devices? What is the offer? How well does it relate to the product or service being offered? To the audience targeted? How much incentive is there to respond promptly?

3. Write a direct-response letter based on the "List of Lists" on page 236. Use all available tactics to interest the prospect. And don't forget the offer—develop one that will make the prospect want to respond. Don't "give away the store," but suggest a premium, special price, limited deal, or other device that relates to your prospect and to what your product represents to the prospect. Check how specifically you are targeting the direct-response package for your product. Remember, you can target more narrowly using a good list than you can through typical mass media. That means you can restrict your appeal through direct response to the "ideal prospect." To narrow your search, assume that you can buy any type of list you might dream of. Beside each applicable entry, specify precisely what characteristics you are seeking in that particular category.

---

[10] Douglas Quenqua, "Friends, Until I Delete You," *The New York Times*, 29 January 2009, p. E1.

Now summarize who is going to be on your list. How will this affect the nature and tone of your copy?

4. Develop a direct-marketing piece for a nonprofit campus organization. Target your mailing to college students most likely to become members or supporters of the organization. Before you begin, interview the staff of the organization, asking what might compel other students to use the services of this organization, join the organization, or donate money to it.

5. You've been hired by a new company that sells socks. Create a site map for your new client, outlining how the site would come together.

6. Visit at least five websites and ask yourself the following questions:

   a. Was the navigation consistent from one page to the next, making it easy for you to move through the site?

   b. Was it easy to find what you were looking for? Why?

   c. Which site did you think had the best design? Why?

   d. If you could change anything about the sites, what would it be?

A Big Idea for a Small Space

The Grant, an art deco building in Washington, DC, was converted into updated condominiums with hardwood floors and carpet, granite countertops, and new appliances, including a washer and dryer in each unit. The building is centrally located on Massachusetts Avenue and is walking distance to mass transportation and lots of restaurants, bars, and clubs. And the price is reasonable—from $189,000 for a studio—in a city where some condos downtown sell for $1 million or more. So what's the catch? They are not very big. To further complicate matters, housing and condo sales started to decline just before this condo conversion hit the market.

Clearly, price is the hook. With the client, the Nasuti & Hinkle Agency determines there are two targets for The Grant. The primary target is first-time buyers—young people earning $40,000 a year or more who currently rent and likely live with roommates. The secondary target includes businesses that want to provide housing for extended-stay visitors from out of town, long-distance commuters who want a weekday home, airline flight crews, and so on. The proximity to mass transit and restaurants appeals to both targets. And neither group needs—or even wants—a large unit. But that's where the similarities end. The lifestyles and media habits of these two targets are quite different. So how does Nasuti & Hinkle reach them? It uses two different creative and media approaches.

The messages for first-time buyers focus on the evils of renting and on roommates. To add a creative twist to the campaign, Nasuti & Hinkle registered a dozen URLs, which became the headlines for the ads that ran in the local alternative and gay newspapers and on their websites, as well as on bus shelters in areas near The Grant. The URLs were also printed on 12,000 beer coasters, which were distributed to local bars.

Each URL forwards to the same bridge page, where the copy speaks directly to the needs of first-time buyers. Part of the copy reads: "Condominium pricing in DC these days seems like some sort of conspiracy designed to keep anybody normal and under 35 out of home ownership. But wait. It is actually possible to buy a place of your own and forget about living at home, renting or roommates. We're talking condos that start at $189,000 for studio units."

With special thanks to Woody Hinkle of Nasuti & Hinkle.

www.BeTheFirstToEverUseYourFridge.com

Affordable condos at 13th and Mass, NW
Available this fall.

The Grant from $189,000

Courtesy of Nasuti & Hinkle Creative.

Sales and marketing by PN Hoffman Realty

www.StopLabelingYourFood.com

Affordable condos at 13th and Mass, NW
Available this fall.

The Grant from $189,000

Courtesy of Nasuti & Hinkle Creative.

Sales and marketing by PN Hoffman Realty

www.IWantSomeTaxDeductions.com

Affordable condos at 13th and Mass, NW
Available this fall.

The Grant from $189,000

Sales and marketing by PN Hoffman Realty

Courtesy of Nasuti & Hinkle Creative.

www.IAmT●●OldToBeRenting.com

Affordable condos at 13th and Mass, NW
Available this fall.

The Grant from $189,000

Sales and marketing by PN Hoffman Realty

Courtesy of Nasuti & Hinkle Creative.

Courtesy of Nasuti & Hinkle Creative.

Businesses were reached by an ad in the *Washington Business Journal* and a direct mail piece. Visually, the ad is the same as the one that targets first-time buyers, but the attitude is different. Here, the big idea is to make the executives feel at home even when they are miles from their families. The URL is www.AHotelIsNotAHome.com. The bridge page for business people is sophisticated and invites interested buyers to schedule an appointment with a sales representative. Part of the copy on this page reads, "New again. The Grant. A classic art deco building beautifully restored with contemporary finishes. This is a perfect condominium opportunity for a first-time buyer, distance commuter or a downtown business with regular extended-stay visitors from out of town."

The campaign for The Grant is a wonderful example of creativity in advertising. Notice how the messages for The Grant make relevant connections to the two distinct audiences. They seem to say, "We understand your problems, and we can help." For the younger audience, the problems are the hassles of renting and roommates. For the older, established executives, the problem is the feeling of being disconnected from home when traveling for business. The campaign makes a relevant connection to its target audiences.

It's unexpected. And it's persuasive. Now *that's* creative.

Courtesy of Nasuti & Hinkle Creative.

INTEGRATED MARKETING COMMUNICATIONS
BUILDING STRONG RELATIONSHIPS
BETWEEN THE BRAND AND THE CONSUMER

12

Throughout this book you've been told: "Great advertising is inspired by insights about brands, consumers, and how the two interact. It starts with a problem from the client and ends with a solution for consumers." This chapter takes the concept one step further and asks that you think beyond the traditional advertising media of print, broadcast, and direct marketing as you come up with ideas to solve your client's problems. The answer to your client's problem may lie in public relations, sales promotion, events marketing, guerilla marketing, and traditional advertising.

For example, Goodby, Silverstein & Partners (GSP) realized it needed to reposition Häagen-Dazs from a brand that's known for "glitz 'n glamour" to one that's known for the all-natural ingredients that go into its ice cream. Along the way, GSP discovered that honeybees, which are vital to pollinating plants, were disappearing at an alarming rate. In a period of two years, one-third of all the honeybees in the United States had disappeared. Without the bees to pollinate them, close to one-third of the natural foods we eat would disappear. And 40 percent of the all-natural flavors that go into Häagen-Dazs would no longer be available.

Beginning in February 2008, Häagen-Dazs launched a fully integrated marketing communications effort to help bring back the honeybee. The company donated $250,000 to Penn State and UC Davis to fund their honeybee research programs, and based upon the recommendation of GSP, Häagen-Dazs created a new bee-dependent flavor—Vanilla Honey Bee—and donated proceeds to Colony Collapse Disorder research.

HelpTheHoneyBees.com gave visitors a space to learn about the problem, donate to the research program, buy a shirt, send a "bee-mail," and help spread the word. "Bee dance" videos brought the problem of Colony Collapse Disorder to the attention of Earth-conscious YouTubers. The dances generated more than 1.2 million hits.

The "HD Loves HB" advertising campaign illustrated the plight of the bees and let consumers know they could help by enjoying Häagen-Dazs Vanilla Honey Bee ice cream. A magazine insert made of seed paper even allowed people to grow wild flowers by burying the ad.

The ultimate demonstration of its commitment to the plight of the honeybee came when Häagen-Dazs testified before the House Subcommittee on Horticulture and Organic Agriculture on June 26, 2008, to urge Congress to allocate more funding for additional honeybee research.

In addition to helping the honeybees, the integrated marketing communications effort helped Häagen-Dazs. The HD Loves HB campaign captured the attention of the national media and generated more than 270 million media impressions worth $1.2 million. Overall unit volume, which had been declining prior to the campaign, jumped 18 percent in the first year of the campaign.[1]

> Integrated Marketing Communications

Integrated marketing communications (IMC) is the coordination and integration of all marketing communications tools within a company into a seamless program that maximizes the impact on consumers and others at a minimal cost.[2] IMC includes direct marketing, Internet marketing, sales promotion, public relations, promotional products, sponsorships, cause-related marketing, guerilla marketing, and, of course, advertising.

> Sales Promotion

A consumer may prefer brand X yet buy brand Y or Z. One explanation for this seemingly odd behavior is sales promotion, the use of short-term incentives such as coupons, rebates, sampling, free offers, contests, and sweepstakes. Done right, sales promotion can inspire trial of your brand, reinvigorate the relationship between your brand and loyal customers, and help reinforce your advertising message.

Ivory Soap's famous slogan, "99 44/100% Pure . . . It Floats," inspired a promotion celebrating the brand's 120th anniversary. Customers were asked to find the sinking bar of Ivory Soap to win a grand prize of $100,000. To commemorate this important anniversary, individual bars of Ivory Soap

---

[1] www.goodbysilverstein.com/#/work/haagen-dazs-helpthehoneybees-campaign-tv and http://www .effie.org/winners/showcase/2009/3595

[2] Kenneth E. Clow and Donald Baack, *Integrated Advertising, Promotion, and Marketing Communications* (Upper Saddle River, NJ: Pearson Prentice Hall, 2004), p. 322.

Photo by Debbie Garris.

Figure 12-1
Ivory Soap brought back an original package design for a limited time. This old design helped break through the clutter on the store shelves and reinforce the brand's image of purity.

were wrapped in limited edition wrappers that looked like the original package (see Figure 12-1). Multiple bars of soap were packaged together with an outer wrapping that gave a little tweak to the brand's slogan: "Ivory Soap: 120 Years and Still Floating."

Contests, Sweepstakes, and Games

Contests require skill, ability, or some other attribute. For example, Oscar Mayer sponsors contests among its local sales mangers to see who can generate the most publicity when the Wienermobile visits their area. The results of this type of contest are easy to tally through press clippings and tapes of local news shows. Also, the relatively small number of sales managers involved makes the contest manageable.

Other competitions receive too many entries to make it feasible to judge each one. That's when sweepstakes make the most sense. The Ivory Soap "Find the Sinking Bar" promotion is an example of a sweepstakes because everyone has an equal chance of winning. In another sweepstakes, Kraft Foods offered pizza lovers an opportunity to win a "job" as the DiGiorno Delivery Guy. The grand prizewinner received a $100,000 "salary," a car, a customized DiGiorno Delivery Guy uniform, and all the pizza one could possibly eat for an entire year. And, because "It's not delivery. It's DiGiorno," the winner never had to deliver a single pizza. Not bad work, if you can get it.

It's luck, not skill, that makes a person win a sweepstakes. Unlike a contest, you don't need to have anyone judge the merits of a sweepstakes entry, other than to ensure that the entry form is filled out properly.

Games are also based on luck but reward repeat visits. McDonald's Monopoly game requires customers to collect game board pieces to win the grand prize. To fight the consumer perception that "I'm never going to win," McDonald's also has "Instant Win" game stamps and includes a code on every Monopoly game piece so that people can go online and register for another chance to win. McDonald's wins every time consumers go to its website to register because it gathers information about the players, including name, zip code, e-mail address, and date of birth (to make sure the player is old enough for McDonald's to collect such information, per the Children's Online Privacy Protection Act). Some players are even willing to share their cell phone numbers by choosing to opt in for mobile communications.[3] See Chapter 13 for information about laws governing games and lotteries.

Premiums

A premium is an item given free, or greatly discounted, to entice you to purchase a brand. If you've ever ordered a Happy Meal at McDonald's for the toy, dug through a box of Cracker Jack's for the prize, or collected proofs of purchase for a gift, you know what a premium is.

A self-liquidating premium offers consumers something at a reduced price when they buy the primary brand. During the Christmas holiday season, many retailers offer stuffed toys at a nominal charge when customers spend a certain amount in the store. The stuffed toys Macy's offers as a premium during the holiday season are inspired by the balloons from the store's annual Thanksgiving Day Parade.

Sometimes the packaging itself can be a premium. Keebler packages its cookies in a container that looks like one of its elves. Planters Peanuts puts its nuts in a glass jar that resembles Mr. Peanut. Tootsie Rolls come in a bank that looks like a giant Tootsie Roll. Popular advertising icons can make great premiums, too.

Coupons

Approximately 78 percent of all U.S. households use coupons, and 64 percent are willing to switch brands with coupons.[4] An advertisement for the Gynecological Cancer Foundation uses the power of a coupon to attract the attention of its target audience (see Figure 12-2).

However, coupons are not foolproof. Brand-loyal users may be the ones redeeming the coupon, not new users. Also, if you run coupons too often, you may "train" customers not to buy your brand when it's full price.

---

[3] Beth Negus Viveiros, "A Big Mac and $1 Million, Please," 12 September 2006, www.directmag.com.
[4] Clow and Baack, *Integrated Advertising*, p. 322.

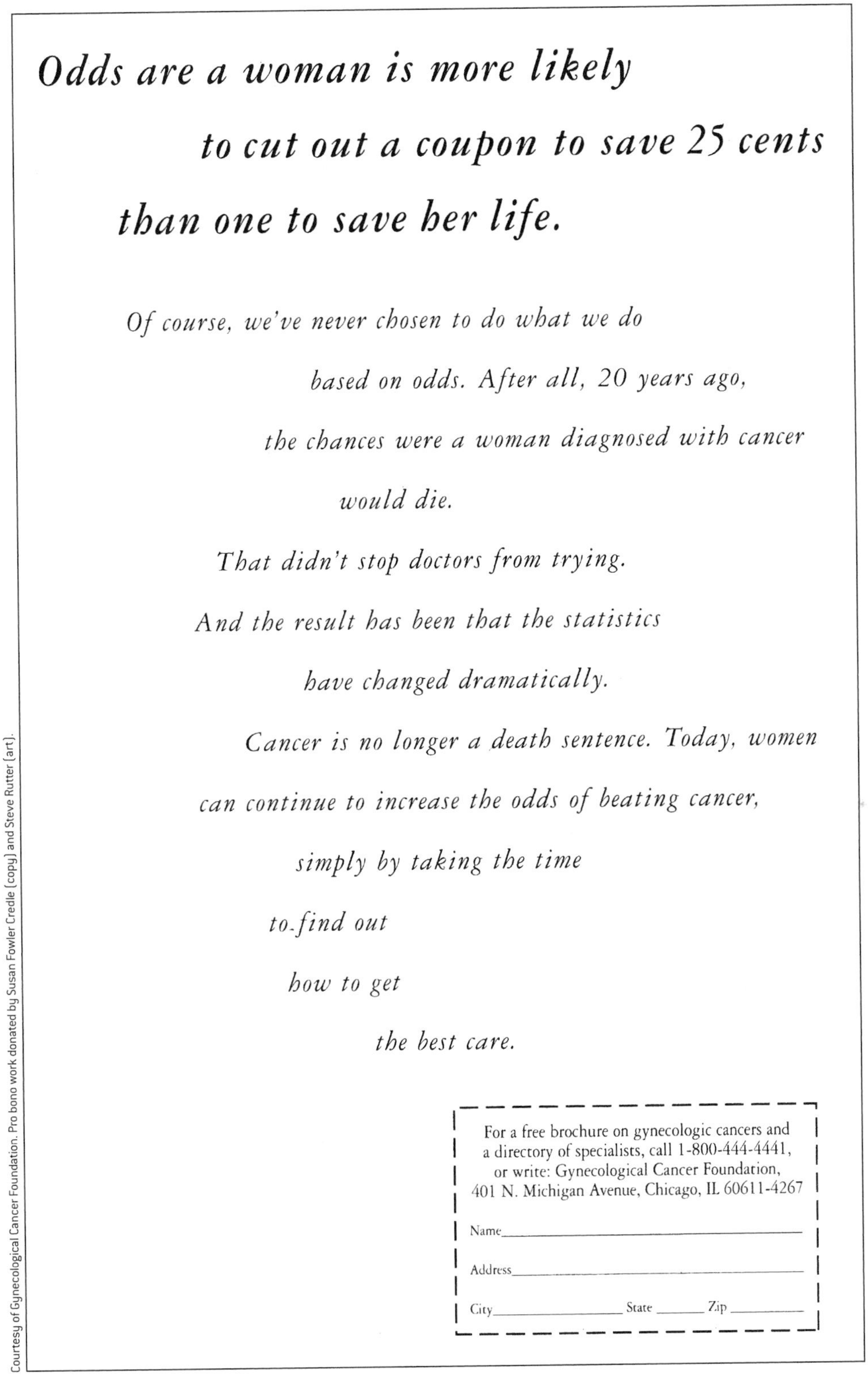

Odds are a woman is more likely to cut out a coupon to save 25 cents than one to save her life.

Of course, we've never chosen to do what we do

based on odds. After all, 20 years ago,

the chances were a woman diagnosed with cancer

would die.

That didn't stop doctors from trying.

And the result has been that the statistics

have changed dramatically.

Cancer is no longer a death sentence. Today, women

can continue to increase the odds of beating cancer,

simply by taking the time

to find out

how to get

the best care.

> For a free brochure on gynecologic cancers and
> a directory of specialists, call 1-800-444-4441,
> or write: Gynecological Cancer Foundation,
> 401 N. Michigan Avenue, Chicago, IL 60611-4267
>
> Name_____
>
> Address_____
>
> City_____ State _____ Zip _____

Courtesy of Gynecological Cancer Foundation. Pro bono work donated by Susan Fowler Credle (copy) and Steve Rutter (art).

Figure 12-2
Before this pro bono (for the public good) ad for the Gynecological Cancer Foundation ran in space donated by *People Weekly,* the foundation was receiving an average of 500 calls a month to its 800 number. The month the ad ran, 1,278 women called for information, and an additional 425 responded by mail. Even two months later, the number of calls (974) was still well above the monthly average before the ad. Despite budget restraints on production and the absence of visuals, the ad worked. What made so many women respond to this ad?

Additional problems include counterfeiting, improper redemptions, and reduced revenues.

Sampling

As the saying goes, "Try it. You'll like it." Sampling can be distributed at special events, given in-store, inserted on or in packages of related products, mailed, or delivered directly to the consumer's home.

Ferrero U.S.A. developed an innovative approach to persuade college students to sample Nutella, a chocolate hazelnut spread that's popular in Europe but less known in the United States. Working with the Public Relations Society of America, they developed a case study and invited public relations students to develop and implement a plan for their Nutella brand. Schools that formed teams of four or five students were sent samples to distribute at their campus events. Students summarized their results in plan books, and the top three teams presented their plans in person to Ferrero executives. The students gained great experience (some may have gained a pound or two of weight in the process). Public relations programs had an interesting case study to use as a teaching tool and the opportunity to gain recognition for their school. In return, Ferrero executives saw college students sample their brand. As a bonus, they heard some great ideas for future events.

To convince people to sample its products, Procter & Gamble created Potty Palooza, portable restrooms driven to outdoor festivals. Unlike the typical portable potty, Procter & Gamble's versions are immaculate and come equipped with running water, wallpaper, hardwood floors, and Charmin Ultra toilet paper, Safeguard hand soap, and Bounty paper towels. Procter & Gamble estimates that Charmin sales increased by 14 percent among those consumers who used the facilities.[5]

Like all integrated marketing communications efforts, sampling requires planning. When KFC offered two free pieces of grilled chicken, two sides, and a biscuit to anyone who downloaded a coupon within a 2-day period, they didn't anticipate the huge response. The offer was announced on the Oprah Winfrey show as part of an effort for consumers to rethink KFC. About 10.5 million coupons were downloaded and more were photocopied. The chain couldn't keep up so the promotion was pulled. The bungled promotion became a hot topic on Twitter and blogs reported "riots" at New York City KFC restaurants.[6]

Continuity Programs

These promotions instill repeat purchases and help brand loyalty. Rent 12 movies and your 13th rental is free. Buy $25 worth of groceries each week for four weeks and receive a turkey at Thanksgiving. Use a certain charge card and accumulate air miles on your favorite airline.

[5] Jack Neff, "P&G Brings Potty to Parties," *Advertising Age*, 17 February 2003, p. 22.
[6] Emily Bryson York, "Grilled Chicken a Kentucky Fried Fiasco," *Advertising Age*, 11 May 2009.

Kirshenbaum Bond & Partners uncovered an interesting insight about members of frequent miles programs. Some people love the thrill of racking up the miles, even if they never use them.[7] This insight led to an ad for the Citibank American AAdvantage card that showed a bouquet of roses with the headline, "Was he sorry? Or was it the miles?"

Rebates

Send in required proofs of purchase, and you'll receive a rebate check in the mail. It sounds simple enough. However, many people fail to redeem the offer, so they end up paying more than they originally planned. Others take the time to cut out bar codes, photocopy sales receipts, fill out forms, and mail it in, only to wait months for the rebate check. Sometimes it never comes. The rebate application may be rejected if there is missing information or if the consumer has failed to comply with an offer's conditions. Approximately 60 percent of purchasers never receive a rebate because they don't send it in or don't supply the necessary information.[8]

Many consumer advocates have ethical concerns about rebates. Manufacturers that take too long to send out rebate checks sometimes attract the attention of the Federal Trade Commission, who may charge offenders with unfair and deceptive practices. Some companies have abandoned rebate offers to avoid tampering with customer goodwill.

Point-of-Purchase Advertising

Advertising at the point of sale—in the store where the buyer is about to choose between one brand and another—represents the last chance the advertiser has to affect the purchasing decision. Common forms of point-of-purchase (POP) advertising include window posters, permanent signs inside and outside the store, special display racks and cases, wall posters and "shelf talkers" (those ubiquitous reminders popping from the place where the product is shelved), coupon dispensers at the point of sale and checkout, shopping cart signs, and signs on aisle floors.

POP displays can be effective because many purchasing decisions are made at the store. In fact, 50 percent of the money spent at supermarkets and mass merchandisers is unplanned.[9] The right display can motivate consumers to make an impulse purchase or choose one brand over another. To be effective, the display needs to grab attention and have a clear selling message that ties into other advertising and promotional messages. But even the most creative display won't work if the retailer won't put it in the store. Your display should be easy to assemble, easy to stock, and versatile so that retailers can adapt it to their individual needs.

---

[7] Jonathan Bond and Richard Kirshenbaum, *Under the Radar: Talking to Today's Cynical Consumer* (New York: Wiley, 1998), p. 34.

[8] Howard Millman, "Customers Tire of Excuses for Rebates That Never Arrive," www.nytimes.com, 17 April 2003.

[9] Clow and Baack, *Integrated Advertising,* p. 322.

Push and Pull Strategies

A push strategy encourages retailers and other intermediaries to promote, or push, the product to consumers. A pull strategy puts its emphasis on the consumer, who is expected to demand that the retailer offer the promoted product. Many successful plans combine these two approaches. For example, on days when the giant Wienermobile is parked outside a supermarket, Oscar Mayer products fly off the shelves. In one promotion, customers received a free Oscar the Bean Bag toy by presenting the Wienermobile staff with a receipt for the purchase of three Oscar Mayer products. To drive excitement inside the stores, Wienermobile pedal cars were made available to retailers who agreed to erect 150-case displays. Plush toys were given to those who bought a minimum of 75-case displays.

As the previous examples illustrate, sales promotion tactics can help an organization see immediate, measurable results. They can instill goodwill among consumers and intermediaries. And unlike traditional advertising, sales promotion tactics give consumers an incentive to buy now. But there are dangers with sales promotions. Creative guru Luke Sullivan likens the dependency on promotions to drug addiction:

> *Similarity No. 1: Both give short bursts of euphoria and a sense of popularity.*

> *Similarity No. 2: A promotion will likely get you through the night with lots of jovial activity, but when morning comes and money is needed for food and rent (or brand awareness), the coffers are empty.*

> *Similarity No. 3: After the stimuli are removed, depression ensues, and there is an overpowering need for another jolt of short-term spending.*[10]

> Public Relations

Public relations practitioners manage the communication between an organization and its "publics." For Oscar Mayer, publics include grocery store managers, restaurant owners, parents, children, food columnists, employees, unions, stockholders, and financial analysts.

News Releases

One of the most common ways of delivering an organization's message is through stories that run in the media. Before the Oscar Mayer Wienermobile rolls into any community, the public relations department sends news releases to the local media to help ensure that the story will run. The media seem happy to cover the giant hot dog because it's a fun human-interest story. Stories about the Wienermobile have appeared in the *Wall Street Journal, USA Today,* the *Los Angeles Times,* the *Chicago Tribune,* and local papers from coast

---

[10] Luke Sullivan, "Natural High: Getting Off Those Addictive Promotional Drugs," *Adweek,* 9 September 2002, p. 10.

to coast. And when it comes to TV coverage, Hotdoggers, the folks who drive the giant wiener, have appeared on *The Tonight Show with Jay Leno, MTV, Oprah,* and NBC's *Today Show.*

Unfortunately, most releases aren't greeted with the same enthusiasm as are ones about the Wienermobile coming to town. In fact, 90 percent of releases are tossed away by editors and producers because they're too promotional or aren't relevant to the medium's audience.[11]

Like a news story, a release should have the tone of an impartial reporter and include the basics of who, what, when, where, and why. It should be written in an inverted pyramid, where the most important points come first and the least important facts last, to allow the editor to cut from the bottom without hurting the message. Follow the format shown in Figure 12-3 when writing your release.

Ann Wylie offers these additional suggestions[12] as a way to get your release published:

- Grab attention in the headline. Telegraph a single newsworthy story in eight words in less so that editors and reporters can understand your point at a glance.
- Sell the reporter on the story in the subhead or summary by offering a secondary news angle or reader benefit.
- Answer "What happened?" and "Why should the reader care?" in your first paragraph.
- Keep your release to 500 words or less.

In addition to a release, you may wish to send a media kit containing a fact sheet, backgrounder, brochure, photos, product samples, or any other item that will help the journalists make an informed decision about the newsworthiness of your story. A fact sheet is a who-what-when-where-why-how breakdown of the news release. Some journalists prefer a fact sheet to a release because they want to write the story themselves, without any bias. A backgrounder may contain information on the history of your organization, biographies of key people in your organization, and testimonials from satisfied customers. Photos can increase the chances of your story running and should have captions attached to them. You may also want to include a photo opportunity sheet, which lets the media's photographers know where and when they should be to capture a photo of a breaking story.

Video news releases, commonly known as VNRs, are distributed to TV stations and are designed to look like TV news stories, ready to air. Most VNRs include a section called b-roll, which contains unedited video footage of the story, thus allowing the station to create its own version. Actualities are sound bites for radio stations and are often accompanied by news releases.

Procter & Gamble hired Manning, Selvage & Lee (MS&L) to encourage media coverage for Potty Palooza. Concert-style T-shirts with the message

---

[11] David W. Guth and Charles Marsh, *Public Relations: A Values-Driven Approach* (Boston: Allyn and Bacon, 2003), p. 274.
[12] Ann Wylie, "Anatomy of a Press Release," *Public Relations Tactics,* September 2003, p. 16.

Figure 12-3
Follow this format when writing a release.

Format for News Releases

- *Use one side of the paper and double-space the copy.* Keep the release short, preferably one page. If the release continues onto a second page, write "more" at the bottom of the first page.

- *Identify your organization,* with your company name or logo at the top.

- *Identify when the story should be released.* Most stories are "for immediate release," but there are times when you want to specify an exact time and date. For example, a company may want to announce a new product to the public on a certain date but will want to prepare the media ahead of time. This information is usually set in capital letters and boldfaced type.

- *Date of release.* This is usually placed under the previous date.

- *Contact information.* Write "CONTACT:" followed by the name, title, phone number, and email address of the person to contact for additional information. This information may be single-spaced.

- *Headline.* Skip two lines after your contact information and give a summary of what your story is about. Boldfaced type is optional but suggested.

- *Dateline.* This is the city of origin for your press release, followed by the state abbreviation if it is not a major city or if it could be confused with another city by the same name. The dateline is written in capital letters plus a dash, followed by the first line of the lead.

- *Lead.* This is the opening line of your story and usually includes who, what, when, and where.

- *Body.* This is the rest of the story and may include quotes from a company official. In the last paragraph, you may include a website or other relevant source for information.

- *Ending.* Skip a line after the last sentence and type a symbol for the ending: "# # #" or "-30-" to indicate the conclusion.

- *Photos.* Attach a caption for each photo to the bottom border. The back of the photo should give the name, address, and phone number of the contact person. Scans of photos may be sent on disk or email in TIFF or JPEG format.

"Potty Palooza . . . It's Loo-La-La" were sent to local media in advance of each appearance. The shirts were compressed and shrink-wrapped into the shape of an 18-wheel trailer, making them even more intriguing to reporters who, before Potty Palooza, may never have considered toilet paper and portable restrooms to be newsworthy. In addition, MS&L sent press releases to local media two days before each festival or fair's opening day. A media alert inviting press to visit Potty Palooza was blast-faxed to the media the day before each event. The potty hoopla worked. Stories ran on television and in print in all local market stops. In addition, three national news stories covered the "event." Procter & Gamble and MS&L won a Bronze Anvil award from the Public Relations Society of America for this creative approach to media relations.

Special Events

Whether it's a major event such as the Macy's Thanksgiving Day Parade or a community cookout to raise money for volunteer firefighters, you need to answer the following questions:

- How will the event benefit your organization? Will it bring you more customers? Build goodwill in the community? Give you a venue for product sampling?
- How will you measure the success of the event? Will it be through formal research methods, such as surveys or focus groups? An increase in sales? Or the amount of media coverage you receive?
- What is the best venue? For instance, Oscar Mayer brings its Wienermobile to state fairs, parades, and grocery store parking lots because that's where its publics eat and buy hot dogs. Macy's prefers to invite its valued customers to its store for private events to put them in a shopping mood. Syracuse University holds numerous receptions in Manhattan because that's home to many of its students and alumni.
- Who should be reached? You need to define your target audience, just as you would in an advertising campaign. Are you thanking loyal customers? Going after new customers? Trying to reach gatekeepers such as teachers and politicians?
- How many should be reached? Bigger is not always better. An exclusive retailer like Neiman Marcus won't want a massive crowd traipsing through its store to see a fashion show because Neiman Marcus isn't about serving the masses. In addition, a large crowd could damage merchandise and raise security concerns.
- What can go wrong? You name it, bad things can happen even when you have the best of intentions. Speakers and celebrities can cancel on you. Guests can contract food poisoning from your hors d'oeuvres. And Mother Nature can wreck your outdoor plans. Beverage maker Snapple hoped to break a Guinness record by creating the world's largest Popsicle. However, when a crane attempted to lift the 17-ton frozen

kiwi-strawberry Snapple treat before a crowd of New Yorkers on a hot summer day, something unexpected happened: sticky pink fluid oozed out of the gargantuan Popsicle, flooding Union Square and sending pedestrians scurrying.[13]

Crisis Management

One of the most important functions of public relations is that of crisis management. You hope that you'll never need it, but you should have a crisis management plan prepared so that your organization will know how to respond to emergencies, which experts need to be consulted, and who should be in contact with the media and the various publics involved.

A crisis plan starts with a risk assessment. Food manufacturers need to know how to respond to food contamination, airlines need to know how to respond to plane crashes, and all companies need to know how to respond to financial difficulties, on-the-job accidents, fires, and natural disasters. Your plan should designate a media spokesperson and identify other experts you may need to call upon for counsel, including lawyers, technical experts, and financial advisers.

Once the crisis occurs, you need to tell the truth, tell it completely, and tell it promptly. Any delays or half-truths will only make the crisis worse. You should also identify ways to make the situation better, whether it's support for grieving family members, product recall, or another appropriate action.

One of the best examples of crisis management is what Johnson & Johnson did after someone laced Tylenol capsules with cyanide, killing seven people. Johnson & Johnson's chief executive responded immediately, admitted the problem, launched a nationwide recall, and presented the company's plan for dealing with the crisis: triple-sealed packaging and tamperproof caplets. The Tylenol brand could have gone into extinction if the crisis was handled differently. Today, Tylenol is back on top.

> Promotional Products

Go to a job fair, outdoor concert, or any major event, and you're bound to come home with a load of free stuff with companies' logos plastered all over it. You may realize you've collected pens, pencils, coffee mugs, T-shirts, and coolers from companies you don't even know. This isn't an effective use of a promotional budget.

However, promotional products can help further your brand's image if they're used strategically. A newspaper that guarantees delivery by 6 a.m. may want to give subscribers an alarm clock with its delivery promise printed on it. A grocery store that promises great savings may want to give calculators

[13] Anthony Ramirez, "Giant Snapple Popsicle Has Meltdown in N.Y." *Berkshire Eagle,* 23 June 2005, p. A7.

to customers when they sign up for the store's savings card. A car dealer in the South may want to give automobile sun protectors, whereas northern dealers may want to give ice scrapers. The key is relevancy and consistency with the brand message.

Often, promotional products will be a part of a public relations effort. For example, Union Pacific Railroad wanted to bolster safety awareness among its 6,200 employees, so it sent a direct mail piece to each employee's home. The mailer featured a photo frame magnet with a postcard and the message, "Be Safe. It's right for you and me." At work, the message was reinforced on posters, floor decals, and banners. Managers also presented scratch-off game cards to employees exhibiting safe workplace behavior. Prizes included Swiss Army knives, insulated coolers, thermoses, binoculars, and customized Fossil watches with the "Be Safe" logo. The campaign generated a 30 percent reduction of on-the-job injuries.[14]

A local hardware store used messages on yardsticks to position itself as more personal than the big box hardware chains. Messages on yardsticks included:

> *No forklifts. No in-store ATM. No aisle 39. Smith Hardware 721-5168*
>
> *Shopping carts are for stores that sell cantaloupes. Smith Hardware 721-5168*
>
> *Smithhardware.com? Don't hold your breath. Smith Hardware 721-5168*

> Special Packaging

How do you make a brand that's been around since 1869 seem cool? That's the challenge Leo Burnett faced with Heinz ketchup, a brand that was losing market share. Research showed consumers knew and liked the brand but just weren't buying it as much as they once did. To add further insult, the ketchup category had dropped from the number one condiment to number two, with salsa leading the way. Something had to be done.

Heinz didn't want to lower the price or offer price incentives that might cheapen the image of the brand, nor did it want to allocate a huge advertising budget. The first thing Leo Burnett did was identify the target audience. Mothers were the buyers, but teenagers were the heavy users. Burnett needed to find a way to project the individualism teens covet by giving the brand a quirky, self-confident voice. It needed to give the brand "attitude." Wisecracking labels did the trick. Funny lines appeared on the bottle labels, including: "Instructions: Put on food;" "Taller than mayonnaise;" "Will work with mustard if it has to;" "Desperately seeking Tater Tots;" "On a first name basis with onion rings;" and "14 billion French fries can't be wrong." The Heinz campaign, which also included television, print, and book covers, was a huge hit. Market share rose 15 percent, and the bottles are so popular

---

[14] "Walk Like a Winner," *PROMO*, 1 April 2003, p. 16.

Figure 12-4
How do you convince people to talk about a 100-year-old brand? By having the brand do the talking. Heinz first introduced "talking labels" on the world's best-selling ketchup in 1999. These versions feature winning statements from the "Say Something Ketchuppy" contest. The name of the person who came up with the expression appears under each quote.

people buy them on eBay (see Figure 12-4). The campaign won a gold Effie, an award presented annually by the New York American Marketing Association in recognition of the year's most effective advertising campaigns.[15]

Innovative packaging is becoming increasingly important as a result of media fragmentation and the proliferation of new products on store shelves.

> Sponsorships

Corporations spent $25 billion in 2001 for the rights to put their names on everything from local AIDS walks to sports stadiums, and that's just for naming rights. Sergio Zyman reports that companies typically spend three times more than that to create, advertise, promote, and implement their sponsorship programs. In his book *The End of Advertising as We Know It*, Zyman lists a series of questions companies need to answer before signing a sponsorship agreement:[16]

- Is the sponsorship relevant and persuasive to your consumers?
- What specific business results are you trying to achieve?
- Does the sponsorship possess the associate equity you need to meet your objectives?
- What will the sponsorship cost, and how much business will it need to generate to achieve your objectives?
- What are the opportunity costs (how else could you be spending the money)?

[15] Adapted from a lecture by Edward Russell at Syracuse University on 17 March 2003 and from www.leoburnett.com.
[16] Sergio Zyman, *The End of Advertising as We Know It* (Hoboken, NJ: Wiley, 2002), pp. 151–154.

The right sponsorship can expose your brand to your target audience, give you a venue for product sampling, and generate positive publicity. But sponsorships can become confusing to the average consumer. For example, do you know what beer company owns the sponsorship to the Super Bowl? Did you think it was Anheuser-Busch? If you did, there's a reason. Anheuser-Busch has been the exclusive Super Bowl beer advertiser since 1989. Despite this, Anheuser-Busch isn't allowed to use the words "Super Bowl" in any of its advertising or promotions. The reason? Coors is the official beer sponsor of the NFL, which makes it the only brewer allowed to use the coveted "Super Bowl" trademark.

> Cause-Related Marketing

Cause-related marketing associates a company or brand with a social cause in an attempt to build customer goodwill. A Cone/Roper study found that consumers consider a company or brand's price, quality, and social involvement as major criteria in their decision of which brands to use.[17] A Roper Starch study confirmed this, with 92 percent of respondents agreeing it's important for marketers to seek ways to become good corporate citizens.[18]

A good example of cause-related marketing is Chiquita's commitment to the rain forest. *Audubon* magazine covered a special event sponsored by Chiquita:

> *Her hat was adorned with a Carmen Miranda-esque assortment of fruit; her lipstick, fire-engine red. The real-life Miss Chiquita recently appeared at the Copacabana, New York City's tropical watering hole, to celebrate a milestone: The Rainforest Alliance has certified 100 percent of Chiquita's farms in Latin America as environmentally and socially responsible. Under the alliance's Better Banana Project, farmers follow strict guidelines to conserve soil and water and minimize the use of pesticides and other agrochemicals.*[19]

Do you think Audubon Society members care about these issues? You bet they do. So do many average consumers. But do you think the average person even knows what an agrochemical is? Probably not. That's why Chiquita uses a different tactic when communicating its respect for the environment to moms and children. A Chiquita banana display in grocery stores promoted an opportunity to win a family vacation for four to a rain forest in Costa Rica. To enter, children under 12 years were asked to color a rain forest drawing that had images of tropical plants, birds, animals, and Miss Chiquita. Interesting facts about rain forests and Chiquita's good deeds appeared throughout the drawing.

Unfortunately, there are bad examples of cause-related marketing. Some companies jump on the "cause du jour" and fail to make a relevant connection

---

[17] Sonia Reyes, "Hotdoggin' Cross-Country," *Brandweek,* 3 April 2000, p. R16.
[18] Carol Krol, "Consumers Note Marketers' Good Causes: Roper," *Advertising Age,* 11 November 1996, p. 51.
[19] David Seideman, "Miss Chiquita Takes a Stand," *Audubon,* March 2001, p. 17.

between the brand and the cause. These transparent efforts usually produce equally transparent results. Sometimes they can even backfire, as a major retailer learned when it asked customers to bring in used jeans; in return, the store would give them a discount on a new pair and then donate the old jeans to a charity. The concept sounds like a good idea. However, the store ran the ad before asking the charity. As it turned out, the charity had no way to distribute used clothing and sued the retailer for wrongfully using its name.

Before developing a cause-related program, answer the following questions:

- How does the cause relate to the brand? Is there a natural tie-in?
- How do consumers feel about the cause? Do you need to educate them about the importance of the issue?
- What are the expectations of the charitable organization?
- How may you promote your involvement with the cause?

> Guerilla Marketing

Coined by Jay Conrad Levinson, guerilla marketing is the use of unconventional marketing intended to pull maximum results from minimal resources. Suppose you want to make a particular brand of alcohol the next trendy drink. You might want to send hip-looking people into the coolest bars and have them order a drink made with the brand, in the hopes that others will take notice and try it themselves.

Want people to realize what harmful ingredients are in their cigarettes? Consider this approach: A man dressed up in a rat costume and pretended to die on the streets of New York to alert people that cigarettes contain cyanide, the same stuff that's used to poison rats.

How do you show people how compact your car is? Crispin Porter + Bogusky placed Mini Coopers in unexpected places, including atop a Ford SUV that rode around major streets and in the place of the coin-operated kiddy car rides outside of grocery stores ("Rides $16,850").

> Product Placement and Branded Content

Watch the James Bond movie *Die Another Day,* and you'll see at least 20 product pitches. Ford is reported to have paid $35 million to have Pierce Brosnan, who plays Bond, behind the wheel of its $228,000 Aston Martin Vanquish and to have Halle Berry, who plays the Jinx, drive a Thunderbird whose coral color matches her bathing suit.[20] In the movie, Bond wears an Omega wristwatch, drinks Finlandia martinis, flies first-class on British Airways, and wears Ballantyne turtleneck sweaters and suits from Brioni Roman Style.

---

[20] Guy Trebay, "Make It a Finlandia and 7Up, Shaken, Not Stirred," www.nytimes.com/weekinreview, 27 October 2002.

Product placement can range from a background shot to a product-centered episode, such as when *Seinfeld* devoted an entire episode to Junior Mints. Some companies even produce their own movies, TV shows, and video games.

Branded content can be extremely expensive and is far from foolproof. Ford and its agency, J. Walter Thompson, created an outdoor-adventure TV series for the WB network. The show's title, *No Boundaries,* was the same as Ford's SUV ad slogan. The show bombed and was quickly yanked off the air.

Product placement also has its share of risks, from being so subtle that most people don't pick up on it to being so blatant that it can turn off viewers and devalue the brand. The trick is to make the brand seem natural to the characters and plot of the story.

> Suggested Activities

1. Develop an idea for a special event for a company you admire. Include details of the event, such as who will be reached, where the event will be held, how it will be promoted, and how much it will cost. Also, indicate how you will evaluate the success of the event.

2. Write a news release for the special event you described in the previous activity.

3. Develop a sales promotion idea for your favorite soft drink or snack food.

4. Go to a movie or watch two hours of prime-time television. Take note of how many brands were recognizable within the film or programs and how they were incorporated into the storyline.

IKEA Embraces Change

IKEA is known for its inspired home furnishings. Walking into an IKEA store is like walking into a home decorating magazine. The mega-size stores showcase hundreds of room settings, and shoppers are welcome to take their time to sit, lie down, open and close doors, and imagine the possibilities.

After being in the Washington, DC market for close to 20 years, the local IKEA stores were showing some wear-and-tear and experiencing sub-par performance compared to other IKEA stores. It was time for change. The Woodbridge, Virginia, store was completely renovated and the College Park, Maryland, store was upgraded. Customer service was enhanced at both stores.

IKEA turned to Deutsch NY to create a campaign that generated buzz and awareness about the changes that had taken place at their Washington-area stores. The timing was fortuitous. The changes at the IKEA stores coincided with the historic 2008 Presidential election. Playing off of the incoming administration's promise of change, "Embrace Change '09" became IKEA's campaign theme, which ran the week before the inauguration.

IKEA extended an offer to the Obamas to furnish any room in the White House free of charge. To give the incoming First Family a sense of the type of inspired design they could create for the White House, IKEA decorated an Oval Office replica with their furniture and home furnishings. The 20-by-25 foot Oval Office replica—complete with mock "Secret Service" protection—was on display in Union Station. People were invited to sit behind IKEA's version of the most powerful desk in the world and everyone was invited to sign a guestbook welcoming the Obamas to their new home.

The Embrace Change '09 microsite (www.embracechange09.com) gave consumers the chance to offer their own interior design solutions by creating a virtual Oval Office with images of IKEA furniture. Once completed, the designer wannabes could send their creations to a friend or even to the White House. They could also enter to win one of three $1,500 IKEA gift cards to bring change to their own oval, square, or rectangular home offices.

The microsite included a letter addressed to President and Mrs. Obama: "At IKEA, we believe that change begins at home. Given your commitment to openness and listening to the American people, we have created a forum where the public could make suggestions on a topic of great importance: the Oval Office. Please take a moment to view some of the thousands of

© Inter IKEA Systems B.V. Reprinted with the permission of Inter IKEA Systems B.V.

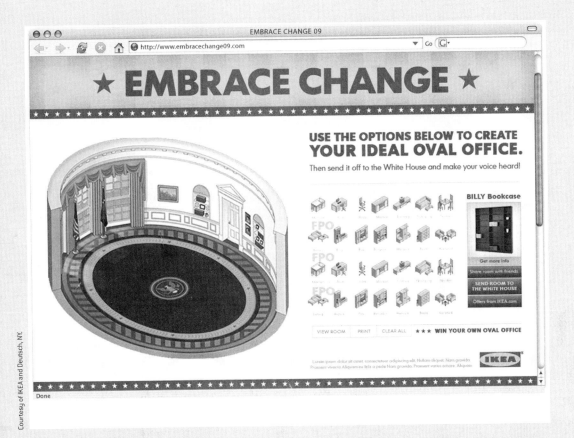

Courtesy of IKEA and Deutsch, NY.

Courtesy of IKEA and Deutsch, NY.

Courtesy of IKEA and Deutsch, NY.

Courtesy of IKEA and Deutsch, NY.

Courtesy of IKEA and Deutsch, NY.

designs created and, perhaps, find the inspiration to embrace change in your new home."

With the assistance of TH Outdoor & Events, Deutsch staged a mock presidential motorcade that cruised past more than 40 historical sites, including the Lincoln Memorial, Washington Monument, U.S. Capitol, and White House. IKEA boxes were strapped to the roof of the limo and an upholstered chair protruded from its trunk. Two Chevy Suburbans followed closely behind to protect the important cargo inside the stretch limo.

The Embrace Change '09 campaign slogan was seen all over DC. Buses, trains, and billboards featured presidential-sounding promises including "Fiscally responsible home furnishings for all" and "The time for domestic reform is now!"

The campaign generated nearly 500 million impressions, with 400 unique media placements. It garnered more than 60 minutes of broadcast coverage and was featured on *The Today Show, Late Night with Conan O'Brien, Inside Edition*, as well as local and national news programs.

Deutsch promised—and delivered—a campaign that generated buzz and awareness. It's nice to know that at least one campaign promise has been kept in DC.

13

THE LAW AND CREATIVITY
MAKING SURE YOUR GREAT IDEA IS A GOOD IDEA

By Carmen Maye, J.D., University of South Carolina

© 2009 Carmen Maye

An award-winning 1969 commercial for Shiseido Toilet Soap features Japanese schoolboys marching into the communal bath. They each grab a bar of soap and begin to wash. The boys are subdued at first, but before long the soap takes effect. The routine efficiency of the bath gives way to good, clean fun and the bathers enthusiastically scrub each other's backs.

The scrubbing accomplished, the bathers return to the tub for a final soak, quite pleased with themselves and their teamwork. But then, the fun is rudely interrupted: one of the boys breaks wind! Telltale bubbles ruin the moment, the offender's schoolmates scatter, and he is left, sheepish and isolated, to ponder his transgression.

In some ways, the creative process is like the bathing ritual depicted in the soap commercial. Gee, this collaborative endeavor can be quite fun! Unless, of course, someone breaks the rules and a telltale lawsuit ruins the moment, causes clients to scatter, and leaves the offending agency isolated and pondering what went wrong.

The creative process is fun. Lawsuits are not fun. Lawsuits are time-consuming and expensive, and they require creative people to spend time dealing with lawyers instead of cultivating the next great idea. And, what's worse, clients don't like them. Few things make clients scatter like being served with a lawsuit because of something their advertising agency did or failed to do on their behalf.

Does that mean fear of a potential lawsuit should control the creative process? No—absolutely not. It does mean, however, that as a campaign concept unfolds, the creative team should be aware of potential legal issues to resolve before production begins. Does the campaign include music? Are you planning to feature a celebrity spokesperson? Does the message make specific product claims about your advertiser or a competitor? Is the client introducing a new tagline? Is the photography original or stock? Are you shooting in studio or on location?

These examples, all of which have potential legal implications, are typical of the types of creative decisions made daily in advertising. Knowing the details of the law in these areas is not required, but being able to recognize where potential legal issues exist is crucial for a clean, creative process.

The ads and campaigns discussed and reproduced in this book were selected because of their relevance to particular creative strategies—not because of their ability to illustrate legal concepts. Nonetheless, many of the examples in this book also serve as excellent points of reference for legal issues that often arise in advertising. In other words, legal issues sometimes lurk in unexpected places.

> Who Worries About Advertising?

When advertisers and their agencies get into legal hot water, it's generally for one of two reasons:

1. *The message or the way in which the message was delivered violated a government law or regulation and resulted in a penalty or fine.* When advertisers' messages mislead consumers or disrupt or have the potential to disrupt the orderly operation of society, governments can step in to regulate or punish those bad acts. State and local laws govern advertisers where they do business; each state, for example, has laws that address individual privacy and reputational interests, contracts, unfair trade practices, and activities like sweepstakes and lotteries—all of which may affect an advertiser's strategy. In some cases, federal law comes into play. For example, when products are promoted across state lines, the Federal Trade Commission (FTC) has the authority to oversee the advertising content. And when copyright disputes arise—as they often do in creative endeavors—they are governed by federal law and resolved in federal court.

2. *The advertisement or something used to create an advertisement violated an individual's rights in some way and prompted that person (or company) to pursue a lawsuit.* Infringing someone's copyrights, invading someone's privacy, compromising someone's right to publicity, and damaging someone's reputation are the kinds of harms that tend to result in legal action against advertising agencies.

   Individuals (including corporate entities) who are harmed in some way by advertising rely on civil laws that allow them to seek compensation (usually in the form of money) for their injuries. With the exception of copyright and some instances of trademark infringement, most of these advertising lawsuits take place in state courts.

> Government Regulation of Advertising

Government restrictions on advertising are either related to the content of advertising messages or the way those messages are presented. Although much advertising is "protected speech" under the First Amendment, false and deceptive ads or ads that promote an illegal product or service may be banned altogether or heavily regulated. Gambling is a heavily regulated activity in most states, and ads promoting gambling may be banned. Similarly, private (as opposed to state-run) lotteries are usually illegal. As discussed in Chapter 12, contests, sweepstakes, and games are popular sales promotion techniques and can be effective parts of an integrated campaign. But sometimes well-intended promotions unwittingly resemble lotteries. For example, if a customer must pay to enter these types of promotions, then that's an illegal lottery and any related advertising would be illegal as well. To avoid problems, advertisers who create these types of promotions should tell consumers how to receive a free entry piece, which may require sending in a self-addressed, stamped envelope.

Advertisers who mislead consumers may face sanctions from the FTC, the Food and Drug Administration (FDA), or other government agencies that have authority to regulate advertising-related messages. An unusual illustration of governmental reach involves Cheerios® cereal, made by General Mills. You may recall the Cheerios commercial in which a grandfather explains to his grandson that he's studying the Cheerios box to prepare for his next cholesterol test. The commercial got high marks for creativity and is a great example of an ad with a clear "selling idea": Cheerios is the only leading cold cereal proven to help lower cholesterol. Subsequent commercials and the Cheerios box also emphasized this selling idea. Interestingly, the FDA, which has regulatory authority over food products and drugs, has indicated that Cheerios' statements that its product is "clinically proven to help lower cholesterol" transform Cheerios from a cereal to a drug and therefore invite the same rigorous testing and bureaucratic hoop-jumping that new drugs undergo prior to reaching the market.[1] Could General Mills' creative team and packaging designers have anticipated this additional regulatory scrutiny? Hard to say, but the bottom line is, advertising messages may have consequences beyond their ability to affect sales.

The Cheerios situation is a little extreme in that General Mills is not alleged to be making false health claims about Cheerios, yet still may be faced with abandoning a very effective creative strategy. Where the FTC is concerned, the focus usually is on making sure consumers aren't deceived by advertisers who play fast and loose with factual claims. An exception is ads that use "puffery." Puffery is "an exaggeration or overstatement expressed in broad, vague and commendatory language and is distinguishable from misdescriptions or false representations of specific characteristics of a product and, as such, is not actionable."[2] In other words, an ad for spaghetti sauce may claim

---

[1] Jennifer Corbett Dooren, "Cheerios' Health Claims Break Rules, FDA Says," www.wsj.com/article/SB124216077825612187.html#printMode, accessed August 22, 2009.
[2] J. Thomas Russell and W. Ronald Lane, *Kleppner's Advertising Procedure* (Upper Saddle River, NJ: Prentice Hall, 2002), pp. 635–636.

it's "as good as mom's." Few people would regard this as a statement of fact, and reasonable people are not likely to be deceived by this type of statement.

Factual claims in advertising, however, especially those presenting data about your product or a competitor's, must be demonstrably truthful. You may be tempted to promote a health benefit (à la Cheerios) or state your product is better than another company's. If you do, you must be able to substantiate any claims you make prior to actually making them. If you can't back up your advertising assertions, the FTC, the FDA, and the National Association of Attorneys General have a number of remedies at their disposal to bring you in line, including pulling the ad in question, running corrective advertising or, in extreme cases, imposing criminal sanctions. In 2009, drugmaker Bayer HealthCare reached a settlement agreement with the FDA and attorneys general in 27 states over advertising claims for Yaz®, an oral contraceptive. The original advertising mentioned clearer skin and reduced mood swings associated with PMS. Bayer agreed to spend $20 million on corrective ads to counter these advertising claims and also to seek prior federal approval for all Yaz ads until the year 2015. The FTC also has targeted Kmart and other companies for making false and unsubstantiated claims that some of their paper products were biodegradable.

In addition to requiring substantiation of factual claims, the FTC frowns on ads that misrepresent product capabilities. If a product-demonstration ad shows a product performing in an unexpected way, the advertiser may not deploy a substitute. The print ad for Stren fishing line, reproduced in Chapter 1, shows a rear view of a portly man on a barstool; the fishing line is holding together a split down the back of his pants. A Stren TV commercial, also described in Chapter 1, suggests the good fairy in the children's play would have remained suspended over the stage if Stren fishing line had been used. In cases like these, the FTC requires that the product actually be used as depicted or that it be capable of the suggested use.

If celebrities endorse a product, the FTC also requires that they actually use the product in such a way that allows them to reasonably endorse it. Celebrity endorsements are discussed at some length in Chapter 1; as you ponder using celebrities in your advertising, the "actual usage" requirement is another factor to consider.

Although rare, in egregious cases of misconduct, the government has the authority to charge advertisers and/or their agents with crimes. Laws governing copyrights and trademarks, for example, allow for criminal sanctions in addition to the civil remedies given to individuals and organizations.

Even though the FTC and its sister agencies have broad reach, they are, after all, agencies of the federal government: this means limited staff and resources to deal with a tremendous volume of advertising.

> Advertising Regulations: Time, Place, and Manner

Most government regulation of advertising is designed to make sure messages are delivered safely and don't unreasonably interfere with important societal interests. Recall the example in Chapter 1 of the major fast-food restaurant that was forced to lower its neon sign on a highway in the

Berkshires because it ruined the vista of rolling hills. The restaurant was allowed to erect a sign, but not in a way that conflicted with local aesthetic interests. That is but one of thousands of instances when the interests of advertisers and the interests of local government have clashed; usually, such clashes result in additional expense and trouble for advertisers.

Local governments typically cannot ban advertising messages altogether, but they may dictate the size, materials, and fasteners used in fabricating and displaying a sign or the volume at which products or events may be promoted. Signs that impede pedestrians on the sidewalk, signs that could be dislodged by a brisk wind and strike passersby or whose flashing lights could distract drivers are all subject to regulation. Staging a commercial shoot in a public park may require permits, as may construction of a special exhibit or display. Before you build your creative strategy around a novel venue or technology, do your homework to see if what you want to do can actually be done lawfully.

Even when you don't technically need a permit from the government to execute your creative strategy, there are times when you should inform government authorities about your plans and seek their "blessing" anyway. Failing to do so could backfire in disastrous ways. A notorious example of a creative strategy gone awry occurred in 2007. A guerilla-marketing firm, hired to promote Cartoon Network, placed lighted electronic devices on bridges and other public structures in major U.S. cities, including Boston. The devices, which were described as resembling "an oversized circuit board with wires hanging beneath,"[3] caused quite a negative stir, especially in Boston. Boston's Logan airport was the originating point of the terrorist-hijacked plane attacks on September 11, 2001, that killed thousands of people in New York, Washington, D.C., and Pennsylvania; as one might imagine, Boston takes security issues very seriously.

After concerned citizens reported seeing the strange electronic devices in key places around the city, local and federal law enforcement agencies—who had no knowledge of the devices—shut down bus stations and highways and evacuated nearby areas. The stunt inconvenienced thousands of people, wasted valuable public resources, and caused Cartoon Network's parent company Turner Broadcasting to issue public apologies and pay millions of dollars in reimbursement and fines. If that weren't bad enough, the architects of the campaign were arrested and the head of Cartoon Network ultimately resigned over the fallout. Creative, perhaps. A good idea? Definitely not.

The majority of advertisers and agencies may never tangle with the FTC or its kin. Instead, legal skirmishes are most likely to arise over everyday dealings with individual vendors, freelancers, models, clients, and others with whom advertising agencies interact.

> Avoiding Individual Disputes

The majority of advertisers and agencies may never tangle with the FTC or its kin. Instead, legal skirmishes are most likely to arise over everyday dealings with individual vendors, freelancers, models, clients, and others with

[3] Michael Learmonth, "Cartoon Network Scares Boston," www.forbes.com/2007/02/01/cx_ml_0201varitytv_print.html, accessed August 21, 2009.

whom advertising agencies interact. Also, advertising is a deadline-driven business. Agencies and creatives get recognized for "big ideas," but the success of those big ideas involves a gazillion small details—details that are handled on a deadline. The devil—or in this case, the potential lawsuit—is in the details.

Review the three print ads for DuPont featured in Chapter 5. This series of ads, featuring farmers in the field, implicates almost every legal issue an advertiser may encounter. When the creatives devised these ads, they probably did not begin with, "Hey, let's see how many legal issues we can implicate with this print campaign!" Yet, this series of ads just sprouts legal issues.

The DuPont ads feature standard advertising elements: a visual (in this case, an illustration), copy (headline, body copy, and a cutline that resembles a long tagline), the product itself, and a couple of trademarks (one for the company and one for the product itself).

Although you copywriters may object, let's start with the visuals. The issues with these and all print or broadcast visuals are

1. If the people depicted in these illustrations are recognizable, do you have their permission to use their likeness (or name, etc.) in this way? If not, you risk a misappropriation lawsuit.

2. Do you own the copyright in these illustrations (or photographs or computer-generated art), or do you have the permission of the copyright owner to use these illustrations in your ads? If not, you risk a copyright infringement lawsuit.

Before you can proceed with this type of ad, you must be able to answer "yes" to both questions.

> Invasion of Privacy and Right of Publicity

Like many ads, the DuPont series features people. In this case, the people are in an illustration rather than a photograph, but assuming these illustrations are of real people and not complete figments of the artist's imagination, the legal issues are the same as if photography were used. The print ads for Whitewater in North Carolina in Chapter 1 and Bell Helmets in Chapter 5 feature photographs of recognizable people, and these ads raise the same issues.

Laws in every state regard the misappropriation of another's name, voice, or likeness for commercial purposes as something worth suing over. If you misappropriate an ordinary person's likeness, you may be sued for invading his or her privacy. The thinking is that using an ordinary person's likeness for commercial purposes is offensive and an invasion of privacy. If you misappropriate the likeness (or name, or voice) of a celebrity or professional model—someone who actively seeks to make money off of his or her likeness—you may be sued for diminishing their "right of publicity." Oprah Winfrey and Dr. Mehmet Oz sued more than 50 businesses for allegedly using their names and images to sell dietary supplements and beauty products without their permission. Tom Waits won a $2.4 million lawsuit against Frito-Lay and ad agency Tracy Locke after they used someone who sounded like Waits in a radio campaign for Doritos. Vanna White won $400,000 from Samsung after it used a female robot dressed in an evening gown and blond wig, standing in front of a letter board. If your proposed print ad will feature or purport to feature an actual person (or people), you must make sure you have the legal authority to use them in your commercial message.

> About Photographs

Photographs and other images used in advertising are either created just for use in advertising or they're already existing "stock" or "file" photos adopted for a particular ad or campaign.

Stock photos are available for sale or license to advertisers and others who need a particular image but aren't inclined to shoot their own. The licensing fee for using stock photography varies depending on the intended use of the photo. A license for a stock photograph often includes blanket permission from any people pictured for that photo to be used in advertising or other purposes, but some restrictions may apply. Before using stock photography, you should verify that the terms of your license allow you to use the photo in the desired manner and geographic area. You should also determine that the subjects in the photos have given a release for their use.

File photos are photos the agency (or perhaps the client) has in its files from previous projects. If you're using a file photo from a previous project or campaign in a new way, you must confirm that the permission previously granted covers the new use. The fit-looking man in the photo who 10 years ago gave permission for his image to be used in an ad for a gym may have packed on 40 pounds and no longer approve of his former, thinner self being featured in advertising. It may be necessary to renew the consent if some time has passed since it was given.

Using file photos also tends to result in "false light" problems. In some states, presenting someone in a false light is another type of invasion of privacy that can generate a lawsuit. In advertising, this typically occurs when a file photo originally shot for one purpose is used to illustrate something else. For example, a photograph of a teenaged girl that accompanies a news story is later used without permission in an ad promoting a teen-pregnancy-prevention program. (And yes, this also could be libel—discussed later—or misappropriation.)

Presumably, the photos in the Whitewater rafting ads in Chapter 1 are original photos commissioned especially for these ads. The basic process should have gone something like this: (1) the creative team proposed using an action photo of people whitewater rafting; (2) the designer produced a comp for the client's approval; (3) the agency hired a freelance photographer to set up and capture just the right image; (4) prior to the shoot, the photographer (or someone from the agency) obtained written releases from everyone in the photograph to use the photograph in the ad, in the campaign and in any other materials related to the campaign; (5) the agency received the photograph (and, one hopes, a licensing contract for the copyrights) from the photographer; (6) the designer dropped the photo into the layout; and (7) the ad appeared in print. From a legal standpoint, step 4 is the most important for avoiding an invasion-of-privacy or right-of-publicity lawsuit.

Consider the Bell Helmets print ads in Chapter 5. One of the ads features a young girl with braids. Another features head-and-shoulders photos of three living Bell employees and a skeleton. (To underscore the seriousness of head trauma, the skeleton is identified as "VP of Research & Development, John Doe.") These ads are terrific for illustrating the issues with obtaining model consent. The child in the "shoes" ad could be a professional model, or she could be the offspring of someone connected with the ad agency or client who agreed to model for the ad. (The same goes for the child in the second DuPont ad in Chapter 5.) Again, any time models—professional or not—are used in advertising, it is necessary to obtain their signed consent. When the model is a minor child, written consent must come from the child's parent or legal guardian; this is true even if the child's parent or guardian arranged for the child to be at the photo shoot. Make sure the parent signs a written release allowing you to use the photograph in an agreed-upon manner and keep a copy of the consent form in the job jacket in case questions arise down the road.

What about the actual Bell employees in the "skeleton" ad? In this case, the employees' voluntary participation in the photo shoot is some indication of consent, but do not rely on this. Employees sometimes become disgruntled former employees, and their recollection of events may differ from yours. Even models who are employees of the client or agency should sign a written release prior to sitting for the photo shoot. The photo of John Doe in the Bell ad illustrates one of the few instances when photos of ordinary "people" can be used in advertising without their consent. Ordinary dead people—and you cannot get more ordinary than "John Doe"—cannot bring lawsuits for invasion of privacy. (Unfortunately, this means the photo of the deceased child featured in the anti-drunk-driving ads in Chapter 3 could technically be used without permission of the child's parent or guardian, and there would be no claim for invasion of privacy. But why would you want to do something as insensitive as that? If you would, revisit the ethics discussion in Chapter 1.)

On the other hand, the estates of famous dead people can—and often do—file misappropriation suits. If one of the Bell ads had used a photograph of a famous, deceased athlete, it would have been necessary to obtain permission from the athlete's estate prior to using the photograph in this way. Celebrities and professional models retain their "right of publicity" even after death, and their estates may continue to control and profit from their images as long as there is a market for doing so.

> Copyrights

Assuming you have signed releases from any people to be featured in an ad, you also may have to clear copyright hurdles before you can incorporate photos, music, video footage, illustrations, drawings, or other graphics into your ads.

Copyrights protect "original works of authorship," including literary, dramatic, musical, artistic, and certain other intellectual works.[4] Authors of "original works" own the copyright beginning at the moment of authorship; they may keep the copyrights for themselves, they may sell or lease them to someone else for a short time or forever or they may give them away if they choose.

Practically speaking, copyright law protects the ads you create, the songs you write and perform, and the artwork you produce. It also protects other people when they create these things. In a nutshell, copyright law requires

Figure 13-1
Copyrights protect "original works of authorship," including literary, dramatic, musical, artistic, and certain other intellectual works . . . including the ads you create.

Courtesy of Carmen Maye.

[4] "Copyright Office Basics," www.copyright.gov/circs/circ1.html#wci, accessed August 29, 2006.

that you identify the owner of copyrighted works you want to use and contact them to obtain permission. And it requires that others do the same for you.

A common misconception is that if you don't see the copyright symbol (see Figure 13-1) or other copyright notice, you are free to use the work as you wish. This is wrong; original works are protected as soon as they're fixed or recorded on paper, film, in bronze, in electronic bits, or any other tangible medium used for expression.

Say, for instance, you write a TV storyboard that just calls out for a particular piece of music. Without the music, the spot could work, but *with* the music, the spot could be really special. A great example of this is a Pepsi spot in which a Coca-Cola delivery guy reaches for a Pepsi. As he does this, "Your Cheatin' Heart" plays in the background. What if the advertising agency had been denied permission to use this song in the commercial? The short answer is that the creative team would have had to pick another song or go with another idea. Using the song without permission would surely have invited a copyright infringement lawsuit, or the least, a nasty letter from a corporate lawyer. The commercial would almost certainly have been pulled from circulation and a very effective creative strategy (along with client funds and probably your job) would have fizzled out.

Because music licensing can be complicated, there are firms that specialize in this area. The Harry Fox Agency in New York is one of the most prominent music licensing agencies; it's been representing music publishers since 1927. In other cases—if, for example, you want to use a particular artist's sound recording of a musical composition—you'll need to contact the record company or artist directly. Whether you go through an agency or deal directly with the copyright holders, do so prior to using the music. The price of the license will vary depending on the scope of the intended use, but you can be sure that it's less expensive to ask permission ahead of time than pay for costly litigation (and maybe punitive damages) after the fact.

On a typical advertising project, the creative elements are either produced in-house, provided by the client, or come from third parties. Consider the following photography examples (keep in mind that the ownership options are the same for music, photography, words, and other creative elements that appear in ads):

1. *Photograph produced in house.* If the photograph was shot in-house by someone employed full time by *the advertising agency*, then *the agency* owns the copyright. (These works of authorship are called "works made for hire." The employer owns copyrights in works made for hire.)

2. *Photograph produced by the client.* If the photograph was shot by someone employed full time by *the client*, then *the client* owns the copyright. (This is another "work made for hire.")

3. *Photograph produced by a third party.* If the photograph was shot by *a freelancer* hired by the agency just for that project or by *a stock photography vendor* or *another supplier*, then *the freelancer, the vendor,* or *the supplier* owns the copyright unless he/she/it sells, leases, or gives it to the agency or the client. Ownership of the copyright will remain with

the photographer unless there is a written contract transferring the copyrights.

Consider again the Whitewater ads from Chapter 1. If the agency hires a freelance photographer for the project, the agency must secure the photograph itself and also the *copyrights* in the photo. In other words, contracting for, paying for, and possessing a print of a photograph does not give someone a right to copy or otherwise reproduce it in an ad. When the freelancer hands over the photograph, the advertiser or agency should agree—in writing—about how the photograph may be used. Too often, agencies hire freelancers to shoot a photo—or write copy—for a single print ad, then later use that photo or copy in a series of ads or on billboards, etc. Yes, the fact that the freelancer handed over the photo for the print ad he thought he was working on probably allows you to use the photo for the originally planned print ad, but unless the original agreement with the freelancer covered all these additional uses, you must obtain a license—that is, written permission—before proceeding.

> Ad Copy

As for the ad copy itself, the same copyright rules apply: if someone other than a full-time employee of the agency or the client writes the copy, the advertiser or its agent must obtain a license that covers every intended use. And if multiple freelancers contribute to an ad—say a second freelance photographer did the product shots for the DuPont ads and a second freelance copywriter wrote the captions or the tagline used in the ads—you need to negotiate with each of them for each anticipated use of their work.

> Trademarks

Like most ads, the DuPont ads in Chapter 5 feature product logos or trademarks. This book contains numerous examples of trademarks, but be aware that sounds, short phrases (including taglines), and, sometimes, colors can identify the source of goods and therefore function as trademarks. (A quirky note about trademark law: symbols, sounds, short phrases, or colors that identify the source of *services* are called service marks. Yes, "trademark" is one word, and "service mark" is two words. No one knows why. It's just that way. The law is the same for each.)

Trademarks and service marks are important because they help consumers identify the source of goods and services and make judgments about the quality, service, etc. associated with those products (See Figure 13-2). Products that compete directly with each other may not use trademarks that are so similar they may confuse consumers. Tony the Tiger and the Exxon tiger coexisted peacefully for more than 30 years. But when Exxon started using its tiger to sell food, Kellogg's sued for infringement of its tiger trademark.

Courtesy of Carmen Maÿe.

Figure 13-2
Trademarks and service marks help consumers identify the source of goods and services and make judgments about the quality, service, etc. associated with those products.

Trademarks can be valuable commodities (see the discussion of names, logos, taglines, colors, and sounds and their role in branding in Chapter 2). Great examples are the word Nike, the symbolic Nike "swoosh," and the phrase "Just do it." The three-note chime that introduces NBC is a trademark, as is the robin's-egg blue of packaging by Tiffany & Co. And there are many more.

Logos (and names and phrases and sounds and colors) become trademarks when they are used in association with products actually traded in commerce. When a company's commerce is confined to a single state, the laws of that state apply to trademarks. For example, if your client, "Acme Widgets," a small firm in South Carolina, discovers that another

South Carolina company is doing business as "Acme Widgets," the law of South Carolina would apply. Most companies with particularly valuable trademarks do business across state lines. Federal law applies to interstate commerce, and the federal Lanham Act allows trademark owners to sue people who infringe or dilute their trademarks. Trademark dilution involves using a trademark in a way that detracts from the uniqueness of another trademark, even when there is no likelihood of customer confusion.

Is it trademark infringement to use someone else's trademarks in your advertisements? The law does not prohibit this practice, but it does require using some caution. If you're tempted to show a visible trademark (other than your own) in your ads, here are some guidelines:

1. Don't use the trademark in a deceptive way; don't apply a competitor's trademark to a fake product, don't alter the mark, and don't use the mark in a way that seems like an endorsement on your behalf (unless, of course, you get permission);

2. Don't use the mark in a disparaging way. While it's legitimate to compare your product to the competition, be sure you can substantiate any claims you make.

3. Consider creating a "dummy" product and trademark for use in your ads. For an example of how a South Carolina hospital did this effectively, see the Briefcase at the end of Chapter 8.

It's clear that advertising can help build brand identity. (See Chapter 2 for more on branding.) Ironically, there is a fine line between a strong brand and a weak trademark. Think about words like aspirin, escalator, nylon, and kerosene. These are simple words often used in conversation. What most people don't realize is that these were at one time trademarks with the power of exclusivity. Other manufacturers could not call their medicine "aspirin," their bathing suits "bikini," or even their toy a "yo-yo." Today people don't know what *else* to call these things. These words lost their trademark status because their owners didn't protect them. Although it may seem tempting to have your brand name on the tip of everyone's tongue when talking about the product category, it's damaging to the trademark.

It's not unheard of for brands to advertise their trademark status in journalism trade journals to help ensure that media know to use the trademark as a "proper adjective" in stories—rather than as a noun or verb. Think of the value a brand's name brings to its owner next time you need a Kleenex® facial tissue or you reach into your pocket for a ChapStik® Lip Balm. And give some serious thought to trademarks when you're standing in line to make a photocopy on a Xerox® photocopier. (If you're wondering why in these examples Kleenex®, ChapStik® and Xerox® have the little "R" in a circle, it's because these are federally registered trademarks; these companies have registered their marks with the United States Patent and Trademark Office and are entitled to use the ® symbol.)

The three print ads for DuPont in Chapter 5 illustrate trademarks at work; they include at least five different federally registered trademarks: DuPont®, Synchrony®, STS®, Canopy®, and Basis Gold®.

> Libel and Product Disparagement

If you're part of a creative team, you'll confront privacy and intellectual property issues almost daily. Occasionally, you'll also have to worry about libel and product disparagement. These issues crop up less often but are equally serious. News reporters and others who regularly write about people and organizations are keenly aware of the need to avoid defaming their subjects. Similarly, if you publish—in ads or otherwise—false information about someone that would defame them or harm their reputation, you could be sued for libel. (Libel and slander are types of defamation. Libel is usually fixed in writing or recorded; slander is oral and more fleeting.)

Individuals and organizations can sue for libel if a publication about them exposes them to hatred or contempt, lowers them in the esteem of friends or associates, or hurts their business. An award-winning ad features the names, photographs, and home counties of absentee parents who had failed to pay significant amounts of child support. Clearly, being falsely accused of not paying child support would harm one's reputation. This is a clear example of a defamatory statement. This particular ad was truthful and, therefore, not problematic, but messages like this that accuse people of bad behavior often breed libel suits. The key is to make sure the information in these ads is correct and to take steps to verify the source of your information. If an ad cites statistics or other information gleaned from government sources—such as names of people failing to pay child support—be careful not to make mistakes when transferring the data to the ad. If the advertising agency makes a defamatory mistake, the client and the agency could be sued. If the mistake was contained in the official government data, neither the client nor the agency could be successfully sued for libel.

A related civil harm is "trade libel." This is akin to ordinary libel but involves statements that defame a particular product. You may have heard of "Veggie Libel" lawsuits. These refer to libel suits over statements that harm the reputation and, therefore, sales of perishable goods like apples or, ironically, beef. Trade libel suits are fairly rare. More often, an organization either sues for ordinary libel because its overall reputation has been sullied, or it sues for product disparagement because the quality of a product or service has been questioned. As with regular libel, the truth is the advertiser's best friend. If your message is true or you had no legitimate reason to believe otherwise, you have little reason to worry.

> A Final Word: Keep Creativity Out of the Courtroom

A number of factors determine the success of libel lawsuits and the other types of legal action discussed in this chapter. Creative lawyers can sometimes minimize the negative effects of lawsuits against advertisers and their agencies—at a price. The best strategy is to avoid lawsuits altogether and save the creativity for somewhere other than the courtroom.

> ## Suggested Activities

1. Visit four restaurants that serve Pepsi brand soft drinks and order a Coca-Cola or Diet Coke. Summarize what the waiters told you. Did they explain that their restaurants don't serve Coca-Cola branded soft drinks? Did they suggest a Pepsi as a substitute brand?

2. Develop a list of names for a new brand of bottled spring water. Do a trademark search for your top name by visiting the United States Patent and Trademark Office online at www.uspto.gov.

ITT Industries' Corporate Advertising Campaign: Putting a Face on a Large Corporation

By Sue Westcott Alessandri, PhD Assistant Professor, Suffolk University

Corporate advertising promotes the company rather than any individual product brands. Often, a company develops a corporate advertising campaign because it feels the public is not fully aware of what it does. Such was the case with New York–based ITT Industries. The company launched a campaign in September 1998 in an attempt to raise the level of awareness of itself as an engineering and manufacturing company.

The campaign was intended to reach several audiences, including vendors, the financial community, and ITT's own employees, and ITT wanted to promote itself "in a memorable way," according to Thomas Martin, senior vice president and director of corporate relations, who oversaw the campaign's development.

ITT found the solution to educating the company's diverse audiences beneath the surface—quite literally beneath the surface. The broadcast component of the campaign was launched with a TV ad featuring an assortment of marine life singing Handel's "Hallelujah Chorus." From a strategic perspective, this ad accomplished the goal of any corporate advertising campaign: it promoted the corporate brand by giving an otherwise abstract company a personality. In ITT's case, this particular ad educated the public about the importance of clean water, which ITT can deliver with the help of its Fluid Technology division.

Additional TV spots took a slice-of-life approach, and each was successful in explaining a complicated business in a simple yet creative way. Also, media was chosen that would reach the diverse audiences that ITT needed to educate. Ads aired on CNN, CNBC, and on local news programs in major markets such as New York; Washington, DC; Boston; and Chicago.

Over time, ITT adopted a print campaign that used full-color, vivid photography to highlight its four divisions: Fluid Technology, Electronic Components, Defense Electronics and Services, and Motion and Flow Control. For example, an ad for ITT's Defense Electronics and Services division features the image of a fighter pilot walking away from his jet and into the sunset.

Courtesy of ITT Industries.

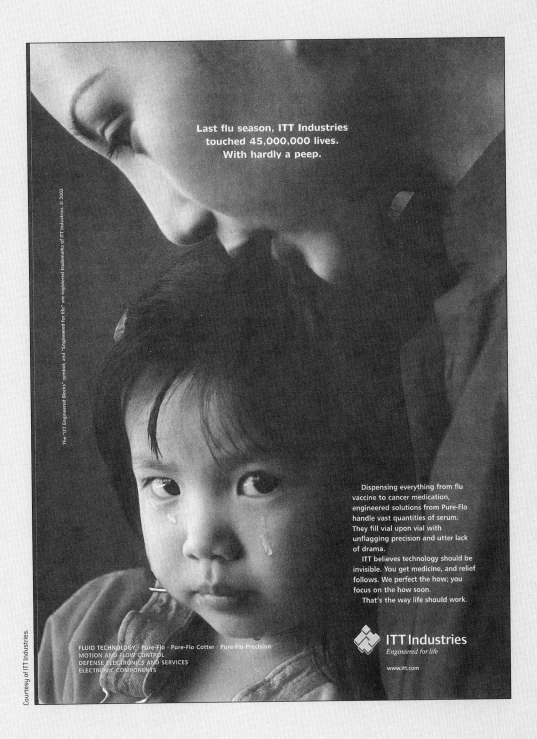

Last flu season, ITT Industries
touched 45,000,000 lives.
With hardly a peep.

The "ITT Engineered Blocks" symbol and "Engineered for life" are registered trademarks of ITT Industries. © 2002

Courtesy of ITT Industries.

Dispensing everything from flu
vaccine to cancer medication,
engineered solutions from Pure-Flo
handle vast quantities of serum.
They fill vial upon vial with
unflagging precision and utter lack
of drama.
    ITT believes technology should be
invisible. You get medicine, and relief
follows. We perfect the how; you
focus on the how soon.
    That's the way life should work.

ITT Industries
Engineered for life

www.itt.com

FLUID TECHNOLOGY · Pure-Flo · Pure-Flo Cotter · Pure-Flo Precision
MOTION AND FLOW CONTROL
DEFENSE ELECTRONICS AND SERVICES
ELECTRONIC COMPONENTS

Strategically, the ad shows how ITT is capable of delivering a global positioning system (GPS) that "responds with positioning information accurate to the foot." An ad for the Motion and Flow Control division features the headline "Over 6,000,000 boaters don't know ITT Industries helps keep them on an even keel." The strategy of using the simple image of a sailor aboard a small vessel illustrates a company that can help keep "water safely at arm's length or comfortably within reach."

During the several years the campaign ran, it became apparent to ITT executives that television was less practical than print in terms of reaching a targeted audience, so in 2002 the company decided not to run additional TV spots. Instead, ITT began to put its media budget to use running the print ads in vehicles that would achieve the company's reach and frequency goals.

ITT and its agency developed a media plan that included a combination of horizontal trades, including *Business Week, Barron's, Forbes,* and *Fortune,* and mainstream titles, such as *Time* and *Newsweek.* And because 30 percent of ITT's revenues are derived from its defense division, the company placed ads in some vertical trades meant to target the Washington leadership, including *Congressional Quarterly* and *National Journal.* The company also used similar trade publications for additional key markets, such as water technology, irrigation, and communication.

During a campaign and at the end of the campaign, a company measures its true success by measuring results. Because it is nearly impossible to make cause-and-effect arguments based on advertising, it is also nearly impossible to directly link the advertising to an increased stock price, but ITT does look at the relationship between the two.

In addition, ITT also uses several other methods to quantify the success of its advertising efforts. For example, in addition to calculating the actual reach and frequency of its chosen media vehicles, the company analyzes the media vehicles' own surveys that measure recall and message retention. By analyzing these two measures, the company is able to prove it is reaching the right audience with the appropriate frequency. More important, these efforts reinforce to the company that the appropriate audience is paying attention. To track more specific results, the company employs familiarity and favorability surveys to measure its success in reaching targeted audience segments.

Finally, the company's own employees represent the company's largest single block of shareholders and therefore are important audience members for the ITT corporate advertising campaign. To reach this target, ITT packaged the campaign on a CD and distributed it to all employees. To measure success among this constituency, the company tracked employees' knowledge of the ads over time in a creative and interactive way. ITT received several hundred responses to a "favorite ad" contest that simultaneously measured recognition and likeability of the ads.

CLIENT PITCHES
HOW TO SELL YOUR IDEAS

14

There's a wonderful scene in the British film *Honest, Decent, and True*—a send-up of advertising—in which the copywriter and art director do their best to convince the client that their TV commercial for his new brand of lager is just what the brand needs to become a success. If the scene didn't strike so close to home, we could enjoy the laughs less guiltily. But as in all good satire, this scene has been played, with variations, in nearly every advertising agency or client conference room. It goes something like this: The writer ardently presents a TV storyboard, which is handsomely mounted and standing on an easel in full view of those present. These include, in addition to the client, members of the agency (the account executive, the planner or head of research, the media analyst, and, of course, the copywriter and art director, who have slaved feverishly for weeks to come up with this concept).

The commercial is risky, however. It tells the story of a group of happy voyagers at the bar of a grand cruise ship. Some order embarrassingly tony drinks, and a few are "brave enough" to order what they want—the client's new lager. Suddenly, there's a loud crash, and the ship begins to sink. In the final shot, we see survivors in a lifeboat, and they're all drinking the client's lager. Only then do we learn the name of the ship—it is the *Titanic*.

The client listens in silence and says nothing, even after the presentation is finished. The tense silence is at last broken by the researcher, who explains that this is a spoof, a big joke. The client answers, "Yes, I suppose some people would find this funny . . . Yes. Well it's just fine. Just fine." There is an audible sigh of relief. Then the client continues: "There are just a few very small things I'm having problems with. Nothing major, mind you. I wonder about the time frame here. After all, this is a contemporary product, and is it appropriate to do it in a period setting? Then there's the question of whether humor is appropriate to the selling of a lager. I also have a bit of a problem with the use of such a historic disaster to advertise our product. But nothing major." Silence again. A few clearings of throats. Then the various agency members attempt to brush these "small" problems aside, telling their conservative client that the young singles who are the market for this product don't care about the *Titanic,* that they will merely laugh at the disaster and get the message. But it's no use. He just isn't buying.

> The Presentation Is Half of the Battle

Coming up with great ideas is a monumental task, but so is convincing your coworkers and your client to "buy" your ideas. When you see great advertising, you can be fairly certain that those ideas saw the light of day because the client was willing to take a risk.

Regardless of your client's proclivity for taking risks, you must be prepared to sell the advertising just as thoroughly as you believe the advertising sells the goods. Generally, the presentation of the creative portion of an ad campaign should come after all other aspects of the campaign have been discussed. These other elements may include a summary of the marketing background for the product or service, a discussion of the research the agency has undertaken to conceive the strategy, and a proposed media plan that justifies the selection of certain media vehicles and the rejection of others.

Because your marketing summary will have touched on target markets and broad marketing goals, your presentation of the ad should be restricted to the communications aspects of your campaign. But where do you begin? Actually, you began weeks or months ago by establishing a comfortable, two-way relationship with your client. Clients don't like surprises. Nothing turns them off faster than walking into a presentation without the slightest inkling of what lies ahead. By staying in touch with your clients and making them feel that they are valued members of your team, you will put them in a more receptive frame of mind. This doesn't mean that you have to reveal your big ideas early, but you should certainly agree on the basic direction of the campaign before the actual presentation. Good clients are risk takers who try not to throw barriers in the way of sound, creative judgment. Part of your job is to nurture this attitude well before the day of the presentation. When that day arrives, here's what should happen:

1. *Begin with a brief recap of the assignment.* You were asked to solve a certain problem. Remind your client of the problem and share your creative exploration of it. You might even share ideas that you rejected; this can indicate that you are concerned about the success of the campaign and not merely about selling your ideas.

2. *Discuss your creative strategy thoroughly.* You're not talking to the consumer, who doesn't need to understand the strategy to like the ads.

You're talking to the people who are going to be paying you handsomely for your efforts. Therefore, you must convince them in a highly logical manner that the ideas you are about to present—which may appear to be highly illogical—are the result of sound, perceptive thinking. So talk about what's going on in the minds of members of the target audience. Tell what they're saying now. Tell what you would like them to be saying. Tell why your campaign will stand out from the competition; you might even want to show competing ads to demonstrate how your campaign breaks through the clutter. Above all, when you present your strategy, link it clearly to the original goals of the project. Does it answer the problem? Exactly how does it do this?

3. *Make a big deal about the campaign's theme.* You may be so familiar with the theme by now that you forget that your client may never have seen or heard it before. Introduce the theme importantly by displaying it on a board or flashing it on a screen. If animation, music, or sound is involved, use it as part of the presentation.

4. *Show how the big idea is expressed.* This involves the various advertisements and commercials, the sales promotion and collateral pieces, and everything else that is part of your campaign. Many agencies will try to have something as finished as possible (a demo CD for radio, a rough video, or a set of computer-generated stills with an audio track for television). Other agencies will sell their idea for a TV commercial by showing a key frame, the one central visual that sums up the ad's idea. When presenting a key frame, explain what action will take place. You may even want to act it out. With regard to the body copy in print ads, most seasoned presenters agree that it's best not to read it to your client. Instead, simply communicate what it expresses and invite them to review it later. What you're striving to communicate is that the big idea—the central theme—runs through all of these ads and that this theme is a result of a well-devised strategy that delivers the intended message perfectly.

5. *Close with a summary statement and ask for the order.* Remind the client how effective this campaign will be, how thoroughly it satisfies marketing and communications goals, and why it is the best choice for the problem at hand.

6. *Answer questions honestly.* If you don't know, say you don't know and promise to find out. Avoid direct confrontations, but don't come off as a "yes-man" or "yes-woman" to your client. Clients don't want that. If you disagree with your client's suggestions, explain why logically and politely. Compromise on minor issues and speak with conviction about those issues that you feel are essential to the spirit and intent of your work. If there is no agreement, your only choice may be to thank the client and go on to another job. Few good agencies will compromise their creative standards to produce what they feel is inferior work. It's a delicate situation. Knowing how to handle a client who disagrees demands a thorough understanding not only of that client's company culture but also of the personalities of the decision makers.

> Pitching with Pizzazz

Advertising is a creative business, so don't try to bore a client into buying your big idea. Have fun with your presentation, but make sure it's relevant. Consider this pitch from Merkley Newman Harty to members of the National Thoroughbred Racing Association. The agency started its presentation with a video that showed close-ups of a typical horse race—pounding hoofs, whips to the hindquarters, flaring nostrils, and a photo finish. Then came the following line: "The function of insanity is doing the same thing over and over again and expecting different results." This helped the agency make the point that the hackneyed approach that racetracks had used for years wasn't working. Racetracks needed a fresh, new approach. They needed Merkley Newman Harty. Members of the National Thoroughbred Racing Association agreed.

Leo Burnett won the Heinz ketchup account by showing ads that made Heinz seem cool and teen-friendly. On the morning of the final pitch, the agency's team set up a hot dog stand in the lobby and lined the escalator walls with ketchup labels with catchy slogans. The conference room was turned into a diner with bar stools, a counter, and a short-order cook.

Zimmerman Advertising won the Six Flags pitch by staging a mock funeral service for Mr. Six, the theme park's geriatric dancing icon. The funeral service was in keeping with Fright Fest, the Halloween event the agency was pitching.

But don't think that elaborately staged events are the best way to win accounts. Like all advertising, you need to consider the audience and the message. Sam's Club, for instance, isn't known for its frills and isn't the right client for stunts. StrawberryFrog, which won the Sam's Club account, had considered installing a giant container labeled "ideas" in its lobby to communicate that the agency had ideas in bulk. However, they abandoned that gimmick and instead sent 12 agency staffers to work at small businesses for a day. Because small-business owners are key customers for Sam's Club, this approach was far more impressive than a giant prop. It showed that the agency understood the brand and its customers.

Elaborate stunts can even backfire. One agency that pitched the 7Up account dressed up like circus characters and danced around the conference room. The stunt took an hour out of the 3-hour meeting and seemed irrelevant to the brand and ideas being pitched. Needless to say, it sent the wrong message and the agency didn't win the account.

Another agency created a 10-minute video of its pitch for the Subway account and uploaded it to YouTube for everyone—including competitors—to see. The video quickly took on a life of its own, and several parody videos soon appeared online that lampooned the agency and its staff. The agency pulled out of the review, stating it had reached the finals of a pitch for a conflicting account.

Why do some agencies go to such elaborate lengths to win accounts? Consider this: A recent article in *Advertising Age* states the average agency/

Courtesy of Nasuti & Hinkle Creative.

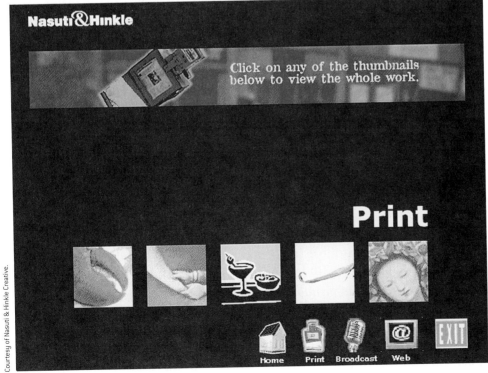

Courtesy of Nasuti & Hinkle Creative.

Figure 14-1

Nasuti & Hinkle's website explains the agency's philosophy and shows examples of its creative work. Also, notice the terrific sales results of the ads.

client relationship is just two years.[1] As Harry Jacobs, chairman emeritus of the Martin Agency, told the *Richmond Times-Dispatch,* "New business is the lifeblood of the advertising agency. Without perfecting it and being proficient at it, the agency is not going to grow."[2]

A great way for prospective clients (and employees) to form a first impression of an agency is to visit its website, which will state the agency's business philosophy, list current clients, profile key personnel, and show examples of creative work (see Figure 14-1). However, even the best website can't compare to the effect of a face-to-face presentation.

> Guidelines for Making Presentations

Whatever area of advertising you eventually choose, you're always going to have to present something to somebody. The more experience you have in presenting, the better you will become. A great place to start presenting is in your classes. The following tips will help you discover how to do so comfortably, enthusiastically, and convincingly:

- *Capture the attention of your audience right away.* Open your talk with something that not only gains the attention of your audience members but also causes them to respect you as an authority and starts them thinking about your topic. Never apologize for yourself as an introduction—that only undermines your credibility.

- *Remember how it feels to be a listener.* You have plenty of practice being a student. What do your most interesting professors do to keep your attention? Use them as role models.

- *Rehearse out loud.* Practice before a mirror, unless that's uncomfortable. If it is, rehearse before a room and pretend the room is filled. Or rehearse by asking one or more friends to listen and give you comments.

- *Listen to your words and inflections.* If they sound wrong to you, they probably are. Underscore words you want to stress. Indicate pauses for a breath if that will help your pacing.

- *Stand tall.* Your arms should be comfortably at your sides. Avoid sweeping gestures. Don't fiddle with rubber bands, paper clips, or pen caps. It will be difficult at first, but you can learn to do it.

- *Make eye contact.* If your audience is large, shift your focus now and then to a different person or a different side of the room. Include everyone. If one person is more important than the rest, spend a good deal of time making contact with him or her.

- *Speak from your diaphragm.* Use one of the lower ranges of your voice. It will carry better and sound more authoritative.

---

[1] Mara Brownstein, "Why Agency-Client Divorce Rates Are Soaring," *Adage.com,* 18 April 2007.
[2] Otesa Middleton, "Here's the Pitch: Ad Agencies Reveal Their Strategies for Getting Accounts," *Richmond Times-Dispatch,* 2 September 1996, p. D16.

- *Use inflection for effect.* Avoid monotones. Emphasize important words as underscored in your notes. Pause for dramatic effect. A pause that seems eternal to you is probably short to your listeners.

- *Use appropriate facial expressions and gestures.* These should be congruent with your spoken words. If something is funny, smile.

- *Be prepared for questions.* Don't let them throw you. No one is out to do that. If you don't know the answer, simply say you don't. Ask team members to answer questions related to their areas of expertise. But don't try to wing it. Cleve Langton, author of *New Business Lessons from Madison Avenue*, says presenters should avoid disclaimers such as "I think . . .", "In my (our) opinion . . .", and "Gut feeling tells us . . ." because they detract from your credibility.[3]

- *Check out the room before you speak.* There's nothing more disconcerting than discovering when you're in the middle of your presentation that you can't use your visual aids. Before you speak, make sure all the audio/visual equipment you'll need is in the room and in working order. Are the seats arranged the way you want them? Is there a podium or table for your notes? If you plan to write key points throughout your presentation, is there an easel with a pad, a whiteboard and appropriate pens?

> Perils and Pitfalls of Presenting

Ron Hoff, who in his long and distinguished career has been associated with Ogilvy & Mather and Foote, Cone & Belding, has a lot of experience with the perils and pitfalls of presenting.[4] Here is what he says

- The biggest problem we face is boring our audience. Sometimes, we even bore ourselves. Seldom do our identities emerge in our professional selves. Perhaps this is why we're so boring when we make presentations.

- Visuals, when added to words, will more than double recall of your message. When you persuade the audience to participate in your presentation, recall will zoom to around 90 percent among the people who have taken part.

- The moment of judgment in presentations occurs within the first 90 seconds. That's when audiences decide to tune in or check out. If the presenter talks entirely about himself or herself, the audience disconnects or daydreams. Audiences are sitting there asking themselves, "When is that presenter going to start talking about me?"

Hoff identifies the following key strategies for effective presentations:

- *Know the people in the opposition, and know your best supporter.* Address your first words to the opponent. Then move to someone you know

---

[3] Cleve Langton, "What Breaks—or Makes—a Presentation," *Advertising Age,* 9 June 2008, p. 18.
[4] The authors thank Ron Hoff for granting them permission to use these ideas.

is favorable. You should feel refueled and reinforced at this point, so you can move on to the others. When you reach a seemingly negative person, go back to a friend. Keep warming up the group until it seems safe to invade the "enemy territory."

- *Start with something you feel comfortable with.* It can be fun, but it must be relevant. Dr. Stephen Zipperblatt of the Pritikin Longevity Center in San Diego opens his workshop with these words: "Man doesn't die . . . he kills himself." He then goes on to tell participants how to live healthier lives. He's off and rolling.

- *Appoint a DSW—a director of "So what?"* This person represents the grubby, selfish interests of the audience. Whenever you say something irrelevant, he or she says, "So what?" and you know you're off course.

- *Start your agency presentations about halfway through.* Halfway through is where most of us stop talking about ourselves and start talking about our clients. Start with the audience's issue of primary concern instead of your issue of concern (get the business). Ask yourself, "How can we help the poor devils?"

Hoff also identifies "what bugs people about presentations," explaining that these examples come from people in the business who've suffered through numerous presentations that flopped:

- "You know so much more about this than I do." (The client wants someone who knows more than he or she does.)

- "I'm so nervous. I hope you can't see how much my knees are shaking." (A true confidence builder.)

- "I've got my notes so screwed up, I don't know what I'm going to do." (The client thinks, "What am I doing here?")

- "We know you're waiting for the creative, so I'll try to fly through the media plan." (And therefore miss many opportunities to sell the package or set the stage for the big idea.)

Hoff also feels that every presentation should have a burning issue. Too often, we fall far short of this. We sputter. He adds that too many presenters act as if they don't know what slide is coming up next and that just as many don't know the first thing about eye contact. What is so interesting about that distant star they're looking at? Is it any wonder there's no connecting going on there?

> How to Correct the Problems

Eye contact and connecting are extremely important. So keep the lights up and move toward members of the audience. Reduce the distance between you and them, both geographically and ideologically. People are nervous at the start of a presentation, when the distance is the greatest.

Don't be upset by interruptions. Answer but never attack. Be professional.

If there are rude people in the audience, continue to be polite. The group will take care of their own. Above all, never lose your temper; this is tantamount to losing the business.

How do you overcome nervousness? Tell yourself that you're the best—and believe it. Relax. Present to yourself in the mirror and watch and listen to yourself. Even better record yourself presenting. Watch it once, a second time with the sound off, and a third time with sound only. Do you like your nonverbals? If not, take steps to improve them. Do you like your voice?

What, if anything, could make you sound more convincing? Exercise your jaw just before presenting. Take several slow, deep breaths.

It all comes out in your voice—your joy, your nervousness, your anticipation, and your boredom. Your voice gives your audience its first real clue about you, yet we often neglect our voices. Deep voices communicate authority. Anyone can, with practice, present in a voice deeper than the normal speaking voice. Spend a day working on your voice by narrating your day into a recorder: "It's 9 a.m. and I'm waiting for the bus. I see it coming now. A few people are here, but it's not a busy day...." Then listen to it. Then do it again and listen again.

Most important, says Hoff, remember that the client may not always be right but that the client is always the client.

> Using PowerPoint Effectively

Picture this: You're sitting in a darkened room. Slide after slide is swirling past you. The presenter is droning on in a monotonous voice, reading everything that appears on the screen. He tells you that he'll give you a handout of the PowerPoint presentation, so you don't have to take notes (or, as you realize, pay attention to what he's saying). Occasionally, a cute graphic or cartoon appears on the screen. You chuckle, even if you don't see the relevance. Finally, the presentation's over and the lights come up. As your eyes try to adjust to the light, the presenter asks, "Any questions?" You're too numb to respond.

Just as in this example, the wrong visuals can sabotage a presentation. So what should you do?

- *Remember you, not the screen, should be the focal point.* There's a reason you were invited to present in person. Otherwise, you would have been asked to e-mail your presentation as an attachment. Use the screen to supplement what you're saying, not say it for you.

- *Keep the bells and whistles to a minimum.* PowerPoint allows you to add all sorts of funky sounds and movements. Sometimes these gimmicks help you make a point, but all too often they're the sign of an inexperienced presenter.

- *Remember the basics of good design.* Readability is key. Have one concept per slide and no more than eight lines per slide. Text should be set in

24-point or larger type and in upper- and lowercase letters to make it easier to read.

- *Use the slides as an aid, not as a script.* Consultant Chris Shumaker cautions, "When a slide with a bunch of complete sentences is shown, the first thing the audience is going to do is read it. And if the speaker is saying something different than what the audience is reading, they have to decide to either listen to the speaker or read the slide, because it's too hard to do both. And if the speaker is saying exactly what's on the slide, then it's not really a slide—it's a script, which is not good."[5]

- *Create a look for your presentation.* Select a typeface and color combination that is easy on the eyes. Sans serif typefaces work best because of their simplicity. Also, consider putting your logo in the corner of your slides.

- *Use numbers, bullets, and lists.* These devices help organize your material and make it easier for your audience to follow. But don't overwhelm your audience with a slide that has every point listed. Start by showing one point at first, then building until you've listed all the points.

- *Keep the visual on screen in sync with what you're saying.* There's nothing more distracting than hearing someone describe the big idea and seeing a media flowchart, or some other unrelated message, on the screen. Even smaller inconsistencies can be irksome, such as hearing someone say, "Save 50 percent" when the screen says "half off."

- *Remember, a slick PowerPoint presentation won't make up for a weak idea.* All the latest bells and whistles won't make up for a presentation that's not smart.

> Suggested Activities

1. Contact an account executive or creative director in an advertising agency, or the advertising manager of a company, and arrange a short interview. During the interview, ask that individual to explain how a particular creative strategy was devised. Make a presentation to your class on your findings.

2. Choose one of the case studies in this book, imagine that you've been chosen to sell the client on the idea, and prepare a presentation of it. Make the presentation to the class as if you were selling the campaign to the client.

3. Read a book on salesmanship or interview a speech professor at your school and prepare a report that identifies the key elements in making a sale. How can you apply these principles to the selling of an idea?

---

[5] Chris Shumaker, "Pitch Perfect: Tips on How to Keep Prospective Clients' Attention," *Adweek,* 9 October 2006, p. 16.

What Does "Urgent" Mean to You?

We've all done dumb things. Like eat food that smells a little funky. Or poke a hornet's nest to see if it's active. Or uncork a champagne bottle without checking to see where it's aimed. Ouch! These dumb moves hurt more than just egos. Although the injuries may not be life threatening, they often need immediate medical attention. So what do you do? Go to the emergency room where people with life-and-death injuries are being rushed in by ambulance? Take a chance that your doctor will squeeze you in between appointments? Lexington Medical Center offers a better remedy.

The Lexington Medical Center has six urgent-care facilities that treat non-life-threatening injuries such as sprains, broken bones, and cuts that need stitches. Created to take some of the burden off the hospital's emergency room, the facilities are strategically located so that urgent care is only 15 minutes from anywhere in Lexington County, South Carolina.

Despite the convenient locations, the facilities were not reaching capacity. So Lexington Medical Center's marketing department turned to the Riggs Agency and Mad Monkey production studio to create a campaign to increase visits to the centers by 5 percent.

Riggs and Mad Monkey developed an award-winning campaign that uses humor to grab people's attention and resonate with its audience. Unlike most medical center ads that boast about state-of-the-art technology or a caring medical team (yawn), Lexington's ads focus on the mishaps of real people. Because none of the injuries featured in the ads is life threatening, the humor is quite appropriate.

"While brainstorming for this campaign, we realized that most of us had hobbled, limped or carried someone into an ER. More times than not, we were there due to a ridiculous lack in judgment. In other words, we were the target—the accident waiting to happen. More importantly, we realized that whether it's a sprain or an unexplained rash, when it happens to you, it's *urgent*. Thus the tag, 'Whatever Urgent Means to You, We're Here,'" explained Lorie Gardner, president of Mad Monkey.

"This stuff was a blast to work on," said art director John Foust. A typical brainstorming session went along these lines: "What's the stupidest thing you've ever tried with a frog gig?" the art director asks, staring into his

Courtesy of Lexington Medical Center.

Courtesy of Lexington Medical Center.

sketchbook. "Clean my toenails?" a copywriter replies, tentatively. The art director pauses, considers, and volleys back, "too expected."

Gardner described how the creative team pitched the idea to the client. "Due to the turnaround time, we wrote scripts and acted them out. Sometimes we create concept boards, with various photos or faces that help us paint the drama. For this project however, we simply became thumb-sucking 'acktors.' Quite scary, I know."

One of the first TV spots in the campaign opens on a mischievous boy who's dressed in a superhero's cape and goggles. We hear his mom calling for him in the background: "Sam . . . turn down the TV. Sammy . . . Sam . . . Oh, please tell me you're not trying to fly again!" As she pleads with him to be careful, he takes a flying leap off the porch, straight into the bushes. A voice-over delivers the tagline: "For whatever urgent means to you." Undaunted, Sam gets up, brushes off his cape, readjusts his goggles, and climbs back on the porch to do it all over again.

The story of the young superhero's misstep came from the life experience of one of the vice presidents of the medical center. Margaret Gregory, then marketing and public relations manager at Lexington Medical Center and mother of a young boy, commented on the commercial: "This spot appeals to parents who know better than anyone what imaginations their children can have and that the end result often means a trip to the urgent care facility."

Another commercial opens on a close-up of a brother and sister, arguing over who'll be the first to try out a new sled. You get the sense that it's just

Courtesy of Lexington Medical Center.

snowed because the kids are bundled in jackets, scarves, and mittens. The boy wins the argument because, as he reminds his sister, "I built it. It's my sled." The sister, nonplused, rolls her eyes and mutters, "Whatever." As the camera pulls back you learn there's not a speck of snow on the hill. And to make matters worse, this is no ordinary sled—it has wheels on the back and sled runners on the front. As the sister gives him a push, you hear the familiar urgent care message: "For whatever urgent means to you."

It's not just kids who need urgent care. Grownups can do some dumb things, too. Another TV commercial features a man opening some leftovers in the middle of the night. You sense that the food has been in the refrigerator for some time by the amount of crinkles in the foil wrapping. The man takes a whiff. Pauses. Takes another whiff and says to himself, "Smells good to me." Tagline: "For whatever urgent means to you."

As the teams from Riggs and Mad Monkey brainstormed, they found themselves showing their scars to one another. Copywriter Michael Powelson mused, "Interesting things happen when you get four or five people around a table discussing the scars they've accumulated. It starts out innocently enough. But at some point the show-and-tell gets pretty competitive. I'm surprised more clothes didn't come off."

A TV commercial features three men around a campfire, each bragging about the ordeal that led to a scar. For one man it was a fishhook gone wrong. Another had appendicitis. And the third guy got his scar from third-degree burns pulling his prize chocolate soufflé out of the oven. As he says

Courtesy of Lexington Medical Center.

this, his marshmallow is burned to a crisp. Guess he won't be a guest chef on the Food Channel anytime soon.

A radio spot captured the numerous reasons people can need urgent care:

LEXINGTON MEDICAL CENTER "STORIES"

MAN:	Here's what happened.
GIRL:	It's a long story.
WOMAN:	You really want to know?
MAN:	I was on the roof . . .
WOMAN:	we were hungry . . .
BOY:	And mom told me not to . . .
MAN:	Everything was OK; at . . .
WOMAN:	first it tasted fine . . .
BOY:	"be that way," I said.
GIRL:	That's when it all happened . . .
MAN:	I only looked away for a second but . . .
WOMAN:	Next thing you know . . .
BOY:	Bam.
MAN:	Pop.
GIRL:	Hsssss.
WOMAN:	Blauuughhh (mock vomit). Uhh, it was so embarrassing.
GIRL:	They were pretty freaked out . . .

BOY:	cause your arm's only supposed to bend one way.
WOMAN:	Yes, OK, I was warned . . .
MAN:	(mocking woman's voice) Use your knees not your back . . .
GIRL:	but I couldn't help scratching it . . .
BOY:	looked like a moldy grapefruit . . .
GIRL:	and the ice wasn't helping . . .
MAN:	I tried to wait but I . . .
WOMAN:	couldn't keep anything down . . .
BOY:	to the Urgent Care Center in . . .
GIRL:	Lexington
MAN:	Chapin
BOY:	Batesburg–Leesville
WOMAN:	Swansea
MAN:	Gilbert
GIRL:	Irmo.
ANNCR:	Every scar has a story. That's why there's urgent care from Lexington Medical Center. With six different locations, urgent care is only 15 minutes from anywhere in Lexington County. It's the perfect solution, for whatever "urgent" means to you.

Billboards feature famous last words spoken before a trip to urgent care:

"A dare is a dare."

"He started it."

"HEY, WATCH THIS."

"Oh, it's not THAT heavy."

"Oh, he won't bite."

"Must've been something I ate."

The ads hit home with people from all walks of life because they trigger memories of similar incidents in our own lives. The campaign began in the summer of 2005 and has won numerous awards. More important, the urgent care centers have seen an average increase of 7 percent in the number of acute care visits over the same period of the previous year. Individual centers have seen increases in ranges from 6 to 14 percent. And that's no accident.

APPENDIX 1
HOW TO LAND A JOB IN THE CREATIVE DEPARTMENT

Here are some key qualities that agencies look for in beginning writers and art directors.

- *Originality in thinking.* Granted, that's highly subjective. But you don't even get an interview unless your work is special. Furthermore, the work and the person being interviewed have to connect in the mind of the interviewer.

- *Passion for the work.* This involves the ability to enthuse about how you come up with the ideas and bounce back from mistakes.

- *Enthusiasm for the world.* More than a fleeting knowledge of music, film, theater, art, and current trends in humor is highly regarded. So is travel, especially to places off the beaten track. Such is the stuff that good ideas come from.

- *A love affair with words and design.* This affair should be ongoing and all-consuming.

- *Raw imagination.* The ideas don't have to be feasible. The agency can pull you back. It's harder to push you further.

- *Knowledge of research and marketing.* This means you can converse intelligently about those subjects but not to the extent that it restrains your creative product.

- *The guts to try the dumbest ideas.* Strike the emotions. Touch people. But don't do too much of a good thing. Too many puns can hurt you. Bad puns can hurt you. Then again, it's subjective.

> Your Portfolio or "Book"

You need more than a good book—you need a *great* book to even be considered by a major agency, according to top creative directors who spoke to a group of advertising educators in a weekend creative symposium. Agencies admire books that break rules instead of complying with them—books that stand apart in smart ways, just as great advertisements stand apart.

What type of portfolio should you use? A spiral book with acetate pages is a popular choice because it allows you to arrange and rearrange your work until everything has the best flow. You may wish to place your mounted works in a compact portfolio or briefcase, arranging them in a way that shows off each piece to its best advantage. However, this approach can become cumbersome. Some students spend extra money to laminate their work so that it has a professional look. Others burn a CD of their work or post it on the Web.

Keep in mind that the quality of your work will be what lands you the job. A typo will hurt your chances whether the piece is laminated, on disk, photocopied, or posted online. However, given a choice between two would-be creatives who both have great portfolios, the individual who puts in the extra effort will probably rate higher.

Also keep in mind that you will often be asked to leave your portfolio for later review. Therefore, you may need to develop several portfolios or create a small "leave-behind" piece consisting of copies of your work. Another great option is to post your work online. There are a number of portfolio hosting sites for creatives, including coroflot.com, foliosnap.com, and carbonmade .com. Your university may have its own site that posts student work.

The Contents of Your Portfolio

John Sweeney offers this advice about what to include in your book:[1]

1. *Demonstrate the campaign concept.* Make sure your first campaign is your best. And close with a flourish. First and last impressions carry weight.

2. *Adjust your portfolio to meet the needs of the interview.* But if you want a simple formula, try this: one package-goods campaign (toothpaste, deodorant, trash bags, and so on), one hard-goods campaign (stereos, cameras, computers, refrigerators, and so on), one food or fashion campaign, one public service or tourism campaign, and one new product idea and an introductory campaign for it. At least one campaign should include television, print, radio, and outdoor—a complete demonstration of the campaign concept. Use music once, demonstration once, and testimonials once. Give a range of solutions to a range of products.

3. *Choose products you like when possible.* Be forewarned, however. It's easy to write for products you like. You won't always have such freedom in the business. Also, if you try to beat American Express, Coke, and

---

[1] John Sweeney, "Step Up Persistence to Get in Agency Door," *Advertising Age,* 2 May 1985.

Macintosh, you will probably fail. Choose products that are not currently celebrated for their creative work. Also, don't do work on one of the agency's accounts. You may choose a strategy rejected by research.

4. *Include at least two long-copy campaigns.* Many creative directors are suspicious of beginners. They are leery of smooth-talking, glitzy TV types who have no fundamental writing skills. Demonstrate your ability to write body copy conclusively by including at least two long-copy print ads that are substantially different in content. Show your ability to handle at least 300 words per ad.

5. *Make sure your scripts time properly.* The first sign of an amateur is a 30-second commercial that runs 58 seconds. Learn the proper scripting format. It's an easy way to look professional.

6. *Keep audience and strategy statements brief.* Agencies are looking for original thinking and strong writing skills, not marketing or research potential.

7. *Monitor your feedback.* If you hear the same comment in many interviews, listen to it. If you hear a range of responses to the same ad, welcome to the business.

Mistakes to Avoid

Based on a survey of top U.S. creative directors, Alice Kendrick and her colleagues report that the biggest mistakes students make in their portfolios include the following:[2]

- Creating fancy storyboards that couldn't be produced for under $500,000 (some even questioned the appropriateness of TV storyboards in portfolios).
- Offering weak ideas or clever pieces that don't demonstrate what advertising can do.
- Failing to develop campaigns.
- Doing what has already been done instead of taking risks with new ideas.
- Doing ads for products that already have great campaigns.
- Revealing a noticeable lack of writing, thinking, and conceptual skills.
- Showing too much work—and having too much finished work.
- Overemphasizing execution and underemphasizing content.
- Overusing puns.
- Forgetting that the real challenge of advertising often involves making small differences important to consumers.
- Putting more weight on polished work than on creative work.
- Showing work that does not apply to advertising.

---

[2] Alice Kendrick, David Slayden, and Sheri Broyles, "Real Worlds and Ivory Towers: A Survey of Top U.S. Agency Creative Directors." Used by permission.

APPENDIX 2
ASSIGNMENTS

> Build a Campaign Step by Step

Choose a client and complete the following assignments as you read each of the chapters in the book. Ideas for clients are listed at the end of this appendix. You may want to choose a client looking for a new agency by referring to *Adweek* and *Advertising Age* magazines.

Chapter 1. Critique the client's current advertising campaign. Does it meet the definition of creativity as discussed in this book? What are the strengths of the current campaign? The weaknesses? How do the client's ads compare to the competitions' ads? Why do you think the client wants a new agency?

Chapter 2. Analyze the strengths of your brand's current identity. Address the following:

- *Name and logo.* Are they unique from those of the competition?
- *Color.* Is there a signature color that represents the brand?
- *Tagline.* Does the brand have one? If so how does it help further the brand's identity?
- *Architecture.* What does the company's headquarters look like? Is it in keeping with the brand's identity?

Now repeat this exercise for the competition.

Chapter 3. Does the client's current campaign reflect diversity? If so, does it do so in a positive way, or does it perpetuate stereotypes?

Chapter 4. Conduct primary and secondary research for this client. Address the following:

- What are trends in the client's industry?
- How does the client compare to its competitors?
- What do consumers think of the client and its competitors?
- What real or perceived differences make the client special?

Chapter 5. Using the research you compiled in the previous assignment, write a creative brief for the client.

Chapter 6. Using the creative brief you completed in the previous assignment, develop 20 ideas for ads for the client. These ideas can be sketches or can be described briefly in words. Present your ideas to the class for feedback. When critiquing other students' ideas, be sure to use the suggestions in the chapter on effective use of criticism.

Chapter 7. Taking the best idea developed in the previous assignment, write copy for a print ad and describe what the visual will look like.

Chapter 8. Draw thumbnail sketches using the copy you just completed. Choose the best thumbnail and develop a detailed layout. Depending upon your computer skills, you may want to scan photos for a more finished look.

Chapter 9. Determine if the idea for your print campaign can translate effectively into radio. If the print ad relies on a visual to be understood, will you be able to communicate that image through sound? If not, develop a new concept for radio, still following the creative brief you completed in the Chapter 5 assignment. Then write a 30- or 60-second spot.

Chapter 10. Determine if the idea for your print campaign can translate effectively into television. If the print ad uses long copy, will you be able to communicate the same points into a visual medium? If not, develop a new concept for television, still following the creative brief you completed in the Chapter 5 assignment. Then develop a storyboard for a 30-second spot.

Chapter 11. Develop a direct mail piece for your client. A letter with an envelope will work best for such clients as credit card companies and non-profit organizations who need longer copy to make their pitch. A catalog makes sense for retailers and business-to-business organizations. Post-cards work for restaurants, hair salons, and other service-oriented clients who don't need much copy to remind consumers that they're ready to be of service.

Look at your client's current website. Does it reflect the brand image of your client? Is it easy to navigate? Develop a site map and look for the home page that reflects the new image you've created for the client.

Chapter 12. Determine which alternatives to traditional advertising work best for your client. Then develop at least one of these ideas. It's not necessary to produce things such as store displays, special packaging, or premiums—just illustrate an image of what they will look like on an 8½- by 11-inch sheet of paper.

Chapter 13. Review the work you've created to make sure it protects your brand's trademark and is in keeping with legal requirements. If anything is amiss, revise before finalizing.

Chapter 14. Take the individual ads you've just completed and refine them, using feedback from your professor and classmates. As you revise your work, make certain that your ads have continuity and work as a campaign.

Once you've revised your work, make a pitch to the class, pretending that they are the client. Address the following:

- The insights you have uncovered about the client's business and consumers.
- The campaign theme and why it works.
- Three to five examples from the campaign.
- Why the client should hire you as its new agency.

> Ideas for Clients

American Classic Tea

More than 100 years ago, tea planters brought their finest ancestral tea bushes from China, India, and Ceylon to the Low Country of South Carolina. Now the direct descendants of those very plants have been lovingly restored to their former grandeur at the Charleston Tea Plantation, the only farm in the nation that grows tea. The owners of the farm, Mark Fleming and Bill Hall, have spent their working lives steeped in tea. Hall is a third-generation tea taster who apprenticed in London. Fleming, a horticulturist, began working on the plantation while it was a research-and-development facility for Thomas J. Lipton. Both owners insist on purity and use no pesticides or fungicides to grow the premium black pekoe tea.

Cascade Plastic 2-in-1 Booster

Have you ever tried to wash a plastic container after you stored spaghetti sauce or lasagna in it? The sauce leaves a disgusting orange film that's impossible to remove. Until now. Just add 3 tablespoons of Cascade Plastic Booster to your dishwasher and presto! The plastic container comes out looking new. It's also a great way to clean and freshen your dishwasher.

This product contains benzoyl peroxide. It is not for hand dishwashing, and the label advises against prolonged skin contact. Cost is about $3 for a 6.8-ounce tube. That's a lot cheaper than replacing a Tupperware bowl. But how will you be able to convince people it beats buying the disposable containers and just tossing them if they become stained?

Fizzies Drink Tablets

OK, this is definitely not for those with champagne tastes. It's for kids. Adolescents. Those seventh- and eighth-graders who love to do "yucky" things. And it's called Fizzies. Fizzies are instant sparkling-water drink tablets in cherry, grape, root beer, and orange.

Fizzies have a strong nostalgic appeal for folks who were around in the late 1950s—the "golden age of bomb shelters"—because this is when they were originally introduced. In the intervening years, they faded from the shelves. Now revived, they're an unusual novelty item for children (or perhaps for their parents—or even grandparents—who remember "the good ole days").

One particularly disgusting aspect of a Fizzie—you don't even need a glass of water to get in on the fun—is to just stick a tablet on your tongue; soon you'll "spew blue goo" and have "colored foam oozing out of your mouth." Now how would you advertise this?

Hill Pet Drinks

Think of them as a cross between Gatorade, Evian, and Ensure . . . for dogs and cats. Dr. George Hill Pet Drinks are beef-flavored concoctions for dogs and cats (two formulations). They can be added to dry food or lapped up as a treat. Both are fortified with 12 vitamins and minerals and with brewer's yeast, commonly used to control fleas.

The products are packaged in 32- and 64-ounce "milk jug" bottles. The smaller ones sell for $1.39. Dr. Hill is a veterinarian from Salisbury, North Carolina, who thinks that dogs and cats don't receive a balanced diet.

Meanwhile a competitor, Original Pet Drink Co., has signed four beverage bottlers to make and distribute its Thirsty Dog! and Thirsty Cat! products. These vitamin- and mineral-enriched waters are intended to replace tap water in a pet's bowl. A 1-liter bottle of either the Crispy Beef flavor Thirsty Dog! or the Tangy Fish flavor Thirsty Cat! sells for $1.79. Two new flavors are in the making, as are formulations for puppies, kittens, and older pets. Research shows that many pet owners give Evian and Perrier to their pets. "Once you give people more than water to drink, they do. Why shouldn't pets have that option, too?" asks president Marc Duke.

The Koolatron Portable Refrigerator

It looks like a cooler. It's just as portable, but it's really a refrigerator and food warmer all in one. NASA developed the technology for the Koolatron. It needed something less bulky and more dependable than traditional refrigeration coils and compressors. It found this in a solid-state component called the thermoelectric module, no bigger than a matchbook, that delivers the cooling power of a 10-pound block of ice. Aside from a small fan, this electronic fridge has no moving parts to wear out or break down. It costs the same as a good cooler plus one or two season's supply of ice (about the same as five family dinners out).

With the switch of a plug, the Koolatron becomes a food warmer for a casserole, burger, or baby bottle. It heats up to 125 degrees. Empty, it weighs only 12 pounds. Full, it holds up to 40 12-ounce cans. On motor trips, plug the Koolatron into your cigarette lighter. For picnics or fishing, it holds its cooling capacity for 24 hours. If you leave it plugged into your battery with the engine off, it consumes only 3 amps of power. $99 plus $12 shipping and handling. An optional AC adapter lets you use it in your recreation room, on your patio, or in a motel room. 1-800 number for orders.

Lawn Makeup

Possibly inspired by those infomercials for spray-on hair, this aerosol can of colored spray is for folks who don't want their lawns to look "browned out" come fall and winter. You can even choose the color to match your lawn or your mood, from Palm Green, to Cedar Green, to Spring Green, to Kentucky Blue. The label promises that Lawn Makeup is virtually nontoxic and suggests that you spray a test area for color match. Definitely not for nature purists, so don't target them. Find your market and convince them it's better to have a healthy-looking lawn than a healthy lawn (just kidding).

Marshmallow Fluff

It's a spreadable marshmallow concoction made by Durkee-Mower and sold primarily in New England and upstate New York. This gooey, sticky delight has just four ingredients: corn syrup, sugar, dried egg white, and vanilla. Dollops of Fluff can go in hot chocolate, be used as the base for cake frosting, or add extra sweetness to sweet potato soufflé. It makes great Whoopie Pies and fudge. But it's the Fluffernutter sandwich, a favorite among New England children, that has put Fluff in the news. In 2006, in its home state of Massachusetts, a state senator proposed limiting its availability in school lunchrooms to once a week. After his constituents rebelled, the senator withdrew his anti-fluff legislation. Another lawmaker jumped to Fluff's defense, nominating the Fluffernutter as the official state sandwich. As this book goes to press, the Massachusetts legislature is debating whether to make the gooey delight the official state sandwich.

Pizza Chef Gourmet Pizza

Locally owned and operated. Recipes prepared fresh on premises. Fresh herbs and spices used in sauce and on pizzas. Gourmet salads of fresh romaine lettuce are tossed with homemade salad dressings. Bakes its own sub buns and offers pizzas on freshly made whole-wheat dough or traditional hand-tossed dough. All pizzas available baked or unbaked. All made to order.

Eat in, delivery, or pickup. Beer and wine on premises. Traditional pizza toppings plus "designer pizzas." Garden, Caesar, antipasto, southwestern chicken salads. Set this operation apart from the giants: Pizza Hut, Domino's, and so on.

Soundmate Personal Safety Device

Out with the old-fashioned way to locate your lost youngster—that is, by shouting his or her name at a volume that blows out store windows. You can now track your child electronically. The Child Safety Corporation of Miami markets a child-tracking monitor system. The system consists of a battery-operated transmitter, attached with a safety pin to the child, and a receiver carried by the parent. Each system sells for $99.

The device allows parents to log in an alarm range of 30 to 60 feet on the child's transmitter, which he or she wears like a pendant about the size of a silver dollar. If the child wanders farther than the preset range, an alarm is triggered on the parent's receiver. The alarm also sounds if the transmitter is switched off or immersed in water.

Tabasco 7-Spice Chili Recipe

For more than 100 years, the world's premier marketer of red pepper sauce has been churning out its mainstay product with no sense of urgency about diversifying its line. The family-owned McIlhenny Co., makers of the Tabasco sauce that all but owns the hot-sauce market, started marketing other products only in 1973, when it introduced a Bloody Mary mix, followed by a picante sauce in 1982. Now it offers Tabasco Brand 7-Spice Chili Recipe mix, which plays off the strong heritage and widespread awareness of the Tabasco brand.

Tabasco is to red pepper sauce what Xerox is to copiers. Despite repeated buyout offers, the McIlhenny family has remained dedicated to preserving the old family recipe. The sauce is aged in oaken vats on remote Avery Island, deep in Louisiana Cajun country and headquarters for the company.

The fiery sauce is difficult to duplicate because of the Central American capsicum peppers used in the aging process, which involves mixing them with the local salt and vinegar.

Tabasco got its start in 1865 when Henry McIlhenny used peppers brought from Mexico's Yucatan Peninsula to create the sauce. For four generations, each patriarch has taken a daily walk, dressed in suit and tie, through the fields of peppers during the fall harvest to personally inspect the crop's quality, examine the mash in the vats, and watch the shipment of bottles.

For more than a century, the bottle, the name, and the logo have not changed.

The chili is made from the finest vine-ripened tomatoes, green chilies, diced onions, genuine Tabasco pepper sauce, and a blend of seven herbs and spices known only to the company. All you add is fresh beef. The sauce comes in a "spaghetti sauce" jar. The label reads, "Tabasco Brand 7-Spice Chili Recipe. McIlhenny Co."

Tabasco dominates the hot-sauce category with 30 percent of the market. It is a growing market, riding the crest of a wave of popularity for spicy foods.

The Value of Independent Higher Education

America's private (or independent) colleges are doing well but see that they must strive to increase enrollment. So they have decided to pool funds to advertise their advantages and thereby increase inquiries and enrollments. One region, the Midwest, is combining its efforts through the Midwest Partnership of Independent Colleges (Illinois, Indiana, Michigan, Ohio, and Wisconsin) and needs to develop a campaign.

The facts will run in regional editions of national newsweeklies, which have agreed to run some of the ads as a public service. This information on private colleges is not well known:

- Independent colleges perform an important service to our society, although many of their contributions go unrecognized, perhaps because of the stronger "clout" of major state-funded colleges and universities.
- They have an average faculty-to-student ratio of 14 to 1. Their enrollments represent all races and income brackets.
- The Midwest group enrolls 390,000 students, of which 48,000 are minorities. Eighty percent of students receive some form of financial aid, 20 percent of which comes from the schools' budgets—double that of 10 years ago.
- They award 30 percent of all bachelor's degrees in the region, and 66 percent of their students go on to postgraduate studies.
- They contribute an estimated $10 billion and 350,000 jobs each year to their local economies.
- Six out of 10 Fortune 500 CEOs attended an independent college.

It is therefore clear that these colleges are strong contributors to the educational, cultural, and economic well-being of our society.

The Audience.   Several choices are appropriate, but for this campaign think in terms of parents of junior and senior high school students in the Midwest region served by this group of colleges. Because financial aid is available, it is important to reach middle- and low-middle-income families, especially those who find it difficult to believe they can afford to send their children to anything but a large state university, where tuition tends to be more affordable and where grants are often available for lower-income levels.

Because roughly 5 out of 40 college students are minorities, this is an audience that should not be overlooked. Essentially, the message should appeal to whites and minorities who believe in the value of diversity and who see or can be made to see the value in low faculty–student ratios and other appealing features of these schools that set them apart from the competition.

The Competition.   This is a broad category. People in the target market might consider the competition to be large state universities and community and technical colleges (lower cost). But you might also think of the competition as not going to college. Remember, this is an era of inflated costs for everything, and education is no exception. Students from this pool will almost certainly have to finance part of their education, either by working or through grants and scholarships. The general perception is that the smaller and more private the school, the less opportunity for any sort of financial support.

Create and Market a New Product

Think up a new product that satisfies certain needs of a particular group of consumers. Use the following guidelines to help you determine what your new product should offer. Then develop an advertising campaign for it.

- What is the nature of the product? Give uses, description of packaging, approximate selling price, type of store carrying it, sizes available, and general shape and appearance.
- What is its name? What does the name signify?
- Who is the target audience in demographic, lifestyle, and relationship terms? Is there a secondary audience?
- What products will this one replace for this audience? In what ways will it be better than the products they were using before?
- What is the key selling idea for this product?

Index

A

Absolut vodka, 141
active voice in ad copy, 158
ad campaigns, 95
ad layouts, 178–179
Adamson, Allen, 153–154
Adidas AG, 15
advertising
    consumer inspired, 5
    government regulation of, 4
    regulations, 277–278
    as a team sport, 166
    trade characters, 121–122
affluent consumers, 50–53
AFLAC
    advertising, 122, 222
    concept research, 85
    duck sound trademark, 32
African American consumer
    demographics, 40–43
age-related marketing tips, 51–53
alliterative phrases in radio
    advertising, 198
Allstate Insurance, 120, 142–143
Ally & Gargano, 95
American Association of Retired
    Persons, 51
American consumer demographics,
    50–53
American Dream, 210
American Family Association, 54
American Family Life Insurance
    Company, 32, 85
American Red Cross, 80
American Standard, 120, 121
Americans with Disabilities Act, 54
America's Dairy Farmers and Milk
    Processors, 117
analogy
    and creativity, 118–119
    in headlines, 145–146
Anheuser-Busch
    advertising, 14, 124
    sponsorship agreements, 267

animation in banner ads, 244
annual reports, 70
Apple ad campaigns, 13–14, 26, 27
Arab American consumer
    demographics, 47–48
architecture as identity element,
    30–31
Arenas, Gilbert, 15
Asian American consumer
    demographics, 45–46
asymmetrical balance, 168–169
Audi advertising, 119
Avis advertising, 142
axial layout, 178, 181

B

backgrounder, 261
balance, 168–169
Bamboo Lingerie, 115
band layout, 178, 181
*Bang: Getting Your Message Heard
    in a Noisy World* (Kaplan
    Thaler and Koval), 222
banner ads, 244
Baruch, Bernard, 51
Bayer HealthCare, 277
BBDO NY, 17, 211
behavioral targeting, 245
Bell, Ted, 16
Bell Helmets
    ad strategy, 99, 100, 101
    television script, 212
Ben & Jerry's Ice Cream, 173
Berman, Jeff, 245
Bernbach, Bill, 97
biased research results, 86
big ideas, 77, 84, 97, 111–113,
    248, 279
billboard advertising, 225
Blackwood, Stephanie, 54
bleed area, 175
Blue Ocean Strategy (Kim and
    Maugorgne), 95
Bodett, Tom, 202, 205–207

body copy, 147–150
boom shot, 217
Boone/Oakley, 161
Boost Mobile, 51
Bougdano, Steve, 124, 209, 210
brainstorming, 122–125, 211
brand identity
    elements, 28–32
    localizing, 34
    patent law and, 35
    protecting, 34–35
    research, 33
    and trademarks, 286
brand loyalty, 256, 258
brand names and creativity, 122
brand negatives and creativity, 118
branded content, 268–269
branding, 26–37
breaking the rules, 150–151
Breeze Exec, 231
Briefcases
    on big ideas, 132–135, 248–252
    on branding, 36–37
    California cows, 132–137
    on client pitches, 303–307
    on consumer diversity, 58–60
    on creativity, 21–25, 88–90,
        90–93, 163–165, 289–291
    Eat Mor Chikin, 105–110
    Grant condominium building,
        248–252
    Icelandair and Baltimore
        Washington International
        Airport, 88–90
    IKEA ad campaign, 21–25
    IKEA home furnishings,
        270–273
    on integrated marketing
        communication, 270–273
    ITT Industries, 289–292
    Lexington Medical Center,
        303–307
    Motel 6, 205–207
    North Carolina, 163–165

Briefcases (*continued*)
Papa John's pizza, 36–37
on print advertising, 186–190
on radio commercials, 205–207
Riverbanks Zoo and Garden, 224–228
on strategy, 105–110
on television, 224–229
Verizon Wireless, 58–68
weight loss, 186–190
Bud Light
ad campaigns, 14, 113
radio, 196
Budweiser, 209, 210
bulleted body copy, 148, 243
Burger King, 17, 120, 245–246
Burke, James Lee, 138
Burnette, Leo
on creativity, 124
on writing, 141
bus-board ads, 94
Business Source Premier, 74
business-speak, 156

C
California cows, 132–137
California Milk Advisory Board (CMAB), 132–137
camera action, 216–217, 219
campaign presentation strategies, 294–295
campaign themes, 113–114
Carlson, Janine, 240
Carmichael Lynch, 3
Carnival Cruise Lines, 56
Carper, Christie, 186
Cartagena, Chiqui
Latino Boom!, 43
Cartoon Network, 278
Castlewood Builders, 95, 96
catalogs, direct mail, 234–235
catchall phrases, 156
cause-related marketing, 267–268
Cee, Heidi, 245
celebrity endorsements, 12–16, 277
celebrity rights of publicity, 281
Center for Media & Democracy, 245
centered layout, 179
Cesar dog food, 82
Champion sportswear, 15

characters, advertising trade, 16–17, 121–122
Charlotte Checkers, 4
checklist
for creative briefs, 104
for radio copy, 203–204
for television commercials, 223
for writing copy, 161
Cheer laundry detergent, 220
Cheerios commercial, 276
Cheetos, 1–2, 81, 121–122
Chernoff Newman agency, 186–190, 224–228
Chester Cheetah, 1–2, 121–122
Chick-fil-A, 105–110, 114, 117, 184, 214
Children's Food & Beverage Advertising Initiative, 1
Chippers Funeral Home, 68
Chiquita, 267
Chunky Soup, 81
circus layout, 178, 181
clichés, 159
client photography, copyright issues for, 283
client pitches, 293–307
client relations, 294–295
Clorox, 116, 140–141
close-up (CU), 216
closure, 172
Clydesdales in Budweiser advertising, 210
Coca-Cola
advertising, 12–13, 43–44, 220
color palette, 30
copyright issues, 283
market research, 85
Coleman gas grills, 82
collective Gestalt, 172
Colonel Sanders, 16
Colonial Supplemental Insurance, 155
color
palette as identity element, 30–31
as trademark, 285–286
vs. black and white, 184
color field layout, 178, 181
Columbia Inferno, 73
Columbia Sportswear, 148
commands in headlines, 143

Communication Abstracts, 74
Compact Disclosures, 74
company records, 70
competitions, creative, 5–9
compilation cutting, 218
computers and design, 182
concept testing, 85
Condos, Rick, 2
Cone, Steve, 153
consumer diversity, 38–67
consumers, 50–53, 75, 231
contests, 255–256
context, creativity and, 116
Continental Airlines, 4
continuity programs, 258–259
contractions in ad copy, 160
contrast in design, 169, 172
cookies, ethical use of, 245
Copland, Richard M., 50
copy
length, 152
mistakes, 151
as story, 148
copy-heavy layout, 178, 181
copyright law, brand identity and, 34
copyright symbol, 283
copyrights, 194, 279, 281–284
corporate advertising, 289–292
Country Time Lemonade, 55
County and City Data Book, 74
coupons, 256
Cracker Jack's, 256
Crain, Rance, 10
crane shot, 217
Crate & Barrel, 118
creative ads
challenges of, 18
characteristics of, 2–5
creative briefs, 84, 92–97, 113
Creative Circus, 115, 118
creative competitions, 5, 6, 9
creative process, 138, 274
creative resources, 129
creative strategy statements, 84
creativity, 1–25
and criticism, 125–126
and cultural context, 120
and the law, 274–292
mental exercise and, 124
opposites and, 122
spokespersons and, 121–122

crisis management, 264
Crispin Porter and Bogusky, 17, 115, 268
criticism and creativity, 125–126
crosscutting, 218
cultural context and creativity, 120
cultural differences, ad campaigns and, 46, 48
cultures, identity and, 34
curiosity and headlines, 143
current events and creativity, 117
Curves, 95
customer profiles, 70
cuts, in television commercials, 217

D

Daffy's advertising, 142
data, interpreting, 84
Dawn dish detergent, 221
DDB Chicago, 196, 209
dead people, signed consent from, 281
deceptive advertising, 276
defamation, 287
Della Femina, Jerry, 52
demographic markets, 55–57
demonstration television, 213
design
    common questions about, 183–185
    computers and, 182
    concepts in Internet marketing, 239–240
    functions of, 166–168
    principles of, 168–171, 172
desktop publishing software, 182
Deutsch NY, 21, 101–102, 132–137, 270–273
DeVito/Verdi, 195
dialog in radio commercials, 198
Die Another Day (James Bond), 268
digestion as part of creative process, 112
DiGiorno Pizza, 84, 114, 153, 255
direct benefit in headlines, 142
direct marketing, 229–252
    advantages of, 230–231
    ethical aspects of, 245–246
    mail packages, 232–233
    requirements for successful, 231–233

dissolves, in television commercials, 217
diversity, consumer, 38–67
dolly in/out, 217
Dove Campaign for Real Beauty, 39, 40, 41, 42
Dow Chemical, 55
down time and creative, 124
dramatization in radio commercials, 199
DSW (director of "so what?"), 300
Dundas, Kevin, 92
Dunkin' Donuts, 48
DuPont, 98, 99
Dusenberry, Phil, 81
Duval, Robyn, 59

E

"Eat Mor Chikin" cows, 105–110
editing for continuity, 218–219
effective copy, guidelines for, 154–161
elephants and death, 68
Emerald Nuts, 5
The End of Advertising as We Know It (Zyman), 266
endorsements, celebrity, 12–16
Erwin-Penland (EP), 58
ethical issues in advertising, 17–18
ethnic Americans, 38, 48–49
ethnography, 82
experience, firsthand, 77–78
experimentation, 83
external audiences, 33
extreme close-up (ECU), 216
Exxon tiger, 284

F

Facebook, 245
fact sheets
    for live radio advertising, 201
    for news releases, 261
factual headlines, 142
fades in television commercials, 218
false advertising, 276
"false light" problems, 280
Federal Trade Commission (FTC), 14, 275
FedEx®, 29, 30, 120
Felton, George, 209

Ferrero U.S.A., 258
Feuer, Jack, 52
file photos in advertising, licensing, 280
firsthand experience, 77–78
five Rs of design, 173–175
flush left or right layout, 179
focus groups, 80–81
Food Bank advertising, 128, 129, 130, 131
Foote, Cone and Belding, 102–103, 103
Ford Motor Company, 54
Foust, John, 303
Fox Hill Village, 52
frame layout, 178, 181
freelancers, copyrights and, 283, 284
Freeman, Michael, 133
Frito-Lay, 279

G

games, 255–256
Gardner, Lorie, 303, 304
Garfield, Bob, 16, 53
Gargano, Amil, 95
gay and lesbian demographics, 54–55
General Electric, 153, 154
General Mills, 276
General Motors, 5
generalities in ad copy, 159
geographic location and creativity, 120–121
"gestalt," 27
Gestalt theory, 171, 172
Glidden color palette, 31
golden mean, 169, 172
Gone With the Wind, camera shot in, 217
Goodby, Silverstein & Partners (GSP), 81, 83, 121–122, 253
Got Milk? campaign, 12
government regulation, 276–277
Grant condominium building, 248–252
Greene, Joe, 12–13
Greenspon Advertising Southeast, 4
Gregory, Margaret, 304
grid layout, 178, 181
Grunberg, Andy, 184
guerilla marketing, 268

guidelines
    for banner ads, 244
    for effective copy, 154–161
    for presentations, 296
    for radio spots, 192–198
Gynecological Cancer Foundation,
    256–257

H

Haagen-Dazs advertising, 253
Hammer, MC, 14
Happy Cows ad campaign, 132–137
Happy Meals, 256
Harley-Davidson
    ad campaigns, 53
    sound trademark, 31
harmony in design, 169, 172
Harry Fox Agency, 283
Haubegger, Christy, 43
Hayden, Ann, 2
Hayden, Steve, 122
headlines, 140–147
    length, 151
    parallel construction in, 146, 147
    punctuation, 182
    selective, 142–143
    similes in, 145
Hebrew National Hotdogs, 153
Heinz ketchup, 265, 296
Herbert, Dave, 5
Herd, Stan, 36
Hershey Resorts, 232
Hinkle, Woody, 96
Hiram Walker & Sons, 54
Hirshberg, Eric, 132
Hispanic American consumer
    demographics, 43–45
history and creativity, 118
Hitchcock, Alfred
    North by Northwest, 208–209
Hodgman, John, 26
Hoff, Ron, 299, 300
Home Depot, 31
Honest, Decent, and True (film), 293
Hoover's, 74
horizontal trade magazines, 292
"How Sweet the Sound," 58–68
H&R Block, 13
human experience, 10
human-speak, 156
humor in advertising, 10–12, 244

I

"I" statements, 126
IBM, 4
Icelandair, 88–90, 142
ideas, 111–137, 293–307
identity and image strategy, 26–37
IKEA
    ad campaigns, 21–25, 117, 121
    Brooklyn ad campaigns, 102
    home furnishings, 270–273
    radio campaigns, 192–193
illumination as part of creative
    process, 112
illustration software, 182
image strategy, identity and, 26–37
images in advertising, licensing, 280
immersion as part of creative
    process, 112
importance scales and strategy,
    102–103
in-house photography, copyright
    issues, 283
in-use rewards, 96
incidental-to-use rewards, 96
incubation as part of creative
    process, 112
InfoTrac Business Index, 74
insight, creativity and, 68–90
integrated marketing
    communications (IMC), 33,
    253–273
intellectual property, brand
    identity as, 34
interior design as identity element,
    30–31
internal audiences, 33
International AntiCounterfeiting
    Coalition, 245
International Newspaper
    Promotion Association, 159
Internet direct mail, 235–243
InterTrend Communications, 46
interviewer bias, 86
interviews
    one-on-one, 81
    in radio advertising, 200
invasion of privacy, 279–280
inverted pyramid style copy, 243
Ipsos-ASI, 85
ITT Industries, 289–292
Ivory Soap, 254–255

J

J. Walter Thompson, 269
Jackson, Michael, 12
Jacobs, Harry, 298
James Bond (*Die Another Day*), 268
Jell-O gelatin, 86
JetBlue, 29
jingles in radio advertising, 200
Johnson, Julie, 242
Johnson, Lyndon, 122
Johnson and Johnson, 264
jokes, humor and, 10
Jolly Green Giant, 16
justification of text, 177
justified layout, 179

K

Kang, Elliot, 45
Kaplan Thaler, Linda, 222
Kaplan Thaler Group, 85
Kay, Allen, 10
Kay Jewelers, 153
Keebler premiums, 256
Kellog Co.
    ad campaigns, 15, 113, 143
    trademark infringement
        lawsuit, 284
kerning, 177
key insight, 97. *See also* big ideas
keywords, 242–243
KFC, 258
Kim, W. Chan
    Blue Ocean Strategy, 95
King, Stephen, 138
Kirshenbaum, Bond & Partners,
    115–116
Klein, Russ, 17
Kmart, 15
Knight, Phil, 28
Knoll, Patrick, 209, 210
Koval, Robin, 222
Kraft Foods, 255

L

Lacoste, 28
Landor Associates, 29
Lands' End, 142, 152, 229, 234
Lang, Steven, 159
Langton, Cleve
    New Business Lessons from
        Madison Avenue, 299

language
    nuances in advertising, 49, 50
    to tell a story, 209
Lanham Act, 286
Latino Boom! (Cartagena), 43
lawsuits, advertising and, 275
layouts, print, 166–190
leading, 177
Leo Burnett, 113, 220, 265, 296
letter spacing, 177
Levinson, Jay Conrad, 268
Lexis-Nexis, 74
libel, 287
library resources for research
    information, 74
licensing process for photography,
    280–281
life experience and creativity, 124
listings as body copy, 148
lists, direct mail, 231–232, 236
live donuts in radio
    commercials, 201
Loeffler Ketchum Mountjoy, 114,
    163–165
logos
    as identity element, 28–29
    as trademarks, 285–286
logotype, 28
Lonesome Town (Nelson), 221
Long, Justin, 26
Longo, Jeff, 4
L'Oreal Paris, 4
lotteries, 276
"Lovemark," 27–28
Luntz, Frank, 156
luxury cars, 83
Lynch, Lee, 53
Lyons, John, 91

M

Mac vs. PC, 26
Mackay, Hugh, 85
Macy's Department Stores, 118, 153
Mad Men, 116
Mad Monkey production studio,
    303–307
Magic Fridge, 210
majority-minority states, 38
mandatories, 149–150
Manning, Selvage & Lee, 261
market data, syndicated, 74–75

Martin, Thomas, 289
Mass, Jane, 92
Massachusetts Society for the
    Prevention of Cruelty to
    Animals, 148
MasterCard, 5
Mauborgne, Renee
    Blue Ocean Strategy, 95
Mazda, 32
McCabe, Ed, 68–69
McCann Erickson, 97–101, 118
McDonald's, 49, 53, 120, 256
McKee, Steve, 158
meaningless words, 158
media, identity and, 34
media kits, 261
Mediamark Research, Inc.
    (MRI), 74
medium
    creativity relative to, 114–115
    relevance of, 4
mental exercise and creativity, 124
Merkley Newman Harty, 296
message, direct mail, 232
metaphors in headlines, 144
MetLife Insurance, 153
MGM lion trademark, 32
Miami Rescue Mission, 115–116
Microsoft, 4
Midas, 51
Ming, Yao, 15
Mini Cooper, 268
minor children, signed consent
    for, 281
Mintel, 74
Minute Maid, 114–115
misappropriation for commercial
    purposes, 279–280
Missouri Corn Growers
    Association, 48
M&M characters, 17
mnemonic devices, 196
moment of judgment, in
    presentations, 299
Mondrian layout, 178, 181
Montgomery Ward Company, 229
Morrison, Margaret, 93
Moseley, Larry, 186
Moss, Mark, 53
Motel 6, 202, 205–207
movement in design, 171

Mr. Peanut, 16–17
MTV, 118–119
multi-voice radio commercials,
    199, 201
music and sound effects, 194,
    219–220

N

names
    as identity element, 28
    as trademarks, 285–286
Nasuti & Hinkle Creative Thinking,
    88–90, 96, 123, 248–252, 297
National Hispanic Consumer Study,
    76–77
national texting champion, 230
National Thoroughbred Racing
    Association, 195
Nationwide Insurance, 5, 14
Native American consumer
    demographics, 46–47
NBC chimes sound trademark,
    32, 285
Neeleman, David, 29
negative space, 171–173
Neiman Marcus holiday
    catalog, 235
Nelson, Ricky, 221
Nelson, Willie, 13
*New Business Lessons
    from Madison Avenue*
    (Langton), 299
New York State Lottery, 153
news and headlines, 143
news releases, 260–263
Nielsen, Jakob, 242
Nielsen National Marketing
    Survey, 75
Nike
    advertising, 4, 15, 28
    trademarks, 285
North by Northwest (Hitchcock),
    208–209
North Carolina ad campaigns, 114,
    139–140, 152, 163–165
novelty type, 176, 177
Noxema advertising, 116
numbers
    insight in, 76–77
    in radio advertising, 196
Nutella, 258

O

Obama, Barak, 48
Oberlander, Bill, 86
objective point of view, 219
O'Brien, Conan, 14
observation, 79–80
offers, direct mail, 232
Ogilvy, David, 200
Ogilvy & Mather, 112–113
on-air personalities, 200
one-voice exposition, 198
online research, 83
opposites and creativity, 122
original works, ownership of, 282
Oscar Mayer Wienermobile, 260, 263
outdoor advertising, 183, 225
Oval Office, decorated by IKEA, 270–273
overused words, 158
Oz, Mehmet, 279

P

Pace Picante Sauce, 120
packaging, 265–266
page templates, 240
pan R/L (camera move), 217
Papa John's pizza ad campaign, 36–37, 230
parallel construction in headlines, 146, 147
patent law, brand identity and, 35
PC ad campaign, Mac vs., 26
Pennsylvania ad campaigns, 55
People for the Ethical Treatment of Animals (PETA), 16
PepsiCola
    advertising, 117, 211, 220, 221
    brand identity research, 33
    celebrity advertising by, 12
    color palette, 30
    copyright issues, 283
Pepto-Bismol, 116
Perel, Matias, 45
permissions, 279
permits for special use, 278
personalized messages, 230
Peters, Tom
    The Pursuit of Wow!, 160
Phelps, Michael, 15

photographs in advertising, licensing, 280
photo manipulation software, 182
phrases as trademarks, 285–286
picture window layout, 178, 181
Planters Peanuts, 256
poetic body copy, 149
point-of-purchase advertising, 259
point of view, 219
points, type measured in, 177
Polamalu, Troy, 13
Polk Multi-dimensional Intelligence, 71
Poltrack, Terence, 111
popsicle, world's largest, 263–264
Pordy, Melissa, 50
Porsche, 97
postscripts in direct response advertising, 232
Potty Palooza, 258, 261
Powell, Colin, 48
Powelson, Michael, 305
PowerPoint technique, 301
Pozgar, Morgan, 230
premiums, 256
present tense in ad copy, 158
presentation guidelines, 298
presentation strategies, 294–295
presenters in television commercials, 215
Price, Heather, 186, 224
primary research, 75–84
privacy
    Internet issues, 245
    invasion of, 279–280
Prizm, 75
Pro Dent bus-board ads, 94
Procter & Gambel
    advertising, 220, 235–236, 258
    research, 82
product
    appearance and creativity, 120
    disparagement, 287
    placement, 268–269
    as star in television commercials, 213
production
    Internet site, 243
    television commercial, 222–223
professional models and rights of publicity, 281

Project Host, 130, 131
projective techniques, 82–83
promotional products, 264
proofreading, 160, 161
"proper adjective," trademark as, 286
proportion in design, 169, 172
prospects, pinpointing, 230
protected speech, 276
proximity, 172
public relations, 260–264
Public Relations Society of America, 258
Publix grocery chain, 56
puffery, 276–277
punctuation, 182
The Pursuit of Wow! (Peters), 160
push and pull strategies, 260

Q

Quaker Oats man, 16
questions in headlines, 143

R

R. J. Reynolds, 148
Rabinowitz, Josh, 12
Rachel Ray, 48
radio advertising, 106–107, 191–207
radio commercials
    approaches to, 197–200
    live versus produced, 200–201
radio script format, 201–202
Rampton, Sheldon, 245
rational benefits, 97
readability, on-screen, 243
readership, type selection and, 179–182
ready, as part of design process, 175
reality testing, 112
rebates, 259
relevant connections, 2–3
repetition in headlines, 144
reputation, brand, 27–28
research
    data interpretation, 84
    defining questions and problems, 69–70
    and design process, 173–174
    methods, 49
    mistakes, 85–86

primary sources, 75–84
   secondary sources, 70–75
restroom advertising, 4
results-of-use rewards, 96
reverse benefit in headlines, 142
reverse type, 182
revision
   copy, 160, 213
   and design process, 174–175
Revson, Charles, 97
rewards, types of, 96
rhyme in headlines, 147
rhythm in design, 171, 172
Richards Group, 105–110, 205–207
Ricoh advertising, 230–231
Riggs Agency, 303–307
right of publicity, 279–280
Riswold, Jim, 124
Riverbanks Zoo and Garden,
   224–228
Roberts, Kevin, 2009
role-playing approach to strategic
   planning, 97–101
Roman, Kenneth, 92
Roper ASW, 51
Rossman, Marlene, 46
roughs and design process, 174
Rouston, Tom, 222
Royal Caribbean, 147
run, as part of design process, 175

S
Saatchi & Saatchi, 27, 117, 120
Sabena Qualitative Research, 84
sales promotion, 254–260
sampling, 258
Sam's Club, 296
Samsung lawsuit, 279–280
Scarborough Research, 75
Schenck, Ernie, 138
Scotchgard headlines, 141
scripts
   in radio advertising, 201
   in television advertising, 221
Sears, Roebuck & Company, 153, 229
secondary sources and creative
   insight, 70–75
Seinfeld, product placement and, 269
selective headlines, 142–143
Selig Center for Economic
   Growth, 38

selling ideas, creative, 2
selling points, emotional and
   rational, 2
sentence variety in ad copy, 159
service marks, 284, 285
"set solid," 177
7-Eleven advertising, 117
SFX (sound effects), 203, 221
Shannon, Dan, 16
Shiseido Toilet Soap, 274
Shumaker, Chris, 302
sight, sound, and motion, 209–210
signed consent, 281
silhouette layout, 178, 181
Silverman, Paul, 176
similarity, 172
similes in headlines, 145
Simmons Bedding Company
   advertising, 118
Simmons National Consumer
   Survey, 75, 76–77
sisomo (sight, sound, and
   motion), 209
site maps, 238, 239
Six Flags presentation, 296
slander, 287
slice-of-life television commercials,
   214–215
slogans, 153–154
small print, 149–150
Smokey Bear, 16
Snap, Crackle, and Pop, 16
Snapple, 263
software and design, 182
Sony, 4–5
sound devices in radio advertising,
   199–200
sound effects, 193–195, 219–220, 221
sounds
   as identity element, 30–31
   as trademarks, 285–286
special events, 263–264
Spence, Roy, 111
spherical branding process,
   105–110, 205
spokespersons and creativity,
   121–122
sponsorships, 266–267
SRI, 75
Standard & Poor's Industry
   Surveys, 74

Statistical Abstract of the United
   States, 74
Steel, Jon, 85–86, 93
Stevenson, Seth, 5
stock photos in advertising,
   licensing, 280, 283
storyboards, 221–222
storytelling in television
   commercials, 209, 210, 216
Stove Top stuffing, 49
strategic planning, 91
strategy
   defined, 91
   and importance scales, 102–103
   and thinking/feeling scale,
      102–103
strategy statements, creative, 84
StrawberryFrog, 296
Stren fishing line, 2, 3, 10, 277
student ADDY competition, 6–8
stunts, 296
subheads, 243
subjective point of view, 219
Subway, 296
Sullivan, Luke, 125
Sunbeam, 82
Super Bowl
   commercials, 5, 10, 12–13,
      14, 117
   sponsorship agreements, 267
Survey of Buying Power, 75
surveys, 80
sweepstakes, 255–256
Swilley, Esther, 229
swipe files, 124
symmetrical balance, 168–169
syndicated market data, 74–75
Syracuse University, 30

T
taglines, 29–30
Talbots clothing stores, 84
target audience, 21, 93–94
Target department stores
   ad campaigns, 27
   logo, 29
   website, 54
Taylor Guitars, 156, 157
technical reports, 70
technology for Internet direct
   marketing, 237

television advertising, 208–228
    commercial formats, 213–214
    production, 222
    scripts, 221
    testimonials in, 216
testing copy, 160
TH Outdoor & Events, 273
theater of the mind, 192
thinking/feeling scales and
    strategy, 102–103
third-party photography, 283
Thompson, Edward T., 156
Thoroughbred Racing
    Association, 296
thumbnail sketches, 181
Tide advertising, 117
Tiffany & Co.
    color palette, 31, 285
    use of white space, 172–173
tilt U/D (camera move), 217
time considerations in radio
    advertising, 197
timing and creativity, 116–117
Tony the Tiger, 16, 284
Tootsie Roll premiums, 256
tracking, 177
Tracy Locke agency, 279
trade associations, 73–74
trade characters, 16–17
"trade libel," 287
trademarks
    and brand identity, 34
    and copyright rules, 284
    loss of status, 286
    phrases as, 285–286
transit ads, 183
transitions
    in ad copy, 158
    in television commercials,
        217–218
trim size, 175
truck R/L (camera move), 217
Tylenol crisis management, 264
type, 175–178, 179
type selection and readership,
    179–182

type specimen layout, 178, 181
typical audience, 86

U

unexpectedness, of creative ads, 2
unified message, 33–34
Union pacific Railroad, 265
United States Patent and
    Trademark Office, 286
U.S. Census, 74
U.S. Postal Service, 229

V

vague generalities, 159
VALS 2, 75
Vanilla Honey Bee ice cream,
    253–254
Verizon Wireless
    ad campaigns, 58–68
    taglines, 29
vertical trade magazines, 292
Vick, Michael, 15, 16
Vicks' NyQuil advertising, 117
video news releases, 261
vignettes
    in radio advertising, 199
    in television commercials,
        214
Vinten Browning, 68
Vinton Studios, 17
Visa ad campaigns, 15
Visconti, Luke, 48
visuals, value in presentations,
    299
Vogel, Nadine, 53
voice-over, 221
Volkswagen, 49, 151, 152
Volpp, Leti, 48

W

Waits, Tom, 279
Walmart, 53
warranty cards, 71–72
Weather Channel, 4
websites, 70, 238
weight-loss seminars, 186–190

Westcott Alessandri, Sue, 26,
    289–292
"what if" thinking, 123
White, Vanna, 279–280
White House, IKEA decorates the,
    270–273
white space, 171–173
white-water rafting campaign, 11
Wild Turkey, 116–117
Williams, Doug, 159
Williams, Hank, 220
Winfrey, Oprah, 279
Woods, Tiger, 15
word play in headlines, 144
works made for hire, 283
writing, 138–140
    for the ear, 192
    for the Internet, 242–243
    for news releases, 262
    "out loud," 160
    for radio, 192–197
    for television, 210–213
writing guidelines
    for banner ads, 244
    for effective copy, 154–161
    for presentations, 296
    for radio spots, 192–197
Wylie, Ann, 261

Y

Yaz oral contraceptives, 277
Young, James Webb, 112–113
Your Cheatin' Heart, 220, 283
youth, advertiser obsession with,
    50–51
YouTube, 296

Z

Zamboli's Italian restaurant, 120
Zimmerman Advertising, 296
Zipperblatt, Stephen, 300
Zoeller, Fuzzy, 15
zoom in/zoom out, 217
Zyman, Sergio
    *The End of Advertising as We
    Know It*, 266